THE ROCKEFELLER COLLECTION OF AMERICAN ART

THE ROCKEFELLER COLLECTION
OF AMERICAN ART

at The Fine Arts Museums of San Francisco

Marc Simpson
with the assistance of Patricia Junker

THE FINE ARTS MUSEUMS OF SAN FRANCISCO
in association with
HARRY N. ABRAMS, INC., PUBLISHERS

This catalogue has been published in conjunction with the exhibition
The Rockefeller Collection of American Art at The Fine Arts Museums of San Francisco.

The Fine Arts Museums of San Francisco
M. H. de Young Memorial Museum
25 June–13 November 1994

Funding from the Ednah Root Foundation has made this exhibition possible.

The Blanchette Hooker Rockefeller Foundation has generously underwritten the exhibition catalogue.

First published in 1994 by The Fine Arts Museums of San Francisco. Distributed by Harry N. Abrams, Incorporated, New York. A Times Mirror Company

Library of Congress Cataloguing-in-Publication Data

Simpson, Marc.
　The Rockefeller collection of American art at the Fine Arts
　Museums of San Francisco / Marc Simpson; with the assistance of
　Patricia A. Junker.
　　p. 316
　　Published in conjunction with an exhibition to be held 25 June–
　13 November 1994.
　　Includes bibliographical references and index.
　　ISBN 0–8109–3774–3 (cloth) / ISBN 0–88401–079–1 (paper)
　　1. Painting, American—Exhibitions.　2. Painting—United States—
　Exhibitions.　3. Rockefeller, John D., 1906–1978　—Art collections—
　Exhibitions.　4. Rockefeller, Blanchette Hooker, 1909–1992　—Art
　collections—Exhibitions.　5. Painting—Private collections—
　California—San Francisco—Exhibitions.　6. Painting—California—
　San Francisco—Exhibitions.　7. Fine Arts Museums of San Francisco—
　Exhibitions.　I. Junker, Patricia A.　II. Fine Arts Museums of San
　Francisco.　III. Title.
　ND205.S544　1994
　759.13′07479461—dc20
　　　　　　　　　　　　　　　　　　　　　　　　94-4367
　　　　　　　　　　　　　　　　　　　　　　　　CIP

FRONT COVER
John Singleton Copley, *Mary Turner Sargent* (Mrs. Daniel Sargent), 1763, catalogue number 7 (detail)

BACK COVER
William J. McCloskey, *Oranges in Tissue Paper*, ca. 1890, catalogue number 105

ON THE TITLE PAGE
Grant Wood, *Dinner for Threshers*, 1934, catalogue number 132

Permission to quote from the letter from Marsden Hartley to Shaemas O'Sheel, 19 October 1908, is given by the Marsden Hartley collection, Yale Collection of American Literature, Beinecke Rare Book and Manuscript Library, Yale University. Publication from the letter by William Page to Frank G. and Sarah Shaw is by permission of the Houghton Library, Harvard University.

Printed and bound in Italy

CONTENTS

The gift of 140 works of American art, among them some of the icons of our national heritage, would be cause for celebration in any art museum in the country. This is especially the case when the works are of the quality, and collectively have the breadth, of the paintings, drawings, and watercolors donated to The Fine Arts Museums by John D. Rockefeller 3rd and Blanchette Hooker Rockefeller. The current exhibition and its accompanying catalogue, which document the Rockefellers' accomplishments as collectors and their generosity as donors, serve as tokens of this institution's appreciation for their vision and extraordinary goodwill.

When the Rockefellers decided to leave their American art collection to The Fine Arts Museums of San Francisco, they did much more than simply augment the selection of American paintings that could be seen on the walls of the M. H. de Young Memorial Museum. Instead, they radically altered the course of this institution and this community. We cannot yet calculate all the ramifications of the gift. But it seems apt, fifteen years after the first portion of the collection arrived in the city, to begin an accounting of the ways in which the community has responded to the challenges and opportunities it presents.

In a letter of 16 January 1978 announcing his intention of making the gift to San Francisco, Mr. Rockefeller wrote of the impact he hoped the collection would make, both in building the Museums' survey of American art and in encouraging the Museums' already expressed commitment to make the field a major focus in the future. It is unquestionably the momentum generated by his announcement and subsequent gift that has prompted the growth of the historic American paintings collection, including gifts (full, partial, and promised) from community members of works by such artists as George Bellows, William Bradford, Mary Cassatt, Childe Hassam, and Edward Hopper (to mention but some of the most notable painters not represented, or at least not characteristically so, in San Francisco's Rockefeller Collection). Likewise, the presence of this strong collection has, at least in part, justified the institution's acquisition of major works (using both endowment funds and generous gifts, again from the community) to broaden and extend the scope of our story of American art. In this manner, exemplary objects by Mary Cassatt, Charles Demuth, Thomas Wilmer Dewing, Edwin Dickinson, Thomas Doughty, Arthur Dove, George Henry Durrie, Frank Duveneck, William Stanley Haseltine, Georgia O'Keeffe, and James McNeill Whistler (again, to note only a portion of the purchases of paintings by artists not among the San Francisco Rockefeller works) have entered the collection. The growing collection of American decorative arts, ranging from colonial times to the present, also finds a context and challenge from being seen in the company of the pictorial works.

The Rockefeller Collection served as an important catalyst in prompting Ednah Root, a San Francisco artist and philanthropist, to support a curatorial chair in American art. From annual support in 1979 for one position, she gradually advanced her commitment to the program until her various gifts and her posthumously created foundation could underwrite four staff positions and a continuing series of exhibitions, seminars, and associated programs connected to American art at The Fine Arts Museums. Thanks to this staff and the resources Ednah Root provided, the past decade has seen a series of important exhibitions—generated both here and elsewhere—that have widened our understanding of key figures and moments in the history of American art.

Two relatively recent events at the Museums grow from the pleasurable duties of sharing, caring for, and researching the Rockefellers' collection: much expanded gallery space at the de Young for the display of American art, and the establishment of the American Art Study Center. Opening initially in 1977, the de Young's new American Galleries had grown over their first decade to a suite of seven handsome galleries in the east wing of the building. Even this space, however, left many important works in storage. Therefore, as one element in the reorganization of the de Young and California Palace of the Legion of Honor galleries, in 1988 and 1989 we dedicated most of the central core of the de Young to American art. Twenty-two galleries, the hallway cases at the back and left sides of Hearst Court, Hearst Court itself, and occasional access to yet other galleries, have allowed the American collections to be far more fully seen in recent years, with over twice as many paintings now generally on view than before, and a much greater increase than that in the number of decorative arts and sculptures on display. The American Art Study Center is another area of signal growth. When the Smithsonian Institution decided to consolidate the Archives of American Art's West Coast branches in San Marino, we determined to try and maintain an active research facility here, where members of the public could use the unrestricted microfilm of the Archives in conjunction with the printed materials of the Museums' Bothin Library. Partially supported since 1992 by the benefit proceeds of *USArt*, an annual exposition and fair of American art, the Study Center welcomes hundreds of users each year—students, academics, museum professionals, and members of the general public. Taken together, these changes have allowed the community ready access to the institution's rich holdings of American art objects and a means of understanding them in their historic contexts.

With the institution's own expanding sense of the central role of education in our public mission, the collection has become the focus of art, art history, history, and cultural history classes for students throughout the region. As an example of the range of educational opportunities of the past several years, American art is a key feature in the curriculum of every fifth grader in the San Francisco Unified School District, an element in the Advanced Placement Art History course offered in the museum to high school students from the district, is now being taught in colleges and universities throughout the Bay Area, and has been the subject of Elderhostel courses held in the galleries. It is a resource, that is to say, for everyone, from child to retired citizen.

If a look at the past fifteen years yields a roster of opportunities and achievements emerging from the presence of the Rockefeller Collection at the de Young, it also makes clear that much remains to be done. Principal, especially from the vantage of this centennial season, is the consideration of the institution's future. The physical structure of the de Young has recently been reinforced, in order to protect people and objects in the event of a major earthquake. But I hope and believe that we are soon going to undertake a much more thorough review of our facilities and services. Because of the presence of the Rockefeller Collection, American art will be a prime component in these deliberations.

Among the priorities to be established, I believe a full presentation of American art—based on the foundation provided by the Rockefeller Collection—has to be one of our goals. In recent years we have worked hard to build our modern and contemporary art program through acquisitions and exhibitions, believing that we have a responsibility to extend the historical survey of American art to the present day. Moreover, we have come to realize how crucial it is to represent the rich artistic heritage of our own region, Northern California. Building the collection in both areas, noting that they overlap significantly, needs to receive our continuing and concerted attention.

As we build our American art holdings and foster scholarship, we must heed the calls for greater ethnic and gender diversity that are, rightly, part of our contemporary world. We need to refine and expand our teaching efforts and educational materials so as to make the museum experience more rewarding, elucidating the complex meanings and history of these objects for our ever-broadening audiences. Underlying all is the responsibility to understand the physical properties of these objects and thereby to preserve them, so that generations beyond our own will be able to study and enjoy them. These are exciting tasks, ones that we can undertake in the assurance that, thanks to the generosity of the Rockefellers, a historic survey of great quality is in place for us to build upon.

In February 1978, John D. Rockefeller 3rd wrote:

> American art will only attain its rightful place in American museums and universities by the efforts of many people. Each of us must do his or her bit as appears wise and right to the individual. I have felt that concentrating my efforts on the collecting was perhaps the best contribution I could make and that others would become interested in making their contribution in different but supplementary ways. . . . Let's each of us in our own way continue to pursue our respective efforts toward strengthening and building the field of American art in this country.

This vision of collective effort is clearly at the core of what the Rockefellers hoped to accomplish with their great gift of art to the people of San Francisco. The next step is our responsibility.

HARRY S. PARKER III
Director of Museums

When selections from the American art collection of Mr. and Mrs. John D. Rockefeller 3rd were first shown in San Francisco, as part of the nation's Bicentennial festivities, the "Foreword" to the catalogue began with a quotation from Mr. Rockefeller's 1973 book, *The Second American Revolution*:

> For my part, give me the decision to become involved by more and more people, and I will gladly take my chances as to the quality of their choices and actions.

The current presentation of the collection puts this philosophy to the test, for it grows out of the involvement of literally hundreds of people. It is our pleasure to acknowledge here some few of them.

Principally, of course, we must acknowledge the Rockefellers for assembling the collection and envisioning it as a means of doing public good. Over the years, the Rockefellers opened their collection to an ever wider circle of people, first through the special exhibition of 1976, then by means of extended loans of specific objects to The Fine Arts Museums. This was in turn followed by the public announcement in 1978 of their intention to give the collection to the people of San Francisco, and culminated with the gift itself, made largely in two groups in 1979 and 1993. One hundred and forty important objects of American art now reside as the core of the institution's historical American art collection. We at The Fine Arts Museums owe our deepest debt of gratitude to the Rockefellers and their family, who have entrusted to us this great legacy and responsibility.

The present exhibition is the first time that all the works of the Rockefeller Collection of American Art now in San Francisco will be seen together. We are grateful to the trustees of the Ednah Root Foundation for providing the funds necessary for the institution to mount this important exhibition. Taking place during the M. H. de Young Memorial Museum's Centennial Season, the project aptly encapsulates one of the crucial moments of the institution's first one hundred years—the entwined legacy of the Rockefeller Collection and Ednah Root's response to support American art projects at the institution.

The present catalogue has been underwritten by the Blanchette Hooker Rockefeller Fund. We are deeply thankful to the trustees of the fund for their encouragement and confidence.

Aspects of the Rockefeller Collection have been examined in special exhibitions twice before. In 1976, as noted above, *American Art: An Exhibition from the Collection of Mr. and Mrs. John D. Rockefeller 3rd* served as Bicentennial celebration both in San Francisco and at the Whitney Museum of American Art in New York. The exhibition was accompanied by a "Narrative and Critical Catalogue" written by E. P. Richardson, premier scholar in the field and the Rockefellers' American art advisor. His elegant and informative text provides a rock on which we now build. In 1982, a different grouping of works was gathered for *American Painting 1730–1960: A Selection from the Collection of Mr. and Mrs. John D. Rockefeller 3rd*, an exhibition that toured in Japan under the auspices of the National Museum of Western Art, Tokyo, the Japan Society, New York, and The Fine Arts Museum of San Francisco. The catalogue for that project, written by Margaretta Lovell (The Fine Arts Museums' Ednah Root Curator of American Art, 1981–1985, and on the faculty of the University of California, Berkeley) was the first to attach the scholarly apparatus of provenance, exhibition history, and selected bibliography to works in the Rockefeller Collection. Lovell's insightful catalogue entries and "A Short History of American Painting" provided one of the earliest histories of American art widely available in Japanese. The informally circulated English version of the text has been an important resource for this project. All three catalogues—of 1976, 1982, and 1994—have relied on material gathered and organized by the Rockefellers' curators, first Berthe Saunders and, for more than the past decade, Meg Perlman.

This catalogue bears the fruit of further concentrated research. A grant from the Henry Luce Foundation, announced in November 1984, allowed the Museums to recruit staff members whose principal responsibilities were to assemble and fill in the object files begun by Lovell. Two inspired researchers expanded our knowledge of the entire American paintings collection dramatically: Sally Mills (beginning in 1985 as Assistant Curator for Research, Mills ultimately was named Associate Curator in the department before leaving in 1991 to further her graduate studies) and Jennifer Saville (who served as Assistant Curator for Research from 1985 to 1987 before leaving to join the staff of the Honolulu Academy of Arts). Their labors are reflected in the provenance, exhibition, and publication histories for each work and in much of the primary source material we have extracted for the catalogue entries. Student interns from the University of California, Berkeley (Linda Graham, Christina Yang, Celeste Connor, Corinna Fong, Yolanda Starczak, Kirk Savage, F. Lindsay Macbeth) and Stanford University (Susan Dennis, Leslie Wright, Michelle Korjeff), and a series of National Endowment for the Arts interns (M. Elizabeth Boone, Koren Sawyer, Derrick Cartwright, Kelly Ebeling, Catherine A. Johnson, Catherine Coulter) each added greatly to the materials in hand, as have Jared Goss, Ruth Clausen, and Juli Cunningham.

The magnitude of this project, and the richness of the works, has led these researchers and us to institutions and scholars throughout the country and abroad. Nearly every line of information in the following catalogue entries depends on the efforts and cooperation of academics, curators, researchers, registrars, librarians, archivists, genealogists, dealers, collectors, and descendants of artists. We cannot here list each and every one, but it is with deep gratitude that we acknowledge their generosity and collegiality.

Throughout the forming of this text, we have relied heavily on two major components of the American Art Study Center at The Fine Arts Museums of San Francisco. The first of these is the Smithsonian Institution's Archives of American Art Depository for Unrestricted Microfilmed Collections. The second is the Museums' Bothin Library of American Art, which in recent years has grown to include such invaluable materials as microform copies of rare nineteenth-century serials along with a significant holding of surveys, monographs, exhibition and auction catalogues, and current periodicals. The Study Center thus provided us with essential access to millions of primary documents and a fine selection of secondary materials.

Our colleagues at The Fine Arts Museums have given generously of their time and expertise to bring this publication and exhibition to fruition. A major effort was put forward by the conservation staff, who conducted a comprehensive survey of all the Rockefeller works and treated many of the pictures prior to the exhibition. Carl Grimm, Senior Paintings Conservator, with Jenny Sherman, Kress Fellow and Assistant Paintings Conservator, and Cynthia Lawrence, Associate Paintings Conservator (through June 1993), examined all 109 paintings and treated a significant number of them. They were assisted by Ria German and Valya Natcheva-Hristova. At the Western Regional Paper Conservation Laboratory, Robert Futernick, Head Conservator of Prints and Drawings and Chairman for Conservation; Debra Evans, Conservator of Prints and Drawings; and Pauline Mohr, Associate Conservator of Prints and Drawings, examined and prepared the twenty-nine works on paper. Elisabeth Cornu, Head Objects Conservator, along with Margaret Thomas, Tracy Radeff, and Robert Rosenberg merit special mention for their efforts to treat many of the frames in the Rockefeller Collection in time for this celebration. A generous gift from Patricia Ann Schindler helped underwrite some of this important work.

In the American Art Department, Jane Glover, Secretary, carries the responsibility of maintaining the now voluminous object record files. She has played an integral part in organizing material for this publication, preparing manuscript drafts, and maintaining order in our contacts with the outside world. Rob Krulak, 1994 NEA Intern, arrived in San Francisco in time to read galley proofs and make several welcome suggestions regarding the form and content of the catalogue entries. Our colleagues in the Achenbach Foundation for Graphic Arts—Robert Flynn Johnson, Curator in Charge; Karin Breuer, Associate Curator; and Maxine Rosston, Assistant Curator—are responsible for the drawings and watercolors in the Rockefeller Collection, and have been models of cooperation.

Kathe Hodgson, Coordinator of Exhibitions, demonstrated the fitness of her title as she worked tirelessly to mount this celebratory exhibition of the Rockefeller Collection. William White, Director of Exhibition and Technical Production, designed the temporary exhibition and supervised the superb technical staff in its installation and with the rehanging of permanent collection galleries necessitated by the removal of so many key works. We especially thank Ron Rick, Chief Graphic Designer, for his handsome layout of the text materials seen throughout the exhibition. Without the combined professionalism and goodwill of each department in the institution—Accounting, Audience Development, Custodial, Development, Education, Engineering, Membership, Museum Stores, Operations, Press Office, Public Programs, Public Relations, Registration, Security, Special Events, Technicians, *Triptych*, as well as Docents and Volunteers—the project as a whole would not take place.

This publication has been carefully shaped by Karen Kevorkian, Editor, and Ann Heath Karlstrom, Director of Publications. Fronia W. Simpson brought order and consistency to the catalogue entries. Designer Robin Weiss has integrated a wide array of documentary material into a handsome and, we hope, usable whole. Photography was provided by Joseph McDonald and coordinated by Mary Haas.

The introductory essay on the Rockefeller Collection grows out of a talk given in 1989. It has changed much since then, at least in part owing to suggestions offered by past and present members of the American Art Department, and such wise outside readers as Charles Eldredge, Meg Perlman, Mrs. E. P. Richardson, and Ian McKibbin White.

Finally, we want to express our appreciation for the support and encouragement of this project extended by four key people. On an institutional level, Harry S. Parker III, Director of Museums, and Steven A. Nash, Associate Director and Chief Curator, have consistently assisted and promoted the enterprise, allowing us to devote necessary time and resources to its completion. On a more personal front, our respective spouses—David and Fronia—have been models of support and patience. We thank them all.

P. J. and M. S.

A SOURCE OF PLEASURE AND SATISFACTION

The American Art Collection of Mr. and Mrs. John D. Rockefeller 3rd

My wife and I began collecting oriental art in the early 1950s and this we supplemented with a number of French Impressionists to give variety. After a while we came to realize that we had no representation of American art and this was disturbing to us particularly in connection with foreign friends and guests. And so we decided in 1964 to buy a few American paintings.

JOHN D. ROCKEFELLER 3RD TO WALTER S. NEWMAN, 16 JANUARY 1978

ORIGIN OF THE COLLECTION

John D. Rockefeller 3rd and Blanchette Hooker Rockefeller made their first recorded purchase of a nineteenth-century American work in spring 1960, when they acquired Winslow Homer's watercolor *Backgammon* (cat. no. 79).[1] The stark and elegant depiction of two young women—its rhythmic composition and vignette format along with the more obvious homages of fan and eccentric signature revealing the artist's appreciation of things Japanese—understandably appealed to collectors sensitive to Asian art But this work's position at the starting point of one of the twentieth century's most noteworthy collections of historic American art is ironic. For the quiet Victorian interior stands well apart from the best-known subjects of the artist. By acquiring it, rather than a more typical outdoor scene observed by Homer the sportsman, seafarer, or tourist, the Rockefellers revealed that personal response to the individual object would always outweigh the opportunity to gain a representative example of a given artist's work.

After the acquisition of *Backgammon*, nearly four years passed before the Rockefellers again turned in a significant way to American art. In this regard, as Rockefeller noted, the start of collecting, rather than owning individual objects, can be said to date from January 1964. For it was then that the Rockefellers acquired their first nineteenth-century landscape painting, a crowning achievement of American landscape art, *Approaching Storm, Owl's Head*, by the then little-known Fitz Hugh Lane (fig. 1).[2] As the scholar Joshua Taylor observed, the work's "enigmatic quality could hardly fail to fascinate a sensibility schooled on Oriental art."[3] The location depicted in the work, Maine's Penobscot Bay, may also have spoken to the Rockefellers; nearby Mount Desert, site of the family's summer home for over a generation, was where they had become engaged.[4] With wry understatement Rockefeller reminisced of these first American works: "As it happened, we had good luck in obtaining some quite outstanding ones. This stirred our interest."[5]

RISING INTEREST IN NINETEENTH-CENTURY AMERICAN ART

The early 1960s was a propitious time to collect historic American art. In the ways it touched the world of collectors, scholars, dealers, and museum administrators, the field was changing, reflecting both the budding of scholarly interest in historic American art as well as its increased prestige in the market.[6] As one noted critic observed when looking back at this period from 1976:

> The classics of 19th-century American painting, which not so long ago were gathering dust and contempt in the storerooms of American museums, have lately been enjoying a new vogue. Art historians no longer risk their reputations by specializing in this material, and art collectors no longer earn the condescension of their peers for investing sizable sums of money in the pictures.[7]

A look at principal texts on nineteenth-century American art reveals the scope of the change. From 1900 to 1950 the surveys and monographs published on the subject were barely enough to fill a single small shelf. Inaugurated by E. P. Richardson's *Painting in America* of 1956, however, a series of overviews, monographs, dictionaries, museum and

exhibition catalogues, and reprints of nineteenth-century texts appeared in quick order, establishing the conceptual and documentary outlines of the discipline and becoming standard, crucial references.[8] In 1970 one scholar could write:

> More studies of American painting have been published in the past decade than in the previous century. The major exhibitions of the past several years in particular have been reawakening millions of Americans to the treasure of their heritage.
>
> This is hardly to suggest that American painting has been thoroughly understood. The bibliography is still the smallest on any major nation in the Western World. We are only at the threshold of discovering the depth and breadth of its richness.[9]

Indeed, it was only in 1970 that the greatest resource for scholars of American art, the Archives of American Art, affiliated itself with the Smithsonian Institution and so became a national resource through its network of regional centers (the Northern California branch opened at the M. H. de Young Memorial Museum in 1973).

Moving in step with this advance in research capability in the 1960s and 1970s was a more specialized market and apparatus.[10] Over the full first half of the twentieth century, Doll & Richards, Childs, and the Vose galleries in Boston, and Babcock, Ferargil, Graham, John Levy, Macbeth, Milch, and Montross galleries, along with a scant handful of others in New York (Norman Hirschl, Victor Spark, and Rudolph Wunderlich were especially important toward the end of the era) could be said to specialize, at least part-time, in nineteenth-century American art. Starting in the 1960s, however, the field grew dramatically. Contributing to this commercialization was the rise of the specialized American art auction, regularly scheduled and heavily promoted, with attendant crowds, headlines, and what might be called "news spasms" dedicated to ever-advancing price records. The newsworthiness of American art not only encouraged purchasers but, equally, alerted owners to the spiraling values of paintings, inspiring fresh works to enter the market.[11]

What the rise in scholarly and commercial attention signaled was the belief in the worthiness of nineteenth-century American art. No longer the stuff of ancestor worship and historical societies, American paintings came to be seen as valid objects of aesthetic and historical merit.[12] As Thomas Hoving wrote in the preface to the Metropolitan Museum's landmark exhibition of 1970, *Nineteenth-Century America: Paintings and Sculpture*, itself an important index of the reappraisal of the field: "Looking at this exhibition, we can assess the folly of the genteel neglect and snobbish disdain that has until recently been the lot of much of this work."[13]

John Davison Rockefeller 3rd (1906–1978; fig. 2, with Blanchette Hooker Rockefeller, his wife) was a member of one of America's most distinguished families, whose fortune derived from the Standard Oil Corporation founded by his grandfather.[14] He was the eldest son of John D. Rockefeller, Jr., and Abby Aldrich Rockefeller (a descendant of Roger Williams and the daughter of Senator Nelson W. Aldrich of Rhode Island).[15] Rockefeller's younger brothers eventually held such visible positions as governor of New York and vice-president of the United States (Nelson; 1908–1979), conservationist (Laurance; b. 1910), governor of Arkansas (Winthrop; 1912–1973), and chairman of Chase Manhattan Bank (David; b. 1915). The eldest child of the family was the sole daughter, Abby (1903–1976).[16] His son, John D. Rockefeller IV, was governor of West Virginia and is now a United States senator from that state. John D. Rockefeller 3rd, however, chose a less public sphere of action. His following a more private path in the midst of one of America's most public families prompted his wife to observe, "What the other brothers have done is natural; what Johnny has done is remarkable. His philosophy of life is based on doing things in a quiet, unostentatious way."[17] He was described in a *New Yorker* profile of 1972 as "a tall (six feet one), intense, handsome man with penetrating blue eyes, a determined chin, and a striking profile somewhat on the order of the Presidential busts carved on the Mount Rushmore National Memorial." The writer then recited a series of adjectives that recurred in others' descriptions of the man: "polite, serious, gentle, diffident, non-circulating, naturally withdrawn, . . . shy, modest, . . . patient, tactful, earnest, conscientious, orderly, idealistic, persistent, constrained but graceful, deliberate, frugal, courtly, stubborn, Calvinistic, and Puritan-ethic-ridden."[18]

A 1929 graduate of Princeton University, where he studied economics, Rockefeller in later life traveled widely, especially in Asia, consistently seeking to foster international well-being and understanding.[19] A thoughtful observer of American society, Rockefeller addressed the split between the Establishment and the country's underprivileged in his 1973 book, *The Second American Revolution: Some Personal Observations*.[20] There, reflecting on political, economic, cultural, educational, and moral issues, Rockefeller revealed his sympathies to be not with the status quo, but with those seeking to make the world a place in which each individual could develop his or her fullest potential. One of his principal efforts in this was the establishment and support of the Population Council, which he initiated in 1952 "to stimulate, encourage, promote, conduct, and support significant activities in the broad field of population."[21]

Rockefeller changed the cultural life of this country by developing the Japan Society (he was elected a director and president in 1952 and later donated the land in Manhattan for Japan House) and by founding such important institutions for New York as the Asia Society, as well as orchestrating the conglomeration of enterprises located at Lincoln Center, serving as its president or chairman for thirteen years (both projects were initiated in 1956).[22] Throughout his life, Rockefeller followed the precept of his philanthropist father, who observed, "Giving is the secret of a healthy life. Not necessarily money, but whatever a man has of encouragement and sympathy and understanding."[23]

Rockefeller had grown up in an environment rich in art treasures.[24] His mother, in addition to being co-founder of the Museum of Modern Art in New York, was one of the earliest and most important collectors of American folk art. "To me," she wrote to another of her sons, "art is one of the great resources of my life."[25] His father, in addition to the founding and decades-long involvement with the Cloisters (the medieval art collection housed in Fort Tryon Park, New York City, which is a branch of the Metropolitan Museum of Art), and collecting K'ang Hsi ceramics, began the restoration and development of Colonial Williamsburg, a project that Rockefeller eventually oversaw from 1939 to 1951.[26]

Mrs. John D. Rockefeller 3rd, Blanchette Hooker Rockefeller (1909–1992), was a significant presence in New York's modern art and philanthropic worlds for fifty years. She was descended on both parents' sides from seventeenth-century settlers and was raised in a family that valued education, individuality, and public-spiritedness.[27] Described by one admirer as "a cool, pale beauty with a regally poised head,"[28] she graduated from Vassar College in 1931 with a degree in music. After her marriage in 1932, she immediately began

FIG. 2.
Blanchette Hooker Rockefeller and
John D. Rockefeller 3rd at Room
5600, Rockefeller Center, 1974
(photo: Elizabeth Gee)

an active life in New York's civic and charitable communities, in addition to undertaking the responsibilities of raising the couple's four children (Sandra, b. 1935; John D. IV, b. 1937; Hope, b. 1938; Alida, b. 1949). Although her interests ranged from the Juilliard School of Music to the welfare of underprivileged children, Mrs. Rockefeller's principal public energies were reserved for the Museum of Modern Art. Inspired by her mother-in-law's involvement there,[29] and persuaded by her brother-in-law Nelson to organize the institution's Junior Council in 1948, she later served in various leadership capacities on the board, including president and chairman. In part because of her activities at MoMA, she began to collect contemporary art.[30] As her husband found the material unsympathetic (as had his father before him when Abby Aldrich Rockefeller was involved at MoMA), in 1950 she commissioned Philip Johnson to design a guest residence on Manhattan's East 52nd Street to hold portions of the collection.[31]

In spite of growing up and living in an art-rich environment, it was only in 1951 that Mr. and Mrs. Rockefeller together began seriously to collect art. There were two focuses: Asian and American.[32] The catalyst for the Asian collection was a trip to Japan in 1951, when Rockefeller served as consultant to John Foster Dulles's Peace Treaty Mission.[33] Two years later, Mr. and Mrs. Rockefeller traveled through much of South and Southeast Asia, meeting many of the regions' political and cultural leaders. "Thanks to that trip," Rockefeller later said, "we found ourselves very drawn to Asia—its peoples, its countries and their cultures. Our collecting has always been closely related to our feeling for these Asian friends. It also expresses our hope of gaining a deeper understanding and appreciation of these older civilizations."[34] With focuses on metal sculpture and porcelain, much of the collection assembled by the Rockefellers over the next twenty-five years is now housed in the Asia Society in New York.[35]

The American collection began a decade later. It grew at least in part as a response to a perceived social need. Rockefeller reminisced:

[The American collection's] origin . . . is found in our collection of Oriental art. Many people who have no background in Oriental art are uncertain about how to respond to it when they encounter it in one's home or office. Its style and feeling are quite different.

So my wife and I thought it would help to make our non-Oriental guests feel more at ease if we added a few French Impressionists. They are known, respected and enjoyed by everybody, and they fit in well with the Oriental.

But that didn't quite solve the problem. We suddenly realized that we had nothing that represented our own country, our own culture, our own heritage. We thought we should since we have quite a few people from other countries come to our home. Therefore, we decided to acquire just a few American paintings. And that is how we began.[36]

The collection started, that is to say, almost as a diplomatic entity—a goodwill ambassador revealing American culture and values to visitors from abroad.

THE ADVISOR

When it became clear that the American collection was going to exceed four or five objects, the Rockefellers sought a knowledgeable advisor to work with them. The man they turned to was Edgar P. Richardson (1902–1985). Director for many years of the Detroit Institute of Arts and a pioneering scholar of American art, Richardson had made notable contributions to the field, writing the first major survey of American art to appear in fifty years, seminal monographic studies, and generating, with Lawrence A. Fleischman and Mrs. Edsel Ford, the idea of the Archives of American Art.[37] Rockefeller evidently contacted Richardson, who was then director of the Henry Francis du Pont Winterthur Museum in Delaware, in late 1964, seeking advice and counsel. Richardson visited the Rockefeller apartment in midtown Manhattan. On 24 December, Rockefeller summarized that meeting:

I asked you if you would be good enough to send us a list of American painters who you felt we should particularly consider in terms of our thought of buying, say, fifteen or twenty paintings which would be representative of American artists and, at the same time, of first quality.

As we mentioned to you, our approach is to buy few things, whether they be American, Oriental or European and to constantly have as our objective items, on the one hand, that are especially fine and, on the other, that we really like ourselves. Also, of course, there is the question of their fitting in with the other things in our apartment. . . .[38]

We do look forward to working with you and we will count on your speaking frankly. Your judgment will be helpful not only in terms of quality, but also as to the importance of the picture in relation to the artist's work generally and as purely an esthetic product.[39]

A week later, on 31 December, Richardson responded. In addition to listing eighteen artists whom he found particularly important,[40] he also committed to paper a credo concerning nineteenth-century American art:

What makes American nineteenth-century painting keenly interesting to explore, at least to me, is that it is so varied and unexplored. The French in the nineteenth century had a few great figures in painting, surrounded by a mass of mediocrity, just as in France there is Paris surrounded by the provinces. Our country is a big and varied continent and our painting is somewhat of the same kind: there are many interesting figures but none dominant. The good men sometimes did bad pictures. This makes it fun to try to pick the enchanting pictures but it discourages an attempt to draw up a canon of twenty names.

Your letter corresponds exactly with my understanding. I shall call your attention to things that interest me and which I think might be worthwhile and shall let you know when I expect to be in New York, in case you wish to ask me to look at something you have found. And don't be surprised if I call attention to painters not on this list at all.[41]

Appropriately, both men wrote on the eve of festival days, for this exchange of letters marked the beginning of a spirited and clearly enjoyable relationship shared over the years.[42]

The manner in which the Rockefellers and Richardson worked together merits retelling. The Rockefellers frequently visited galleries (most often on Saturday mornings) and the occasional auction preview, and, of course, once their interest in the field was known, they were presented with numerous opportunities to acquire works. If works struck them as interesting, they would sometimes ask Richardson's opinion or response. Richardson in turn brought works to their notice from his weekday visits to New York and Philadelphia dealers. Collector and advisor rarely, if ever, visited commercial establishments together.[43]

The Rockefellers and Richardson used a gradually developed classification system to rank candidates for purchase—A, B, C, D, X, and O. "A" paintings were judged to be of exemplary beauty and great historical importance, and could be considered "one of the two or three best by a particular artist"; "B" were of a quality that any first-rate museum would be proud to possess; "C" paintings were "good paintings by the individual artist which a good museum would be glad to have"; the "D" category was for "perfectly respectable works of an individual artist but without any particular distinction and which a museum would take in lieu of a better painting being available."[44] The last two categories were evolved to deal with surprises: the "X" label was for rare works of extraordinary attractiveness by little-known artists; the "O" rank was given to exquisite, small-scale works that, no matter the artist's fame, generated sufficient pleasure to prompt the exclamation, "O, what a delightful little picture!" The works from these last two classifications are crucial in giving the Rockefeller collection its personal, idiosyncratic flavor—what Richardson called its "note of individual taste and connoisseurship, and of a love of the arts for their own sake, independent of fame or price."[45]

Of course there was not always unanimity on the ranking of the works. In the case of disagreement, Rockefeller's was the deciding voice. As they appear to have done in other endeavors, the Rockefellers sought the best advice available on a subject and listened to it gladly, but final responsibility remained with the collectors—especially with Rockefeller. Although Mr. and Mrs. Rockefeller worked together in forming and donating the collection, his was the dominant voice; she most often in later years referred to it as "Johnny's collection."[46] Richardson, too, in public stressed this point: "Mr. Rockefeller has never, in my experience, acquired a work he has not himself enjoyed and found significant, often after long study. The exhibition [organized in 1976 by The Fine Arts Museums of San Francisco— see below] thus represents a thoughtful, personal view of our [nation's] art by an observer of unusual experience and perspective. . . . All [the works] speak from the heart."[47] The scholar was even more adamant on the point in private. He wrote to Ian McKibbin White, director of The Fine Arts Museums, as plans for the opening the 1976 exhibition were progressing:

> Mr. Rockefeller asked my opinion about your suggestion of a news conference. . . .
> I support your suggestion. He talks well in an interview and his personality always makes a good impression. But I also said I do not want to be there or have a part in the press conference. I think it very important to make clear that this is his personal collection and that the credit for it should be his. I have enjoyed finding things for him, and enjoyed working with him. But the choice has always been his. There are many other collections which have been formed by someone, engaged to buy a collection, who has made the selection and done the buying for the collector. That is not the case here at all and I am determined, so far as I can, to see that the credit goes where it belongs, to him. . . . A truly great collector, whose things have never before been seen; a great name, unknown in this aspect. What a story! Concentrate on that.[48]

THE GROWTH OF A PRIVATE COLLECTION

With a system in place, the collection began to grow. In spring 1965 the Rockefellers acquired three small paintings—a Thomas Sully portrait sketch of Charles Carroll (cat. no. 31) and William Michael Harnett's jewel-like *Still Life with "Le Figaro"* (fig. 3), both of which Richardson brought to Rockefeller's attention in a letter of 9 March, and Eastman Johnson's diminutive *The Mother* (cat. no. 73), which the Rockefellers asked Richardson about in a letter of 19 April, their interest in a maternal theme perhaps kindled by the birth of their second grandchild in 1964. It would seem that for the first years of the collection the standard American acquisition was small in scale, simple in composition, and exquisite in handling— works that would speak to their personal interests and readily sympathize with the Asian works already on display in their home.

In addition to opinions about specific works of art, Rockefeller and Richardson exchanged views in this early correspondence of an exhibition both had visited, at separate times, at the Metropolitan Museum of Art: *Three Centuries of American Painting.* Their comments, rich in ramifications for the future of the collection, are also indicative of the relatively lowly status of American art in the museum hierarchies (although not necessarily the public sensibility) of the time. Rockefeller wrote first:

> Last week I had a chance to stop in and see the Metropolitan Museum's show. I must say I was particularly impressed by some of the examples of John Singleton Copley whose works I had not really known before. Also I thought especially well of some of the examples of Thomas Cole, Albert Bierstadt, Eastman Johnson, Thomas Eakins and Winslow Homer.[49]
>
> It is a good show and I enjoyed very much seeing it, although I do think it might have been more effective if there were not quite so many paintings all at once.[50]

Richardson responded:

> I agree with you that there are too many pictures to be seen in the Metropolitan's exhibition: there were also, when I saw it, too many people. It was like trying to look at works of art in the middle of the commuters' rush in Grand Central terminal. The Metropolitan Museum has a very important collection of American painting, perhaps the most comprehensive collection in any museum. It has been in storage for nearly twenty years. I was glad to have a chance to see it but it should be a part of their permanent galleries, not a temporary exhibition, so that a collector like yourself could use it as a work of reference. It always seemed to me most unfortunate that the greatest museum in the greatest city of this country should not enable both Americans, and the stream of foreign visitors passing through, to see what this country has done in the arts. . . . Only in America do we treat the tradition of our own civilization as a poor stepchild.[51]

The theme of these two letters—the importance of museum collections in awakening knowledge of and enthusiasm for a nation's cultural achievements—would resonate long in Rockefeller's consideration.

One of the key moments in the collection's early history took place in fall 1965. Rockefeller wrote on 20 September, "I have had a letter from Mr. Wunderlich of the Kennedy Galleries stating that they are in the process of acquiring some important American paintings and offering to show them to me which, of course, I want to do."[52] The works were the American paintings collected by Lawrence and Barbara Fleischman of Detroit. Richardson responded immediately. He knew the collection extremely well, having been in Detroit during some of the years when the Fleischmans were building it, and having organized several exhibitions from it.[53] He noted that it "was, or is, the largest and most distinguished collection of American paintings, watercolors, prints and drawings I know and I can't help but feel sad to see it broken up."[54] Yet it presented a tremendous opportunity for the Rockefellers. Richardson singled out Thomas Cole's *View near the Village of Catskill* (cat. no. 32), Frederic Church's *Twilight* (cat. no. 51), Charles Willson Peale's *Mordecai Gist* (cat. no. 10), and Raphaelle Peale's *Blackberries* (cat. no. 27)[55] as of particular merit, but added: "In short, I haven't seen so large a group of paintings of this quality on the market since we have been discussing American painting. The question is simply whether you and Mrs. Rockefeller enjoy them."[56] Later, in response to Rockefeller's further questions, he added William Page's *Cupid and Psyche* (cat. no. 38), Grant Wood's *The Perfectionist* (cat. no. 133), and Thomas Eakins's *Frank Jay St. John* (cat. no. 118) to his list of recommendations. The Rockefellers eventually purchased all of these.[57] They, and other objects that Rockefeller picked out by photograph in December (such as William McCloskey's *Oranges in Tissue Paper* [cat. no. 105]) but did not act on until later the next spring, transformed and simultaneously signaled the expanding ambition of the collection. The general characteristics that all these works share is a resolved composition and carefully crafted surface—they project a considered retelling of the visual world rather than recording an artist's particular temperament or assertive technique.

The concentration of potential acquisitions prompted by the dispersal of the Fleischman collection sparked the need for Rockefeller actively to consider the parameters of the collection, rather than letting them evolve. Discussions started in October 1965 as Rockefeller contemplated the first three of the Fleischman paintings—Peale's *Mordecai Gist*, Church's *Twilight*, and Cole's *View near the Village of Catskill*. Rockefeller wrote:

> We have the Peale portrait and the Church and Cole landscapes at home now and are studying them carefully. The first two have much appeal to me, but I do have trouble getting up enthusism for the third—the Cole. To me it is a little bit bleak or bland and does not stir me the way I somehow feel a really good painting should.
>
> As you know, my wife and I have in mind the purchase of only a relatively limited number of paintings by Americans; hence we obviously cannot have representatives of all the better painters even if we could find them. . . .
>
> Obviously, there is no "must" as to who we should or should not purchase since our approach is the quality of the work and the appeal of the particular painting to us. On the other hand, if one is attempting to put together a group, there are undoubtedly certain painters one should try and add. My own feeling, however, is that I would rather add an exciting picture by a relatively unknown painter than a less-appealing one by a man of greater reputation and stature.
>
> This letter is somewhat philosophying but I guess this is understandable when we are entering a new field of painting and hence grooping [sic] to find our way.[58]

Richardson's reply was immediate and firm:

> It would be a great mistake to buy the Cole, or any other picture, unless you genuinely enjoy it. You are not creating a museum of the history of art in the United States. You are creating your own private collection which should reflect your own temperament, and your personal exploration of the long story of art in America. It will be a much more interesting collection for you, and for visitors to your apartment, if it remains truly personal. . . .
>
> . . . I would far rather see you buy a fine work by an artist no one has ever heard of than a work by *Cole*, simply because the name Cole is one that is known to almost everyone. The picture, not the name on the label, is what counts.[59]

Rockefeller purchased both the Peale and the Church paintings in February 1966. Only in May did he reconsider the Cole, acquire it, and grow eventually to value it above many other of his paintings.[60]

In part due to purchases such as these, by early 1966 it was apparent that a major exercise was underway and that both Mr. and Mrs. Rockefeller were, to use his word, "stirred" by American art.[61] The year was also a significant one for Richardson who, after decades of museum administration, had decided to retire in late spring, move to Philadelphia, and lead the life of an independent scholar. Rockefeller, who had from the first felt uneasy about the informal, non-paid consulting that Richardson was doing for him, moved to regularize the relationship. On 3 October, he put into writing a conversation they had earlier carried on:

> We agreed that you would continue for another year as my advisor concerning American art. We mentioned the year only so that at the end of the period we would both feel free to review the question on the light of developments during the year.
>
> We further agreed that not only would you be available to advise me in connection with paintings which might come to my attention, but also that you would take initiative keeping in touch with galleries and auctions handling American paintings. . . .
>
> Finally, we agreed that I would pay you an honorarium and that any out-of-pocket expenses would be charged to me in addition. . . .
>
> I greatly look forward to continuing to work with you in this area of special interest to me.[62]

From early in their correspondence, Rockefeller had written to Richardson that he was interested in the works of two particular artists: John Singleton Copley, whose paintings at the Metropolitan Museum of Art had proved to be a revelation; and Charles Burchfield, admittedly a twentieth-century artist but not an "extremely modern" one.[63] Works by both artists entered the collection late in 1966—Copley's *Dr. Nathaniel Perkins* (fig. 4) and Burchfield's *Railroad in Spring* (cat. no. 131)—becoming centers of significant clusters of works that joined them over the course of the next decade.

Other opportunities arose during the year, which the Rockefellers acted on at least fifteen times, establishing concentrations in colonial portraiture and nineteenth-century landscape, genre, and still-life painting. Two works by Eastman Johnson, *Cranberry Pickers* (fig. 5) and *What the Shell Says* (cat. no. 76), joined *The Mother*, becoming the second and third of what would be ten works by the artist in the collection.[64] But the acquisition that most thoroughly signaled the Rockefeller's increasing seriousness of purpose in 1966 was the purchase of George Caleb Bingham's recently rediscovered masterpiece, *Boatmen on the Missouri* (cat. no. 41). This in many ways epitomizes the virtues that appealed to the collectors: quietness of spirit, historical importance, distinctively American subject matter. Its purchase from Kennedy Galleries for $225,000 involved, by far, the Rockefellers' largest financial commitment for American art to date.

The correspondence between Rockefeller and Richardson sometimes gave way to Rockefeller's "philosophying." These paragraphs of reflection and speculation reveal much about the sixty-plus-year-old men, each thoughtful, quiet, and gentle in their private lives yet, especially in Rockefeller's case, well informed of the public sphere. They wrote about art, but also about the larger world around them. Richardson, for example, wrote of Martin Johnson Heade's *Twilight, Singing Beach* (cat. no. 59), which Rockefeller had asked after:

> I like the Heade at Hirschl and Adler. It has an almost uncanny stillness: your word was *surrealistic*. But in Salvador Dali the mysterious quality is contrived. In an artist like Heade, the note of mystery is a response by the artist to the wonder and mystery of nature. It is, in other words, a part of that modesty in the American artists of the past which makes them so attractive to me; altho today, I fear, it also stands in the way of their appreciation. Our eyes today [are] accustomed to pictures which are displays of the artist's art, skill and inventiveness—the subject they are painting does not count.[65] Men like Copley, Bingham, Church, Durand (in your portrait) or Fitz Hugh Lane, were not trying to make us admire their skill and artistry—they were trying to make us see something admirable which they had observed in a man or a phase of nature. This leads,

FIG. 4.
John Singleton Copley, 1738–1815.
Dr. Nathaniel Perkins, ca. 1773–
1774. Oil on canvas, 30 x 25 in. Private collection

FIG. 5.
Eastman Johnson, 1824–1906.
Cranberry Pickers, ca. 1879. Oil on paperboard, 22½ x 26¾ in. Private collection (photo: O. E. Nelson)

at its best, to a beautiful simplicity of statement, which yet says a great deal. Like some of Lincoln's speeches, for example, in the art of words.[66]

For both men, nostalgia informs patriotism. Yet, as Rockefeller especially was well aware, they lived in a world of challenging problems that demanded resolute and well-considered action.[67] The recognition of problems was not a cause for despair:

My belief is that it is quite possible to understand fully the gravity of our situation today and yet continue to be basically hopeful and optimistic about the future. . . . I feel this is an exciting time to be alive. Virtually everything seems to be wide open for change. I look upon this positively for to me it means that everything is wide open for improvement and progress. It means to me that each person has the opportunity to influence the course of events, in however small or large a way. I would much rather be alive during a time of challenge such as this than during a sedate and static period of history.[68]

Engaged with the challenges of the world, intent on its betterment, when Rockefeller turned to art, he inclined toward works of refinement and repose rather than those revelling in the questing sublime. "It is those [works] of the simplest form, he thinks, that usually give him the greatest satisfaction," wrote one scholar of the Asian objects.[69] Richardson, referring to the American collection, noted that it "passes by works representing a purely esthetic impulse or mode, in favor of those expressing a response to human life and to nature."[70]

In their appreciation of nostalgic pastoralism,[71] Rockefeller and Richardson moved a step ahead of the leading scholars of American art. In their glowing response to Heade's *Twilight*, for example, they were writing two years before the principal scholar of Heade's work, Theodore E. Stebbins, Jr., organized the artist's first monographic exhibition, and eight years before his extended examination of Heade's works and biography appeared.[72] Barbara Novak's pathbreaking study, *American Paintings of the Nineteenth Century: Realism, Idealism, and the American Experience*, which positioned the quietist landscapes of Heade, Lane, Kensett, and Gifford at the center of American nineteenth-century artistic accomplishment, was first published only in 1969. *American Light: The Luminist Movement, 1850–1875*, the exhibition organized by John Wilmerding for the National Gallery of Art in Washington, codifying a generation's debate on the importance of this group of painters (and using the Rockefellers' Fitz Hugh Lane as the cover of the catalogue), opened in 1980.

Such private collectors as the Rockefellers (and their few colleagues in the pursuit)[73] were in the vanguard of the appreciation of historic American painting. Richardson wrote of this phenomenon:

> Private collectors always lead the way in change of taste, ahead of institutions & the public; and a change of taste is over due in our country. By acquiring great examples of the most famous American artists, and by making discoveries among those who have been perhaps unjustly overlooked by fashion—in our X class—a collector like yourself can exert a strong and useful influence. We need, as a people, to know ourselves. Our heritage in the arts needs to be understood and valued, as does our heritage of nature and of history. And a sense [of] our history can have a steadying influence in a time of rapid change. So this is a useful thing to do. I am glad to be of such help as I can.[74]

The fact that the collection now seems so magisterial testifies not, as we might at first suspect, that the Rockefellers simply purchased the art-world equivalent of blue-chip stocks.[75] Rather, many of their acquisitions have proven to be, in the decades since their purchase, exceedingly prescient, leading scholars and the market in an appreciation (in both laudatory and financial senses of the word) of a given artist or style.

COLLECTION AS PUBLIC ENTITY

In trying to understand Rockefeller's intentions concerning his collection, it is worthwhile to note that to 1967 the acquired works are generally on a domestic scale—the largest being Burchfield's watercolor *Railroad in Spring*, at twenty-eight by forty-two inches. Several important paintings that appealed to both Mr. and Mrs. Rockefeller were passed over because of their concern that the works could not be readily displayed in the New York apartment. It was still a distinctly private enterprise.

Gradually, over the next four years, a significant change occurred. First of all, in an impressive display of momentum, nearly eighty more works were added. A few of the highlights in the approximate order of acquisition reveal the level of achievement that the Rockefellers considered: John F. Peto's *Job Lot Cheap* (cat. no. 109), Albert Pinkham Ryder's *The Lone Scout* (cat. no. 84), William Morris Hunt's *Governor's Creek, Florida* (cat. no. 75), J. G. Brown's *On the Hudson* (cat. no. 67), Robert Feke's *Grizzell Eastwick Apthorp* (cat. no. 4), Eastman Johnson's *A Day Dream* (cat. no. 80), Thomas Cole's *Sunrise in the Catskills* (fig. 6), William Michael Harnett's *After the Hunt* (fig. 7), Elihu Vedder's *The Sphinx of the*

FIG. 6.
Thomas Cole, 1801–1848. *Sunrise in the Catskills*, 1826. Oil on canvas, 25½ x 35½ in. National Gallery of Art, Washington, Gift of Mrs. John D. Rockefeller 3rd

FIG. 7.
William M. Harnett, 1848–1892.
After the Hunt, 1883 (first version).
Oil on canvas, 52½ x 34 in. The Hun-
tington, San Marino, California

FIG. 8.
Albert Bierstadt, 1830–1902. *Winter
—Yosemite*, ca. 1870. Oil on canvas,
26 x 36 in. Private collection. Photo
courtesy Gerald Peters Gallery

Seashore (cat. no. 82), Edward Hicks's *The Peaceable Kingdom* (cat. no. 42), Albert Bierstadt's *Winter—Yosemite* (fig. 8), Eastman Johnson's *Girl Picking Waterlilies* (fig. 9), Martin Johnson Heade's *Orchid and Hummingbird* (cat. no. 97), Frederic Church's *Snow Scene, Olana* (fig. 10), John F. Peto's *The Cup We All Race 4* (cat. no. 120), and Grant Wood's *Dinner for Threshers* (cat. no. 132).

Although the quality of these works is consistently high, their range in terms of artist, period, and subject is broad. Even a complete roster of them does not provide any overt, rational ordering or easy summarization. Rockefeller recognized and valued this serendipitous aspect of the collection:

> You see, so much really is happenstance. By that I mean that when something happens to become available, we try to see it, and, if we like it, we try to acquire it. Once or twice I have written a collector to say that, if at any time he or she was considering the disposition of any of the pieces in the collection I had seen, I would be pleased to be informed. But that has never produced any results. . . . We have purchased somewhat inspirationally or coincidentally as items came to our attention and as we responded to them.[76]

Moreover, in addition to their sheer number, the scale of the works during these years increased. This was in part allowed by the fact that American paintings were no longer being acquired solely for display in the apartment and offices in Manhattan but also for the Rockefeller country home, Fieldwood Farm, on the Hudson River near Tarrytown.[77] American art was coming to be a pervasive and important part of the collectors' lives— not merely decorative or ambassadorial, but of real importance in an emotional way. As Rockefeller wrote to Richardson in July 1968: "For some reason this spring has been a particularly active one as far as art is concerned for my wife and myself both in the Oriental field as well as American. It has been lots of fun but we have gotten in a little deeper than we expected." He closed his note with the conflicted emotions well known to every collector:

FIG. 9.
Eastman Johnson, 1824–1906. *Girl Picking Waterlilies*, 1865. Oil on paperboard, 18⅝ x 14¾ in. Collection of Jo Ann and Julian Ganz, Jr. (photo: Helga Photo Studio)

"Maybe this summer will be somewhat quieter but do not hesitate at any time to bring to our attention something which you feel is really appealing and/or important."[78]

There was a more important reason for the loosening up of concern with scale. Already by 1970, Rockefeller began to perceive—or at least began to articulate his perception—of the collection as no longer solely a private activity for the sake of himself and his family. Instead, in a fashion consistent with Rockefeller family tradition, he began to explore what public good it could achieve. This was very much in keeping with the fate of his cherished Asian art collection, which he was to commit to the Asia Society in Manhattan. As regards the American art, he broached the topic, in a purely hypothetical mode, in correspondence with Richardson early in 1970. By May it had begun to have concrete ramifications on the shape of the collection. Rockefeller wrote:

> Obviously we are not set up to handle these very big pictures. You mentioned this in connection with the portrait of the cardinal to be sold at auction [Thomas Eakins's *His Eminence Sebastiano Cardinal Martinelli*, 1902, The Armand Hammer Museum of Art and Cultural Center, Los Angeles]. On the other hand, if we are to give the collection to some museum in due course, maybe we should not rule out the very large picture if it is uniquely good.[79]

Together, Rockefeller and Richardson began to explore the notion of a responsible gift, discussing as possible recipients institutions of various sizes across the country, ranging from such private museums as that of Stanford University (where the Rockefellers' youngest daughter, Alida, was a student) to the Smithsonian Institution. Quickly they concluded that they should seek a large public museum, and that it should be a facility where there was evidence of a concerted interest specifically in historic American art, and yet where the Rockefeller collection would make a real impact on the cultural life of the community. Their discussions soon focused on Washington, D.C.—as the nation's capital—and a site in the West or Midwest—where there was a perceived need for a significant American art collection. Very informally, they began to canvass institutions, their programs in American art, and their staffs—including the major museums in Los Angeles, San Francisco, Seattle, Denver, Kansas City, and Minneapolis.

FIRST CONTACT WITH THE FINE ARTS MUSEUMS

In summer 1970, Rockefeller made a trip to San Francisco. He visited in the company of a cousin, Mary Homans, who was then on the Board of Trustees at the California Palace of the Legion of Honor. Together they met with the newly appointed director, Ian McKibbin White, looked at the historic American collections, discussed plans for an exhibition of the San Francisco collection that would show the combined American works of the Legion of Honor and the de Young,[80] and spoke of the possible merger of the two museums (which was accomplished in 1972 with the creation of The Fine Arts Museums of San Francisco). One point of apparently great interest was Frederic Church's *Rainy Season in the Tropics* (1866), which the Legion of Honor had just acquired. This purchase, at $165,000 an institutional record price for an American work, clearly signaled an administrative commitment to historic American painting. This impression was bolstered by a string of recent acquisitions at the de Young, including the purchase of works by George Bellows, Maurice Prendergast, Robert Henri, and John Singer Sargent (made possible in part with funds from the Charles E. Merrill Foundation), along with gifts received from the folk art collection of Edgar William and Bernice Chrysler Garbisch and a major donation from Dr. T. Edward and Tullah Hanley that included significant paintings by Gilbert Stuart, Everett Shinn, and Marsden Hartley.

Rockefeller took all this in, and later in the summer began corresponding with White, congratulating him on institutional plans and, in closing, asking: "As a matter of curiosity, is this field of art [historic American painting] of any special interest to you personally?"[81] Nicely, White was able to respond: "I must admit to a special interest myself in the 19th Century Americans. My wife and I have collected very modestly in this area. . . . I cannot claim a scholarly interest, only an enthusiastic one."[82] A dialogue, which White has lately described as a seven-year-long walk, was begun.[83] But Rockefeller was careful to remain determinedly neutral, trying to avoid the possibility of "raising hopes and then having them dashed to the detriment of all concerned."[84]

FIG. II.
John Singer Sargent, 1856–1925.
The Oyster Gatherer, 1877. Oil on
canvas, II x 10 in. Private collection
(photo: O. E. Nelson)

EMPHASIS ON MAJOR WORKS

During the early 1970s the collection continued to grow, with Mrs. Rockefeller taking an increasingly active role. She wrote to Richardson in September 1970:

> Johnny wanted me to send you the enclosed transparency of a Thomas Sully portrait of his son which is at Hirschl & Adler and with which I was very much impressed [*Alfred Sully*, cat. no. 37]. . . .
>
> I am doing my best to act as a go-between for Johnny while he is stuck in Tarrytown and unable to get around to the galleries.[85] We are having the Childe Hassam from the Newhouse Galleries [*In the Garden*, which the Rockefellers acquired but traded in 1974] sent to the country as we all like it very much and wish to study it further. The Eastman Johnson we voted down.[86]

As the Rockefellers wrestled, albeit privately, with the collection's potential as a public resource, they slowed the pace of acquisition. They aimed, it seems, for fewer but more demonstrably important paintings. As Richardson wrote early on in the deliberations:

> Your collection long since out-grew your original goal of enough American art to show, at home and in your office, something of our own people's contribution to the world of art. The idea of leaving the collection to a museum—and with a national purpose in mind— has changed the dimensions of the project. Or has it?[87]

Thus in the next year—1971—fewer than ten pictures are documented as entering the collection, although they included such critical works as Bingham's *Country Politician* (cat. no. 43), Sanford R. Gifford's *Windsor Castle* (cat. no. 56), Winslow Homer's *The Bright Side* (cat. no. 61), Eastman Johnson's *Sugaring Off* (cat. no. 66), and—in the "X" category— Dennis Miller Bunker's *A Bohemian* (cat. no. 94). Roughly the same number of works joined the collection in 1972, some of such considerable importance as Charles Willson Peale's *Self-Portrait* (cat. no. 30) and Eastman Johnson's *The Brown Family* (cat. no. 70), although there were also smaller-scale works such as John Singer Sargent's *The Oyster Gatherer* (fig. II) and Thomas Hovenden's *Taking His Ease* (cat. no. 96).

During these two years of relative inactivity, Rockefeller characterized his mood as "somewhat constrained as to buying at the present time."[88] But in retrospect it seems clear that during this period of quiet they were simply mustering the great reserves of determination and resource in order to make a maximum impact on the collection, which they did in

1973 with the purchase of at least a dozen canvases—among them the most important and the most expensive works they were to acquire. Rockefeller's early fascination with the works of John Singleton Copley came to stunning realization with two three-quarter-length portraits of the highest interest, the well-known *Mary Turner Sargent* and the recently rediscovered double portrait of *William Vassall and His Son Leonard* (cat. nos. 7 and 9). Sanford Gifford's *Sunset on the Hudson* (fig. 12) joined the collection in March. This and J. G. Brown's *On the Hudson* are probably the works Blanchette Rockefeller had in mind when, speaking of her husband, she said, "he started in with the Hudson River School, reminiscent of his grandfather's day. We have several paintings that look as though they were painted from our porch."[89] William Sidney Mount's two small panels showing views of Setauket (figs. 13 and 14) spoke to a similarly bucolic, in some sense proprietary, sensibility.

The pastoralism of these three landscapes stood in direct contrast to the mood of the major nineteenth-century acquisition of the year—*The Ironworkers' Noontime* by Thomas Anshutz (cat. no. 83). Richardson had tried to tempt Rockefeller years earlier with this work. Writing in June 1965 he noted:

> I have heard indirectly that a really admirable genre painting, *Steelworkers' Noontime* by Thomas Anshutz, may come on the market. I recommended it years ago, when I was in Detroit, to a Detroit collector, Lawrence Fleischman. . . . If it should come on the market, I hope that you will think about it. You will find it reproduced in my *Painting in America*, Fig. 133, although the black and white illustration gives no idea of the subtlety of the color. It is unique, to my knowledge, as an industrial subject in American nineteenth-century genre.[90]

But the Anshutz stayed in Michigan, entering a private collection there. It came onto the open market only in 1972, when that collection was sold on 18 October at auction in New York. The painting brought $250,000, thus earning, for a short time, the distinction of being the most expensive American painting yet sold publicly.[91] The Rockefellers were not participants in that rise of attention. Rockefeller later recalled: "Although Anshutz was not then too well known, the picture somehow came to the fore very suddenly. . . . We were aware of it when it was sold at auction, but for some reason didn't bid on it."[92] Instead, after being in the hands of another private collector, the painting was acquired by Kennedy Galleries. Only then, in the incredibly ambitious year of 1973, did the Rockefellers acquire what has come to be seen as one of the signature works of the collection (they paid only 15 percent more than the auction price). Rockefeller explained that the draw of the work was, finally, that it "seemed to us to present an aspect of the American story through art that was intriguing and significant to have."[93]

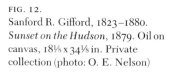

FIG. 12.
Sanford R. Gifford, 1823–1880. *Sunset on the Hudson*, 1879. Oil on canvas, 18⅛ x 34⅛ in. Private collection (photo: O. E. Nelson)

But the major effort of the year was reserved for a small-scale, dark, colonial portrait by an artist whose name is not yet known—*The Mason Children* (cat. no. 1). Initially in August 1973 Vose Galleries of Boston, acting for the family in which the painting had descended for over three hundred years, had sought to sell it for one million dollars. Neither Rockefeller nor Richardson seriously considered the opportunity. Indeed, Richardson responded to Rockefeller's questions on the work with an air of incredulity: "It was bound to happen and now it has; the first American picture priced at a million dollars. Interesting, though, that Vose, who used to be a conservative, modest-priced dealer, should be the one to do it."[94] Repeatedly in his correspondence, Rockefeller writes to the effect that, in spite of their liking a given work, if the asking price was too high they would pass.[95] In mid-November, the Voses again came forward, writing to Richardson:

> We would like to reopen discussion of the group portrait of the Mason Children on a more practical basis.
>
> We do still believe that, if time were no object, the million-dollar price goal for that painting could be achieved. However, the family who own it are interested in moving it now and, after a number of lengthy conferences, have agreed to let us offer it at a firm price of $500,000.
>
> I think we are correct in stating that this is the earliest known group portrait painted in this country, and an item that would add considerable interest to Mr. Rockefeller's collection.[96]

The painting was brought to New York on 27 November, where it was examined by the Rockefellers, Richardson, and the paintings conservator William Suhr. The Voses prepared a portfolio of photocopies citing early references in the literature and, in the accompanying letter, reiterated their belief in the work: "The painting is unique. It will some day be nationally known as the cornerstone of a collection. We hope it will be yours."[97] Discussions— as well as a cleaning test to remove discolored varnish and overpaint—continued into the following February. Finally, on the 8th of that month, the dealer was able to write: "Doctor Richardson has told us that you have made what we sincerely believe you will long consider a wise decision: To keep the 17th Century American portrait of the Mason Children."[98] It would prove to be the most expensive American painting the Rockefellers purchased; it would also be, as Vose had predicted, a cornerstone of the collection. As Richardson later

wrote: "It remains, and it is, probably the greatest and rarest thing that any collector of painting in America could own. And it has great charm, in spite of the accidents and wear of time."[99]

There are two significant revelations in the purchases of 1973 and early 1974. On the level of the Rockefellers' considerations, it is clear that they were still involved in buying beautiful works—often of modest scale and relatively modest price—that appealed to their love of nature and the exquisitely crafted object. These attributes parallel what John Russell had written of the Rockefellers' Asian art collection:

> Rooted in private taste and private affection, it is made up of works of art of high quality and manageable size. . . . [F]undamentally it consists of pieces that it would be a pleasure to come home to, rather than of pieces that demand to be sent straight to a museum.[100]

The Gifford *Sunset on the Hudson* and the two panels by Mount of Setauket, each work tied to an appreciation of New York State's natural beauty and providing great visual pleasure, demonstrate this continuity with the start of the collection. But the involved and difficult acquisition of the *Mason Children*, a painting of immense historic value but of an aesthetic sensibility far removed from most of their collection, indicates a very different kind of purpose. Such an important pilgrimage picture, added to the decision to acquire the Anshutz, passed over at auction only a little more than a year earlier, seems to indicate that the Rockefellers were increasingly considering the public, educational role that their collection could play—even if, as of yet, there was no resolution as to where precisely that future home would be.

Museum directors and curators throughout the country were becoming increasingly aware of the collection, in part through the many loans to special exhibitions that the Rockefellers made during these years. As the collection began to develop a public profile, representatives from the National Gallery of Art, the Whitney Museum of American Art, the Amon Carter Museum in Fort Worth, the National Collection of Fine Arts, and The Fine Arts Museums of San Francisco all approached the Rockefellers, seeking to organize exhibitions drawn from the single collection and thus forge an alliance with these collectors noted for their philanthropy. The nation's 1976 Bicentennial began, in these years, to exert a further pressure on museums to generate projects on American themes.

Rockefeller took the nation's impending two-hundredth anniversary very seriously. He both served as chairman of the National Committee for the Bicentennial Era and wrote at length of the need for the occasion "to stimulate a sense of renewal and rededication, even an American renaissance."[101]

In San Francisco, White sought to unite his double aim of hosting a national celebration and establishing closer ties to the Rockefellers by proposing that an exhibition drawn from their collection serve as the institution's major Bicentennial program. On 19 November 1973, Rockefeller responded favorably to the proposal:

> While I am of course still aware of the problems which the lending of so many pictures at one time will create for me, I am very much intrigued at the thought of seeing a good part of the collection shown under your ideal museum conditions. And most importantly, it is gratifying, as you mention in your letter, to think of so many of your Museum visitors enjoying the pictures.[102]

A press release was drafted and, on the day after Christmas, sent to Rockefeller for review. White wrote to him:

> If "the aim is freshness" as Richardson says, what a way to celebrate the American birthday. Sweep across the land to our farthest continental frontier and focus on a hundred American images together for the first time. Exhibit and publish them so we can take a fresh look at ourselves. . . .
>
> I hope your decision will afford you the pleasure it will bring to so many others. I am pleased personally and for the museum that we can participate in this adventure.[103]

Meanwhile, White continued in his drive to demonstrate his seriousness about a concerted American art presence at the de Young Museum. In February 1974 he introduced a resolution before The Fine Arts Museums' board of trustees to create a suite of galleries for the institution's American collection, asking them to designate this their "major Bicentennial renovation effort" (the American Galleries at the de Young eventually opened on 4 July 1977). As Ransom Cook, then President of the Board of Trustees, wrote to Rockefeller after a congenial meeting over plans for the Bicentennial exhibition:

> We seem to have a unique meeting of interests. We are laying great stress on the development and housing of our American collection. And you want to encourage the study and appreciation of American art. Your recognition of our efforts has been enormously stimulating to all of us in pushing ahead with our plans to give American art the importance it deserves on the West Coast.[104]

As word of the Bicentennial project spread, other museums sought to serve as auxiliary venues—Tom Armstrong, then newly appointed as director of the Whitney Museum of American Art, was finally successful in persuading Rockefeller to place the collection in New York in the fall. Over the course of the year, much energy in San Francisco, New York, and Philadelphia was expended on developing the components of the exhibition. Richardson, in Philadelphia, was at work on the exhibition's catalogue, which he wanted to make "narrative and critical." Writing at a time when there were few opportunities for the general public to see American art, and when even fewer colleges and universities offered courses in the field, he opined:

> One must start with the realization that an American audience, even of the educated, will know little in general and nothing in detail of the history of their country, and next to nothing about its artists. I try, therefore, to make each entry a little window into a moment of the American past, into the creative intention and achievement of the artist, and (if a portrait) of the person seen. And to be as brief as possible. . . .
>
> I must add that as I study each picture in detail, the collection grows more interesting. Out of the stream of pictures pouring through the art market, we have been fortunate to cull some very significant ones; more fortunate than I realized as we went along step by step. You have done something pretty swell, in my judgment at least.[105]

In San Francisco, White and curator Lanier Graham were busy trying to coordinate the exhibition and production of the catalogue. Across the Bay, Wanda Corn, professor of art history at Mills College, began her years-long effort to create a multidisciplinary educational program for college and university students throughout the area.[106]

And in New York, the Rockefellers continued to add to the collection, undoubtedly keeping several things in mind. Collecting for pleasure was complicated by the equally pressing awareness that a large number of the works were going to be on display within the next several years and, given the Bicentennial nature of the event and the Rockefeller family name, they would provoke considerable scrutiny. So a degree of self-consciousness as collector must have risen to the surface. Likewise, the growing conviction that the collection would end ultimately in a museum must have provided a further element to their deliberations over a given acquisition.

The Rockefellers did not, however, respond to the pressures of public collecting by succumbing to a "stamp-collector's" mentality, where an example by all famous artists was necessary. Rockefeller later addressed this point: "Also, obviously our purchases have been affected by the availability of items of quality and appeal. As a result of this approach, there are notable gaps in the collection which have not concerned us."[107] Thus there were no works by, among others, James McNeill Whistler or Mary Cassatt.[108] On the other hand, there were multiple works by Copley, Eastman Johnson, Bierstadt, and Elihu Vedder. The two criteria of quality and personal appeal continued to outweigh any other concerns. Mark Stevens, the art critic from *Newsweek*, writing in 1978, understood and appreciated this fact:

> Because it was put together for personal pleasure, the collection seems untroubled by too many imposed ideas. As a result, the paintings become beautifully suited for browsing, one of the most overlooked pleasures in an era that often prefers razzle-dazzle shows. Browsing in a good collection ought to resemble an old-fashioned solitary walk in the country: thoughts float freely and connections come to mind, looking and thinking mingle, enriching each other.[109]

PUBLIC DEBUT OF THE COLLECTION

After more than two years of concerted activity on both coasts, the exhibition of the Rockefeller collection opened in San Francisco in April 1976. Planned as "a Bicentennial tribute to the city of San Francisco," *American Art: Selections from the Collection of Mr. and Mrs. John D. Rockefeller 3rd* gathered together 106 paintings, watercolors, and sculptures.[110] Rockefeller spoke briefly at one of the opening events:

> Three or four years ago I wrote a book called "The Second American Revolution, Some Personal Observations" and one of the chapters in that book was called "A Learning Society" and the thrust of the chapter was that the learning process should be a lifelong process. . . . [E]ducation should be reaching out for new knowledge right through one's life in order to attain the full potential of each individual, and the thing I wanted to say was how much a museum and a great museum such as yours can contribute to this process of making available to people who want to broaden their horizon, who want to keep on learning, giving them the facility through which they can continue to broaden themselves and develop. And, of course, the collecting factor is a terribly nice means of broadening one's education but everybody cannot do that and the museum is an ideal focal point for such interest and development. It is really, I think, what a museum is all about. . . . [A]nd the other point I wanted to make was, is how little we Americans know about ourselves. . . . [T]he interest in American Art has grown very encouragingly across the country. This is a wonderful thing, I think, although there are certain disadvantages that my fellow collectors will appreciate [this last being a wry reference to the attendant rise in prices].[111]

The exhibition and educational programs developed to accompany the exhibition were successful. In spite of a citywide municipal crafts union strike, no public transportation, and an alleged sabotage of two water mains in Golden Gate Park that deprived the museum and a significant portion of the city of water for a day, White was able to write:

I am pleased to report that your exhibition is averaging 1,000 visitors a week, an average that I am sure will increase as we get our influx of summer visitors. . . . [T]he people who visit the exhibition appear to be seriously interested in what they see and learn. The response to the Acoustiguide recorded tour is excellent. Catalogue sales are averaging 15 a day and the special American Art Bookstore is a great success.[112]

And, indeed, as White had foreseen, high summer visitation rates and enthusiasm prompted the museum to extend the showing for an extra two weeks—to 15 August—"because of the extraordinary public interest in the exhibit."[113] Over 92,000 people attended, nearly two-thirds of those being non-museum members, who were asked to pay a newly instituted museum admission fee of $.75, as well as a special exhibition charge of $1.00.

The project prompted enthusiasm in the national press. Mahonri Sharp Young closed his review of the exhibition for the magazine *Apollo* with the encomium, "This is the finest collection of American painting of our day; and one of the finest collections ever assembled."[114] Joshua Taylor summarized the exhibition by writing for *Smithsonian*: "Such a group of paintings provides endless questions and infinite satisfactions. The collection has been put together less with a sense of possession than with a delight in knowing."[115] William Wilson, critic of the *Los Angeles Times*, found the exhibition to be "rewarding," filled with pictures that "seem to inspire affection."[116] Martha Hutson, who wrote one of the most extensive reviews of the exhibition and interviewed Rockefeller at length for the *American Art Review*, concluded: "This exhibition could be described as a classic painting collection of basically two centuries made up of medium-sized canvases. There is nothing excessive about it except the high quality."[117]

Later, when the exhibition was seen in New York, Emily Genauer, writing in the *New York Post* toward the end of her distinguished career, caught at the newsworthy threads of the story with a series of rhetorical questions that focused on the biography of the collector:

> "What American art does a man buy for himself who was brought up to see in his home each day that set of the Unicorn Tapestries, now at the Cloisters branch of the Metropolitan Museum, and counted among the world's greatest medieval treasures? What does a man buy for himself when his mother was one of the three founders of the Museum of Modern Art almost a half-century ago, and a lover and buyer—long before most people ever heard of them—of works by Cezanne, Gauguin, Seurat? When his father loved and bought Oriental art?". . .
>
> Whatever they've bought for the Modern Museum, the Cloisters, the Asia Society and the Oriental collections of other institutions, what the Rockefellers live with . . . are simple, modest, generally small, genteel and even homely works by American artists from the 17th century to the present.[118]

Genauer, suggesting that, among other revelations, the exhibition showed that the Rockefellers possessed a sense of humor, closed her review with an attempt at wit:

> The picture that fascinates me most in the whole show is one of the very earliest, an 18th century portrait by Joseph Badger of Anna Porter Brown [cat. no. 5]. There is no suggestion of a smile or warmth in her plain, long severe face. Her costume is mostly gray, as I recall it. She carries in her hand what must be a Bible. The one person she calls to mind more than anyone in the world is John D. Rockefeller Sr.[119]

The senior art critic for the *New York Times*, Hilton Kramer, not known for his love of nineteenth-century American art, painted a generally positive picture in his review devoted to the show, finding "many delights, of course—and some surprises." He did, however, find the sudden popularity of American historic painting somewhat suspect, as an unthinking patriotic response to the nation's Bicentennial: "The momentum of revival, which was swiftly gaining speed before the Bicentennial celebration, has this year reached avalanche force as the result of that event." Nonetheless he praised particularly the eighteenth-century works, choosing, as did Genauer, to illustrate Joseph Badger's *Anna Porter Brown* as exemplary, and found much pleasure in the works of the nineteenth-century genre painters. Kramer continued, however, by opining that the Rockefellers' taste "for small pictures of human interest and picturesque view," with a tendency toward the "the placid and the genteel," inclined

their collection "to the temptations of nostalgia."[120] Within a month, Kramer returned to
discuss nineteenth-century American paintings in a review of *The Natural Paradise*, the
Museum of Modern Art's Bicentennial contribution. As an introductory aside to his article
(which was illustrated by Frederic Church's *Rainy Season in the Tropics* from San Francisco's
collection), he characterized the Rockefeller collection in much harsher tones as

> a very pleasant, placid, unspectacular exhibition of (mainly) small 19th-century American
> realist painting guaranteed to act as a soothing poultice for sensibilities inflamed by a
> surfeit of modernist art. . . .
>
> The Whitney show, it is safe to say, will influence nobody's thinking about anything.
> It is a sop to Bicentennial piety that affords us, almost inadvertently, a glimpse of some
> very nice pictures. By design, as it were, it makes no distinction between significant and
> insignificant works of art, and with ideas of any sort it has absolutely nothing to do.[121]

E. P. Richardson responded to all the New York reviews with a draft of a letter to
Rockefeller (it is unknown whether a final version was ever sent):

> The Whitney Museum's publicity department has sent me a number of "reviews" of the
> exhibition and I have been debating with myself whether to write you about them. Their
> tone does not surprise me, for I have no illusions about the New York critics and I rather
> expected a hostile or patronizing reception. I do not write to complain that their taste is
> different from mine—for that is in[evi]table. But what impresses me and leaves me a
> feeling of dust and ashes in the mouth, is the ignorance of the New York critics. They do
> not know what is good or bad, what is a fascinating new discovery, what throws a new
> light upon an important artist, what the exhibition tells us of the emotional experience
> and the imaginative life of our country. They do not know—and they do not care.[122]

The renovation of historic American art as a worthwhile subject was, at least in Richardson's
view, decidedly not complete.

Throughout all of this, the Rockefeller collection was enmeshed in a political contro-
versy. In December 1975, as soon as the New York venue of the exhibition was announced,
over fifty artists picketed the Whitney Museum and circulated petitions calling on the
institution's administration to cancel the project:

Petition from the American Art Community and Others to the Whiteney [*sic*] and De Young Museums:

Next September, as one of its four Bicentennial exhibitions, the Whitney Museum of American Art in New York City will present a show entitled "Three Centuries of American Art," an exhibition originating at the M. H. De Young Museum in San Francisco. This show is culled entirely from the private collection of John D. Rockefeller III. It will include *no Black artists and only one woman artist* [Susan Macdowell Eakins's *Girl with Fan* (fig. 15)]. Presumably, other minorities in United States culture will also be underrepresented or excluded.

Demonstrably, therefore, the exhibition is a blatant example of large cultural institutions determining the history of art in the United States.

We, the undersigned, strongly object to the collusion of the De Young and Whitney Museum and John D. Rockefeller III in using a private collection of art, with its discriminatory omissions, to promote ruling-class values and a socially reactionary view of art. WE DEMAND THAT THIS SHOW BE CANCELLED.[123]

A number of media voices registered the protest, and comparable pressure was exerted in San Francisco. Critics, such as the writer for the *Berkeley Barb*, reported:

A New York based "umbrella" group called Artists Meeting for Cultural Change (AMCC) has set up "a national network to protest (the) misuse of art and artists for the Bicentennial—and afterwards." The AMCC and a Bay Area group known as the Ad Hoc Committee of the San Francisco Art Workers' Coalition (SFAWC) view the collection as "a history of art from the complacent viewpoint of the power elite"—a celebration of one man's reactionary taste. . . .

The Bicentennial is the common property of all Americans. One moneyed individual's taste, represented by his art collection, is inappropriate material for [a] Bicentennial exhibition.[124]

In part to respond to these concerns, the proposed title of the exhibition was changed from *Three Centuries of American Art* to the less anniversary-oriented *American Art: Selections from the Collection of Mr. and Mrs. John D. Rockefeller 3rd*, echoing the title of the Rockefeller's Asian art exhibition organized at Asia House in 1970. Bicentennial references, however, remained in the general promotional material connected with the show.

Pickets demonstrated outside both museums, passing out brochures that in San Francisco reminded visitors of the racial and gender disparities of the works on display. The leaflets proclaimed the show to represent but one elitist point of view; called on the museum to change its exhibition policies to include more works by California artists, women, and non-whites; and urged visitors to become involved at all levels of public discourse concerning the institution. In New York, pickets at the opening confronted the invited guests, providing art and society columnists with attitude-full stories and caricaturish photographs.[125] Although the protesters did not affect the program to the extent they desired,[126] they succeeded in forcing nearly every critical response to the exhibition to question the biases implicit in the museums' programs. Much of the debate during the time of the exhibition divided between calls on one side for a more expansive representation of American art and, on the other, the assertion that private collectors have the right to assemble collections to reflect their individual tastes. Most observers concurred with the view expressed by Roberta J. M. Olson, who wrote:

Obviously the Rockefeller Collection does not and cannot be expected to reflect the total spectrum of American art, although it certainly gives a feeling for many of its important trends, as well as supplying the viewer with cultural history, which our nation does not pay sufficient attention to, and a tangible hint at what this new world, with its metaphoric comparison to the garden of paradise, was like to our predecessors. Rather it allows us, through the relatively calm and serene choices of the Rockefellers, the privilege of viewing works of art we might never be exposed to, while illustrating one of the principal rights that our nation was founded on: individual freedom of choice. Mr. and Mrs. Rockefeller have made their choices; hopefully the exhibition of their private collection marks the beginning of a number of shows which will explore the phenomenon of American art and expand our knowledge of it.[127]

That is to say, responsibility for presenting the full picture of American art lay with the public institutions and not with the Rockefellers.

In 1977 the AMCC published a response and overview to the entire enterprise, an *anti-catalog*, which called upon artist action in a mode that became popular and even expected in the 1980s and early 1990s. The cover of the catalogue boldly announced the manifesto of the organizers:

> Because it calls the neutrality of art into question, this Anti-Catalog will be seen as a political statement. It is, in reality, no more political than the viewpoint of official culture. The singularity of that viewpoint—the way it advances the interests of a class—is difficult to see because in our society that viewpoint is so pervasive. In this Anti-Catalog, we have attempted to elucidate some of the underlying mechanisms and assumptions. Our effort is not intended simply as a critical exercise. Culture has the power to shape not only our view of the past but also the way we see ourselves today. Official culture can only diminish our ability to understand the world and to act upon that understanding. The critical examination of culture is thus a necessary step in gaining control over the meaning we give our lives.[128]

Within, the seventeen authors/designers/producers (and two collaborators)[129] developed an articulate and visually enticing text, with reproductions from *American Art: Selections from the Collection of Mr. and Mrs. John D. Rockefeller 3rd, Smithsonian Magazine*, and various historical sources. The impetus for the project was not only a response to the Rockefeller exhibition[130] but as well "the more general issue of the use (or more aptly the *misuse*) of art and art institutions to serve the interests of a wealthy minority sector of the population at the expense of the majority." The writers continued:

> Some of us, who had felt that good art couldn't be "political," were faced by the realization that our institutions were politicizing our work for us, and more importantly: those "politics" were against our interests.[131]

Sounding a call that would reverberate in the art world through the coming decades, they wrote:

> Official culture, through its monopoly of cultural institutions, defines what is and what is not art. It does this by conferring institutional legitimacy. This process of legitimatizing art ultimately functions ideologically. Via the institutions of official culture, the corporate-government elite projects an image of the past that justifies the present social order and its unequal divisions of wealth and power. In this manner, as the Rockefeller collection so clearly illustrates, history is portrayed as solely the work of the wealthy and powerful. Their visibility in art is predicated upon the invisibility and powerlessness of the majority. Official culture thus raises the inequalities of the present social system to the level of eternal law. Under the cover of the neutrality of art, official culture certifies the claim to power of those who now possess it.[132]

To at least a limited degree, museums of the 1980s and 1990s have sought to address the issues raised by the AMCC—in part through work of AMCC members within museum and academic communities.[133]

THE FATE OF THE COLLECTION

Neither the public exhibition, culminating over a decade of activity, nor the controversies surrounding its showing, provoked the Rockefellers to stop collecting. They did encounter, however, a problem met by nearly every pathbreaking collector. As Rockefeller wrote to Richardson just after the exhibition opened in San Francisco: "It really has been a pleasure and satisfaction working with you and I look forward to continuing the relationship even though the number of our purchases may be somewhat diminished because of the excessively high prices."[134] Even so, at least eleven important paintings were acquired in 1976 and 1977, varying in theme and time, among them those by artists already represented in the collection—such as Albert Bierstadt's *Roman Fish Market. Arch of Octavius* (cat. no. 50), Elihu Vedder's *Death of Abel* (cat. no. 72), and Charles Burchfield's *Spring Flood* (cat. no. 130)—and others by new voices, such as Benjamin West's *Genius Calling forth the Fine Arts* (cat. no. 18), John Quidor's *Tom Walker's Flight* (cat. no. 48), Joseph Wright's *John Coats Browne* (cat. no. 15), Horace Pippin's *The Trial of John Brown* (cat. no. 135), and Cecilia Beaux's *Little Lamerche* (cat. no. 119). The latter two—by, respectively, an African American and a woman artist—seem particularly relevant to the discussions initiated by the AMCC.

The major question for the collection during these years, however, was not what to add to the works already in hand, but the matter and manner of its final disposition. Considerable time and effort were expended on the issue, trying to determine where this important group of objects would have the greatest positive impact. As early as 1970 Rockefeller had looked hard at San Francisco as a potential home for his collection; he surely intended his agreement to the de Young's Bicentennial exhibition as a form of encouragement. Ian White continued to press the case for San Francisco, seeking to augment established ties by requesting the long-term loan of eight paintings to hang in the de Young Museum's new American Galleries; Rockefeller granted the request.[135] And in November 1976, Rockefeller was again in San Francisco and met with the newly appointed President of the Board of Trustees, Walter S. Newman.

In the large question of disposition, Rockefeller sought the advice of Richardson, of course. As early as October 1970 Richardson had visited both Los Angeles and San Francisco to explore the suitability of each as a possible home for the collection. In two momentous reports dated 20 and 29 October, he weighed the merits of the two western cities and of the National Collection of the Fine Arts (now the National Museum of American Art) in Washington, D.C. Fifteen points were discussed in the balance between Los Angeles and San Francisco, with greater weight going to the latter because of its central location on the West Coast, its popularity as a destination for tourists, the large number of visitors from Asia who entered the country through San Francisco, the foundation of American art already in place, the management of the institution, its large attendance, its facilities (which would allow of space for an expanded American showing), and a past record of good American purchases. As between San Francisco and Washington, apparent benefits were nearly equal. Richardson concluded: "On balance, the West seems to represent a more open field and greater need. . . . The balance seems slightly in favor of the West. The decision, and the pleasure, are yours."[136]

Nothing over the years altered this point of view, nor is there any extant correspondence between Rockefeller and Richardson on the question of disposition from 1971 until after the exhibition. If the administration of The Fine Arts Museums was looking for hopeful auguries, they may have perceived one in Rockefeller's decision in 1973 to trade his large Harnett *After the Hunt*, acquired in 1969.[137] Among the major examples of the artist's work in private hands, it could be seen as redundant if the collection were to come to San Francisco, which already possessed the fourth and most famous version of the work. But it was not until 1976 that we have further extant discussion on the fate of the collection. It was initiated by a somewhat surprising source—Rockefeller's art advisor for Asian material, Sherman Lee. In November 1976, Lee proposed an unusual and creative scheme for the Rockefeller American art collection:

> It would take a considerable amount of work and analysis, but I think it would be eminently worth-while in the long run to seriously consider the concept of giving individual or groups of pictures to various museums where that individual work or group would have an effect like that of placing a key stone in an arch. I think such a concept would be a truly creative and revolutionary one which might well set donors to thinking of such a method and thereby generally improving the level of understanding of American art throughout the country.[138]

This did not sit well with Richardson. He responded to Rockefeller: "I take pride in your collection as a magnificent ensemble. It is a great monument, still growing. As Williamsburg is a monument to your father's interests, and Rockefeller University to your grandfather's, Asia House and this collection are monuments of yours. I should not like to see any of these dismembered."[139] Rockefeller evidently pondered these options and, before the end of the year, determined that a unified gift would better serve his interests. He questioned Richardson:

> Assuming that the collection should be given as a whole, the other question that remains is the timing of the announcement. I will have to admit that I vacillate in relation to this. I cannot see that it would necessarily make too much difference in my satisfaction in collecting if the announcement were to be made soon provided it was understood that the transfer of the collection would only take place on my death and provided it was understood that I would continue to collect for my own pleasure and satisfaction and not as an agent for the museum.
>
> As you suggest in your letter, there would be certain satisfaction if an early announcement were made in working with the recipient museum in connection with the development of their plans in the American field.
>
> While I still am open minded in the subject, I think I am leaning a bit at the present time towards announcing soon. I recognize that such action would make the institution selected irrevocable and, as you point out, circumstances within the institution might change some years hence. However as I see it there is some risk however we decide to handle the matter and that maybe the risk factor should weigh less heavily than the satisfaction factor.[140]

By the end of January 1977, Rockefeller had reached a decision in favor of donating the collection to San Francisco. He drafted, but did not send, a letter to this effect, instead showing it to his close associates for their review. In the spring, he sent a version of the letter to FAMSF Board Chairman Newman, clearly marking it as a provisional communication to help, as Rockefeller phrased it, "clarify" his thinking. In response, on 22 March Newman sent him a detailed history of the institution in San Francisco, its governance, its plans regarding American art, and the current state of its collections. On 22 August Rockefeller drafted a further version of his letter. In October he again visited San Francisco, meeting with Newman, White, and the city's legal counsel. He wrote to Richardson that they "had a good session and we are about to agree on wording of the final statement."[141]

The matter came to public resolution in January 1978. Rockefeller wrote to Richardson:

> I should mention that the announcement of my collection eventually going to the San Francisco Museums is scheduled for next Thursday, January 19th. This obviously is a major event for me and I do want you to know how grateful I am to you for having had your wisdom and judgment as well as friendship in building the collection. I like to feel that we will keep on with the effort but certainly the main accomplishment is behind us.[142]

Richardson responded:

> Thank you for your kind words about our work together and what it means. I do hope the announcement on the 19th goes well. The museum people know what they are being promised and understand their good fortune. But one never knows about the journalists. . . . [I]t would be a delightful surprise if, for once, they would be moved to appreciate your generosity of spirit and to respond appropriately. Ah well, whatever the journalists say, this is a great gift to the nation and a great enrichment of life for the whole west. A great opportunity for enrichment, I should say, perhaps. It will take years for the public to absorb what this offers.[143]

On the morning of 19 January 1978, Mayor George R. Moscone, Dianne Feinstein (then President of the Board of Supervisors), Walter S. Newman (President of the Museums' Board of Trustees), and Ian McKibbin White, Director of Museums, gathered with trustees, staff, and assembled members of the press at the M. H. de Young Memorial Museum in Golden Gate Park to hear Rockefeller make what would be one of the most important announcements in the cultural history of San Francisco (fig. 16).

Newman introduced the proceedings by circulating copies of a letter Rockefeller had written him earlier in the week, in which Rockefeller stated his intention of eventually giving his American art collection to The Fine Arts Museums (the full text follows). Always

FIG. 16.
Dianne Feinstein, John D. Rockefeller 3rd, Walter S. Newman, George Moscone, press conference, The Fine Arts Museums of San Francisco, 19 January 1978 (photo: Oliver Goldsmith)

emphasizing the personal nature of the enterprise, Rockefeller wrote of the collection's origins, its development, and the careful search he and Richardson had undertaken to find a suitable public home for it. He closed the letter, one of most momentous documents in the history of the institution, by noting that

> the thought of giving my collection to The Fine Arts Museums of San Francisco is a source of pleasure and satisfaction to me. That I am helping in this way to foster your great Museums' commitment to the American field of art makes me feel my efforts in building the collection will have lasting meaning and value.[144]

The press conference went smoothly and the announcement was met with nearly universal acclaim. There followed a special meeting of the Board of Trustees, the sole order of business being to commit the institution "to the stewardship of this wonderful collection consistent with the desires of Mr. Rockefeller and the purpose for which the Museums were founded," and to express "profound appreciation to Mr. and Mrs. John D. Rockefeller 3rd for selecting The Fine Arts Museums of San Francisco as the ultimate repository of their American collection."[145]

Announced in newspapers and magazines across the nation, when the story was reported in the *New York Times* the Rockefeller collection was cited as "generally regarded by specialists in the field as the finest holding of American art in private hands"; the *Times*'s article closed with a series of laudatory comments from curators and directors of major East Coast institutions.[146] The art critic for *Newsweek* summarized the general response in closing his account of the day: "A lucky city, San Francisco."[147]

The one qualifying note was sounded by the art critic and scholar Alfred Frankenstein, who asked at the press conference: "Mr. Rockefeller, will any provision be made for the scholarly study, analysis (or publication?) of American art for this gift."[148] He elaborated on his point in the *San Francisco Chronicle* two days after the announcement:

> What I am driving at here is that all the things Richardson stands for [having mentioned the Archives of American Art, the first chair in American art history at Wayne State University, and the first and, to that date, only general history of American art written by a museum director], with the exception of the collecting of the works of art, are ignored in the statements issued by Rockefeller and the officials of the Fine Arts Museums, and there is no indication that they are thinking of carrying forward his work. The Fine Arts Museums do not even have a curator of American art.
>
> Rockefeller has a John D. III Fund, dedicated to cultural and scholarly exchanges with the Orient, but he leaves the cultural and scholarly work associated with his American collecting to happenstance and luck. . . .
>
> We need a lively, vigorous institute for the study of American art.[149]

The clear implication was that, at least in Frankenstein's mind, it was Rockefeller's responsibility to create such an institute.

Frankenstein sent copies of his article, along with letters, to both Rockefeller and

Richardson, seeking to establish a dialogue with the former and hoping to find an ally in the latter. In both he was disappointed. Rockefeller responded simply and deliberately:

> In order to obtain your objectives it would seem to me that two factors were important: (1) An increasing awareness of and interest in the field of American art by the American public. This, it would seem to me, has been occurring at an encouraging rate. (2) The building of sufficient collections in the American field to justify the outlay of funds for adequate personnel and research. This I would feel has been encouraging also, but at a slower pace.
>
> What disturbed me concerning your article is that you tend to blame me for what I have not done rather than being gratified and encouraged by what I have tried to do. To me American art will only attain its rightful place in American museums and universities by the efforts of many people. Each of us must do his or her bit as appears wise and right to the individual. I have felt that concentrating my efforts on the collecting was perhaps the best contribution I could make and that others would become interested in making their contribution in different but supplementary ways.
>
> When we talked at the Museums and in your letter, you suggest the possibility of our talking further. I cannot see how at such a meeting I could add to what is already said in this letter, namely, that I am in complete accord with your objectives. Let's each of us in our own way continue to pursue our respective efforts toward strengthening and building the field of American art in this country.[150]

Frankenstein responded with thanks for "your exceedingly kind letter," but filled two pages of single-space type to pursue his point, closing with "I find it very difficult to understand— and not at all hopeful for the future collecting of American art—that you refuse to see this obvious point."[151]

Richardson, on the other hand, responded two weeks later than had Rockefeller, and with considerably more edge in his prose:

> But in what you say of Mr. Rockefeller's attitude toward teaching American Art History, I must tell you that you do not understand the man you are dealing with. He has spent his life administering his family's benefactions—the Rockefeller Foundation, The United Negro College Fund, Lincoln Center, Williamsburg, etc.; and in creating new foundations such as the Agricultural Council, the Population Council, the Japan Society, the Asia Society, etc. He is not an amateur scattering largesse. He is an old pro in the difficult business of giving money wisely.
>
> As I understand his philosophy, it is to define a problem very carefully, then adopt a very clear objective when you move to meet it. Second, to act so that you enable people to help themselves, which is the only way to confer a permanent benefit. . . .
>
> If I were in his place, and the response of San Francisco was: "Well, fine, yes; but we want MORE"—I think I should be a little irritated and feel more inclined toward other's needs. Since I hope he will continue his interest in San Francisco and American art, I too am a little disappointed in your reaction.[152]

This was the final volley in the debate.

THE CLOSING OF THE COLLECTION

Rockefeller's letter of 16 January to Walter Newman proposed future collecting activity that he and Mrs. Rockefeller would undertake for their own "pleasure and satisfaction," but in which the needs of the Museums would inevitably arise. Yet they acquired only a very few paintings in 1978. One was the watercolor *Sunday Meeting* by Andrew Wyeth, an artist whom they had long admired (cat. no. 136).[153] They looked seriously at a number of works in the Sotheby Parke-Bernet auction of 21 April, acquiring Charles Burchfield's *September* (cat. no. 137). They added a small, precious panel by Charles Curran, *In the Garden of the Cluny Museum* (fig. 17)—an "X" on the Rockefeller-Richardson scale—to their collection. There was also a major drawing by Homer, *A Little More Yarn* (cat. no. 91). With this acquisition, the collection closed as it had begun, with a work on paper by Winslow Homer. On 10 July 1978 Rockefeller was killed in an automobile accident near the family estate at Pocantico Hills.

FIG. 17.
Charles C. Curran, 1861–1942. *In the Garden of the Cluny Museum*, 1889. Oil on wood panel, 9 x 12 in. Mrs. E. P. Richardson (photo: O. E. Nelson)

THE COLLECTION COMES TO SAN FRANCISCO

In 1979, in accordance with Rockefeller's wishes, the Rockefeller family sent over one hundred American paintings, watercolors, and sculptures to The Fine Arts Museums of San Francisco. His will read, in part:

> I have given considerable thought to the disposition of my American art. It is my belief that there is a greater need for the location of a significant collection of American art in the Western part of the United States than is the case in the East where a number of important collections are already available to the public. For this reason I have concluded that the most appropriate and meaningful disposition of my collection would be achieved by a gift to a significant museum in a leading Western city. I have chosen The Fine Arts Museums of San Francisco because of this and because it has committed itself to the building of an important American collection and because I have confidence in its leadership.[154]

The group of works immediately catapulted the institution to the national forefront of American collections, creating the most comprehensive gathering of historic American art in the West. The community, as Rockefeller had hoped, responded. The Museums outlined a program that included expanded gallery space and curatorial staff dedicated to American art. Beginning in 1980, the Bothin Foundation (a San Francisco–based philanthropic trust) supported a major drive to build a research library of American art materials. San Franciscan collectors stepped forward to promise such major gifts as Mary Cassatt's *Mother and Sara Admiring the Baby* to the institution. And Ednah Root, a local artist and philanthropist, undertook the support of curatorial positions and special programs devoted to American art. Appropriately enough, given his vociferous demands for such a position, Alfred Frankenstein was appointed as the first of the institution's Ednah Root curators of American art.[155] Major acquisitions of nineteenth- and twentieth-century American paintings, the institutional transitions made since 1989 under the leadership of director Harry S. Parker III (with increased space and central focus at the de Young given to the American collections), and the creation of the American Art Study Center in 1991, have followed upon these leads.

In later years, Blanchette Rockefeller continued to support the collection in San Francisco, visiting in 1980, 1984 (fig. 18), 1986, and again in 1987. On occasion, she gave to the

FIG. 18.
Ednah Root, FAMSF Board of Trustees President Leonard Kingsley, Blanchette Rockefeller, and Ian McKibbin White, American Galleries, de Young Museum, June 1984 (photo: R. Valentine Atkinson)

museum other paintings from the collection she and her husband had formed (Irving Wiles's *The Sonata* [cat. no. 102] in 1985, John Wesley Jarvis's *Philip Hone* [cat. no. 23] in 1986, and Worthington Whittredge's *From the Harz Mountains* [cat. no. 45] in 1989). Upon her death, on 29 November 1992, she bequeathed a group of twenty-eight extraordinary objects to join the collection in San Francisco, further strengthening the work she and her husband had begun in the late 1970s.

CONCLUSION

When asked, in 1976, whether he would like to acquire an artist's masterpiece, Rockefeller responded: "Those of that quality are probably in museums. I think that about all a private collector can aspire to is to feel that a painting is a masterpiece."[156] Aware of the subjective nature of the collector's enterprise, of the ego and sense of proprietorship that animate discussions where indeterminate terms such as "quality" dominate, Rockefeller knew that opinions toward works within the collection would change. In his letter to Newman, he thus made provision for changing his mind, and for the institution to act similarly:

> During the remaining period of my ownership, I may choose to dispose of such items from the collection as I feel do not measure up in quality or which have lost their special appeal to me. . . .
>
> Once items from the collection have been transferred to the Fine Arts Museums, it would be understood that they would not be de-acquisitioned by the Museums except upon recommendation of the director and with the approval of the board of trustees after consideration at two regularly scheduled meetings. And it would also be understood that works of art from the collection would be sold or traded by the Museums only to improve the quality of the collection donated by me.[157]

These two paragraphs allow for the reevaluations that are an inevitable part of studying historic art. Sadly, aside from exchanging some few objects in the course of building the collection—notably Harnett's *After the Hunt*, Edward Hopper's *New York Office*, and Hassam's *In the Garden*—Rockefeller did not have a chance to refine the collection to the degree he might have liked.[158] Nor, given its status as a historic entity, is the collection likely to be broken apart by The Fine Arts Museums, in spite of Rockefeller's generous and unusual provision allowing for prudent deaccessioning.

Even without the impetus of potential trade or deaccessioning, however, the present exhibition and catalogue provide the opportunity to assess the accomplishment of Mr. and Mrs. Rockefeller as collectors of American art from the perspective of 1994. From this vantage, the level of their achievement seems to be exceedingly high. One question to ask of collectors is, what were their mistakes? Did they acquire works that were not what they purported to be? Did they gather minor examples or emphasize artists whose accomplishments do not seem of the highest caliber?

As with nearly all collectors, some of the works the Rockefellers acquired now appear to be by hands other than those they initially believed. Among the works now at The Fine Arts Museums, however, this is a very small number. The *Richard Yates* said to be by Gilbert Stuart (cat. no. 22), for example, can now be seen to be an early copy, probably of about 1800, after the original at the National Gallery of Art.[159] The delightful small panel *Horse Chestnut Blossom* (cat. no. 77) was acquired as the work of John La Farge and came with a distinguished, albeit recent, provenance and testimony from the acknowledged experts of the time. Now, however, with a thorough catalogue raisonné coming to conclusion, it is evident that the ascription to La Farge was hopeful; a leading scholar of still life has recently ascribed the work to Walter Gay.[160] The Rockefellers acquired several of Thomas Hovenden's most accomplished paintings, but when they bought what was supposed to be the artist's self-portrait, they misstepped. Although the work indeed shows Hovenden, it is not by his hand but rather by his friend the Irish-born William Magrath (cat. no. 115), whose signature on the panel had simply gone unnoticed over the years. For some works, the jury is still out—Abbott Thayer's *David* (cat. no. 114) has elements, especially the handling of the boy's face and the flesh painting throughout, that are unlike any well-known work by the artist; there are no mentions of the work in the bibliography or the known archival materials relating to Thayer; and one of the leading scholars of the work has called it into question.[161] On the other hand, in conception, color, and handling of elements of the costume the painting seems characteristic of the artist and not readily ascribable to anyone else. So the nature and extent of Thayer's involvement with the canvas remain unknown. Likewise, some scholars have questioned whether Asher B. Durand is the artist of the Rockefellers' handsome portrayal of the key patron of nineteenth-century American painting, Luman Reed (cat. no. 34).[162] Further work is required to evaluate the merit of these questions. That there are only five paintings of the 140 at the museum whose authorship has been queried in the quarter century since their purchase speaks highly of the care with which they were acquired. Especially when in at least two instances they are simple misattributions and another, the *Richard Yates*, is an almost contemporary replica of a work by a painter whose stylistic changes have baffled connoisseurs for over a century.

A more interesting, although less quantifiable measure, for evaluating the collection is to look at the forecasting successes of the collection. Especially among the "X" and "O" paintings, are there works by artists little known who have now gained in reputation? Here the answer is unqualified acclamation. The Rockefellers' belief in certain key painters—Albert Bierstadt, Eastman Johnson, Martin Johnson Heade, and Elihu Vedder—years before their contemporary revival, allowed them to gather significant selections of work, providing an in-depth look at some of the nineteenth century's major talents. In other instances, particularly with such late nineteenth-century works as Charles Ulrich's *Moment Musicale* (cat. no. 89), Dennis Bunker's *A Bohemian* (cat. no. 94), William McCloskey's *Oranges in Tissue Paper* (cat. no. 105), and the paintings of Jefferson D. Chalfant (cat. nos. 107 and 117), the Rockefellers' works have either generated admiration for an artist or era or else have come to be seen as defining the period. Only in a very few instances, as with the work of Harry Roseland, has current opinion failed to validate their choices.

On the other end of the recognition scale, the Rockefellers, working in the decades of the 1960s and 1970s, acquired a number of paintings that are, in themselves, pilgrimage paintings of the highest importance in the history of American art. Those now at The Fine

Arts Museums would certainly include *The Mason Children*, Robert Feke's *Grizzell Eastwick Apthorp*, John Singleton Copley's *Mary Turner Sargent* and *William Vassall and His Son Leonard*, Charles Willson Peale's *Mordecai Gist* and much later *Self-Portrait*, Raphaelle Peale's *Blackberries*, Thomas Hicks's *The Peaceable Kingdom*, both paintings by George Caleb Bingham, Frederic Church's *Twilight*, Albert Bierstadt's *Sunlight and Shadow*, the works by Winslow Homer, Thomas Anshutz's *The Ironworkers' Noontime*, Thomas Hovenden's *The Last Moments of John Brown*, John La Farge's *The Great Statue of Amida Buddha at Kamakura*, the two works by John Frederick Peto, the powerful group of images by Charles Burchfield, Grant Wood's *Dinner for Threshers*, Charles Sheeler's *Kitchen, Williamsburg*. These are not simply representative or characteristic works but show the artists at the very height of their powers. And while each curator or collector would probably shape this list somewhat differently—Rockefeller did not admit of his collection being dominated by any one "masterpiece"[163]—it nonetheless seems safe to assert that this group would form an outstanding element in any survey of historic American painting.

Finally, in evaluating the collection and the gift, there is the simple question that seemed to be preeminent for Rockefeller: Do the individual works and the collection as a whole yield pleasure and satisfaction? For Mr. and Mrs. Rockefeller, the answer was clearly positive—he articulated the point no fewer than three times in his letter of 16 January 1978. Now, thanks to the marked generosity of the Rockefellers, visitors to The Fine Arts Museums of San Francisco will be able to experience these objects and answer that most important question for themselves.

———————

Letter from John D. Rockefeller 3rd Announcing the Donation of His Collection to The Fine Arts Museums of San Francisco

January 16, 1978

Mr. Walter S. Newman
President, Board of Trustees
The Fine Arts Museums of San Francisco
Lincoln Park
San Francisco, California 94121

Dear Mr. Newman:

When you, Ian White and I had lunch together in San Francisco a year ago in November, I indicated that for some time I had been considering the ultimate disposition of my collection of American paintings and that The Fine Arts Museums of San Francisco had come to the fore in my thinking. More recently you and I exchanged letters to help clarify our thinking as to the questions that such a gift might raise and found ourselves generally in accord. And then the three of us met again in October with your counsel to finalize our understanding.

The purpose of this letter is to advise you of my intent to give my collection to the Fine Arts Museums. First, let me give you certain background information as to the basis of my decision and then outline the conditions under which I would make the gift.

My wife and I began collecting oriental art in the early 1950's and this we supplemented with a number of French Impressionists to give variety. After a while we came to realize that we had no representation of American art and this was disturbing to us particularly in connection with foreign friends and guests. And so we decided in 1964 to buy a few American paintings.

We were fortunate in that the first paintings we acquired turned out to be both important and appealing with the result that we were stirred to buy others. And before we knew it we were under way with what has turned out to be a reasonably substantial collection.

From the beginning the criteria for the selection of each item in our collection have been on the one hand quality, and on the other that my wife and I responded to it—that we were moved both aesthetically and emotionally. Also, obviously, our purchases have been affected by the availability of items of quality and appeal. As a result of this approach, there are notable gaps in the collection which have not concerned us.

In the beginning we showed the pieces acquired in our home and then, as the number increased, in my office as well. And as the collection became better known, we found that we had an increasing number of requests for loans to exhibitions.

I mention all of this so that it will be understood that our collection has been a very personal matter for my wife and myself as well as a source of genuine pleasure and satisfaction. Hence the question of continuing ownership seems important.

Dr. Edgar P. Richardson, as you know, has been an important factor in the building of the collection both as a friend and advisor. He has also been most helpful to us these past many months in approaching broadly and realistically the question of ultimate disposition. First, obviously, one thinks of one's family but in today's world this is not practical tax-wise, except for a very few items. Then one thinks of museums and where a collection such as ours would have the most impact. Dr. Richardson has been especially helpful in this connection as he is familiar with the museums of the country and where American paintings are primarily located. Obviously here in the East we are very fortunate, particularly of course in the Washington-New York-Boston area.

After carefully studying the distribution of American paintings in museums across the country, we increasingly became convinced that a gift of our collection to your museums would have greater impact than elsewhere, partly because it would help you in your efforts to build a great collection of American art in a most important part of the country, and partly because we are appreciative of your museums' commitment to make American art a major focus in the years ahead.

Having decided on the ultimate disposition of the collection, the next question is the timing of such a gift. What would be the impact on me as owner and collector should a commitment be made and announced now as against later, possibly in my will; and what would be the impact on the recipient as to the two alternatives. Some of the questions we considered were: If we commit the collection to a museum at this time, would it undercut our interest in further collecting? Would we then be collecting for the museum and not ourselves?

We came to feel that a solution was possible which would be satisfactory to both parties: that is, make a strong statement of intention now, but retain ownership, transferring some items from the collection to the Fine Arts Museums over a period of time, and completing the transfer in my will.

Thus further collecting by my wife and myself will continue to be in terms of our own pleasure and satisfaction and not, so to speak as agents for someone else. This is important to us and should not involve risk to the Fine Arts Museums since the quality and character of the collection has already been established. Inevitably however we would think in making a purchase about the needs of the Museums, but this would not be overriding.

With this background let me now speak about the future. What I have to say covers both items already in the collection as well as those that we may acquire later. To me there should be no distinction between them.

Although I will retain ownership of the collection, together with complete freedom to dispose of it during my life and at my death, I hereby declare my every intention to donate the collection to The Fine Arts Museums of San Francisco with the following understandings:

1. I very likely will transfer a number of pieces to the Museums over the years. With some exceptions referred to below, such items as have not been transferred at the time of my death I intend to transfer to the Museums under my will.

2. During the remaining period of my ownership, I may choose to dispose of such items from the collection as I feel do not measure up in quality or which have lost their special appeal to me.

3. I may choose to give paintings from the collection to members of my family or to other individuals or institutions. I would not anticipate that the number would exceed fifteen percent of the total number comprising my collection. In due course, I will send you a list of the works of art now in the collection. I will be pleased to keep you informed from time to time as to changes in the collection and as to any decisions I might make not to include specific works in the gift to the Museums.

4. Once items from the collection have been transferred to the Fine Arts Museums, it would be understood that they would not be de-acquisitioned by the Museums except upon recommendation of the director and with the approval of the board of trustees after consideration at two regularly scheduled meetings. And it would also be understood that works of art from the collection would be sold or traded by the Museums only to improve the quality of the collection donated by me.

May I say in closing that the thought of giving my collection to The Fine Arts Museums of San Francisco is a source pleasure and satisfaction to me. That I am helping in this way to foster your great Museums' commitment to the American field of art makes me feel my efforts in building the collection will have lasting meaning and value.

Sincerely,

John D. Rockefeller 3rd

Notes

1. They purchased the work from Hirschl & Adler Galleries. The majority of the Rockefeller paintings were acquired from commercial galleries in New York, Boston, and Philadelphia. For specific information on the sources of the 140 works now at The Fine Arts Museums, see the provenance section of the catalogue entries following this essay.

2. The first major monograph devoted to Lane, John Wilmerding's *Fitz Hugh Lane, 1804–1865, American Marine Painter* (Salem, Mass: Essex Institute), appeared later in 1964. Writing in 1971, Wilmerding called it "a small book, [which] brought together previously scattered pieces of information on Lane, some already published and much not." He continued by noting the "enormous expansion of scholarly and popular interest in nineteenth-century American art during the last ten years" (*Fitz Hugh Lane* [New York: Praeger Publishers, 1971], 11, 12).

3. Joshua Taylor, "A Personal and Distinctive Collection of American Art Makes Its Debut," *Smithsonian Magazine* 7, no. 1 (April 1976): 41.

4. For Rockefeller family involvement with the establishment of Acadia National Park on Mount Desert, see Peter Collier and David Horowitz, *The Rockefellers: An American Dynasty* (New York: Holt, Rinehart and Winston, 1976), 147–148. North Haven Island, where the John D. Rockefeller 3rd family had their summer home from 1955 onward, lies about halfway between Owl's Head and Mount Desert.

5. Martha Hutson, "An Interview with John D. Rockefeller 3rd," *American Art Review* 3, no. 4 (July–August 1976): 94.

6. Wanda Corn's overview of scholarship in American art, published in the College Art Association's *Art Bulletin*, opens with an appreciation of the burgeoning of the field during the past three decades and closes by assuring us that the discipline has "come of age." She cites increased numbers of historians, publications, exhibitions, specialized museums, endowments, graduate programs, symposia, and specialized journals—characterizing the increases in available resources with the just phrase, "a quantum leap" (Wanda M. Corn, "Coming of Age: Historical Scholarship in American Art," *The Art Bulletin* 70, no. 2 [June 1988]: 188–207).

7. Hilton Kramer, "Art of the American Past Gets Its Due," *New York Times*, 17 September 1976.

8. See Corn, "Coming of Age," passim; and Elizabeth Johns, "Scholarship in American Art: Its History and Recent Developments," *American Studies International* 22 (October 1984): 3–40. Among the now standard texts that were not available at midcentury: Groce and Wallace, *The New-York Historical Society's Dictionary of Artists in America* (1957); John McCoubrey's compilation, *American Art: Sources and Documents* (1965); the incredibly rich catalogues of the *American Paintings from the Metropolitan Museum of Art* (1965/1980/1985); Maria Naylor's compilation of *National Academy of Design Exhibition Record, 1861–1900* (1973), or such fully documented exhibition catalogues as *A New World: Masterpieces of American Painting* (1983). And how troubling it would be to try to work without access to the many reprints of crucial texts that have been recently reissued—William Dunlap's *A History of the Rise and Progress of the Arts of Design in the United States* (1834/1965), Mantle Fielding's *Dictionary of American Painters, Sculptors, and Engravers* (1926/1965), Henry T. Tuckerman's *Book of the Artists* (1867/1966), and the superb Garland series of nineteenth-century texts written by, among others, S. G. W. Benjamin, Walter Montgomery, and Clarence Cook. Throughout the field, detailed monographic and thematic studies, exhibition catalogues, and catalogues raisonnés have blossomed since the 1950s.

9. F. Lanier Graham, "The New Perspective: An Introduction to the History of American Painting," *Three Centuries of American Painting*, exh. cat. (San Francisco: M. H. de Young Memorial Museum and the California Palace of the Legion of Honor, 1971), 9.

10. Linda Henefield Skalet notes in her work on the American art market: "Though art galleries in general multiplied in New York City in the decades following the Civil War, dealers in American painting were virtually non-existent. There were a few who were willing to sell them on commission, but none who would deal exclusively in American art or invest their capital in it" ("The Market for American Painting in New York: 1870–1915" [Ph.D. diss., The Johns Hopkins University, 1980], 186).

11. E. P. Richardson observed in 1971: "The art market in American art today makes me think of the art market in Dutch and Italian paintings in the 1920s and 30s. The war, inflation in Germany, the depression resulted then in breaking up of the great, old collections of central Europe, rich in Italian and Dutch art. . . .

The rise in values, and taxes, are bringing old family possessions on the market now in America" (Richardson to Rockefeller, 2 December 1971, FAMSF departmental files).

12. The contrast with the immediately preceding period can be illustrated by a tale that Roger Howlett, of Boston's Childs Gallery, delights in telling. In 1948, Charles Childs had in his possession Fitz Hugh Lane's *Entrance of Somes Sound from Southwest Harbor* (1852, private collection), one of the great works in the oeuvre. Childs offered the painting to a distinguished museum, asking a seemingly modest price of $600.00. The museum declined the offer, responding: "Dear Mr. Childs: Thank you for offering your little picture to the Metropolitan Museum, which we must decline. Please keep in mind that we are a museum of art, not Americana" (Roger Howlett, telephone conversation with the author, 12 September 1989).

13. *Nineteenth-Century America: Paintings and Sculpture*, exh. cat. (New York: The Metropolitan Museum of Art, 1970), v. The exhibition included five paintings that the Rockefellers would eventually own: Raphaelle Peale's *Blackberries* (cat. no. 27), William Page's *Cupid and Psyche* (cat. no. 38), Fitz Hugh Lane's *Schooners before Approaching Storm* (fig. 1), Eastman Johnson's *The Brown Family* (cat. no. 70), and Thomas Anshutz's *The Ironworkers' Noontime* (cat. no. 83).

14. The fullest biography of the man is the excellent work by John Ensor Harr and Peter Johnson, *The Rockefeller Conscience: An American Family in Public and in Private* (New York: Charles Scribner's Sons, 1991). For another extended biographical account, see Geoffrey T. Hellman, "Profiles (John D. Rockefeller 3rd)—Out of the Cocoon on the Fifty-Sixth Floor," *The New Yorker* (4 November 1972): 56–103. For the family in general, see William Manchester, *A Rockefeller Family Portrait: From John D. to Nelson* (Boston: Little, Brown & Co., 1958); and Collier and Horowitz, *The Rockefellers*.

15. For an extended biography of Abby Aldrich Rockefeller, see Bernice Kert, *Abby Aldrich Rockefeller: The Woman in the Family* (New York: Random House, 1993).

16. For an early account of the brothers, see Joe Alex Morris, *Those Rockefeller Brothers: An Informal Biography of Five Extraordinary Young Men* (New York: Harper & Brothers, 1953). Rockefeller is the focus of pp. 4, 41–50, and 242–247.

17. Hellman, "Profiles," 68. Stories abound of Rockefeller's trying to keep his and his family's life in touch with the daily strains of New York City—walking or riding public transportation across town to the office; for examples, see Harr and Johnson, *Rockefeller Conscience*, 268–271.

18. Hellman, "Profiles," 60.

19. Travel to Kyoto the year after college (as a member of the Institute of Pacific Relations) and service in the Navy during World War II (where Rockefeller's responsibilities included working toward the establishment of a U.S. military government in Japan) turned his attention to Asia. In 1946 the Rockefeller family donated the land for the United Nations headquarters in Manhattan. In 1949 he was among those asked by the State Department to study U.S. trade relations with Communist China. In 1953 he began the Council for Economic and Cultural Affairs, later renamed the Agricultural Development Council, which encouraged scientific research on crops and rural economics throughout Asia. In 1963 he established the John D. Rockefeller 3rd Fund, "to stimulate, encourage, promote, and support activities important to

human welfare"; a chief purpose of this program was the support of individual artists and scholars throughout East Asia.

Among his decorations and awards were the Grand Cordon Order of Sacred Treasure, Grand Cordon Order Rising Sun (Japan); First Class, Most Noble Order of Crown, Thailand; and Commander Order Thousand Elephants and White Parasol, Laos; as well as a Special Tony Award (1960) and a silver plaque from the Federation of Jewish Philanthropies (Hellman, "Profiles," 56).

20. John D. Rockefeller 3rd, *The Second American Revolution: Some Personal Observations* (New York: Harper & Row, 1972), xiv. See the favorable review by Eric Pace, *The New York Times*, 26 February 1973. For Rockefeller's establishing of the Task Force on Youth in 1970 and its concerns, see Harr and Johnson, *Rockefeller Conscience*, 305–332.

21. Hellman, "Profiles," 56. Hellman quotes Rockefeller from a speech given at a 1967 National Institute of Social Sciences Family Award Dinner, where he received a gold medal for "distinguished service to humanity": "It is true . . . that the field of population and family planning has occupied much of my thought and energy for a number of years. But tonight's occasion makes me wonder. If my parents had been exposed to today's ideas of family planning, brothers Win and Dave might not have made it" (Hellman, "Profiles," 58). For an overview of Rockefeller's work as co-chair of the federal Advisory Committee on Population and Family Planning, and on the Population Council's achievements, see Harr and Johnson, *Rockefeller Conscience*, 31–45, 158–179, 395–442.

22. For an extended review, see Harr and Johnson, *Rockefeller Conscience*, 120–157. One colleague has said, "There's something kind of miraculous about the fact that Lincoln Center exists. I credit John's bull-headedness and tenacity. It was a very demanding, time-consuming, and, in my opinion, distinguished effort. If he hadn't been determined to include education in the concept of the Center, the Juilliard School and the Library and Museum of the Performing Arts might not be there today" (Hellman, "Profiles," 94–95). See also the obituary articles in the *New York Times*: Robert

D. McFadden, "John D. Rockefeller 3d Is Killed in Auto Collision near His Home," 11 July 1978; Wolfgang Saxon, "John D. Rockefeller 3d —Philanthropist, 72, Aided Arts and Population Planning," 11 July 1978; Grace Glueck, "In World of Art, Rockefeller Left Imprint in 2 Main Fields," 12 July 1978.

23. Quoted in "Heroes: The Good Man" [a profile of John D. Rockefeller, Jr.], *Time* (24 September 1956): 20.

24. For an overview of the family as collectors, see Aline B. Saarinen, *The Proud Possessors: The Lives, Times and Tastes of Some Adventurous American Art Collectors* (New York: Random House, 1958), 344–395; Kenneth Clark, "Introduction," *Great Private Collections*, ed. Douglas Cooper (New York: Macmillan Co., 1963), 16.

25. Abby Aldrich Rockefeller to Nelson Rockefeller, quoted in Kert, *Abby Aldrich Rockefeller*, 253. See also Beatrix T. Rumford, "Uncommon Art of the Common People: A Review of Trends in the Collecting and Exhibiting of American Folk Art," in *Perspectives of American Folk Art*, Ian M. G. Quimby and Scott T. Swank, eds. (New York: W. W. Norton for the Henry Francis du Pont Winterthur Museum, 1980), 13–53; and Beatrix T. Rumford and Carolyn J. Weekley, "Preface: Celebrating Fifty Years: The Abby Aldrich Rockefeller Folk Art Center Collection," in *Treasures of American Folk Art from the Abby Aldrich Rockefeller Folk Art Center*, exh. cat. (Boston: Little, Brown and Company, 1989), 8–15.

26. "In John's view, Williamsburg is not just a place of beauty and tourist interest, but a stage for a deeper spiritual presentation of the inspiring story of early democracy in America. 'We are,' he said, 'thinking increasingly of the broader significance of this community as a reflection of the character and faith of the people of colonial America by whom it was built. Williamsburg was a vital force in the life and thought of eighteenth-century America. We hope and intend that it shall be a living force in the twentieth century'" (Morris, *Those Rockefeller Brothers*, 244–245).

27. Kert, 330.

28. Saarinen, *Proud Possessors*, 368. See also Kathleen Teltsch, "Blanchette Rockefeller, 83, Philanthropist, Dies," *New York Times*, 1 December 1992.

29. See Harr and Johnson, *Rockefeller Conscience*, 227–229. It was probably in part the inspiration of Abby Aldrich Rockefeller that prompted Rockefeller and Blanchette Rockefeller to acquire a group of Charles Demuth watercolors in the 1930s (one in 1931 from Abby Aldrich Rockefeller, and three from Kraushaar Gallery in 1939). It was certainly her mother-in-law's patronage of Charles Sheeler, commissioning him to paint two scenes in Williamsburg, that allowed Blanchette Rockefeller in 1937 to acquire that artist's *Kitchen, Williamsburg* (cat. no. 134) from the Downtown Gallery.

30. As she later recalled: "I wasn't up on modern art. But I learned" (Blanchette Rockefeller, interview with Bernice Kert, 19 March 1986, quoted in Kert, 333).

31. Many of these objects have since been donated to the Museum of Modern Art, New York, and the Vassar College Art Gallery. For the house itself, see *Philip Johnson: Architecture, 1949–1965*, intro. Henry-Russell Hitchcock (New York: Holt, Rinehart and Winston, 1966), 46–47; "House Sale," *The New Yorker* (29 May 1989): 29–30.

32. The distinguished scholar of Asian art, Sherman E. Lee, who advised the Rockefellers after 1963, later reminisced: "One learned to respect [Rockefeller's] deeply felt response to the often contemplative ideals of Eastern art and to understand the creative tension existing between these ideals and the more pragmatic and concrete achievements of his other artistic love, American painting. This tension was a true meeting of East and West, and to me it epitomized the character of the man, rooted in the traditional American virtues, but increasingly aware of other transcendental realms" (Sherman E. Lee, "Words of Commemoration," *John D. Rockefeller 3rd, 1906–1978* [privately printed, 1978], n.p.).

33. Rockefeller is quoted as saying, "I was surrounded by art at home, and the arts were strong at Princeton in my day, but I did nothing more about art until my wife and I started to travel in the Far East in 1951, when I began to collect" (Hellman, "Profiles," 70).

34. Rockefeller, quoted in Gordon Bailey Washburn, "Foreword," *Asian Art from the Collection of Mr. and Mrs. John D. Rockefeller 3rd*, exh. cat. (New York: Asia House, 1970), 8.

,35 Fred Ferretti, "New Asian Art Gallery from a Rockefeller," *New York Times*, 7 October 1981; John Russell, "A Splendid New Home for Rockefeller's Treasures," *New York Times*, 11 October 1981; John Russell, "Art: Asia Society Opens New Gallery to Public," *New York Times*, 13 October 1981.

36. Hutson, "An Interview," 93–94.

37. Richardson served at the Detroit Institute of Arts from 1930 until 1962 (director from 1945), and, from 1962 to 1966, as director of the Henry Francis du Pont Winterthur Museum. His principal texts were *Painting in America: The Story of 450 Years* (1956: reissued 1965), *American Romantic Painting* (1944), *Washington Allston: A Study of the Romantic Artist in America* (1948 and 1967), *A Short History of American Painting* (1963), and key contributions to several exhibition catalogues, most notably *Charles Willson Peale and His World* (1982). For a review of his career, see William E. Woolfenden, "E. P. Richardson," *Archives of American Art Journal* 17, no. 3 (1977): 2–4; and "E. P. Richardson: A Bibliography," *Archives of American Art Journal* 17, no. 3 (1977): 12–14.

38. Mrs. Rockefeller referred to their collections from many cultures as a "mishmash" (Teltsch, *New York Times*).

39. Rockefeller to Dr. Edgar P. Richardson, 24 December 1964, FAMSF departmental files.

40. The list was broken into eight categories: *Early-nineteenth-century Romantic painters*: Allston, Audubon, William Page; *Early Landscape*: Kensett; *Early Genre*: Bingham, Mount; *Early Still Life*: James Peale, Raphaelle Peale; *Painters of the West*: Bierstadt; *Later nineteenth century*: Whistler, Sargent, Homer, Eakins, La Farge, Vedder; *Still-life painters*: Peto; *Early twentieth century*: Hopper, Burchfield. In smaller type he added to some of these categories with the names Whittredge, F. E. Church, Sanford Gifford, Thomas Cole, Heade, Fitz Hugh Lane, other members of the Peale family, S. Eastman, Catlin, Hassam, Dewing, Twachtman, Eastman Johnson, Ryder, Harnett, Habarle, Cope.

41. Richardson to Rockefeller, 31 December 1964, FAMSF departmental files.

42. They referred to it often. As one example, in January 1968 Rockefeller wrote to Richardson: "Again my warmest thanks to you for your interest and your assistance. I do greatly enjoy working with you and lean heavily on your knowledge and wise counsel. I only hope that you too are deriving pleasure and satisfaction from the relationship" (Rockefeller to Richardson, 2 January 1968, FAMSF departmental files). Speaking of Richardson in a more public fashion, Rockefeller said in 1976: "We have been working together for nearly 12 years now. He has been very helpful and, of course, he is a wonderful person" (Hutson, "An Interview," 99).

43. On occasion, Blanchette Rockefeller would accompany Richardson and his wife as they visited New York galleries. Rockefeller would note such outings in his correspondence, as for example: "My wife enjoyed so much her luncheon with you and your wife and your visit together to two or three galleries" (Rockefeller to Richardson, 10 March 1966, FAMSF departmental files).

44. Rockefeller proposed these categories, based in part on his work in the Asian collection with Sherman Lee, in a letter to Richardson of 12 January 1967 (FAMSF departmental files).

45. Richardson to Rockefeller, 23 January 1967, FAMSF departmental files. Richardson proposed the "O" category in a letter of 1 September 1970, in part as a response to Albert Bierstadt's *River Scene* (cat. no. 49): "Would you be willing to accept an O category? designating things that you might enjoy, as a private collector, and *only* because I think they might give you pleasure?

You do not wish to dilute your collection by too many small and unimportant things, I know. Your own good judgment will keep you from doing so. However, the arts offer so many different kinds of pleasure; and American life is so diverse, so rich in interest, often so difficult to fit into categories, that I don't want to miss calling anything to your attention as we go along, because it doesn't fit into our scale" (FAMSF departmental files).

46. Conversation with the author, 16 March 1987.

47. Richardson, "Preface," *American Art: An Exhibition from the Collection of Mr. and Mrs. John D. Rockefeller 3rd*, exh. cat. (San Francisco: The Fine Arts Museums of San Francisco, 1976), n.p.

48. Richardson to White, 12 November 1975, FAMSF departmental files. Richardson made much the same point to Rockefeller himself: "I would make only one suggestion: I do not want to be there. This is for a very good reason. It is your collection. It represents your interests, taste, decisions. No one else formed it. I have helped along the way, finding things, supplying an element of professional experience—and have enjoyed very much working with you—but the credit for the collection is, and should be, yours alone.

There are other collections of which this is not true: they are really formed by someone else for the collector. It is important that no one should think this to be the case here" (Richardson to Rockefeller, 10 November 1975, FAMSF departmental files).

Not all critics recognized the truth of this, of course. Thomas B. Hess, writing in the magazine *New York*, praised the collection enthusiastically, but opined that it "beautifully articulates the sensibility, passion, and scholarship of one man. And his name is Edgar P. Richardson" ("Seeing the Light," 18 October 1976, 94).

49. It is important to remember, in reading this letter from the perspective of the 1990s, the tremendous amount of activity—within museum, academic, and commercial settings—that now provides a much broader knowledge of American historical art than a neutral observer thirty years ago would have thought possible. Rockefeller wrote of Copley in early 1965. Only later in the year was a major retrospective of the artist's work held in New York, Boston, and Washington, D.C. Published later still, in 1966, was the major scholarly work on the artist, Jules Prown's two-volume catalogue raisonné. Nor had images by Copley entered the public's visual vocabulary of images through the intense use in advertisements and general proliferation of visual materials that we now take for granted.

50. Rockefeller to Richardson, 19 April 1965, FAMSF departmental files. Rockefeller held a place in his affections for smaller exhibitions.

He once said: "I would stress my sincere belief. . . that the [Asian] society s collection should always remain small. In this age of ever-growing museums of major importance, there is a particularly useful role for the small specialized museum of high quality. Not only can it serve as an initial point of contact with a great culture for the casual visitor, but it can raise the sights of those knowledgeable in the field by the sheer beauty and quality of the items on display" (John Russell, "Splendid New Home," *New York Times*, 11 October 1981).

51. Richardson to Rockefeller, 26 April 1965, FAMSF departmental files.

52. Rockefeller to Richardson, 20 September 1965, FAMSF departmental files.

53. Single-collection exhibitions include: *Mr. and Mrs. Lawrence A. Fleischman Collection of American Paintings*, exh. cat. (Ann Arbor: University of Michigan Museum of Art, 1953); *Collection in Progress: Selections from the Lawrence and Barbara Fleischman Collection of American Art*, exh. cat. (The Detroit Institute of Arts, 1955); *American Painting 1760–1960: A Selection of 125 Paintings from the Collection of Mr. and Mrs. Lawrence A. Fleischman, Detroit*, exh. cat. (Milwaukee, Wisc.: Milwaukee Art Center, 1960); *American Painting 1765–1963: Selections from the Lawrence A. and Barbara Fleischman Collection of American Art*, exh. cat. (Tucson: University of Arizona Art Gallery, 1964). *Small Pictures of Large Import from the Collection of Lawrence A. and Barbara Fleischman of Detroit, Michigan*, exh. cat. (Philadelphia: Pennsylvania Academy of the Fine Arts, 1964).

54. Richardson to Rockefeller, 4 October 1965, FAMSF departmental files. Fleischman is a key figure in the revival of nineteenth-century American painting. With Richardson, he brought the Archives of American Art into existence. As an omnivore collector—Richardson had earlier categorized him as "a compulsive buyer" and teasingly noted that if "there were a Buyers Anonymous, he should join it" (2 June 1965)—Fleischman and his wife, Barbara, acquired many of the greatest American paintings available on the market. He disposed of

the collection when he acquired a major portion of Kennedy Galleries, one of the nation's oldest firms specializing in American art. As Richardson wrote to Rockefeller on 13 May 1966: "A piece of news is out to which I was sworn to secrecy until now. Mr. Wunderlich told me some time ago that he had offered Mr. Fleischman a half interest in his business, if he would come to New York and turn from a collector into a dealer. . . . The news is out that he is moving from Detroit to New York. . . .

This will be a formidable combination, if the two men can work harmoniously together. Larry Fleischman has a flair for making discoveries and is a natural salesman; while Wunderlich has great experience. The other dealers in American art will find them formidable competitors" (FAMSF departmental files).

55. The Rockefellers initially passed on the *Blackberries*, but upon it being mentioned again in response to their questioning Richardson, they moved to acquire it: "My wife was pleased that you mentioned again the Raphaelle Peale *Still Life with Blackberries* as we both liked it very much but I had decided against it because of the very high price and because it is so small that it seemed to me that it might be difficult to show effectively in our apartment" (Rockefeller to Richardson, 10 March 1966, FAMSF departmental files).

56. Richardson to Rockefeller, 4 October 1965, FAMSF departmental files.

57. Richardson to Rockefeller, 25 October 1965, FAMSF departmental files. Among the works urged by Richardson but not acted on were: James Peale, *George Washington* (a miniature that was not shown them for many months); Washington Allston's *Samuel Williams* (Cleveland Museum of Art), Albert Pinkham Ryder's *Self-Portrait* (Mr. and Mrs. Daniel W. Dietrich II), Eakins's *A. W. Lee* (Reynolda House), and John Haberle's *Japanese Doll* (private collection).

58. Rockefeller to Richardson, 11 October 1965, FAMSF departmental files.

59. Richardson to Rockefeller, 14 October 1965, FAMSF departmental files.

60. Joshua Taylor noted this hesitancy with praise, saying: "In his office hangs an early painting by Thomas Cole, *View near Catskill Village*, a quiet painting that somehow mingles Claude Lorrain and the American landscape. At first he was not especially taken with the painting, he admits, but now it has a place of honor, satisfying by the subtlety with which it presents its half-concealed beauties. So each new painting is an adventure in seeing, a new personality to get to know" ("A Personal and Distinctive Collection," 46).

61. "The basic question that Mr. Rockefeller asks himself before an available piece is 'Does it stir and lift me?'" (Washburn, *Asian Art*, 7).

62. Rockefeller to Richardson, 3 October 1966, FAMSF departmental files. Richardson apparently responded in the affirmative on 6 October. The year was to be such an active one that on 28 June 1967 Rockefeller wrote: "We have been working together now on this basis for nearly a year. I do want you to know how much I appreciate your help. It has been a real pleasure working with you. The way things have worked out you have spent considerably more time in regard to my purchases than I had anticipated and I guess this is to a large extent due to the number of paintings which I acquired during the period.

Under these circumstances I would like very much to increase the honorarium for this year. . . . It is a pleasure in this tangible way to express my satisfaction and appreciation for what you are doing for me" (FAMSF departmental files).

63. Rockefeller used the phrase to describe those twentieth-century painters who interested him— Hopper, Burchfield, Sheeler, Prendergast, and Sloan (Rockefeller to Richardson, 15 October 1965, FAMSF departmental files). Concerning Copley, he wrote, after visiting the National Gallery of Art in order to see the Chester Dale collection: "I was interested to see that it included a few eighteenth and nineteenth century Americans. Also, the National Gallery itself has some, although mainly portraits. I must say I do increasingly come to respect and admire John Singleton Copely [*sic*]" (Rockefeller to Richardson, 2 August 1965, FAMSF departmental files).

64. "Then there are the genre paintings that have real appeal. Eastman Johnson specialized in them. There are two or three on exhibit in San Francisco. We like them particularly" (Hutson, "An Interview," 95).

65. Writing of the period, Barbara Rose has observed: "The frantic search for technical, formal, and conceptual breakthroughs that had become the staple of the radical rhetoric pervasive in both formalist and non-formalist late sixties' criticism, made it seem as though innovation were the proof of quality" (*American Art since 1960* [1967; New York: Praeger, 1975], 221).

66. Richardson to Rockefeller, 6 January 1967, FAMSF departmental files.

67. The sense of this was conveyed in *Prospect for America: The Rockefeller Panel Reports*, a series of papers commissioned by The Rockefeller Brothers Fund and published individually in the late 1950s. The writers claimed to be at a crucial point in the nation's history: "The signs are all around us. Probably never have these signs—of growth and change, of danger and dilemma—so abounded in all spheres of national life. From the security of our nation to the renewal of our cities, from the education of our young to the well-being of our old, from the facts of military might to the subtle substance of spiritual strength—everything seems touched by challenge.

The number and the depth of the problems we face suggest that the very life of our free society may be at stake" (Rockefeller Brothers Fund, *Prospect for America: The Rockefeller Panel Reports* [New York: Doubleday & Doubleday, 1961], xix.

68. *The Second American Revolution*, quoted in John D. Rockefeller IV, "Words of Commemoration," *John D. Rockefeller 3rd, 1906–1978* (New York: privately printed, 1978), n.p.

69. Washburn, *Asian Art*, 7.

70. Richardson, "Preface," n.p.

71. This is as opposed to appreciating the individual assertiveness of more operatic works of the nineteenth century—large-scale paintings by Bierstadt, Church, or Moran, for example—that were finding a tentative respectability in such writings as Robert Rosenblum's "The Abstract Sublime: How Some of the Most Heretical Concepts of Modern American Abstract Painting Relate to the Visionary Nature-painting of a Century Ago," *Art News* 59, no. 10 (February 1961).

72. Theodore E. Stebbins, Jr., *Martin Johnson Heade*, exh. cat. (College Park: University of Maryland Art Gallery, 1969); Theodore E. Stebbins, Jr., *The Life and Works of Martin Johnson Heade* (New Haven, Conn.: Yale University Press, 1975).

73. Arthur Altschul, Daniel and Rita Fraad, and Herbert Goldstone in New York, Lawrence A. and Barbara Fleischman in Detroit, and Meyer and Vivian Potamkin in Philadelphia began collecting American art in the 1950s. Raymond and Margaret Horowitz of New York began in about 1960. In Los Angeles, Jo Ann and Julian Ganz made their first purchase in 1964. For a review of American art collectors of this generation, see Linda Ayres, "Introduction," in Linda Ayres and Jane Myers, *American Paintings, Watercolors, and Drawings from the Collection of Rita and Daniel Fraad*, exh. cat. (Fort Worth, Tex.: Amon Carter Museum, 1985), xi. Others who should also be noted as active during these decades include Lee B. Anderson, Dr. John McDonough, Paul Magriel, Ambassador and Mrs. William Middendorf, James Ricau, and Graham Williford.

74. Richardson to Rockefeller, 21 December 1968, FAMSF departmental files (pencil draft only). Thomas Hoving, when director of the Metropolitan Museum of Art, later wrote in a parallel vein concerning the collectors' lead in taste: "In recent years American painting has enjoyed one of the most lively, interesting, and deserved revivals in the art world. . . . Although art museums have good reason to be pleased with this activity, it should be remembered that private collectors have often been the pioneer, reviving force in American art. They, through their enthusiasm and acumen, have shown the way for the museums" (Thomas Hoving, "Foreword," in Dianne H. Pilgrim, *American Impressionist and Realist Paintings and Drawings from the Collection of Mr. & Mrs. Raymond J Horowitz*, exh. cat. [New York: The Metropolitan Museum of Art, 1973], 5).

75. This is parallel to what Mrs. Rockefeller said of the Asian art collection: "'It is not merely the purchasing of a rich man,' she approvingly declares, 'but that of an individual collector who has studied the material and made his own sensitive choices'" (Washburn, *Asian Art*, 7).

76. Hutson, "An Interview," 96.

77. Richardson wrote to Rockefeller on 3 June: "Our weekend on the Hudson left a very pleasant savor behind. . . . It was certainly a help to me to see so many of the pictures you have been acquiring in the setting where you intend to use them" (FAMSF departmental files). Hellman wrote of Rockefeller as "more relaxed in the country than he is in the city. He has a place—Fieldwood Farm, full of Shaker furniture, just outside the family park at Pocantico Hills—where, 'Mr. John' to the tenantry, he breeds Aberdeen Angus cattle and, weekends and summers, likes to ride, play golf, chop wood, and trim trees. 'He works on the view to the Hudson to get it at its artistic best,' one of his daughters has said" ("Profiles," 65).

78. Rockefeller to Richardson, 8 July 1968, FAMSF departmental files. At the end of the year, the collector wrote to the advisor: "As you know, I am enjoying the collecting very much. As you also know, I hope, I am sincerely appreciative of your help and count heavily on your sound judgement and wise advice" (12 December 1968).

79. Rockefeller to Richardson, 19 May 1970, FAMSF departmental files.

80. *Three Centuries of American Painting*, exh. cat. (San Francisco: M. H. de Young Memorial Museum and California Palace of the Legion of Honor, 1971).

81. Rockefeller to White, 18 August 1970, FAMSF departmental files.

82. White to Rockefeller, 1 September 1970, FAMSF departmental files.

83. "First conversations about the Rockefellers' own collection went gingerly indeed. 'He said, "Now, we're not really talking about anything; we're just walking around the subject",' White recalls. 'It was a walk that lasted seven years'" (Bruce Porter, "Doers and Donors: The Making of the Best Museum Board in America," *Connoisseur* [December 1984]: 73).

84. Rockefeller to Richardson, 17 July 1970, FAMSF departmental files.

85. Rockefeller was recovering from a fall from a new horse (Harr and Johnson, *Rockefeller Conscience*, 464–465).

86. Blanchette Rockefeller to Richardson, 17 September 1970, FAMSF departmental files. The Eastman Johnson that was voted down was probably *Fiddling His Way*, being offered by the newly formed Coe Kerr Gallery.

87. Richardson to Rockefeller, 25 May 1971, FAMSF departmental files.

88. Rockefeller to Richardson, 24 May 1972, FAMSF departmental files.

89. Hellman, "Profiles," 68.

90. Richardson to Rockefeller, 2 June 1965, FAMSF departmental files.

91. Ruth Bowman, "Nature, The Photograph and Thomas Anshutz," *Art Journal* 33, no. 1 (Fall 1973): 32.

92. Hutson, "An Interview," 95.

93. Hutson, "An Interview," 95.

94. Richardson continued: "The *Mason Children, David, Joanna and Abigail* is of great interest *historically*. It is dated 1670 and is one of the best of the small group of paintings done in Massachusetts before the year 1700. Only about 35 such portraits are known. Many are dark and ruinous; many are of grim-faced Puritan preachers in black gowns; only a few are of the kind to give pleasure over and beyond their value as rarities from that early time. This is one that can give pleasure. And it is a great rarity. But when I say that, I have said all that I can in its favor. It is a distant, provincial echo of English provincial portraiture. And even in such a crazy country as ours, should one pay a million dollars for a secondary work? A top price for a work of great artistry, yes. For this, no. . . .

It seems a picture for a museum with a historical aim, rather than a private collector" (Richardson to Rockefeller, 16 August 1973, FAMSF departmental files).

95. Sometimes, although we do not know which objects were involved, this response provoked Mrs. Rockefeller to exclaim: "Get it, Johnny. It's *good*" (quoted in Hellman, "Profiles," 65).

96. Robert C. Vose, Jr., to Richardson, 17 November 1973, FAMSF departmental files.

97. Vose to Rockefeller, 26 November 1973, FAMSF departmental files.

98. Vose to Rockefeller, 8 February 1974, FAMSF departmental files.

99. Richardson to Rockefeller, 3 June 1974, FAMSF departmental files.

100. John Russell, "Art: Asia Society Opens to Public," *New York Times* (13 October 1981).

101. John D. Rockefeller 3rd, "More Than 200 Candles," *New York Times*, 19 March 1975.

102. Rockefeller to White, 19 November 1973, FAMSF departmental files.

103. White to Rockefeller, 26 December 1973, FAMSF departmental files. Rockefeller responded: "Now that the decision has been made to go ahead and make the loan, I find myself increasingly looking forward to the event" (Rockefeller to White, 10 January 1974, FAMSF departmental files).

104. Cook to Rockefeller, 14 March 1974, FAMSF departmental files.

105. Richardson to Rockefeller, 10 October 1974, FAMSF departmental files.

106. "Mrs. Corn has made every effort to increase the educational opportunities of the exhibition. She has written an attractive four page handout free for every visitor, arranged for student tours from the various universities in the area, trained students as lecturers to speak to local groups interested in attending, made available seminar rooms and slide projection equipment for interested parties, and helped organize a one-day symposium on American art. Besides all these offerings, the museum is having a multiple art program by subscription with seven meetings that will be *An American Sampler* of music, dance, drama, and readings" (Martha Hutson, "Mr. and Mrs. John D. Rockefeller 3rd Collection of American Art: Exhibition Review," *American Art Review* 3, no. 4 [July–August 1976]: 90).

107. Rockefeller to Newman, 16 January 1978, FAMSF departmental files.

108. Concerning these two artists, Rockefeller noted: "Mary Cassatt, for example, is an artist whose work is not represented in our collection.

We would be pleased to find one that we really liked, but I don't feel any pressure to have a Mary Cassatt"; "I'd be pleased if we had a Whistler, but they are very difficult to find. We saw a tiny Whistler the other day that we didn't particularly like. I think it is the first Whistler I have seen that was available since we have been collecting" (Hutson, "An Interview," 96, 98).

109. Mark Stevens, "A Rockefeller Bonanza," *Newsweek*, 30 January 1978, 60.

110. Ian McKibbin White, "Foreword," *American Art: An Exhibition from the Collection of Mr. and Mrs. John D. Rockefeller 3rd*, 9.

111. "Opening Speech by Mr. John D. Rockefeller 3rd, April 19, 1976," typescript, FAMSF departmental files.

112. White to Rockefeller, 24 May 1976, FAMSF departmental files.

113. Blake A. Samson, "Rockefeller Art Exhibition Extended at SF Museum," *Contra Costa Times*, 14 July 1976.

114. Mahonri Sharp Young, "A Rockefeller Collection of American Art," *Apollo* 103, no. 172 (June 1976): 513.

115. Taylor, "A Personal and Distinctive Collection," 46.

116. William Wilson, "This American Show Is No Turkey," *Los Angeles Times*, 9 August 1976.

117. Hutson, "Exhibition Review," 91.

118. Emily Genauer, "Art & the Artist," *New York Post*, 18 September 1976.

119. Genauer, "Art & the Artist."

120. Hilton Kramer, "Art of the American Past Gets Its Due," *New York Times*, 17 September 1976.

121. Hilton Kramer, "A Great Show on a False Peg," *New York Times*, 10 October 1976. Comparably disparaging responses to the three major private collections of nineteenth-century American paintings shown subsequently present a revelatory consistency toward the subject matter on the part of the newspaper. See Hilton Kramer, "Are the Standards Too Low for American Art?" *New York Times*, 1 November 1981 (review of the Jo Ann and Julian Ganz collection); John Russell, "Art: A Two-pronged Survey of American Masters," *New York Times*, 17 August 1985 (review of the Baron

Thyssen-Bornemisza collection); and Michael Kimmelman, "Private Art in Public Places," *New York Times*, 30 July 1989 (review of the Manoogian collection).

122. Richardson continued: "All they wish to do is to needle Mr. Rockefeller, or hit him with a monkey wrench. I suppose that since your name is Rockefeller, you must have grown to expect this kind of smallness; and perhaps to pay it no attention. But the ignorance bothers me!" (Richardson to Rockefeller, draft, ca. 30 October 1976, FAMSF departmental files).

123. The picketing was reported, and the petition reprinted in, "Artists Rights: Artists Demand Whitney Cancel Bicentennial Exhibition," *Art Workers News* (December–January 1976): 3.

124. Robert Atkins, "Politics and Aesthetics Clash in Rockefeller Art Exhibit," *Berkeley Barb*, 16 July 1976.

125. See, for example, Gregory Battcock, "Rien de Plus Eloquent Que l'Argent Comptant," *Soho Weekly News*, 23 September 1976. A considerable amount of attention was devoted to Chythia Hollinsworth, an invited guest, who once inside the Whitney tripped over a Calder statue and had to have her leg packed with ice.

126. The one response to the issues raised by the AMCC from anyone actually involved with *American Art: Selections from the Collection of Mr. and Mrs. John D. Rockefeller 3rd* came from E. P. Richardson. On 30 June 1976, Benny Andrews had written on the letterhead of the Black Emergency Cultural Coalition asking Richardson questions revolving around the lack of black artists in the selected works. At the core of them was the terse, "How do you . . . feel about the exclusion of Black artists from the exhibition?" Richardson responded on 14 July: "Your letter expressing your concern for the well-being of black artists deserves a thoughtful answer.

Your questions are addressed to an exhibition chosen as a national survey of talent today. This is a misunderstanding. When I was director of a public museum in Detroit, we exhibited, and acquired, the works of black artists, past and present . . . as a normal part of our effort to form a representative collection of American art.

The collection of Mr. and Mrs. John D. Rockefeller 3rd is not of that kind. It was acquired over a long period of years with no thought that it would be shown in a bicentennial year. . . . What the exhibition represents is a deep interest in the work of American artists by a thoughtful private collector.

I emphasize the words *private collector*. . . .

. . . I believe you will agree that no one can, or should, say to such a private individual, 'You have no right to lend your pictures to a public gallery unless you lend pictures by artists we are interested in.'" The letter (edited and re-typed onto blank paper, leaving off Richardson's address), and Richardson's response (with Richardson's address masked) were reproduced in facsimile in *an anti-catalog* (New York: The Catalogue Committee, Inc., 1977), 72, 73.

127. Roberta J. M. Olson, "On Art: American Art at Whitney," *Soho Weekly News*, 23 September 1976.

128. *anti-catalog*, front cover.

129. The title page reads: "an *anti*-catalog written, designed, and produced by Rudolf Barabik, Sarina Bromberg, Sarah Charlesworth, Susanne Cohn, Carol Duncan, Shawn Gargagliano, Eunice Golden, Janet Koenig, Joseph Kosuth, Anthony McCall, Paul Pechter, Elain Bendock Pelosini, Aaron Roseman, Larry Rosing, Ann Marie Rousseau, Alan Wallach, Walter Weissman/Jimmy Durham wrote 'Mr. Catlin and Mr. Rockefeller Tame the Wilderness.' Gerald Horne collaborated on 'Black Art and Historical Omission.'"

130. "For this purpose the Rockefeller show has been our consistent focus, although our perspective relates to issues which go far beyond the specific scope of this exhibition" (*anti-catalog*, 6).

131. *anti-catalog*, 6.

132. *anti-catalog*, 7.

133. The continuing explorations of Joseph Kosuth and Alan Wallach have been particularly important in this effort.

Locally, in San Francisco, an expanded board of trustees reflecting the ethnic and political multiplicity of the region, a concerted effort at providing a varied exhibition schedule, increasingly active educational programs, and the development of special exhibition committees drawn from diverse sectors of the community have all moved The Fine Arts Museums along this path. The opening in 1993 of the Yerba Buena Center for the Visual Arts—a major municipal achievement—and the growth of neighborhood museums and arts centers testify to the city's commitment to a diverse view of the contemporary art scene. At the exhibition's other venue, the Whitney Museum, the 1993 Biennial received a barrage of negative criticism precisely because of the overtly activist stance (labeled as politically correct) of many of its components.

134. Rockefeller to Richardson, 20 May 1976, FAMSF departmental files.

135. White to Rockefeller, 5 October 1976, FAMSF departmental files. The works on loan were Albert Bierstadt's *Niagara Falls* (cat. no. 62), George Caleb Bingham's *Boatmen on the Missouri* (cat. no. 41), William Merritt Chase's *A Corner of My Studio* (cat. no. 112), the de Peyster Painter's *Maria Maytilda Winkler* (cat. no. 2), Robert Feke's *Grizzell Eastwick Apthorp* (cat. no. 4), Eastman Johnson's *Cranberry Pickers* (fig. 5), John La Farge's *The Great Statue of Amida Buddha at Kamakura* (cat. no. 100), and Charles Sheeler's *Kitchen, Williamsburg* (cat. no. 134).

136. Richardson to Rockefeller, 29 October 1970, FAMSF departmental files. Coincidentally, also during the month of October, J. Carter Brown, director of the National Gallery of Art, wrote to Rockefeller to explore the option of showing the Rockefeller American collection at the National Gallery. Rockefeller kindly but firmly declined the opportunity (correspondence from Rockefeller of 29 October and 29 December 1970; and from Brown of 23 October, 9 November, and 4 January 1971; FAMSF departmental files).

137. The painting was eventually acquired by the Amon Carter Museum, was deaccessioned, and has been recently acquired by The Huntington, San Marino, California.

138. Lee to Rockefeller, 24 November 1976, FAMSF departmental files.

139. Richardson to Rockefeller, 14 December 1976, FAMSF departmental files.

140. Rockefeller to Richardson, 29 December 1976, FAMSF departmental files. Rockefeller closed the letter: "You are a good friend and I appreciate it." Richardson responded: "I greatly hope that you will keep the collection together. In this matter I have experience: for I know the value and impact of a large, rich collection upon both scholars and public.

In the matter of timing of the announcement, I have no experience: there must be others who can advise you better; but the best guide surely lies in your own feelings" (Richardson to Rockefeller, 7 January 1977, FAMSF departmental files).

141. Rockefeller to Richardson, 14 November 1977, FAMSF departmental files.

142. Rockefeller to Richardson, 12 January 1978, FAMSF departmental files.

143. Richardson to Rockefeller, 23 January 1978, FAMSF departmental files.

144. Rockefeller to Walter S. Newman, 16 January 1978, FAMSF departmental files.

145. Board of Trustees, Special Meeting, 19 January 1978, Resolution No. 144.

146. Wallace Turner, "John D. Rockefeller 3d Wills $10 Million in American Art to San Francisco," *New York Times*, 20 January 1978.

147. Stevens, "A Rockefeller Bonanza," 61.

148. Transcript of press conference, 19 January 1978, FAMSF departmental files. This picked up on a point Frankenstein had earlier raised in February 1974 and again in 1976. Writing in the *San Francisco Chronicle*, Frankenstein noted: "This show will be most interesting, valuable, and instructive, but unless I am badly mistaken Mr. Rockefeller's John D. III Fund is still restricted to students of Oriental art, and no serious study of American art and its place in American culture as a whole is contemplated for the de Young or anywhere else during the Bicentennial year" (Alfred Frankenstein, "Rockefeller Collection at de Young in '76," *San Francisco Sunday Examiner & Chronicle*,

10 February 1974). Frankenstein had again raised the point as the opening of the first of several reviews of the exhibition in 1976, writing: "In 1965, when the Asian Art Museum of San Francisco opened, it was inaugurated with a symposium of 100 of the leading scholars on Asian art from every part of the world. A considerable part of the financial load of this symposium was borne by the JDRIII Fund, a trust established by the lender of the new de Young show and devoted entirely, so far as art history is concerned, to exchanges with the Orient. Rockefeller was not collecting American art at that time. He began to do so shortly thereafter. But the JDRIII Fund never has established a program for the study of American art, and its directors have apparently never given the idea as much as a moment's thought.

Now look: . . .

America had a right to expect more of John D. Rockefeller III than simply another Bicentennial exhibition" (Alfred Frankenstein, "The Rockefeller Collection of American Art," *San Francisco Sunday Examiner & Chronicle*, 18 April 1976, "This World," 30).

149. Alfred Frankenstein, "That Neglected, Essential Side of Art," *San Francisco Chronicle*, 21 January 1978.

150. Rockefeller to Frankenstein, 17 February 1978, FAMSF departmental files.

151. Frankenstein to Rockefeller, 27 February 1978, FAMSF departmental files.

152. Richardson to Frankenstein, 27 February 1978, FAMSF departmental files.

153. The Rockefeller collection included, in addition to *Sunday Meeting*, two temperas by the artist —*Karl* (1948) and *Miss Olson* (1952), both now in private collections—and the drybrush of *Frosted Apples* (cat. no. 139).

154. Quoted in letter from Carroll L. Wainwright, Jr., to White, 1 August 1978, FAMSF departmental files.

155. After Frankenstein, the Ednah Root curatorship was held by Donald L. Stover (1980–1981), Margaretta Lovell (1981–1985), and Marc Simpson (from 1985). In 1987 the Museums designated a second Ednah Root curatorship, dedicated to American Decorative Arts and Sculpture, which Donald L. Stover has held since its inception.

156. Hutson, "An Interview," 99.

157. Rockefeller to Newman, 16 January 1978, FAMSF departmental files. The conditions Rockefeller set upon the museum are, in fact, less stringent than the institution's own deaccessioning policy.

158. There is a memorandum of 29 November 1977 from Rockefeller's curator, Berthe Saunders, to Richardson asking about pruning nine works from the collection: Copley's *Dr. Nathaniel Perkins* (fig. 4), Eakins's *Professor William Woolsey Johnson* (cat. no. 116), David Johnson's *View on Lake George* (private collection), three works by Eastman Johnson (*The Eavesdropper*, *The Mother*, and *What the Shell Says* [cat. nos. 65, 73, and 76]), Irving Wiles's *The Sonata* (cat. no. 102), Abbott Thayer's *David* (cat. no. 114), and Eugene Speicher's *Vase of Flowers* (private collection). Richardson responded: "Now, the list of paintings to be traded in. If these are pictures which no longer give you pleasure, if their interest is gone, I shall make no objection. This is your collection and everything should be such as to enrich your life.

But if the fact that I did not put the Eakins *Professor Johnson* and the three small Eastman Johnsons in the San Francisco exhibition has given you the impression that I consider them secondary, I regret the misapprehension. I had a numerical limit to work within in selecting that show. Some very good things had to be left out.

The Eakins is a portrait of the first quality and of remarkable force. You have nothing else like it and you would find it extremely difficult to find another to replace it. I did not want to put in too many portraits and I left this one out. Looking backward, I judge that to be one of my mistakes" (19 December 1977, FAMSF departmental files). None of these works were then deaccessioned.

159. In spite of Richardson's firm belief that the Rockefeller copy was the superior one, it now appears through conservation examination and close study that it is indeed a copy, the mate to the *Mrs. Yates* at the Museum of Fine Arts, Boston, which is a replica by an unknown hand.

160. William Gerdts in conversation with the author, 6 October 1993; affirmed by correspondence of 27 December 1993, FAMSF departmental files.

161. Ross C. Anderson to Margaretta Lovell, 3 November 1982, FAMSF departmental files.

162. Questions have been raised by, among others, David Meschutt (27 July 1993), Carrie Rebora (2 January 1991), and Barbara Buff (23 March 1985); correspondence FAMSF departmental files.

163. When Martha Hutson asked, "Do you consider any work the masterpiece of the collection?" Rockefeller replied with the eloquent but terse, "No" ("An Interview," 99).

EXPLANATORY NOTE

ARRANGEMENT

The catalogue entries are arranged in chronological order by date of execution, starting with *The Mason Children* of 1670 and moving through Philip Jamison's *Daisies in Maine Studio* of 1970. With very few exceptions (for example, Worthington Whittredge's *From the Harz Mountains*), we have accepted the dates inscribed on the paintings as their execution dates. In instances such as Robert Henri's *The Ice Floe*, which he began in 1901, stopped work on, then completed and exhibited in 1902, we have used 1902 as the execution date. If two or more works were completed in the same year, they are placed in alphabetical order by the artists' last names. Circa dates (ca.) signal our lack of specific documentation, but belief (often based on stylistic grounds or closely related objects) that the works were completed on or near to the date given, certainly within plus-or-minus five years. In ordering the catalogue entries, these follow the firmly dated paintings of a given year.

TITLES

Portrait subjects are identified as fully as possible. Titles of other works are generally those used in their earliest recorded public exhibitions.

DIMENSIONS

All measurements are in inches, height preceding width. For paintings, we have recorded the painted surface. In most, but not all, instances these coincide with the edges of panels and stretchers. Drawing and watercolor measurements document the sheet size.

QUOTED EXTRACTS

We have selected quoted extracts to provide brief biographical reviews of the artists' careers, answer basic questions about subject matter (for example—who is portrayed in a portrait? where is a landscape taken from?), and share the flavor of the responses that the object generated when it was put on exhibition. Some of these extracts will contain statements that are counter to our current understanding of a subject, or even that contradict one another. They should be looked upon not as full and seamless explications, but as documents relevant to constructing an interpretation of a work and its passage through time.

PROVENANCE

The basic format of the history of ownership, moving forward from the past, is: possessor (life dates), cities of residence, dates of possession. Commercial establishments are indicated by square brackets []. The closing date of possession sometimes extends beyond an owner's life dates, accounting for estate settlement and distribution (e.g., Mrs. John D. Rockefeller 3rd died in 1992, but The Fine Arts Museums did not receive her bequest until it was distributed in 1993). In instances where we lack contrary documentation, we have assumed the date of death and the final date of possession to be the same. We have tried to construct the provenance to reflect a continuous history of ownership; instances where that has not been possible will be clear by gaps in the dates of possession.

The number following the abbreviation FAMSF at the end of this section is the Museums' accession number, which can be parsed to reveal the year of acquisition, the order of the donor's transaction with the museum in that year, and the number of the particular object within that transaction. For example, 1979.7.31, John Singleton Copley's *Mary Turner Sargent*, entered the museum in 1979. It came as one of 109 works given by Mr. and Mrs. Rockefeller, which was, as a lot, the seventh acquisition of the year. *Mary Turner Sargent* was the thirty-first object catalogued in that gift (general order of cataloguing was alphabetically by the last name of the artist).

EXHIBITION HISTORY

The basic format of this section is city, organizing institution, *title of exhibition*, the year the exhibition was organized, and the object's number in the exhibition. If the exhibition record includes an alternate title, a lender whose name is otherwise subsumed within the "descended in family" section of the provenance, a price, or a prize award, we include it at the end of the citation within parentheses. We have not here recorded details concerning additional venues and specific dates for exhibitions, trusting that such material is generally available in the publication accompanying the exhibition. In instances where no exhibition numbers were assigned to objects, or where we have been unable to locate records of a publication, or where the object was in the exhibition but not included in any published record, we have used the abbreviations, respectively: no exh. no.; no publ.; not in publ.

Two abbreviations are widely used in this section:

San Francisco 1976
San Francisco, The Fine Arts Museums of San Francisco, *American Art: Selections from the Collection of Mr. and Mrs. John D. Rockefeller 3rd*, 1976

Tokyo 1982
Tokyo, The National Museum of Western Art, *American Painting 1730–1960: A Selection from the Collection of Mr. and Mrs. John D. Rockefeller 3rd*, 1982

SELECTED REFERENCES

This section is an exceedingly limited list of the publications in which the work appears. The list does not, for the most part, include exhibition catalogues, which will be cited in the *Exhibition History*, nor does it generally repeat sources that are among the text extracts.

The one short reference frequently used in this section is:

The American Canvas
Marc Simpson, Sally Mills, and Jennifer Saville, *The American Canvas: Paintings from the Collection of The Fine Arts Museums of San Francisco* (New York: Hudson Hills Press, in association with The Fine Arts Museums of San Francisco, 1989)

RELATED WORKS

Unless otherwise noted, works listed in this section are by the artist of the FAMSF object. They include preparatory or closely related works; portraits of family members; and selected later copies by other hands. The list is not complete.

ABBREVIATIONS USED THROUGHOUT THE CATALOGUE

AAA
Archives of American Art, Smithsonian Institution

FAMSF
The Fine Arts Museums of San Francisco

Oil on canvas, 39 x 42½ in.
Dated and inscribed: *Anno Dom 1670* (to right of David's head); *8* (to left of David's head); *6* (to left of Joanna's head); *4* (to left of Abigail's head)

**ATTRIBUTED TO
THE FREAKE-GIBBS
PAINTER**

Active Boston, Mass. ca. 1670

This group of portraits [depicting the Freake, Gibbs, and Mason families], the most intriguing and most frequently represented in histories of early American painting, is also the most problematical in terms of attribution to artist. Each painting in this group reflects a high degree of professional training in a late Elizabethan or Tudor tradition, which may be identified with a fashionable trend toward neomedievalism. There is nothing uncertain about the manner in which these paintings were made. A fundamental error is to interpret them as examples of outmoded art, cut off from the mainstream of European or English culture. The painter (or school of painters) who made these works was not a self-taught itinerant craftsman but a professional oil painter practicing an art still current in certain parts of England during the 1670s.

> Jonathan L. Fairbanks, "Portrait Painting in Seventeenth-Century Boston: Its History, Methods, and Materials," in *New England Begins: The Seventeenth Century*, exh. cat. (Boston: Museum of Fine Arts, 1982), p. 418

The Mason Children, depicting three full-length figures, is the only painting from seventeenth-century New England to include more than two subjects in a single composition. . . .

Portrayed here are three of Arthur and Joanna (Parker) Mason's five children. Their eldest son David (1661–1724), a figure of abnormally tall proportions for an eight-year-old, is depicted with gloves in his right hand and a silver-headed walking stick in his left. The cane symbolizes his status as male heir. Joanna (b. 1664) stands in the middle of the family group, holding a yellow fan and red and yellow ribbons, props that suggest her position as the daughter of wealthy parents. Four-year-old Abigail (baptized in 1666) bears a rose, the symbol of innocence associated with childhood.

> Joy Cattanach, *"The Mason Children,"* in *New England Begins: The Seventeenth Century*, exh. cat. (Boston: Museum of Fine Arts, 1982), pp. 462–463

[The children's father, whose profession is most often listed in contemporary records as "biscake baker," was later described as]: an officer [constable] of spirit and firmness, whose name was Arthur Mason. . . .

. . . "Mr. Mason, a blunt, honest Christian; will speak his mind, take it how you please."

> Samuel G. Drake, *The History and Antiquities of Boston* (Boston: Luther Stevens, 1856), pp. 374, 464

Vpon a veiw of the Ovens in Arther Masons bake-house neere Mr. Nortons wee finde them to be very insuffitient & hassardous to the welfare of the towne, therefore order and require that noe fire be kindled in the said ovens, after this day, vpon the penaltie of 20s. p. day, vntil they are secured & the causes of the danger be remoued.

> 21 July 1670, *A Report of the Record Commissioners of the City of Boston* (Boston: Rockwell and Churchill, 1881), pp. 55–56

Provenance

Arthur Mason (ca. 1630–1708) and Joanna Parker Mason (1635–1708), Boston, 1670–1708

Descended in family to Nathaniel Hamlen (1905–1967) and Evelyn L. Hollingsworth Hamlen, Boston, by 1947–1973

[Vose Galleries, Boston, 1973–1974]

John D. Rockefeller 3rd and Blanchette Hooker Rockefeller, New York, 1974–1979

FAMSF, 1979.7.3

Exhibition History

Boston, The Copley Society (Boston Art Club), *Loan Exhibition of Portraits by American Painters before the Revolution*, 1922, exh. no. 61

Worcester Art Museum, in collaboration with the American Antiquarian Society, *Seventeenth-Century Painting in New England*, 1934, no exh. no.

San Francisco 1976, exh. no. 1

Boston, Museum of Fine Arts, *New England Begins: The Seventeenth Century*, 1982, exh. no. 438

Selected References

Alan Burroughs, *Limners and Likenesses: Three Centuries of American Painting* (Cambridge, Mass.: Harvard University Press, 1936), pp. 9–10

James Thomas Flexner, *American Painting: First Flowers of Our Wilderness* (Boston: Houghton Mifflin Co., 1947), p. 9

Wayne Craven, *Colonial American Portraiture* (Cambridge: Cambridge University Press, 1986), pp. 55, 61–63

The American Canvas, pp. 20–21, 232

Related Works

Other portraits of Mason family members, sisters of David, Joanna, and Abigail, apparently by the same artist:

Mary Mason, 1668
Oil on canvas, 27 x 36 in.
Adams National Historic Site, Quincy, Mass.

Alice Mason, 1670
Oil on canvas, 33¼ x 24⅞ in.
Adams National Historic Site, Quincy, Mass.

2 MARIA MAYTILDA WINKLER, CA. 1730
(LATER, MRS. NICHOLAS GOUVERNEUR)

Oil on canvas, 30 x 25 in.

THE DE PEYSTER PAINTER

Active New York ca. 1730

Painters working in the Hudson River Valley in the early eighteenth century produced a sizable and impressive body of work that includes portraits of wealthy Dutch patroon families and occasional religious pictures. Nearly all of these paintings are unsigned, and few documents remain from the period to suggest the identities of the artists. . . .

Although the artist has yet to be conclusively identified, the De Peyster style is evident in the portrait of Maria Maytilda Winkler (later Mrs. Nicholas Gouverneur), especially in her delicate features, fine curling locks of hair, and the simplified lines and vivid red and blue of her costume. Although Maria was of Dutch origin—daughter of a merchant who settled in New Amsterdam after dealing in Sumatra, Indonesia—the model for her posture and attributes was English—specifically, the figure of Lady Mary Villiers in Sir Godfrey Kneller's . . . portrait of Lord William and Lady Mary Villiers, which was engraved in mezzotint by John Smith . . . around 1715. The artist uses some invention in the turn of Maria's head and the appearance of the parklike background, but the remainder of the composition—the garland she holds and the lamb that nuzzles against her—are copied from the engraving. Such visual quotations were common practice among artists in the New World.

Sally Mills, in *The American Canvas: Paintings from the Collection of The Fine Arts Museums of San Francisco* (New York: Hudson Hills Press, in association with The Fine Arts Museums of San Francisco, 1989), p. 22

Provenance

Herman Winkler [father of the sitter], New York, ca. 1730

Descended in family to Ella Therese Plate (Mrs. Fritz) Barkan (1887–1982), Palo Alto, Calif., to 1969

[M. Knoedler & Co., New York, 1969]

John D. Rockefeller 3rd and Blanchette Hooker Rockefeller, New York, 1969–1979

FAMSF, 1979.7.34

Exhibition History

New York, M. Knoedler & Co., *American Portraits, 1750–1950*, 1969, exh. no. 2

San Francisco 1976, exh. no. 4

Tokyo 1982, exh. no. 1

Selected Reference

The American Canvas, pp. 22–23, 232

Related Work

Jacomina Winkler [Maria Maytilda's sister], ca. 1730 Oil on canvas, 30 x 25 in. Private collection, St. Louis, as of 1993

3 JOHN NELSON, 1732

Oil on canvas, 44⅜ x 36 in.
Inscribed lower left: *Aet. 78:1732*; Nelson arms surmounted by helmet and crest at upper left

JOHN SMIBERT

b. Edinburgh, Scotland 1688
d. Boston, Mass. 1751

On January 23, 1729, arrived at Newport, R.I., John Smibert, able and conscientious Scottish artist, in the company of George Berkeley, then dean of Derry and later Bishop of Cloyne. The two men had met in Italy and discovered similarity of tastes. Berkeley's brief stay in Rhode Island was destined considerably to influence American colonial metaphysics and theological speculation; Smibert's longer American residence, to aid greatly in establishment of the arts of design in North America. . . .

. . . There were limners in New England, of course, before the Berkeley expedition reached Rhode Island. . . . It is hardly too much to say, however, that the practice of painting as a profession in British North America began with John Smibert's arrival in 1729.

Frederick W. Coburn, "John Smibert," *Art in America* 17, no. 4 (June 1929): 175–176

John Nelson, of Boston, was born in or near London in 1654. . . .

Nelson came to Boston in 1680, and when about thirty-two, married Elizabeth Tailer, a girl of nineteen or twenty. . . . His familiar letters show strong domestic affection and concern for the welfare of his growing family. . . .

John Nelson managed to pack into a merchant's life much of adventure. In 1689 he took part in an uprising against the unpopular royal governor, Sir Edmund Andros. . . . Soon after this event he was in Nova Scotia on business and was captured by French and Indians, led by Villebon, and was well treated as a prisoner by Frontenac. Understanding both French and Indian, he contrived to gather the outlines of a plan to attack Maine and New Hampshire. He bribed two French soldiers, Vignon and Albert, to carry a letter from him to the authorities at Boston. The letters were delivered, but the messengers were eventually caught, were brought back to Canada, where they confessed and, together with Mr. Nelson, were taken out to be shot. Nelson alone was reprieved, and was sent to the castle of Angoulême, in France, where he lived in a hole for two years, being fed through a grating. When England demanded his release, he was transferred to the Bastille as a prisoner of consequence. He was allowed, in 1694, to visit London on parole, a French gentleman going on his bond. King William, who heard his story, forbade him to return to France.

"Will your Majesty, then, pay my bonds?" he asked.

"No," said the King.

"Please God I live, I'll go," Nelson exclaimed.

He went back to France in January, 1698, but was soon permitted to return to his home in Boston.

Charles Knowles Bolton, *The Founders: Portraits of Persons Born Abroad Who Came to the Colonies in North America before the Year 1701*, 3 vols. (Boston: The Boston Athenaeum, 1919), 3:797–798

With a very good understanding, improved by Education and Travel, the Spirit and Temper of an ancient and worthy Family appeared in him; Genteel, Enlarged, Liberal, contemning

mean and sordid Actions. He passed through many Changes and Events of Life, remarkable in their own nature, and though troublesome and dangerous in *Themselves*, and detrimental to his *Family*, yet neither dishonourable in the *Occasion* or the *Improvement* of them. He was unmoveably attach'd to what he tho't just and right, couragious in bearing Witness against and reproving Vice, a Despised of this World, a Lover of his Country, acceptable to his Family, . . . universally affable, courteous, and hospitable. . . . and with this Temper he closed a Life of fourscore and one Years, fearing God, and calmly and quietly trusting in his Mercy.

> Dr. Timothy Cutler, "The Final Peace, Security, and Happiness of the Upright" [sermon on the death of John Nelson], reprinted in Henry Wilder Foote, *Annals of King's Chapel from the Puritan Age of New England to the Present Day*, 3 vols. (Boston: Little, Brown, and Co., 1882–1940), 1:181

Provenance
Captain John Nelson (ca. 1654–1734) and Elizabeth Tailer Nelson (1667–1734), Boston, 1732–1734

Descended in family to Roger Alden Derby, Jr., Cambridge, Mass., and New York, by 1969

[Kennedy Galleries, New York, 1969]

John D. Rockefeller 3rd and Blanchette Hooker Rockefeller, New York, 1969–1979

FAMSF, 1979.7.93

Exhibition History
San Francisco 1976, exh. no. 2

Tokyo 1982, exh. no. 2

Selected References
Henry Wilder Foote, *John Smibert, Painter* (Cambridge, Mass.: Harvard University Press, 1950), p. 172

John Smibert, *The Notebook of John Smibert*, ed. Sir David

Evans, John Kerslake, and Andrew Oliver (Boston: Massachusetts Historical Society, 1969), pp. 22, 90, 109

Richard L. Saunders III, *John Smibert: Anglo-American Portrait Painter*, 2 vols. (Ann Arbor, Mich.: University Microfilms International, 1979), 1:152–153; 2:106

The American Canvas, pp. 24–25, 232

Related Works
James Frothingham (American, 1786–1864)
After *John Nelson*, before 1824
Oil on canvas, 32 x 26½ in.
Alice Borland (Mrs. Orne)
Wilson, Washington, D.C., as of 1959

O. J. Lay (American)
After *John Nelson*, 1879

Temple Prime, Huntington, N.Y., as of 1886

4 GRIZZELL EASTWICK APTHORP, 1748
(MRS. CHARLES APTHORP)

Oil on canvas, 49⅝ x 39¾ in.
Signed and dated lower left: *RF Pinx/1748*

ROBERT FEKE

b. Oyster Bay, N.Y. ca. 1707
d. Barbados (?) ca. 1752

Of native-born American painters before Copley, Robert Feke was the most accomplished. But less is known about him than any eighteenth-century artist of like importance. Surviving portraits that can be definitely attributed to him number only about sixty. Of these only twelve are signed or dated. The dates of his birth and death are unknown, not a letter or a piece of his handwriting has been preserved, no will by him has been found. Contemporary records of him consist only of a land survey, two references in diaries, and his marriage record and those of his two daughters after his death. William Dunlap, the Vasari of early American artists, knew nothing about him.

Lloyd Goodrich, *Robert Feke*, exh. cat. (New York: Whitney Museum of American Art, 1946), n.p.

Grizzell Eastwick was born in Jamaica on 16 August 1709. She went to Boston in 1716 and in 1726 married Charles Apthorp (1698–1758), an English-born merchant who was . . . "the greatest and most noted Merchant on this Continent," according to the obituary published in the *Newsletter* of King's Chapel, Boston, on 16 November 1758. The couple had eighteen children, fifteen of whom survived their father. . . .

In this portrait, Feke has Mrs. Apthorp look up from John Milton's *Paradise Lost*. The page is open to the lines in book 9 where Eve has just told Adam that she has tasted the fruit of the tree of knowledge and has asked that he too eat of it. Speechless and pale, Adam thinks to himself:

> O fairest of Creation, last and best
> Of all God's Works, Creature in whom excell'd
> Whatever can to sight or thought be form'd,
> Holy, divine, good, amiable, or sweet!
>   . . . with thee
> Certain my resolution is to Die;
> How can I live without thee, how forgo
> Thy sweet converse and Love so dearly join'd,
> To live again in these wild Woods forlorn?
>   . . . no no, I feel
> The Link of Nature draw me: Flesh of Flesh,
> Bone of my Bone thou art, and from thy State
> Mine shall never be parted, bliss or woe.

This apostrophe of woman is the human climax of Milton's epic—Adam will shortly follow Eve, eat of the forbidden fruit, and lose Eden for all humankind. But by citing this bold glorification of woman, Feke clearly means to associate Mrs. Apthorp with the qualities in Eve that Adam found so compelling.

Marc Simpson, in *The American Canvas: Paintings from the Collection of The Fine Arts Museums of San Francisco* (New York: Hudson Hills Press, in association with The Fine Arts Museums of San Francisco, 1989), p. 26

Provenance
Charles Apthorp (1698–1758) and Grizzell Eastwick Apthorp (1709–1796), Boston, from 1748–1796

Descended in family to Sargent Bradlee (1898–1987), Beverly Farms, Mass., 1967

[Hirschl & Adler Galleries, New York, 1967]

John D. Rockefeller 3rd and Blanchette Hooker Rockefeller, New York, 1967–1979

FAMSF, 1979.7.42

Exhibition History
Boston, Museum of Fine Arts, extended loan, 1909–1914 (lent by Sarah Apthorp Cunningham Clinch Bond)

Boston, Copley Society, at the Boston Art Club, *Loan Exhibition of Portraits by American Painters before the Revolution*, 1922, exh. no. 22 (lent by Isaac R. Thomas, Esq.)

Boston, Museum of Fine Arts, *Loan Exhibition of One Hundred Colonial Portraits: Exhibition in Honor of the Massachusetts Bay Colony Tercentenary*, 1930, no exh. no. (lent by Mrs. Ben P. P. Moseley)

New York, Whitney Museum of American Art, *Robert Feke*, 1946, exh. no. 3 (lent by Mr. and Mrs. B. P. P. Moseley)

Cambridge, Mass., Fogg Art Museum, *Apthorp House: 1760–1960*, 1960, no publ.

New York, Hirschl & Adler Galleries, *American Paintings for Public and Private Collections*, 1967, exh. no. 3

New York, Hirschl & Adler Galleries, *Retrospective of a Gallery: Twenty Years*, 1973, no exh. no.

Boston, Museum of Fine Arts, *Paul Revere's Boston, 1735–1818*, 1975, exh. no. 45

San Francisco 1976, exh. no. 5

Tokyo 1982, exh. no. 4

Selected References
Frank W. Bayley, *Five Colonial Artists of New England* (Boston: privately printed, 1929), p. 305

Henry Wilder Foote, *Robert Feke: Colonial Portrait Painter* (Cambridge, Mass.: Harvard University Press, 1930), pp. 45, 72, 74, 102 n. 1, 123–124

Ralph Peter Mooz, *The Art of Robert Feke* (Ann Arbor, Mich.: University Microfilms, 1970), pp. 108, 141–142, 218

The American Canvas, pp. 26–27, 232

Related Works
Charles Apthorp, ca. 1748
Oil on canvas, 50 x 40 in.
The Cleveland Museum of Art

Mrs. Barlow Trecothick (Grizzell Apthorp Trecothick), ca. 1748
Oil on canvas, 40⅞ x 40¼ in.
Wichita Art Museum, Wichita, Kans.

5 ANNA PORTER BROWN, CA. 1750 (MRS. NATHANIEL BROWN)

Oil on canvas, 47¾ x 36⅞ in.

JOSEPH BADGER

b. Charlestown, Mass. 1708
d. Boston, Mass. (?) 1765

In the vacuum created by the deaths of John Smibert and Robert Feke, the painter Joseph Badger became the leading portraitist of mid-eighteenth-century Boston. As was true for many other self-taught artisans of the period, Badger began his career in trade as a glazier and painter of houses. Only as he reached his thirties did Badger add portraiture to his professional accomplishments. For some ten years during the 1740s and 1750s, when Boston did not have a major European talent, prosperous families relied on Badger to paint their portraits. . . .

Anna Porter Brown (1718–1781), great-great-granddaughter of the colonial Massachusetts governor Simon Bradstreet, appears in three-quarter length in a landscape setting. Her appearance depends heavily on pictorial conventions that Badger adapted and repeated throughout his career. Placement of the figure high on the canvas, the single tree, and the open book with gilt-leather binding are features that Badger repeated with little variation in several of his portraits.

Jennifer Saville, in *The American Canvas: Paintings from the Collection of The Fine Arts Museums of San Francisco* (New York: Hudson Hills Press, in association with The Fine Arts Museums of San Francisco, 1989), p. 28

Provenance
Nathaniel Brown and Anna Porter Brown (1718–1781), Wenham, Mass., ca. 1750–ca. 1781

Presumably descended in family

[Kennedy Galleries, New York, 1967–1968]

John D. Rockefeller 3rd and Blanchette Hooker Rockefeller, New York, 1968–1979

FAMSF, 1979.7.6

Exhibition History
San Francisco 1976, exh. no. 3

Tokyo 1982, exh. no. 3

Selected Reference
The American Canvas, pp. 28–29, 232

6 KATHERINE STANBRIDGE GREENE, CA. 1760 (MRS. RUFUS GREENE)

Oil on canvas, 24 x 20⅜ in.
Inscribed on reverse of canvas (visible before lining): *This picture of Mrs. Rufus Greene was painted by Mr. John Copley in Boston in the year 1760*

JOHN SINGLETON COPLEY

b. Boston, Mass. 1738
d. London, England 1815

Copley, another American, after enjoying greater advantages for the study of his art, than had been afforded to his countryman West, and after painting better pictures, in the new world, than the Pennsylvanian, followed him to Europe; and with admirable industry and perseverance raised himself nearly to a level with the best portrait painters of England, where portrait painting was at the period of his making that country his permanent place of residence, taking that stand which has rendered England the school for all artists, who desire to excel in a branch of the fine arts, more lucrative (though not so honorable) than history painting. West, as we have seen, chose the more difficult, complicated, and brilliant department, and was acknowledged as its head. Copley only took up the historic pencil at intervals, and was even when so employed, still a portrait painter.

William Dunlap, *A History of the Rise and Progress of the Arts of Design in the United States*, 3 vols. (1834; Boston: C. E. Goodspeed & Co., 1918), 1:116

Katherine Stanbridge married Rufus Greene in 1728 in King's Chapel, that stronghold of the Church of England in Congregationalist Boston. She and her husband and children belonged to the Anglican minority, from which, in the troubled years ahead, came many of the New England Loyalists. One of her daughters, Mrs. John Amory (whose portrait by Copley is in the Museum of Fine Arts, Boston) went into exile when the Revolution came, sailing to join her husband in London on the same ship that took Mrs. Copley and her three children to England. In Mrs. Amory's diary in exile she spoke affectionately of her mother, whose sweet, pious, courageous character Copley painted with great understanding.

The portrait has been cut down [at the sides and bottom] from a larger size because of damage by fire at some point in the past [before 1873].

E. P. Richardson, *American Art: An Exhibition from the Collection of Mr. and Mrs. John D. Rockefeller 3rd*, exh. cat. (San Francisco: The Fine Arts Museums of San Francisco, 1976), p. 36

Provenance
Rufus Greene (1707–1777) and Katherine Stanbridge Greene (1709–1768), Boston, ca. 1760–1777

Descended in family to William Gardiner Prescott, Sudbury, Mass., by 1873–at least 1938

Senator Theodore Francis Green (1867–1966), Providence, R.I., ca. 1938–1966

[Kennedy Galleries, New York, 1967]

John D. Rockefeller 3rd and Blanchette Hooker Rockefeller, New York, 1967–1979

FAMSF, 1979.7.32

Exhibition History
Boston, Copley Hall, *Loan Collection of Portraits of Women, for the Benefit of the Boston Children's*

Aid Society, and the Sunnyside Day Nursery, 1895, no exh. no.

Boston, Museum of Fine Arts, extended loan, 1919–1924

San Francisco 1976, exh. no. 9

Fresno, Calif., Fresno Metropolitan Museum of Art, History and Science, *Visages: Persistence in Portraiture*, 1984, exh. no. 23

Selected Reference
Jules David Prown, *John Singleton Copley*, 2 vols. (Cambridge, Mass.: Harvard University Press, 1966), 1:29, 107, 118, 124, 148–149, 164–165, 217

Related Work
Rufus Greene ca. 1760
Oil on canvas, 24 x 20¾ in.
Kennedy Galleries, New York, as of 1989

---

7 MARY TURNER SARGENT, 1763 (MRS. DANIEL SARGENT)

Oil on canvas, 49½ x 39¼ in.
Signed and dated lower left: *John Singleton Copley/Pinx. 1763.*

JOHN SINGLETON COPLEY

b. Boston, Mass. 1738
d. London, England 1815

Mrs. Daniel Sargent (Mary Turner): 1743–1818. The daughter of John Turner and Mary Osborne, she was born in Salem and was married there in 1763 to her cousin Daniel Sargent, son of Epes Sargent, Jr. She and her husband moved to Boston in 1778 and by 1797 were living in the Bradlee House at the corner of Lincoln and Essex Streets. Her son, Lucius Manlius Sargent, writes of it: "It was accounted a palace; and my father, . . . hired it to gratify my dear mother who was rather more fond of elegant apartments and showy furniture than he."

Barbara Neville Parker and Anne Bolling Wheeler, *John Singleton Copley: American Portraits in Oil, Pastel, and Miniature, with Biographical Sketches* (Boston: Museum of Fine Arts, 1938), pp. 170–171

We will give some anecdotes elucidating Copley's elaborate mode of working: and first, from Mr. [Henry] Sargent [son of the sitter]:

"[Gilbert] Stuart used to tell me, that no man ever knew how to *manage paint* better than Copley. I suppose he meant that *firm*, artist-like manner in which it was applied to the canvas; but he said he was very tedious in his practice. . . .

"Copley's manner," continues Mr. Sargent, "though his pictures have great merit, was very mechanical. He painted a very beautiful head of my mother, who told me that she sat to him fifteen or sixteen times! Six hours at a time!! And that once she had been sitting to him for many hours, when he left the room for a few minutes, but requested that she would not

move from her seat during his absence. She had the curiosity, however, to peep at the picture, and, to her astonishment, she found it all rubbed out."

William Dunlap, *A History of the Rise and Progress of the Arts of Design in the United States*, 3 vols. (1834; Boston: C. E. Goodspeed & Co., 1918), 1:143–144

Provenance
Daniel Sargent (1731–1806) and Mary Turner Sargent (1743–1818 [1813 in some sources]), Gloucester, Mass., and Boston, 1763–1813 or 1818

Descended in family to Mary Elizabeth Sargent MacArthur (Mrs. Thomas R.) Symington (b. 1913), Washington, D.C., and New York, 1959–1973 (although listed in some sources as her property as early as 1923)

[Hirschl & Adler Galleries, New York, 1973]

John D. Rockefeller 3rd and Blanchette Hooker Rockefeller, New York, 1973–1979

FAMSF, 1979.7.31

Exhibition History
Boston, Copley Hall, *Loan Collection of Portraits of Women, for the Benefit of the Boston Children's Aid Society, and the Sunnyside Day Nursery*, 1895, no exh. no.

Boston, Museum of Fine Arts, extended loan, 1897–1906 (lent by Mrs. B. H. McCalla)

Boston, Museum of Fine Arts, extended loan, 1911–1912 (lent by Mrs. B. H. McCalla)

Washington, D.C., The Corcoran Gallery of Art, extended loan,

1935–1972 (lent by Mrs. Arthur MacArthur and Mrs. T. R. Symington)

Washington, D.C., National Gallery of Art, *John Singleton Copley, 1738–1815*, 1965, exh. no. 17

New York, Hirschl & Adler Galleries, *Retrospective of a Gallery: Twenty Years*, 1973, exh. no. 24

San Francisco 1976, exh. no. 10

Los Angeles County Museum of Art, *American Portraiture in the Grand Manner, 1720–1920*, 1981, exh. no. 12

Tokyo 1982, exh. no. 5

Selected References
Jules David Prown, *John Singleton Copley*, 2 vols. (Cambridge, Mass.: Harvard University Press, 1966), 1:38, 113, 116, 119, 124, 132, 140, 190–191, 227

The American Canvas, pp. 30–31, 232

Related Work
Harry Sutton (American) After *Mrs. Daniel Sargent*, (unknown date) Oil on canvas, ca. 50 x 40 in. The House of Seven Gables, Salem, Mass.

Oil on canvas, 80¾ x 57¼ in.

HENRY BENBRIDGE

b. Philadelphia, Pa. 1743
buried Philadelphia, Pa. 1812

Mr. Benbridge was born in Philadelphia about the year 1750. Being left at liberty to pursue the bent of his inclination by the death of [his] parents, he devoted his patrimony in aid of his desire to become a painter, no doubt stimulated by the success of [Benjamin] West; and he was the second American who studied the fine arts at Rome. Mr. Benbridge was a gentleman by birth, and had received a liberal education; . . . and before he left Philadelphia he had shown his love of the arts by painting the panels of a room in his paternal dwelling with designs from history. In Rome he became the pupil of Pompeio Battoni, and received instruction from [Raphael] Mengs.

William Dunlap, *A History of the Rise and Progress of the Arts of Design in the United States*, 3 vols. (1834; Boston: C. E. Goodspeed & Co., 1918), 1:165

Paoli [1725–1807] had become the darling of the Enlightenment and from one end of Europe to the other his name resounded as the Enlightened trumpeted forth their praise: he had brought to a proud, simple and courageous people the reality of a law freed from sectional interest and pettifogging precedent; his faith, deep and unshakable, went hand in hand with his desire for an Erastian Church staffed by an educated priesthood; his love for, and pride in, his country was tempered by an all-embracing tolerance to other creeds and nationalities; he was the founder of cities and begetter of trade; to crown all, he did this consciously and deliberately in accordance with principles that all rational men accepted and in a language which all rational men understood. He had, indeed, made Corsica the cynosure of European eyes.

Peter Adam Thrasher, *Pasquale Paoli: An Enlightened Hero, 1725–1807* (London: Constable & Co., 1970), p. 98

———————

There is just arrived in London a portrait of the illustrious Chief Paoli, painted for Mr. Boswell of Auchinleck. Mr. Boswell sent for this purpose to Corsica last Summer Mr. Bambridge, a young American Artist, who had finished his studies in Italy, and, amidst all the fatigues and dangers of war, his Excellency was pleased to sit, to indulge the earnest desire of his ever zealous friend. When the picture was brought to Leghorn, all who had seen the General, thought it a striking Likeness. The Grand Duke of Tuscany expressed a desire to see it, upon which it was sent to Florence, where it was much admired by the Grand Duke, Duchess, and all the Court. It is a whole length as large as life; the canvass about 7 feet by 5. The Painter has taken great pains, and has finished the face in a very masterly manner.

The London Chronicle 25, no. 1934 (6–9 May 1769): 438

Provenance
Commissioned in 1767 by James Boswell (1740–1795), London and Auchinleck, Ayrshire, Scotland

Descended in family to Mr. and Mrs. John P. D. Boswell, Auchinleck, by 1957–1974

[Thomas Agnew & Sons, London, 1974]

John D. Rockefeller 3rd and Blanchette Hooker Rockefeller, New York, 1974–1979

FAMSF, 1979.7.8

Exhibition History
Exhibited in Florence, Italy, while Benbridge en route from Corsica to London, at the request of the grand duke of Tuscany, 1769

Exhibited in Leghorn, Italy, en route to London, 1769

London, Christie's Great Room, *Exhibition of the Free Society of Artists*, 1769, exh. no. 258

London, National Portrait Gallery, *Mr. Boswell*, 1967, exh. no. 24

Washington, D.C., National Portrait Gallery, *Henry Benbridge, 1743–1812: American Portrait Painter*, 1971, exh. no. 40

San Francisco 1976, exh. no. 6

FAMSF, *A Gentleman's Finery*, 1983, no publ.

Selected References
Anna Wells Rutledge, "Henry Benbridge (1743–1812?): American Portrait Painter," *The American Collector* 17, no. 9 (October 1948): 8–9; no. 10 (November 1948): 11

Frederick A. Pottle, *James Boswell: The Earlier Years, 1740–1769* (New York: McGraw-Hill Book Co., 1966), pp. 306, 397, 534n, 553–554n

The American Canvas, pp. 40–41, 233

Related Work
John Raphael Smith (British, 1752–1812)
After *Pascal Paoli*, 1769
Mezzotint engraving, 20 x 14 in.

———————

9 **WILLIAM VASSALL AND HIS SON LEONARD**, CA. 1771

Oil on canvas, 49¾ x 40⅜ in.

JOHN SINGLETON COPLEY

b. Boston, Mass. 1738
d. London, England 1815

As we have every April an Exhibition where our works is exhibited to the Publick, I advise you to Paint a Picture of a half figure or two in one Piec. . . . And be shure take your Subjects from Nature as you did in your last Piec, and dont trust any resemblanc of any thing to fancey, except the dispositions of they figures and they ajustments of Draperies, So as to make an agreable whole. . . .

. . . As I am from America, and know the little Opertunities is to be had their in they way of Painting, made the inducement the more in writeing to you in this manner, and as

you have got to that lenght in the art that nothing is wanting to Perfect you now but a Sight of what has been done by the great Masters, and if you Could make a viset to Europe for this Porpase for three or four years, you would find yourself then in Possession of what will be highly valuable.

> Benjamin West to Copley, London, 4 August 1766, quoted in Charles Francis Adams, Guernsey Jones, and Worthington Chauncey Ford, eds., *Letters and Papers of John Singleton Copley and Henry Pelham, 1739–1776* (1914; New York: Da Capo Press, for Kennedy Graphics, 1970), pp. 44–45

Your kind favour of Augst. 4, 1766, came to hand. . . . In my last I promis'd to send another peace. the subject You have sence pointed out, but I fear it will not be in my power to comply with Your design. . . . but I shall do somthing near what you propose. . . .

It would give me inexpressable pleasure to make a trip to Europe. . . . the Paintings, Sculptors and Basso Releivos that adourn Italy, and which You have had the pleasure of making Your Studies from would, I am sure, annimate my pencil, and inable me to acquire that bold free and gracefull stile of Painting that will, if ever, come much slower from the mere dictates of Nature, which has hither too been my only instructor. . . . I think myself peculiarly unlucky in Liveing in a place into which there has not been one portrait brought that is worthy to be call'd a Picture within my memory, which leaves me at a great loss to gess the stile that You, Mr. Renolds, and the other Artists pracktice.

Copley to Benjamin West, 12 November 1766, quoted in Charles Francis Adams, Guernsey Jones, and Worthington Chauncey Ford, eds., *Letters and Papers of John Singleton Copley and Henry Pelham, 1739–1776* (1914; New York: Da Capo Press, for Kennedy Graphics, 1970), pp. 50–51

One of my old friends and clients, a mandamus counsellor against his will, a man of letters and virtues, without one vice that I ever knew or suspected, except garrulity, William Vassal, asserted to me, and strenuously maintained, that pleasure is no compensation for pain. A hundred years of the keenest delights of human life, could not atone for one hour of bilious colic that he had felt. The sublimity of this philosophy my dull genius could not reach.

John Adams, quoted in Clifford K. Shipton, *Biographical Sketches of Those Who Attended Harvard College in the Classes 1731–1735* (Boston: Massachusetts Historical Society, 1956), p. 356

I would ask every considerate impartial person, What I, an infirm man upwards of 60 years of age with a large family, could do? I owed natural Allegiance to the King of Great Britain, my liege Lord, and the greatest part of my property lay in Jamaica . . . subject to his Authority, and I had a considerable property in Massachusetts and Rhode Island. . . . Under these Circumstances, I greatly lamented the unhappy disastrous War between two powers, to which I bore the greatest good will, and for which I had the highest regard; and prudence, common Sense, Principle and Affection dictated to me, that the only rational and moral part I could act, was to remain Neuter, and to do nothing inimical or unfriendly to either power.

William Vassall to Simeon Potter, 10 April 1784, quoted in Clifford K. Shipton, *Biographical Sketches of Those Who Attended Harvard College in the Classes 1731–1735* (Boston: Massachusetts Historical Society, 1956), p. 356

This representative [William Vassall] of a conspicuous family in Massachusetts and in Jamaica was born in this West India Island in 1715 and graduated at Harvard College in 1733. He fled to England at the Revolution and died at Battersea in 1800. His will discloses the fact that he bequeathed portraits of himself and his first wife, Ann Davis, of his daughter, Sarah, of his deceased son, William, and of his eldest surviving son, William, all drawn by Smibert, to the latter son, William. All these portraits, with one of himself and his son, Leonard (by his second marriage to Margaret Hubbard), painted in one picture by Copley, had been left behind at Boston on his flight in 1776 in charge of Dr. James Lloyd. None of them can now be traced.

. . . Leonard Vassall, matriculated at Oriel College, Oxford, in 1782, and joined Lincoln's Inn in 1783 and was called to the English bar in 1793.

E. Alfred Jones, *The Loyalists of Massachusetts: Their Memorials, Petitions, and Claims* (London: The Saint Catherine Press, 1930), p. 285

John Singleton Copley's portrait of William Vassal [*sic*] and his son Leonard is one of four excellent Copleys among the Rockefellers' paintings. In the case of Copley, however, his sense of reality was tested by an acute awareness of vision. He saw with a greedy eye, noting each reflection and shadow, each wart and wrinkle, and even the dusting of powder on the older Vassal's shoulders. Since vision was dependent on light, he emphasized the flood of light across his figures, recording how differently it reflected from each individual part. Generalization came slowly to Copley: he believed in the unique instance.

When Rockefeller talks about this painting, he does not attempt to place it in Copley's early style or talk about its formal values. He talks at once about the expression of Vassal and the relationship to his son at his side. Copley would have been pleased. It is evident that, in his early years at least, Copley never separated character from form. That is, he had no preconceptions about what people should look like in order to make a good picture. So his pictorial pleasures had to be found in the actual features of his sitters. Think what it must have been to be a boy painted by Copley, seeing yourself in the sharp light of art, clearer in image than any mirror could reflect, granted a perpetuation not granted to others. The place of the artist was changing, however, and later portraitists were hardly content to leave their clients as they saw them.

Joshua Taylor, "A Personal and Distinctive Collection of American Art Makes Its Debut," *Smithsonian Magazine*, April 1976, pp. 42, 44

Provenance
William Vassall (1715–1800), Boston, ca. 1771–1800

Descended in family to Leonard Samuel Vassall (b. 1899), Cleeve Hall, Cleeve and Little Newlands,

Frenchay, England, before 1959–1972

[Auction sale, Christie, Manson & Woods, London, 23 June 1972, lot no. 95]

[Kennedy Galleries, New York, 1972]

John D. Rockefeller 3rd and Blanchette Hooker Rockefeller, New York, 1972–1979

FAMSF, 1979.7.30

Exhibition History
San Francisco 1976, exh. no. 11

Tokyo 1982, exh. no. 6

Selected Reference
The American Canvas, pp. 34–35, 232–233

---

10 MORDECAI GIST, CA. 1774

Oil on canvas, 29¾ x 24¾ in.

CHARLES WILLSON PEALE

b. Queen Anne's County, Md. 1741
d. Philadelphia, Pa. 1827

Mr. Peale, who seems to have wished to play every part in life's drama, not content with being a saddler, a coach maker, a clock and watchmaker, a silversmith, and a portrait painter, studied while in London modeling in wax, moulding and casting in plaster, painting in miniature, and engraving in mezzotinto. . . .

In the year 1776, Charles Willson Peale established himself in Philadelphia, and as a captain of volunteers, he joined Washington, and was present at the battles of Trenton and Germantown. . . .

From 1779 to 1785, Mr. Peale applied himself assiduously to painting; but about that time some bones of a mammoth having been brought to him, the idea of forming a museum, occurred to his active mind. . . .

Mr. Peale now became a lecturer on natural history . . . but finding that the loss of his front teeth interfered with his oratory, he became a dentist to supply the deficiency; first working in ivory, and then making porcelain teeth for himself and others.

In the year 1791 Mr. Peale attempted to form an association as an Academy of Fine Arts, in Philadelphia [which was finally successful in 1809]. . . .

Mr. Peale, among his many whims, had that of naming his numerous family after illustrious characters of bygone ages, particularly painters. A dangerous and sometimes ludicrous experiment. Raphael, Angelica Kauffman, Rembrandt, Rubens, and Titian, and many other great folks, were all his children.

We shall sum up the trades, employments, and professions of Mr. Peale, somewhat as his biographer . . . has done. He was a saddler; harnessmaker; clock and watchmaker; silversmith; painter in oil, crayons, and miniature; modeler in clay, wax, and plaster; he sawed his own ivory for his miniatures, moulded the glasses, and made the shagreen cases; he was a soldier; a legislator; a lecturer; a preserver of animals,—whose deficiencies he supplied by means of glass eyes and artificial limbs; he was a dentist—and he was, as his biographer truly says, "a mild, benevolent, and good man."

William Dunlap, *A History of the Rise and Progress of the Arts of Design in the United States*, 3 vols. (1834; Boston: C. E. Goodspeed & Co., 1918), 1:158–162

Gist, Mordecai. Soldier. 1742–1792.

Merchant-sea captain of an old Maryland family which had figured in the early border wars of the province, Mordecai Gist turned to soldiering at the first outbreak of the Revolution. With dash, courage and a fanatical devotion to the cause, he rose quickly to the rank of a general officer. He is best remembered perhaps for the pugnacity with which he held together a remnant of the shattered American battle line at Camden. A young Quaker girl has left us our most intimate glimpse of him, "He's very pretty; a charming person; his eyes are exceptional; and he so rolls them about that mine always fall under them."

Charles Coleman Sellers, *Portraits and Miniatures by Charles Willson Peale*, Transactions of the American Philosophical Society, vol. 42, pt. 1 (Philadelphia: American Philosophical Society, 1952), p. 87

———

It was certainly this type of American who won the Revolution. His mind was seemingly cast for this one end, and his whole life was conditioned by the times. . . . Superficially this attitude of mind may be observed in the naming of his sons. The first, called Independent [*sic*—Independence], was born Jan. 8, 1779. . . . His second son, States, was born in 1787.

C[urtis] W. G[arrison], "Mordecai Gist," *Dictionary of American Biography*, rev. ed., vol. 4, pt. 1, pp. 324–325

Provenance
Mordecai Gist (1742/43–1792), Baltimore, and Charleston, S.C., ca. 1774–1792

Descended in family to Mrs. F. LaMotte Smith, Westminster, Md., ca. 1937–1957

[M. Knoedler & Co. and Hirschl & Adler Galleries, New York, 1957–1959]

[Hirschl & Adler Galleries, New York, 1959]

Lawrence A. Fleischman (b. 1925) and Barbara Greenberg Fleischman (b. 1924), Detroit, 1959–1965

[Kennedy Galleries, New York, 1965–1966]

John D. Rockefeller 3rd and Blanchette Hooker Rockefeller, New York, 1966–1979

FAMSF, 1979.7.79

Exhibition History
The Baltimore Museum of Art, *Two Hundred and Fifty Years of Painting in Maryland*, 1945, exh. no. 25

New York, M. Knoedler & Co., *American Paintings of the Eighteenth and Early Nineteenth Century in Our Current Collection*, 1948, exh. no. 12

Columbus, Ohio, Columbus Gallery of Fine Arts, *Sir Joshua Reynolds and His American Contemporaries*, 1958, exh. no. 39

Milwaukee Art Center, *American Painting, 1760–1960: A Selection of 125 Paintings from the Collection of Mr. and Mrs. Lawrence A. Fleischman, Detroit*, 1960, no exh. no.

The Detroit Institute of Arts, *American Paintings and Drawings from Michigan Collections*, 1962, exh. no. 4

Tucson, University of Arizona Art Gallery, *American Painting, 1765–1963: Selections from the Lawrence A. and Barbara Fleischman Collection of American Art*, 1964, exh. no. 75

Washington, D.C., National Portrait Gallery, *A Nineteenth-Century Gallery of Distinguished Americans*, 1969, no exh. no.

San Francisco 1976, exh. no. 12

Tokyo 1982, exh. no. 9

Washington, D.C., National Portrait Gallery, *Charles Willson Peale and His World*, 1982, exh. no. 6

Selected References
Charles Coleman Sellers, *Portraits and Miniatures by Charles Willson Peale*, Transactions of the American Philosophical Society, vol. 42, pt. 1 (Philadelphia: American Philosophical Society, 1952), pp. 87–88, cat. no. 298

Lillian B. Miller, ed., *The Selected Papers of Charles Willson Peale and His Family*, 3 vols. (New Haven: Yale University Press, for the National Portrait Gallery, 1981), 1:529

The American Canvas, pp. 38–39, 233

Related Works
Mordecai Gist, ca. 1774
Oil on canvas, 30 x 25 in.
Maryland Historical Society, Baltimore

Mrs. Mordecai Gist (really *Elizabeth McClure?*), 1774–1775
Oil on canvas, 30 x 25 in.
Milwaukee Art Museum

Luther Terry (American, 1813–1869)
After *Mordecai Gist*, 1837
Oil on canvas, 30 x 25 in.
Maryland Historical Society, Baltimore

11–12 CALLED **ROBERT SHEWELL, JUNIOR** AND **SARAH BOYER SHEWELL**, CA. 1775 (MRS. ROBERT SHEWELL, JUNIOR)

Oil on canvas, diameter each 25⅞ in.

HENRY BENBRIDGE
b. Philadelphia, Pa. 1743
buried Philadelphia, Pa. 1812

After his return to America, Benbridge's style changed; his drawing grew crisper, his chiaroscuro more dramatic. The change is seen in the sharp definition of these two portraits which, looking out from their circular frames, seem almost startlingly real.

The subjects are a young Philadelphia shipmaster, Robert Shewell, junior, and his wife, Sarah Boyer. There was reason for the artist to do his best. Robert Shewell's sister, Elizabeth, was the wife of Benjamin West. Another sister, Mary Shewell, married one of Benbridge's cousins. The two artists considered themselves cousins, and Benbridge had lived as an intimate of the West household in London. These are family portraits, warmed by a sense of kinship and spurred by Benbridge's desire to show his family what he had learned in Europe. The costumes indicate that he painted them in the early 1770s immediately after his return from London.

The portraits descended in the family through five generations. In 1942 William Sawitzky, a pioneer student of eighteenth-century painting, published them as the work of Matthew Pratt. But in 1948 Anna Wells Rutledge put together the work of Benbridge in two articles that established his role in the middle colonies and the south. Mr. Rockefeller acquired these portraits in 1967 as characteristic works of Benbridge, and the exhibition of his work at the National Portrait Gallery in 1971 made it clear that they are among his finest works.

E. P. Richardson, *American Art: An Exhibition from the Collection of Mr. and Mrs. John D. Rockefeller 3rd*, exh. cat. (San Francisco: The Fine Arts Museums of San Francisco, 1976), p. 32

The freeing of Charleston from the British on 14 December 1782 occasioned the flight of British sympathizers as well as Loyalists. At the same time the former prisoners of the British commenced to return home. Some of the released prisoners went to Philadelphia, and

among these was Benbridge. . . . It is likely that the delightful companion conversation pieces of the Edwards Family and the John Saltar Family were executed at this time, as well as the portraits of Robert Shewell and his wife. . . .

[re: *Robert Shewell, Junior*] The picture with its companion is clearly Benbridge at his very finest. . . .

Robert Shewell, Junior, was a ship's captain. In fact, writing to Betsey Saltar on 28 April 1787, Henry Benbridge says:

> I take this opportunity by Captn Sewell, in preference to Captn Strong of sending you a box . . .
>
> Captain Sewell will inform you of many particulars if you ask him, he was up to see me once but he has been so busy that I could not have the pleasure of seeing him at my Lodging . . .

The picture depicts a man about forty-five years old. The portrait is very carefully done; the artist obviously knows his subject well and the portrait is one of his finest. . . . The pictures were painted some time in the late 1780s, perhaps during one of Captain Shewell's trips to Charleston when his wife may have accompanied him.

Robert G. Stewart, *Henry Benbridge, 1743–1812: American Portrait Painter*, exh. cat. (Washington, D.C.: National Portrait Gallery, 1971), pp. 20, 51

Provenance
Purportedly Robert Shewell (b. ca. 1743) and Sarah Boyer Shewell (b. ca. 1745), Philadelphia, ca. 1775

Descended in family to Bernard Hepburn Benson, Washington, D.C., 1908–at least 1942

[Mortimer Brandt, New York, by 1966]

[Hirschl & Adler Galleries, New York, 1966–1967]

John D. Rockefeller 3rd and Blanchette Hooker Rockefeller, New York, 1967–1979

FAMSF, 1979.7.9.1, 1979.7.9.2

Exhibition History
Philadelphia, Pennsylvania Academy of the Fine Arts, *Philadelphia Painting and Printing to 1776*, 1971, not in publ.

Washington, D.C., National Portrait Gallery, *Henry Benbridge, 1743–1812: American Portrait Painter*, 1971, exh. nos. 49, 50

San Francisco 1976, exh. nos. 7, 8

Tokyo 1982, exh. nos. 7, 8

Selected Reference
William Sawitzky, *Matthew Pratt, 1734–1805* (New York: The New-York Historical Society, in cooperation with the Carnegie Corporation of New York, 1942), pp. 68–70

Oil on canvas, 35¾ x 27½ in.
Signed and dated lower left: *R. Earl pi 1784*

RALPH EARL

b. Worcester County, Mass. 1751
d. Bolton, Conn. 1801

[A]lthough [Ralph Earl's] father and brother fought on the Whig side [of the American Revolution], he himself was a Loyalist.

After some politically uncomfortable years in Connecticut, he was able to escape in 1778 to England. There he painted portraits with some success, married and exhibited at the Royal Academy. This portrait of a witty and worldly woman shows the skill and perception of character he attained during his stay there.

E. P. Richardson, *American Art: An Exhibition from the Collection of Mr. and Mrs. John D. Rockefeller 3rd*, exh. cat. (San Francisco: The Fine Arts Museums of San Francisco, 1976), p. 56

———————

Earl's early years in England, from 1778 to 1782, virtually escape historical record. No known mention of the artist exists in written accounts of the day. . . .

. . . By 1783 he had established a residence in London, where he remained, at different addresses, until 1785. In contrast to the seemingly unremarkable beginnings of his English career, Earl painted an impressive number of grand-scale portraits of prominent English subjects while in London, to wit, the sixteen signed and dated or documented works from these years, as well as the eight attributed portraits. He exhibited four of these works at the Royal Academy exhibitions of 1783, 1784, and 1785. The seemingly abrupt shift from virtual obscurity to a relatively high level of artistic activity appears to coincide with Earl's acceptance into the studio of Benjamin West. . . .

In 1784, Earl was living in Leicester Fields, where a number of the most prominent artists of the day lived. Sir Joshua Reynolds, then president of the Royal Academy, lived at

47 Leicester Square until his death in 1792; Copley settled with his family across the street at 12 Leicester Square. . . . Upon his return to America [in 1785], Earl customarily cited Reynolds (in his numerous newspaper advertisements) as one of three artists he received inspiration from during his English years, the others being West and Copley. Unfortunately, the details of Earl's residence in London have remained elusive.

Elizabeth Mankin Kornhauser, *Ralph Earl: The Face of the Young Republic*, exh. cat. (Hartford, Conn.: Wadsworth Atheneum, 1991), pp. 18–21, 30

Provenance
Hulme Art Collection, 1953

[Ira Spanierman Gallery, New York, ca. 1968]

[David David, Philadelphia, by 1968]

[Kennedy Galleries, New York, 1970]

John D. Rockefeller 3rd and Blanchette Hooker Rockefeller, New York, 1970–1993

FAMSF, 1993.35.9

Exhibition History
New York, The Metropolitan Museum of Art, *American Painting, 1754–1954*, 1953, no publ. (as School of Gilbert Stuart)

San Francisco 1976, exh. no. 18

Selected Reference
"American Primitives," *The Kennedy Quarterly* 10, no. 3 (December 1970): cat. no. 182

14 PHILIP CHURCH, 1784

Oil on canvas, 17⅞ x 13¾ in.

JOHN TRUMBULL
b. Lebanon, Conn. 1756
d. New York, N.Y. 1843

He [John Trumbull] was a remarkable man in many ways—even in the matter of longevity. He witnessed the birth of this nation, he saw the smoke and heard the firing from Bunker's Hill from across Boston harbor and he lived under the administrations of the first ten presidents of the United States, the first six of whom he knew well. In 1832 he introduced himself to the Secretary of War as the "senior surviving officer of the Revolution." Though the soldier-painter lived to be eighty-eight he was conditioned, throughout his long life, by four early events.

To begin with, he never got over the fact that he was *well born*, the son of the Colonial and Revolutionary Governor of Connecticut. He was an aristocrat—although of the small town, home-spun, strict Calvinistic variety. He was, shall we say, always something of a social snob. Secondly, he was *monocular*, having lost most of the sight of his left eye at the age of four or five. Consequently, his small scale work, such as his oil miniatures, is best, as the defect of one-eyed vision is least apparent. Thirdly he was *well educated*, a Harvard man. He was a brilliant boy, almost painfully so. He received—and survived—a classical education at Cambridge, graduating at the age of seventeen, the youngest member of the class of 1773. He was to have the distinction of being the earliest college-trained graduate to become a professional painter in the United States. And, finally, he was commissioned a full *colonel* in the Continental Army at the age of twenty and was a member of the great Washington's official family, though only for a matter of weeks, as an Aide-de-Camp to the Commander-in-Chief.

Theodore Sizer, "John Trumbull, 'Patriot-Painter,' in Northern New York," *New York History* 31, no. 3 (July 1950): 283–284

In May, 1777, immediately after my resignation [from the Revolutionary Army], my military accounts were audited and settled at Albany, by the proper accounting officer, John Carter. This gentleman who, soon after, married Angelica, the eldest daughter of General Schuyler, resided in 1778 and 1779, in Boston, where I was studying, and the acquaintance which commenced at Albany was continued. . . . [W]hen I resolved to return to London for the purpose of studying the arts, I purchased from Mr. Carter, a bill of exchange upon a banking house in London, with the full amount of all my disposable means, which were small enough to begin such a course with.

In London, 1784, my acquaintance with this gentleman was renewed, under the name of John Barker Church, (Carter had been but a *nom de guerre*), where he lived in great elegance, a member of Parliament, &c. &c.; and although I was now but a poor student of

painting, and he rich, honored, and associated with the great, Mr. Church continued to treat me on a footing of equality, and I frequently dined at his table with distinguished men, such as Sheridan, &c.

John Trumbull, *Autobiography: Reminiscences and Letters of John Trumbull from 1756 to 1841* (New York and London: Wiley and Putnam; New Haven: B. L. Hamlen, 1841), pp. 96–97

In the letter from [George] Washington [to Philip John Schuyler] quoted he adds: "Your grandson has all the exterior of a fine young man and from what I have heard of his intellect and principles will do justice to and reward the precepts he has received from yourself, his parents and Uncle [Alexander] Hamilton. So far then as my attentions to him will go, consistent with my duties, he may assuredly count upon." This youth was Philip Church, who had been educated at Eton and was now on Hamilton's staff in the Whiskey insurrection [a farmers' revolt in Pennsylvania against a 1791 excise tax on liquor] that had been engaging attention in Pennsylvania. The promise of Washington was afterward handsomely fulfilled when the young man married Ann Stuart, the daughter of General Walter Stuart, and the President gave the bride away and presented her with his miniature surrounded by diamonds.

Mary Gay Humphreys, *Catherine Schuyler* (New York: Charles Scribner's Sons, 1901), p. 238

Provenance
Philip John Schuyler (1733–1804) and Catherine Van Rensselaer Schuyler (1756–1803), maternal grandparents of the sitter, Albany, 1784–ca. 1804

Descended in family to 1945

[Kennedy Galleries, New York, 1945]

Edwin A. Fish (1887–1968), Locust Valley and Southampton, N.Y., and Palm Springs, Fla., ca. 1945–ca. 1969

[Kennedy Galleries, New York, ca. 1969–1970]

John D. Rockefeller 3rd and Blanchette Hooker Rockefeller, New York, 1970–1979

FAMSF, 1979.7.97

Exhibition History
San Francisco 1976, exh. no. 21

Tokyo 1982, exh. no. 11

Selected References
Theodore Sizer, *The Works of Colonel John Trumbull: Artist of the American Revolution*, rev. ed. (New Haven: Yale University Press, 1967), p. 25

The American Canvas, pp. 48–49, 233

Related Works
Philip Church, 1784
Oil on canvas, 31 x 26 in.
Hirschl & Adler Galleries, New York, as of 1982

Mrs. John Barker Church, Child, and Servant, 1784
Oil on canvas, 36 x 28 in.
Mrs. Amy Olney Johnson, Farmington, Conn., as of 1982

Oil on canvas, 61⅜ x 42⅞ in.

JOSEPH WRIGHT
b. Bordentown, N.J. 1756
d. Philadelphia, Pa. 1793

Joseph Wright was born in Bordentown, New Jersey, in 1756, son of Joseph and Patience Lovell Wright. She was the very successful modeler in wax and a secret American spy in London during the Revolution. After her husband's death she settled in London, in 1772, where her family followed her in 1773. She taught modeling to her son and introduced him into artistic circles that led to his admittance, as the first American, to the Royal Academy schools in 1775.

> Michael Quick, "Joseph Wright," in *American Portraiture in the Grand Manner, 1720–1920*, exh. cat. (Los Angeles: Los Angeles County Museum of Art, 1981), p. 120

Students [at the Royal Academy Schools] were probably also directed to examine works of art that had already left artists' studios and gone into private ownership. Such must have been the case when Joseph Wright ventured up to the corner of Greek and King Streets to see Gainsborough's portrait of young Master Jonathan Buttall [*The Blue Boy*, The Huntington, San Marino, Calif.]. He made at least one drawing of it, which he kept with him until he returned to Philadelphia a number of years later. There, in about 1784, he used it as the basis for the design of the full-length portrait of his distant cousin, John Coats Browne.

> Monroe H. Fabian, *Joseph Wright: American Artist, 1756–1793*, exh. cat. (Washington, D.C.: Smithsonian Institution Press, for the National Portrait Gallery, 1985), p. 26

The eldest child, John Coats Browne, was born on October 23, 1774. His early education was acquired at the Episcopal Academy. . . .

Subsequently entering the University of Pennsylvania, he graduated therefrom in 1793. He then engaged in business with his father as an iron-monger, his specialty being the furnishing of the iron-work for ships. Both in the business world and otherwise he attained the same degree of prominence and influence as his father, particularly in that section of Philadelphia now known as Kensington.

He was the first President of the Kensington Bank, which was incorporated April 11, 1826. In 1831 he was chosen President of the Board of Commissioners of the District of Kensington, Northern Liberties, and held this post at the time of his death a year later. He had been elected June 2, 1798, a member of the celebrated First Troop Philadelphia City Cavalry, and had remained in that organization until his resignation, May 7, 1810. From 1803 to 1807 he held the position of 4th Corporal. . . .

His residence was on the bank of the Delaware river, a short distance north of the "Old Treaty Tree."

The death of John Coats Browne took place August 8, 1832. Poulson's American Daily Advertiser for August 11, 1832, contains a memoir of the deceased, couched in eulogistic terms.

He was married, April 27, 1800, to Hannah Lloyd. . . .

The Lloyd family were strict Quakers. The Brownes had been, prior to the Revolution, but Peter Browne [John Coats's father], after bearing arms in the defense of American liberty, had ceased to be a Friend.

> Frank Willing Leach, "Old Philadelphia Families, 148: Browne," *(Philadelphia) North American*, 2 February 1913

Provenance
Peter Browne (1751–1810), Philadelphia, ca. 1784–ca. 1810

Descended in family

[Carlen Galleries, Philadelphia,
1976]

John D. Rockefeller 3rd and
Blanchette Hooker Rockefeller,
New York, 1976–1979

FAMSF, 1979.7.107

Exhibition History
Washington, D.C., National Portrait Gallery, *Benjamin West and
His American Students*, 1980, no
exh. no.

Los Angeles County Museum of
Art, *American Portraiture in the*

Grand Manner, 1720–1920, 1981,
exh. no. 24

Tokyo 1982, exh. no. 12

Selected Reference
The American Canvas, pp. 50–
51, 233

Oil on canvas, each 24 x 18 in.

**WINTHROP
CHANDLER**

b. Woodstock, Conn. 1747
d. Woodstock, Conn. 1790

Chandler worked at about the same time and in the same general vicinity as Ralph Earl and Richard Jennys. He ranks with these two limners . . . as an outstanding provincial painter of the eighteenth century. They represent the early development of the native as against the cosmopolitan tradition in American art, and offer interesting contrast with that great Anglo-American triumvirate, Copley-Stuart-West. Chandler's assembled work proves him to have been one of our greatest portrait and earliest scene painters. . . . Chandler's painting exemplifies, above all else, the independent achievement of the homely native tradition in early American art. . . .

> Jean Lipman, foreword to Nina Fletcher Little, "Winthrop Chandler," *Art in America* 35, no. 2 (April 1947): 75–76

———

Died at Woodstock, Mr. Winthrop Chandler of this town; a man whose native genius has been servicable to the community in which he resided. By profession he was a house painter, but many good likenesses on canvas show he could guide the pencil of the limner. . . . The world was not his enemy, but as is too common, his genius was not matured on the bosom of encouragement. Embarrassment, like strong weeds in a garden of delicate flowers, checked his enthusiasm and disheartened the man. Peace to his manes.

> "Obituary," *Worcester Spy*, 19 August 1790, quoted in Nina Fletcher Little, "Winthrop Chandler," *Art in America* 35, no. 2 (April 1947): 88

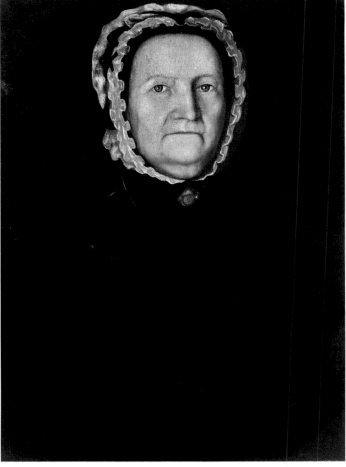

18 GENIUS CALLING FORTH THE FINE ARTS TO ADORN MANUFACTURES AND COMMERCE, 1789

Oil on paperboard (now mounted on canvas), 19⅜ x 24⅝ in.
Signed and dated left of lower center: *B. West/1789*

BENJAMIN WEST
b. Springfield, Pa. 1738
d. London, England 1820

By His Majesty's commands I made nine designs for the ceiling in the Queen's Lodge, Windsor, for Mr. Haas to work the ceilings from. Viz. 1. Genius inspiring the fine arts to adorn the useful arts and sciences. 2. Agriculture. 3. Manufactures. 4. Commerce. 5. Botany. 6. Chemistry. 7. Celestial Science. 8. Terrestrial Science; and 9. To adorn Empire[.] £525. . . .

This is a true statement of the numbers of pictures, cartoons, and drawings of designs, and sketches of scripture subjects, as well as historical events, British as well as Greek, Roman, and other nations, with which I had been honoured by the King's commands, from 1768, to 5th January 1801, to paint for His Majesty.

West, "The Account of Pictures Painted by Benjamin West. . . . A True Copy from Mr. West's Account Books," in John Galt, *The Life and Works of Benjamin West, Esq*. (London: T. Cadell and W. Davies, 1820), pp. 214–215

———

Another project, a ceiling at Queen's Lodge, Windsor Castle, has completely disappeared and must be reconstructed after some drawings. In the late 1770s the royal couple [George III and Charlotte] and nearly all of the fifteen children had moved into Queen's Lodge. The King had put up the ceiling in 1788. The Queen had taken it down during her husband's illness. After his recovery in March, 1789, and his resumption of authority, a confectioner, Haas, painted the ceiling after West's drawings in a week. He used an Italian process, called Marmotinto, the basis of which is marble dust. The ceiling was in a reception room. The subject of the paintings was surprisingly modern: "the utility of the Arts and Sciences, as they are of to this as a commercial nation." This is what the exhibition catalogue of the Royal Academy of 1790 called it. West had followed the division of the ceiling at Whitehall by Rubens, but it was not an apotheosis of the royal house. It showed the needs of a modern nation. There were allegorical figures of Agriculture, Manufacture, Printing and Astronomy. . . . Nothing is more expressive of the transitional character of the eighteenth century than this ceiling. Very modern in content and Renaissance in form.

Helmut von Erffa, "Benjamin West at the Height of His Career," *The American Art Journal* I, no. I (Spring 1969): 20–21

Exhibition History

London, Royal Academy, 1790, exh. no. 110 (as *A sketch: Genius calling forth Arts and Sciences; part of a design in the Queen's Lodge, Windsor, intended to show the utility they are of to this, as a commercial nation*)

Philadelphia, The Art Alliance, *Benjamin West Memorial Exhibition*, 1921, exh. no. 14 (as *Apollo and the Muses*)

The Brooklyn Museum, *Exhibition of Paintings and Drawings by Benjamin West and of Engravings Representing His Work*, 1922, exh. no. 14 (as *Apollo and the Muses*)

Tokyo 1982, exh. no. 10

The Baltimore Museum of Art, *Benjamin West: American Painter at the English Court*, 1989, exh. no. 35

Selected References

John Dillenberger, *Benjamin West: The Context of His Life's Work with Particular Attention to Paintings with Religious Subject Matter* (San Antonio, Tex.: Trinity University Press, 1977), pp. 134, 142, 193, 202, 207

Helmut von Erffa and Allen Staley, *The Paintings of Benjamin West* (New Haven and London: Yale University Press, 1986), pp. 90, 93, 98, 100, cat. no. 435

The American Canvas, pp. 36–37, 233

Related Works

Painted with four companion pictures and several drawings as designs for a ceiling in Queen's Lodge:

Agriculture (Husbandry Aided by Arts and Commerce), 1789
Oil on paper, mounted on panel, oval, 20 x 24 in.

Mint Museum of Art, Charlotte, N.C.

British Manufactory (Manufactory Giving Support to Industry) (Étruria), ca. 1789–1791
Oil on paper, mounted on panel, oval, 20⅛ x 25½ in.
The Cleveland Museum of Art

British Commerce (The Four Quarters of the Globe Bringing Treasures to Britannia), ca. 1787–1791
19½ x 24 in.
Location unknown

Astronomy and *Navigation*, 1788
Sepia ink and blue wash, 5⅞ x 31¼ in.
Victoria and Albert Museum, London

Botany, 1788
Pen and wash, 14 x 18½ in.
Courtauld Institute Galleries, London

Architecture and *Music*, 1788
Pen and ink, approx. 12¼ x 15¾ in.

Delaware Art Museum, Wilmington

Sculpture and *Painting*, 1788
Pen and ink, approx. 12¼ x 15¾ in.
Auction sale, Sotheby's, London, 22 March 1979, lot no. 30

Riches (Marine and Inland Navigation Enriching Britannia), ca. 1788–1789
Oil on paper, mounted on panel, 19 x 21¼ in.
Davis Museum and Cultural Center, Wellesley College, Wellesley, Mass.

Genius Calling forth the Arts, 1787
Black chalk and watercolor, 13¹¹⁄₁₆ x 18¼ in.
Cincinnati Art Museum

Francesco Bartolozzi (Italian, 1727–1815), *Les Beaux-Arts et les Sciences Réveillées par un Génie. D'après B. West*
Engraving
Published 1 October 1789 (de Vesme, cat. no. 557)

19 SARAH PERRY HUBBELL, 1795
(MRS. DAVID HUBBELL)

Oil on canvas, 37 x 30 in.
Signed and dated lower left: *R. Earl.Pinxt/1795*

RALPH EARL

b. Worcester County, Mass. 1751
d. Bolton, Conn. 1801

Ambitious of producing a picture of artistic merit as well as a likeness, Earl arranges his sitters in relationship to their surroundings. Chairs and tables are faithfully depicted and often historically interesting. . . . The more personal belongings—fans, parasols, inkwells, snuffboxes, and now and then a chosen volume—distinctly add to the intimacy of these paintings. . . .

The placing of his subjects near an open window, or out-of-doors, affording a view of local or at least native landscape, has repeatedly been mentioned as being peculiar to Earl. As a matter of fact, in his earlier and more elaborate work, Charles Willson Peale employed the same device. The difference is, that in Earl's paintings these bits of scenery or full landscape backgrounds are often given a very definite, even personal character. One is shown not only Connecticut, but the particular spot associated with the individual subject.

William Sawitzky, *Connecticut Portraits by Ralph Earl, 1751–1801*, exh. cat. (New Haven: Yale University Gallery of Fine Arts, 1935), p. 7

————

I would simply imagine that the wick that Mrs. Hubbell is holding in her lap is for a lamp rather than a candlewick.

Joseph T. Butler, Curator and Director of Collections, Sleepy Hollow Restorations, Tarrytown, N.Y., 16 September 1986, FAMSF departmental files

Provenance
David Hubbell (1747/48–1814)
and Sarah Perry Hubbell (1744–
1826), Greenfield Hill (now Fairfield), Conn., 1795–ca. 1826

Descended in family to Mary
Quintard Meyer (Mrs. Percy
Shelton) Weeks, Oyster Bay,
N.Y., by 1944–1967

[Hirschl & Adler Galleries,
New York, 1967–1968]

John D. Rockefeller 3rd and
Blanchette Hooker Rockefeller,
New York, 1968–1979

FAMSF, 1979.7.39

Exhibition History
New York, Whitney Museum
of American Art, *Ralph Earl,
1751–1801*, 1945, exh. no. 39

Oyster Bay, N.Y., Parish Hall,
Christ Church, *Exhibition of*

American Portraits, 1958,
no publ.

San Francisco 1976, exh. no. 19

Tokyo 1982, exh. no. 13

Selected Reference
Robert L. Harley, "Ralph Earl,
Eighteenth-Century Connecticut
Artist, Comes into His Own," *The
American Collector* 14, no. 10
(November 1945): 13

Related Works
David Hubbell, 1795
Oil on canvas, 35¾ x 28¾ in.
Allison Gallery, New York,
as of 1993

The Hubbell Children (David, Jr.,
and Harriet), 1788
Oil on canvas, 37 x 30 in.
Mrs. Charles C. Lawrence,
New York, as of 1986

20 ELIZABETH RODMAN ROGERS, CA. 1795 (MRS. JOHN ROGERS)

Oil on canvas, 34¾ x 28⅝ in.

JAMES EARL
b. Paxton, Mass. 1761
d. Charleston, S.C. 1796

Died, on Thursday, the 18th instant, Mr. James Earl, Portrait Painter, of Paxton, Massachusetts. This gentleman has resided for nearly two years in this city, in which time he has exhibited so many specimens of his art as to enable us to speak with decision of his talents. To an uncommon facility in hitting of the likeness, may be added a peculiarity in his execution of drapery, and, which ever has been esteemed in his art the NE PLUS ULTRA, of giving life to the eye, and expression of every feature.

He was a Royal Academician in London, where he resided ten years and where his wife and children are; and his name appeared equally prominent with the other American geniuses of the present time, Copeley, West, Trumbull, Savage.

As a man, he must be regreted as possessing a suavity of disposition, benevolence, and good humor. As a husband, a father, we attempt not to reach his merits!

(Charleston) South Carolina State Gazette and Timothy and Mason's Daily Advertiser, 20 August 1796, reprinted in Anna Wells Rutledge, *Artists in the Life of Charleston*, Transactions of the American Philosophical Society, vol. 39, pt. 2 (Philadelphia: American Philosophical Society, 1949), p. 124

A technical duality is frequently operative in James Earl's portraits. Whereas the features of his subjects are generally delineated in a relatively smooth, precise manner and the texture of the hair brought out with wispy accents, the rest of the picture is often rendered quite broadly, even in a pronounced painterly fashion, with the track of the brush and some impasto clearly in evidence. . . . The cursive configurations in his draperies are veritable signatures of the artist and are remarkably spontaneous for one as intent as James Earl on capturing so literally the likeness of a human face. This element of literalness has a special quality. It is as if, at times, the intermediary between the sitter and the image on the canvas were some impersonal agent bent on replication. One is tempted to speculate here about the significance of one item recorded in the inventory made of the artist's effects when he died: a camera obscura.

Harold Spencer, *The American Earls: Ralph Earl, James Earl, R. E. W. Earl*, exh. cat. (Storrs: The William Benton Museum of Art, The University of Connecticut, 1972), pp. xxv–xxvi

---

Daughter of a prominent Newport family and wife of a distinguished Providence attorney [*sic*—merchant], Mrs. Rogers leans casually forward, her chin resting on her hand, and wears a pleasant, engaging expression. The upholstered lolling chair, velvet background drapery, and detailed paneling evoke a rich and substantial setting for the sitter, emphasizing by contrast her informal costume and pose. Earl uses this contrast to create a vivid, apparently spontaneous moment of reality, in which Mrs. Rogers glances up from her book, finger

still holding her place, as if a friend or family member had just entered her chamber. The fashionable effect of intimacy is extremely close to the practice of the British artists Sir Joshua Reynolds (1723–1792) and Allan Ramsay (1713–1784).

Earl's handling of paint in this portrait is particularly fluent. Mrs. Rogers's cap, kerchief, and sash are effectively summarized with thick, continuous strokes of creamy paint, while the strands of her lightly grizzled hair contrast with the lustrous material of her gown. *Mrs. John Rogers*, a painting in which formal and illusionistic qualities give equal pleasure, prompts severe regret at the early death of the artist.

Marc Simpson, in *The American Canvas: Paintings from the Collection of The Fine Arts Museums of San Francisco* (New York: Hudson Hills Press, in association with The Fine Arts Museums of San Francisco, 1989), p. 52

Provenance
John Rogers (1756–1810) and Elizabeth Rodman Rogers (1760–1848), Providence, R.I., ca. 1795–1848

Descended in family to Senator Theodore Francis Green (1867–1966), Providence, R.I., by 1914–1969

[Hirschl & Adler Galleries, New York, 1969–1970]

John D. Rockefeller 3rd and Blanchette Hooker Rockefeller, New York, 1970–1979

FAMSF, 1979.7.38

Exhibition History
Providence, R.I., Providence Art Club, *Portraits of Women Loan Exhibition*, 1895, exh. no. 31

Providence, Museum of Art, Rhode Island School of Design,

Early American Art, 1914, exh. no. 12 (as by Ralph Earl)

Providence, Museum of Art, Rhode Island School of Design, 1936, no publ.

New York, Hirschl & Adler Galleries, *Forty Masterworks of American Art*, 1970, exh. no. 9

San Francisco 1976, exh. no. 17

Tokyo 1982, exh. no. 14

Selected Reference
The American Canvas, pp. 52–53, 234

Related Work
John Rogers, ca. 1795
Oil on canvas (?), size unknown
Senator Theodore Francis Greene, as of 1914 (then attributed to Ralph Earl)

21 CATHERINE LIVINGSTON THORN JOHNSON, CA. 1796
(MRS. HORACE JOHNSON)

Pastel on gray-brown wove paper mounted on paperboard, 9¼ x 7⅛ in.

JAMES SHARPLES

b. Lancashire, England ca. 1751
d. New York, N.Y. 1811

After training in France for the priesthood, [Sharples] returned to England to study art. By 1782 he had moved to Bath, where he taught drawing, and in the following year he moved to London, where on several occasions his work was exhibited at the Royal Academy. About 1793 the family—including his artist-wife Ellen Wallace (1769–1849) and three sons [*sic*—two sons and a daughter] whom he also trained—moved to America; over the next eight years they made a great many small pastels, primarily in New York and Philadelphia. Eventually the family returned to England; however, the popularity of their work enabled James in 1811 to leave an estate of £35,000 [elsewhere reported as $35,000], and a large collection of the family's output makes up the Sharples Collection at Bristol, England.

Even the fine study of 1930 by Katherine McCook Knox, *The Sharples*, failed to unravel completely the problem of trying to separate the hand of James Sharples from that of his wife, from his sons' work, and from later imitators; so uncertainty still abounds in this area.

. . . Working on grainy, gray paper (usually sheets 9 by 7 inches), Sharples used a brush to apply powdered pastels, which he kept in bottles. . . . A pastel normally took about two hours, and the artist charged fifteen dollars for profiles—his most successful mode—and twenty for full-face views.

Theodore E. Stebbins, Jr., *American Master Drawings and Watercolors*, exh. cat. (New York: Harper & Row, in association with The Drawing Society, 1976), p. 44

To secure a fast and accurate representation, he employed a well-known device of the day called the physiognotrace. This machine aided the artist in copying the profile of a sitter, after which modeling could be added. Brushes were then used to apply the pastel in powdered form over the profile tracing.

Robert Flynn Johnson, *Master Drawings from the Achenbach Foundation for Graphic Arts*, exh. cat. (San Francisco: The Fine Arts Museums of San Francisco, 1985), p. 216

Provenance
Possibly Horace Johnson and Catherine Livingston Thorn Johnson (b. 1769) from ca. 1796

Lawrence A. Fleischman (b. 1925) and Barbara Greenberg Fleischman (b. 1924), Detroit, by 1960–1966

[Kennedy Galleries, New York, 1966–1967]

John D. Rockefeller 3rd and Blanchette Hooker Rockefeller, New York, 1967–1979

FAMSF, 1979.7.92

Exhibition History
Milwaukee Art Center, *American Painting, 1760–1960: A Selection of 125 Paintings from the Collection of Mr. and Mrs. Lawrence A. Fleischman, Detroit*, 1960, no exh. no.

Tucson, University of Arizona Art Gallery, *American Painting, 1765–1963: Selections from the Lawrence A. and Barbara Fleischman Collection of American Art*, 1964, exh. no. 90

New York, Kennedy Galleries, *American Drawings, Pastels, and Watercolors: Part One, Works of the Eighteenth and Early Nineteenth Centuries*, 1967, exh. no. 8

FAMSF, *Selected Acquisitions, 1977–1979*, 1979, exh. no. 52

FAMSF, *Faces and Figures: Nineteenth-Century Works on Paper from the Permanent Collection*, 1984, no publ.

FAMSF, *Master Drawings from the Achenbach Foundation for Graphic Arts*, 1985, exh. no. 100

---

22 RICHARD YATES, CA. 1800 (ORIGINAL PAINTED 1793 OR 1794)

Oil on canvas, 30 x 25 in.

AFTER GILBERT STUART
b. North Kingstown, R.I. 1755
d. Boston, Mass. 1828

Stuart landed at and took up his abode for some months in New York. Here he favored the renowned, the rich, and the fashionable, by exercising his skill for their gratification; and gave present éclat and a *short-lived immortality* in exchange for a portion of their wealth. He opened an *atelier* in Stone Street, near William Street, where all who admired the art or wished to avail themselves of the artist's talents, daily resorted. It appeared to the writer as if he had never seen portraits before, so decidedly was form and mind conveyed to the canvas. . . .

In New York, as elsewhere, the talents and acquirements of Mr. Stuart introduced him to the intimate society of all who were distinguished by office, rank or attainment; and his observing mind and powerful memory treasured up events, characters and anecdotes, which rendered his conversation an inexhaustible fund of amusement and information to his sitters, and his companions. Of the many fine portraits he painted at this time we remember more particularly those of the Pollock and Yates family.

William Dunlap, *A History of the Rise and Progress of the Arts of Design in the United States*, 3 vols. (1834; Boston: C. E. Goodspeed & Co., 1918), 1:229–230

Richard Yates (1732–1808) was the senior member of the mercantile firm of Yates & Pollock, 97 Front Street, New York City. . . . In 1757, he married Catherine Brass of New York by whom he had a daughter Catherine, who married in 1787 George Pollock, the junior member of the firm. Mr Edward P. Terry, M.D. married Sophia H. P. Pollock, daughter of Carlisle and Sophia (Yates) Pollock; Carlisle Pollock was the brother of George Pollock, the above named partner and son-in-law of the sitter. Gilbert Stuart in writing on November 2, 1794 to his uncle, Joseph Anthony, in Philadelphia, expressed his obligation to the Pollock family by stating: "To their house I am indebted for more civilities than to the world beside" It was through George and Carlisle Pollock that he met many of the distinguished sitters painted after he returned to New York in 1793.

> *The Harold W. Hack Estate and Other Collections*, sale cat. (New York: Parke-Bernet, 2 December 1938), lot no. 32

Provenance

Edward Pomeroy Terry, M.D. (1800–1843), and Sophia Pollock Terry (granddaughter of the sitter), Hartford, Conn.

Descended in family to Charles Edward Terry (d. 1943), ca. 1886–1926

Thomas B. Clarke (1848–1931), New York, 1926–ca. 1938

City Bank Farmer's Trust Company, New York, as executor, 1938

[Auction sale, Parke-Bernet, New York, 2 December 1938, lot no. 32, sold for $800]

Clarence Dearden (d. 1950), New York, 1938–ca. 1950

Descended in family to ca. 1976

[Kennedy Galleries, New York, by 1976]

John D. Rockefeller 3rd and Blanchette Hooker Rockefeller, New York, 1976–1993

FAMSF, 1993.35.25

Exhibition History

New York, The Century Association, *A Loan Exhibition of Paintings by Early American Portrait Painters*, 1928, exh. no. 2

Related Works

Gilbert Stuart (American, 1755–1828)
Richard Yates, 1793–1794
Oil on canvas, 34½ x 27⅜ in.
National Gallery of Art, Washington, D.C.

Gilbert Stuart (American, 1755–1828)
Mrs. Richard Yates, 1793–1794
Oil on canvas, 30¼ x 25 in.
National Gallery of Art, Washington, D.C.

After Gilbert Stuart
Mrs. Richard Yates, early 19th century
Oil on canvas, 30¼ x 25¼ in.
Museum of Fine Arts, Boston

Oil on wood panel, 34 x 26¾ in.
Signed and dated lower left: *JARVIS/JULY 1809*

**JOHN WESLEY
JARVIS**

b. South Shields, England 1780
d. New York, N.Y. 1840

Jarvis,—John Wesley Jarvis,—named after the celebrated preacher, who was a relative [Methodism's founder John Wesley]. . . .

Beyond all question, Jarvis was the best portrait-painter of his day, within a limited sphere,—that of character when there was in it anything of the humorist. Being himself a humorist in the broadest and richest sense of the word, all his men were . . . distinctly individualized. . . .

In stature he was about five feet seven, with large features, a dark, turbid complexion, . . . and when I knew him he was not far from forty-five years old. He was a man of imperturbable gravity on common occasions, and the best story-teller that ever lived. . . .

But he was a sad dog at the best. In Audubon's Ornithological Biography . . . we have a capital sketch of Jarvis, with an account of his painting and shooting and *naturalizing*, well worth a place here. "As I was lounging," says Audubon, "one fair and very warm morning, on

the levee at New Orleans, I chanced to observe a gentleman whose dress and other accomplishments greatly attracted my attention. . . . His head was covered with a straw hat, the brim of which might cope with those worn by the fair sex in 1830; his neck was exposed to the weather; the broad frill of a shirt, then fashionable, flapped about his breast, whilst an extraordinary collar, carefully arranged, fell over the top of his coat. The latter was of *a light green color, harmonizing well with a pair of flowing nankeen trousers and a pink waistcoat,* from the bosom of which, amidst a large bunch of splendid flowers of the magnolia, protruded part of a young alligator."

Observations on American Art: Selections from the Writings of John Neal, 1793–1876, ed. Harold Edward Dickson (State College: Pennsylvania State College, 1943), pp. 78–80

———

Profusion and confusion, as Dunlap, the historian of the art of that day, expressed it, reigned in the Jarvis menage. . . . [I]n 1808, Jarvis married. He tried to readjust his life and also he raised his prices for large portraits. For a head he charged $100, and for a portrait showing head and hands, or a half length, $150. Instead of his clientele decreasing, as he thought it surely would, this change augmented his income. He set himself to the task of receiving six sitters a day, as Stuart did. Some weeks he completed the likenesses of all of them. Jarvis worked with an astonishing facility and accuracy.

Despite his careless habits he was a very hard worker. From Dr. John Augustine Smith he had taken lessons in anatomy, and he also had made a profound study of the works of the physiognomists and phrenologists of the day. It may be said of him that he was an art-anatomist. His portraits, many of which are highly finished, and others of which show the marks of haste, were vital and vivid.

John Walker Harrington, "John Wesley Jarvis, Portraitist," *The American Magazine of Art* 18, no. 11 (November 1927): 579

———

Hone, Philip (Oct. 25, 1780–May 5, 1851), diarist, was born in New York City of German-French ancestry, his father being a joiner of limited means. At sixteen he began assisting his elder brother John in an auction business, and at nineteen became a partner. The firm rapidly grew to be one of the most profitable in New York, its net profits in the single year 1815 reaching $159,000, and it gave Hone at forty a fortune of at least a half million. Retiring from business in May 1821, he made a tour of Europe, and then settled himself, his wife, Catherine Dunscomb, whom he married Oct. 1, 1801, his six children, his large library, and his art collection in his Broadway house, overlooking City Hall Park. His wealth, his cultivation, his affable personality, and his public spirit, made him a prominent figure in city affairs. Elected mayor for one year when in 1825 the Democratic city counsel split upon two rival candidates, he ably represented the city at the reception of Lafayette and the opening of the Erie Canal. . . .

Hone's claims to repute as an able, honorable, and conservative citizen were known to everyone; but his immortality rests upon the secret diary which he kept from 1828 to 1851, and which furnishes the best extant picture of New York life in that period.

A[llan] N[evins], "Philip Hone," *Dictionary of National Biography,* rev. ed., vol. 9, pt. 1, p. 192

Provenance
Philip Hone (1780–1851) and Catherine Dunscombe Hone, New York, 1809–ca. 1851
Descended in family to 1975

[Hirschl & Adler Galleries, New York, 1975–1976]
John D. Rockefeller 3rd and Blanchette Hooker Rockefeller, New York, 1976–1986
FAMSF, 1986.84

Exhibition History
FAMSF, extended loan, 1979–1986

Selected References
Harold E. Dickson, *John Wesley Jarvis: American Painter, 1780–1840* (New York: The New-York Historical Society, 1949), p. 160
The American Canvas, pp. 62–63, 234

Oil on canvas, 28 x 50⅝ in.
Signed and dated lower right: *R.S 1809.*

ROBERT SALMON

b. Whitehaven, Cumberland,
England 1775
d. between 1848 and 1851

Salmon—This painter's name was once quite familiar to the Bostonians. . . . He was one of the earliest marine painters of reputation in Massachusetts.

Salmon painted with great care, and his pictures are almost miniatures in their detail. He chiefly affected sea-views, and was especially happy in introducing figures therein. His greatest defect was in the treatment of the water, which he usually represented as a succession of short, choppy waves, an effect rarely seen on our coast, though not in itself untrue to nature. His colors are very harmoniously blended, and especially there is in many of them a pearly tone which has a charming effect.

Salmon was a very eccentric man, and lived for years in a little hut on one of the wharves in Boston, studying the subject he most loved. Very many of his views are of familiar localities near Boston, though there are also English scenes from his pencil.

Henry T. Tuckerman, *Book of the Artists: American Artist Life* (1867; New York: James F. Carr, 1966), p. 551

———

In my younger days I knew Robert Salmon very well . . . and I used to go to his studio which was at the lower end of the Marine Railway Wharf, and directly over a boat-builder's shop. His studio and living room, or rooms, were on the same floor, and I recall the fact that he had a bay window built from his studio, and overhanging the wharf, which was so arranged that it gave not only a direct view across the harbor, but also an opportunity to see both up and down stream. He was a small man, most unmistakably Scotch in his appearance and conversation. He was a man of very quick temper, and one who generally called a spade by its proper name.

Salmon's pictures were generally very realistic—he loved to paint what was about him. . . .

Salmon was not an idealist; his pictures were faithful transcripts of what he saw and felt,

and as such they will always have a certain amount of historical value. His preference seemed to be for bright, breezy effects, with plenty of sunshine.

> Henry Hitchings, Proceedings of the Bostonian Society, 1894, quoted in Charles D. Childs, "Robert Salmon: A Boston Painter of Ships and Views," *Old-Time New England* 28, no. 3 (January 1938): 96–97

Topographically the background fits in with the inscribed R.S. 1809 bottom right, which would be during the artist's first visit to Liverpool 1806–11. From left to right: the Townsend Mill (under the tip of the bowsprit), the dome of St. Paul's Church (directly over the figurehead), the dome of the Town Hall (immediately in front of the foremast), the spire of St. George's Church (above the fourth gun) separated by the distant sail from the spire of St. Nicholas. (On Feb 11th the following year, i.e. 1810, this spire collapsed just as the service was about to start causing considerable loss of life. The reconstructed spire was slightly different in design). The final spire is that of St. Thomas's Church (just forward of the mainmast). . . .

To orient the stranger, the sea is off the picture to the left (northwards) and the River Mersey here is a mile wide. To the right it expands considerably becoming much shallower upriver. Although termed a river the Mersey here is best thought of as an 'arm of the sea'. Incidentally the rise and fall at Spring Tide is 32 feet, and with a northerly gale it can be very rough! . . .

Regarding the class of vessel, we concur with your understanding that this is probably not a naval vessel but a powerfully armed merchant ship according to the fashion (dictated by necessity at the time).

We are fairly confident that the ship on the right is a second view of the same vessel. All the features seem to correspond, number of guns, the break of the quarter deck at the mainmast, the quarter stern cabin arrangements etc.

> A. S. Davidson, Honorary Curator (Marine Paintings), Merseyside Maritime Museum, 20 June 1986, FAMSF departmental files

Provenance
[Childs Gallery, Boston, 1956]
Ross Whittier (1893–1973) and Katherine Hamlin Whittier (1899–1982), Beverly Farms, Mass., 1956–ca. 1974

[Childs Gallery, Boston, ca. 1974–1975]
John D. Rockefeller 3rd and Blanchette Hooker Rockefeller, New York, 1975–1979
FAMSF, 1979.7.89

Exhibition History
Boston, Childs Gallery, *American Paintings, 1749–1937*, 1974, exh. no. 4
Boston, Childs Gallery, *Robert Salmon and Other Marine Painters*, 1975, no exh. no.
Tokyo 1982, exh. no. 17

Selected Reference
The American Canvas, pp. 54–55, 234

---

25 LUCY ELLERY CHANNING, 1811 (MRS. WILLIAM CHANNING)

Oil on canvas, 27 x 22⅜ in.
Signed on reverse of canvas (visible before lining)

WASHINGTON ALLSTON
b. Georgetown County, S.C. 1779
d. Cambridgeport, Mass. 1843

Allston's involvement with the relatively small Boston art world in 1808 and subsequent years is not documented. Perhaps the cosmopolitan nature of his training and the lifestyle of his recent years kept him aloof, although he became at this time a good friend and close colleague of [Gilbert] Stuart's; it was a friendship that even deepened when he finally returned again to America in 1818, after his second period abroad. It is interesting, though, that these years in Boston, from 1808 to 1811, saw Allston's greatest production of portraits, a reflection of the continuing thematic preference in America.

> William H. Gerdts, "The Paintings of Washington Allston," in *"A Man of Genius": The Art of Washington Allston, 1779–1843*, exh. cat. (Boston: Museum of Fine Arts, 1979), p. 56

These are portraits, it is said; and with that of Mr. Samuel Williams, Mr. Benjamin West, and the late Mrs. Channing, prove that Mr. Allston can paint portraits. It is said that he painted Mrs. Channing in one day, but that I think impossible. It is a very striking likeness and what is remarkable, bears a resemblance to her son, (Rev. Dr. C.) which could not be discerned so clearly in her living features.

[Elizabeth Palmer Peabody], *Remarks on Allston's Paintings* (Boston: William D. Ticknor, 1839), p. 12

Lucy Ellery Channing was a small person of considerable energy and good sense. Left a widow at the age of forty-three with nine children and a meager inheritance from her husband, she kept her family together, sent four sons to Harvard, and maintained her other children until the older boys, Francis and William, were prepared to share the burden of support.

Madeleine Hooke Rice, *Federal Street Pastor: The Life of William Ellery Channing* (New York: Bookman Associates, 1961), p. 47

The mother, Lucy Ellery, was, like the son [William Ellery], short and elastic, keen, candid, and assertive. From her spirited father [a signer of the Declaration of Independence], she received energy, judgment, and a charm of romance. She was strong. She could be chillingly severe with pretension and fraud. . . .

"The most remarkable trait in my mother's character," Channing later wrote, "was the [rectitude and] simplicity of her mind. . . . She had the firmness to see the truth, to speak it, to act upon it. She was direct in judgment and conversation[.] . . . I cannot recall one word or action betraying the slightest insincerity. She had keen insight into character. She was not to be imposed upon by others, and, what is rarer, she practiced no imposition on her own mind.

She saw things, persons, events, as they were, and spoke of them by their right names. Her partialities did not blind her, even to her own children. Her love was without illusion."

Jack Mendelsohn, *Channing: The Reluctant Radical* (Boston and Toronto: Little, Brown and Company, 1971), p. 21

Provenance
Lucy Ellery (Mrs. William) Channing (1752–1834), Boston, 1811–1834

Descended in family to Henry Channing Rivers, Northeast Harbor, Maine, ca. 1959–1966

[Vose Galleries, Boston, 1966–1967]

John D. Rockefeller 3rd and Blanchette Hooker Rockefeller, New York, 1967–1979

FAMSF, 1979.7.1

Exhibition History
Boston, Harding's Gallery, *Exhibition of Pictures Painted by Washington Allston*, 1839, exh. no. 42

Boston, Museum of Fine Arts, temporary loan, 1915–1916

Boston, Museum of Fine Arts, extended loan, 1917–1959

San Francisco 1976, exh. no. 22

FAMSF, *Viewpoints I: Good, Better, Best*, 1987, not in publ.

Selected References
Edgar Preston Richardson, *Washington Allston: A Study of the Romantic Artist in America* (Chicago: University of Chicago Press, 1948), p. 90, cat. no. 66

William H. Gerdts and Theodore E. Stebbins, Jr., *"A Man of Genius": The Art of Washington Allston, 1779–1843*, exh. cat. (Boston: Museum of Fine Arts, 1979), pp. 57–58

Related Works
Other portraits by Allston of the Channing family:

Francis Dana Channing [Mrs. Channing's son], 1808–1809

Oil on canvas, 30½ x 27½ in. Private collection

William Ellery Channing [Mrs. Channing's son], 1809–1811
Oil on canvas, 31 x 27½ in. Museum of Fine Arts, Boston

Ann Channing Allston [Mrs. Channing's daughter and wife of the artist], 1809–1811
Oil on canvas, 17½ x 15¾ in. Private collection

The Valentine (Ann Channing Allston), 1809–1811
Oil on canvas, 25½ x 22 in. Private collection

26 THE NARROWS, NEW YORK BAY, 1812

Oil on wood panel, 19⅞ x 26¾ in.
Signed and dated lower right: *T Birch 1812*

THOMAS BIRCH
b. Warwickshire, England 1779
d. Philadelphia, Pa. 1851

Thos. Birch.
    This artist is the son of William Birch, the enamel painter . . . , and was brought to this country in 1794, when he was seven [*sic*—ca. fifteen] years of age. Like many others of our subjects, he is English by birth, but an American artist. He could from infancy (to use his own expression) "sketch a little." He of course had his father for an instructor: but, as he advanced in life and art, he preferred the instruction of nature, and studied on the banks of the Schuylkill, his father's place of residence being Philadelphia.

William Dunlap, *A History of the Rise and Progress of the Arts of Design in the United States*, 3 vols. (1834; Boston: C. D. Goodspeed & Co., 1918), 3:25–26

About a year later [1807], he accompanied several pilots to the Capes of Delaware, and the visions of his voyage across the Atlantic were so revived and enlarged by the scenes of this visitation, as to establish within him that love of marine pictures which so distinguished him throughout life.

On his return from the Capes, he painted his first marine sketch in oil. . . .

This may be regarded as the commencement of his career of renown as an artist; but he was obliged, for several years, to devote much of his time to inferior sketches, for the embellishment of old-fashioned looking-glasses, and the like—mainly because pictures on canvas were illy paid for, and in comparatively small demand. Nevertheless, there were some thoughtful patrons of art in that day, who recognized the merit of Mr. Birch, and many fine landscapes, painted more than forty years ago, were prophetic of his future eminence. . . .

In *a critique* written by one more competent to judge in such matters than myself, it is declared that "the principal merits of Mr. Birch consist, as well in the certainty and delicacy of his touch as in his remarkable fidelity to nature. As a painter of storm scenes he has never been equalled either in this country or Europe. His skies and water are also among the most truthful representations ever exhibited, and indeed may be regarded as inimitable, surpass-

ing, we think, the very best productions of the modern English school. His river pieces, and inland landscapes, present the same adherence to facts. Mr. Birch, unlike the majority of the present day artists, is, however, by no means an imitator. All his finer pieces are original compositions, and many of them display a creative genius second to none in the land.

"Living almost all his early life in the country, nature became a second mother to Birch, teaching him those principles which assist so materially in moulding the artist. Besides, no one ever labored harder in his profession. He was the earliest of American Marine painters. He gave that department of art the impetus which has since made it what it is. He also did much to encourage the young artists who were daily springing up around him."

> The Reverend Abel C. Thomas, "Obituary of Artists: Sketch of Thomas Birch," *Philadelphia Art Union Reporter* 1, no. 1 (January 1851): 22–23

————

Re: Narrows, New York Bay 1812 by Thomas Birch

I spoke to a local historian about the same and he feels it could likely be the correct title. The view is looking out to the ocean. Manhattan Island would be to far right and is not visible in this scene. The land in foreground and on the left is Brooklyn, the land on the right with signal pole to the left of the ship is Staten Island.

> Barnett Shepherd, Executive Director, Richmondtown Restoration, Staten Island Historical Society, 18 August 1989, FAMSF departmental files

Provenance
Descended in Bacon family, Philadelphia, from at least the 1850s to Francis Bacon, Philadelphia, to 1973

[Carlen Galleries, Philadelphia, 1973]

John D. Rockefeller 3rd and Blanchette Hooker Rockefeller, New York, 1973–1979

FAMSF, 1979.7.17

Exhibition History
San Francisco 1976, exh. no. 24

Selected Reference
The American Canvas, pp. 60–61, 234

Oil on wood panel, 7¼ x 10¼ in.

RAPHAELLE PEALE

b. Annapolis, Md. 1774
d. Philadelphia, Pa. 1825

Mr. R[embrandt] P[eale] says, "all these children [of Charles Willson Peale] but two were named after painters, though only two of the number adopted the profession. Raphael was a painter of portraits in oil and miniature, but excelled more in compositions of still life. He may perhaps be considered the first in point of time who adopted this branch of painting in America, and many of his pictures are in the collections of men of taste and highly esteemed." He died early in life, perhaps at the age of forty, after severe affliction from gout.

William Dunlap, *A History of the Rise and Progress of the Arts of Design in the United States,* 3 vols. (1834; Boston: C. E. Goodspeed & Co., 1918), 2:181

Dr Sir

My old and inveterate enemy, the Gout, has Commenced a most violent attack on me, two months previous to its regular time—and most unfortunately on the day that I was to Commence still life, in the most beautifull productions of Fruit, I therefore fear that the Season will pass without producing a single Picture. . . . [I]f the disease was only confined to my feet I still would have some hope of doing something, But unfortunately my left hand is in a most dreadfull situation, & my Right Getting so bad as to be scarcely able to hold my Pen—

Peale to Charles Graff, 6 September 1816, Misc. MSS., AAA, roll D9, frames 833–836

One of the most delightful [paintings in the Rockefeller Collection] is also the simplest. Raphaelle Peale's little painting of a few lush blackberries, each daringly isolated in space and picked out by light, is enough to rekindle a belief in the reality of matter. Why paint the

exact image of a handful of berries? In some ways to imitate is to possess, to make one's own. But the artist is not covetous of the berries. He could have eaten them if he wished. It is the sharp clean vision of the rich bright fruit, fresh and dazzling in the clear light and contrasting shade, that he wanted to possess. And he did, allowing us to possess it too.

Joshua Taylor, "A Personal and Distinctive Collection of American Art Makes Its Debut," *Smithsonian Magazine*, April 1976, pp. 41–42

Provenance
Charles Graff (d. 1856), Philadelphia, by 1856

[Auction sale, M. Thomas and Sons, Philadelphia, 17 October 1856, lot no. 80 (as *Still Life*, 10 x 6¾ in., "a branch of red and black blackberries, lying across a saucer")]

Paul Magriel (1906–1990), New York, by 1954–1962

[Kennedy Galleries, New York, 1962]

Lawrence A. Fleischman (b. 1925) and Barbara Greenberg Fleischman (b. 1924), Detroit, by 1964–1966

[Kennedy Galleries, New York, 1966]

John D. Rockefeller 3rd and Blanchette Hooker Rockefeller, New York, 1966–1993

FAMSF, 1993.35.23

Exhibition History
Philadelphia, Pennsylvania Academy of the Fine Arts, *Fourth Annual Exhibition of the Society of Artists and the Pennsylvania Academy*, 1814, exh. no. 92

Philadelphia, Pennsylvania Academy of the Fine Arts, *Sixth Annual Exhibition of the Pennsylvania Academy of the Fine Arts*, 1817, exh. no. 100

Cincinnati Art Museum, *Paintings by the Peale Family*, 1954, exh. no. 60 (as *Dish of Blackberries*)

Washington, D.C., The Corcoran Gallery of Art, *American Still Life Paintings from the Paul Magriel Collection*, 1957, exh. no. 27 (as *Dish of Blackberries*)

New York, The Downtown Gallery, *Art Our Children Live With*, 1957, exh. no. 29

Santa Barbara, Calif., Santa Barbara Museum of Art, *Fruits and Flowers in Painting*, 1958, exh.

no. 47 (as *A Dish of Blackberries*, 1815)

Milwaukee Art Center, *Raphaelle Peale*, 1959, exh. no. 8 (as *Dish of Blackberries*, 1815)

New York, Kennedy Galleries, *The Fabulous Peale Family*, 1960, exh. no. 73 (as *Dish of Blackberries*, ca. 1815)

The Baltimore Museum of Art, *Fruit and Flowers*, 1961, exh. no. 27 (as *Dish of Blackberries*, 1815)

Tucson, University of Arizona Art Gallery, *American Painting, 1765–1963: Selections from the Lawrence A. and Barbara Fleischman Collection of American Art*, 1964, exh. no. 77

Philadelphia, Pennsylvania Academy of the Fine Arts, *Small Paintings of Large Import from the Collection of Lawrence A. and Barbara Fleischman of Detroit, Michigan*, 1964, exh. no. 36

New York World's Fair, The Gallery at the Better Living Center, *Four Centuries of American Masterpieces: An Exhibition Arranged by the Skowhegan School of Painting and Sculpture*, 1964, exh. no. 21

New York, The Metropolitan Museum of Art, *Nineteenth-Century America: Paintings and Sculpture*, 1970, exh. no. 22 (as *Dish of Blackberries*, ca. 1815–1817)

San Francisco 1976, exh. no. 27

Tokyo 1982, exh. no. 18 (as *Dish of Blackberries*, ca. 1813)

FAMSF, *Director's Choice: Twenty Years of Collecting*, 1987, no publ.

Washington, D.C., National Gallery of Art, *Raphaelle Peale Still Lifes*, 1988, exh. no. 44

Selected Reference
Nicolai Cikovsky, Jr., "The Still Lifes of Raphaelle Peale," *The Magazine Antiques* 134, no. 5 (November 1988): 1121, 1128

---

28 DR. JOHN KING, 1814

Oil on canvas, 44⅜ x 33⅞ in.
Signed and dated on reverse (visible before lining): *W. Allston. 1814*

WASHINGTON ALLSTON

b. Georgetown County, S.C. 1779
d. Cambridgeport, Mass. 1843

The first labor in which Mr. Allston engaged on his return to England [in 1811], was his great picture of the "Dead man revived by touching Elisha's bones" [Pennsylvania Academy of the Fine Arts, Philadelphia]. He says to his correspondent, ". . . My progress in this picture was interrupted by a dangerous illness, which after some months of great suffering, compelled me to remove to Clifton, near Bristol. My recovery, for which I was indebted under Providence, to one of the best friends, and most skilful of the faculty, was slow and painful, leaving me still an invalid when I returned to London—and indeed as my medical friend predicted, in some degree so to this day. . . . I went back to Bristol where I painted and left a number of pictures; among these were half-length portraits of my friend Mr. [the poet Samuel Taylor] Coleridge, and my medical friend Mr. King, of Clifton. I have painted but few portraits, and these I think are my best."

William Dunlap, *A History of the Rise and Progress of the Arts of Design in the United States*, 3 vols. (1834; Boston: C. E. Goodspeed & Co., 1918), 2:315–316

95

John King, 1766–1846, is the most impressive and sympathetic figure amongst the so-called amateurs behind the Bristol School. And he was really no amateur at all for he had been, before his arrival in Bristol, a professional artist in London. His wide interests in science and literature brought him into contact with all the major names that can be associated with Bristol around the turn of the century. . . .

John King was born Johann Koenig in Berne of an old and important family. He reacted against his family's idea of a career in the church and turned to physics and the arts. He took up copper plate engraving and moved to Geneva in 1789. After two years he went to Paris and from there to London where he probably arrived in 1791 or 1792. . . .

John King had arrived in Bristol by 1799 when he already knew Dr. Beddoes. Several years he worked with Beddoes and Humphrey Davy at the Pneumatic Institute in Dowry Square before settling at 26 The Mall, Clifton as a surgeon. He married Emmeline Edgeworth, Dr. Beddoes' sister-in-law and Maria Edgeworth's sister.

He was a friend of Coleridge and a very close friend of Southey and Davey. Walter Savage Landor was to write the epitaph on his grave. . . .

In his own profession he was extraordinarily zealous, generous and able. But his religious scepticism, his liberal political views and his refusal to take part in the electoral systems then necessary for advancement in medicine meant that he remained relatively poor. But he did acquire an exceptional library of some three thousand volumes that reflected his wide knowledge in literature, medicine and science, languages and art.

> Francis Greenacre, *The Bristol School of Artists: Francis Danby and Painting in Bristol, 1810–1840*, exh. cat. (Bristol: City Art Gallery, 1973), pp. 183–185

[*Dr. John King* was probably one of two portraits exhibited at the artist's exhibition in Merchant Tailor Hall, Bristol, England, in 1814.]

The Allston exhibition, consisting of eight paintings, opened on July 25. Although not a large exhibition, it represented something of a landmark. It was one of the earliest one-man shows held in England of the work of a living artist. . . . What was especially unusual was Allston's exhibiting in a provincial center. . . . This was also one of the earliest one-man shows of a living American artist.

> William H. Gerdts, "The Paintings of Washington Allston," in *"A Man of Genius": The Art of Washington Allston, 1779–1843*, exh. cat. (Boston: Museum of Fine Arts, 1979), p. 82

Provenance
Dr. John King (1766–1846) and Emmeline Edgeworth King, Clifton, England, 1814–1846

Descended in family to ca. 1973

[Hirschl & Adler Galleries, New York, 1975]

John D. Rockefeller 3rd and Blanchette Hooker Rockefeller, New York, 1975–1979

FAMSF, 1979.7.2

Exhibition History
Probably Bristol, England, Merchant Tailor Hall, 1814

Boston, Museum of Fine Arts, *"A Man of Genius": The Art of Washington Allston, 1779–1843*, 1979, exh. no. 33

Birmingham, Ala., Birmingham Museum of Art, *The Art of Healing: Medicine and Science in American Art*, 1981, no exh. no.

Tokyo 1982, exh. no. 16

Selected References
Jared B. Flagg, *The Life and Letters of Washington Allston* (New York: Charles Scribner's Sons, 1892), pp. 104, 108

The American Canvas, pp. 58–59, 234

---

29 THE REVEREND WILLIAM ELLERY CHANNING, CA. 1815

Oil on canvas, 30 x 25 in.

GILBERT STUART
b. North Kingstown, R.I. 1755
d. Boston, Mass. 1828

I sat to Stuart before and after breakfast and found his conversation very interesting. His own figure is highly picturesque, with his dress always disordered, and taking snuff from a large round tin wafer box, holding perhaps half a pound, which he must use up in a day. He considers himself beyond all question the first portrait painter of the age, and tells numbers of anecdotes concerning himself to prove it, with the utmost simplicity and unconsciousness of ridicule. His conclusion is not very wide of the truth.

> John Quincy Adams, diary entry for 19 September 1818, quoted in William T. Whitley, *Gilbert Stuart* (Cambridge, Mass.: Harvard University Press, 1932), p. 157

Never be sparing of colour, load your pictures, but keep your colours as seperate as you can. No blending, tis destruction to clear & bea[u]tiful effect. it takes of the transparency & liquidity of colouring & renders the flesh of the consistency of buckskin.

> "Notes Taken by M. H. Jouett while in Boston from Conve[r]sations on Painting with Gilbert Stuart Esqr," quoted in John Hill Morgan, *Gilbert Stuart and His Pupils* (New York: The New-York Historical Society, 1939), pp. 82–83

Channing, William Ellery (Apr. 7, 1780–Oct. 2, 1842), Unitarian clergyman, was born in Newport, R.I. His ancestors on both sides were of the best New England stock. . . . Contemporary accounts describe him as a serious, over-thoughtful youth, inclined to self-

inspection but acutely sensitive to the conditions of life about him. After graduation from college [Harvard] in 1798 he accepted a position as tutor in the family of David Meade Randolph in Richmond, Va., and spent a year and a half there. Up to this time he had been in good health, fond of exercise, and a cheerful if rather serious companion. During this Southern residence among people of alien sympathies he acquired habits of overwork and ascetic discipline which undermined his health. Returning to Newport he applied himself with characteristic fervor to the study of theology. In 1802 he was called to Cambridge as "Regent" of Harvard College, a kind of proctorial office which left him abundant leisure for his chosen studies. In 1814 at the age of thirty-four he married his cousin Ruth Gibbs. On June 1, 1803, he was ordained and installed as minister of the Federal Street Church in Boston, and continued in this pastorate until his death in 1842. Channing's semi-invalidism accounts in a large measure for the social aloofness which was one of his great limitations. . . .

On the pedestal of the statue of Channing in the Public Garden of Boston is the inscription, "He breathed into theology a humane spirit." This expresses his real contribution to theology. He had no novelties of doctrine to propose. He was no innovator. . . . It is one of the ironies of history that he should have had an important part in some of the bitterest religious and political controversies of his time. A man whose temper was altogether catholic was forced by circumstances to appear as the standard bearer of a new sect. . . .

Those who heard Channing preach testify to the arresting quality of his voice and the charm of his manner. His style was unadorned by illustration. . . .

The influence of Channing on American literature was very direct. The term "Channing Unitarians," while not precise when applied to a theological party, was very apt when applied to the group of New England writers who flourished in the middle of the nineteenth century. Emerson, Bryant, Longfellow, Lowell, Holmes were all closely associated with the Unitarian movement, and acknowledged their indebtedness to Channing. If "he breathed into theology a humane spirit" it may with equal truth be said that he breathed into literature a religious spirit. . . .

Unlike the members of the society in which he lived, Channing was conscious of the tremendous revolutionary forces which were at work. . . . Slavery, he insisted, is an unspeakable evil. But so also is war and of all wars the most dreadful to contemplate is a civil war. . . . In his discussions of slavery he addressed himself to the conscience of the South rather than to the New England conscience. He was attacked from both sides, but his addresses did much to prepare people to understand and follow Abraham Lincoln.

S[amuel] M. C[rothers], "William Ellery Channing," *Dictionary of American Biography*, rev. ed., vol. 2, pt. 2, pp. 4–7

Provenance
The Reverend William Ellery Channing (1780–1842) and Ruth Gibbs Channing (d. ca. 1858), Boston, ca. 1815–ca. 1858

Descended in family to Henry Channing Rivers, Northeast Harbor, Maine, ca. 1959–1967

[Vose Galleries, Boston, 1967]

John D. Rockefeller 3rd and Blanchette Hooker Rockefeller, New York, 1967–1979

FAMSF, 1979.7.95

Exhibition History
Boston Athenaeum, *An Exhibition of Portraits, Painted by the Late Gilbert Stuart, Esq.*, 1828, exh. no. 209 (as *Rev. Dr. W. Channing*; although crossed out in catalogue by a contemporary hand in copy at Museum of Fine Arts, Boston)

Boston, Museum of Fine Arts, *Exhibition of Portraits Painted by Gilbert Stuart*, 1880, exh. no. 294

Boston, Museum of Fine Arts, temporary loan, 1914–1915

Boston, Museum of Fine Arts, extended loan, 1917–1959

Boston, Museum of Fine Arts, *Gilbert Stuart Memorial Exhibition*, 1928, exh. no. 14

Cambridge, Mass., Robinson Hall, School of Architecture, Harvard University, *Harvard Tercentenary Exhibition*, 1936, exh. no. 8

San Francisco 1976, exh. no. 20

Tokyo 1982, exh. no. 15

Selected References
Charles Henry Hart, "The Stuart Exhibition at the Museum of Fine Arts Boston," *The American Art Review* 1, no. 11 (September 1880): 486–487

George C. Mason, *The Life and Works of Gilbert Stuart* (New York: Charles Scribner's Sons, 1894), p. 157

Lawrence Park, *Gilbert Stuart: An Illustrated Descriptive List of His Works*, 4 vols. (New York: William Edwin Rudge, 1926), vol. 1, cat. no. 147

Related Work
Unknown (American)
After *The Reverend William Ellery Channing*
Mrs. Henry W. Bellows, Boston, as of 1915

---

30 SELF-PORTRAIT, 1822

Oil on canvas, 29¼ x 24⅛ in.

CHARLES WILLSON PEALE

b. Queen Anne's County, Md. 1741
d. Philadelphia, Pa. 1827

Peale was a man of liberal sympathies and public spirit; he not only was an efficient military officer, but served his State worthily in the legislature. He had the prescience rightly to estimate the historical value of native portraiture in the crisis of his country's destiny, and carefully gathered the materials which have since proved so valuable in illustrating the incidents and characters of our brief annals. Although widely dispersed, the best portraits of Peale are cherished memorials. . . .

For a considerable time antecedent and subsequent to the Revolutionary War, Peale was almost the only portrait painter in America known to fame. . . . His conscientious and intelligent labors in the cause of Art merit the grateful remembrance he enjoys. "His likenesses,"

says his son Rembrandt, who has written his life, "were strong, but never flattered; his execution spirited and natural. The last years of his life he luxuriated in the enjoyment of a country life, near Germantown, with hanging gardens, grotto and fountain, and a hospitable table for all his friends. His last painting was a full length portrait of himself, painted at the age of eighty-three. He died in his eighty-fifth year, in 1826."

Henry T. Tuckerman, *Book of the Artists: American Artist Life* (1867; New York: James F. Carr, 1966), pp. 52–53

———

Peale painted this self-portrait in 1822 as a gift to his daughter Sophonisba, Mrs. Coleman Sellers; it was exhibited at the Pennsylvania Academy of the Fine Arts in that year. A note in the catalogue said, "Painted in the 81st year of his age without spectacles." It remained in the family until given in 1972 to the Museum of Northern Arizona, Flagstaff, to be sold for the benefit of its endowment. Peale, who struggled for half his life to establish his own museum on a sound financial basis, would have sympathized. . . .

This portrait of the old artist-scientist has a sober power worthy of a Dutch seventeenth-century painter. Intelligence, searching powers of observation, and firm will are the traits that emerge most strongly; but Peale was also a creature of affection, sensibility and idealism. He was one of the remarkable men of his time.

E. P. Richardson, *American Art: An Exhibition from the Collection of Mr. and Mrs. John D. Rockefeller 3rd*, exh. cat. (San Francisco: The Fine Arts Museums of San Francisco, 1976), p. 46

Provenance
The artist's daughter, Sophonisba Angusciola Peale (Mrs. Coleman) Sellers (1786–1859), Philadelphia, 1822–1859

Descended in family to Harold Sellers Colton (1881–1970), Flagstaff, Ariz., by 1952–1970

Museum of Northern Arizona, Flagstaff, 1970–1972

[Kennedy Galleries, New York, 1972]

John D. Rockefeller 3rd and Blanchette Hooker Rockefeller, New York, 1972–1993

FAMSF, 1993.35.22

Exhibition History
Philadelphia, Pennsylvania Academy of the Fine Arts, *Eleventh Annual Exhibition of the Pennsylvania Academy of the Fine Arts*, 1822, exh. no. 300 or 343 (two related portraits were exhibited, both described as depicting the artist "in the 81st year of his age without spectacles, 1822")

Philadelphia, Pennsylvania Academy of the Fine Arts, *Exhibition of Portraits by Charles Willson Peale and James Peale and Rembrandt Peale*, 1923, exh. no. 94 (erroneously dated 1808)

New York, Kennedy Galleries, *American Masters, Eighteenth and Nineteenth Centuries*, 1972, exh. no. 9

San Francisco 1976, exh. no. 14

Washington, D.C., National Portrait Gallery, *Charles Willson Peale and His World*, 1982, exh. no. 73

Selected References
"The Peale Exhibition/The Pennsylvania Academy of the Fine Arts," *The American Magazine of Art* 14, no. 6 (June 1923): 309

Charles Coleman Sellers, *Portraits and Miniatures by Charles Willson Peale*, Transactions of the American Philosophical Society, vol. 42, pt. 1 (Philadelphia: American Philosophical Society, 1952), cat. no. 633 (dated 1821)

David C. Ward, "Celebration of Self: The Portraiture of Charles Willson Peale and Rembrandt Peale, 1822–1827," *American Art* 7, no. 1 (Winter 1993): 12

Related Work
Self-Portrait, 1822
Oil on canvas, 29 x 23¾ in.
Lester Hoadly Sellers, Radnor, Pa., as of 1952

---

31 CHARLES CARROLL OF CARROLLTON, 1826

Oil on canvas, 19 x 15 in.

THOMAS SULLY
b. Horncastle, Lincolnshire, England 1783
d. Philadelphia, Pa. 1872

Many are the vicissitudes which a portrait painter has to undergo even after he has attained eminence. How necessary is it for him to catch and hold fast a portion of the product of the flood tide, that when the ebb comes he may not be left stranded and destitute like a shipwrecked mariner. Perhaps no painter of Mr. Sully's acknowledged merit has experienced the fluctuations of fashion, or the caprices of the public, in so great a degree. At one time overwhelmed with applications for portraits, at another literally deserted, not because he deteriorated, as some have done, for all acknowledge progressive improvement to the present hour. . . .

Mr. Sully is, as we believe and sincerely hope, anchored safely in port for life. He has portraits engaged in succession for years to come at liberal prices. His fellow citizens of Philadelphia justly appreciate him as an artist and a man. The late wealthy, eccentric, benevolent, and munificent Stephen Girard caused to be built in addition to one of his houses, purposely for the artist, an exhibition and painting room, and in that house he resides surrounded by his numerous family, and by all those conveniences which are so dear and necessary to a painter.

With a frame apparently slight, but in reality strong, muscular, athletic, and uncommonly active, Mr. Sully does not stand over five feet eight inches in height [his passport of 3 October 1837 records Sully's height as 5'6"], but he walks with the stride of a man of six feet. His complexion is pale, hair brown, eyes grey, approaching to blue, and ornamented with uncommonly long eyelashes, and his whole physiognomy marked with the wish to make others happy.

William Dunlap, *A History of the Rise and Progress of the Arts of Design in the United States*, 3 vols. (1834; Boston: C. E. Goodspeed & Co., 1918), 2:275–276

[Charles Carroll of Carrollton] had the distinction of being, among many other things, the last-surviving Signer of the Declaration of Independence, a Maryland state senator from 1777 to 1800, and one of Maryland's first two representatives in the United States Senate from 1789 to 1792. In private enterprise he was one of the organizing members of the Chesapeake and Ohio Canal Company in 1823, on the first board of directors of the Baltimore and Ohio Railroad, and a charter director of the first Bank of the United States. At the time of the Revolution he had one of the largest private fortunes in America—according to some calculations the largest—and during his lifetime his land holdings totaled more than forty thousand acres in Maryland, including a good percentage of the lots in Annapolis and Baltimore, as well as several thousand acres in Pennsylvania and New York.

Ann Van Devanter, "Charles Carroll of Carrollton," *The Magazine Antiques* 108, no. 4 (October 1975): 736

———

May 20 [1826] Left Phila. for Baltimore at 12 o'clock by steamboat. . . . Reached the steamboat at 7 and at 2 o'clock on Saturday morning touched the wharf at Baltimore—At breakfast repaired to Robinson's—delivered sundry letters and called on Chas. Carroll of Carrolton and arranged to begin his portrait next Monday.

Monday.—Begun Mr. Carroll's portrait

Tuesday.—Made sketches of his person for a whole length. . . .

Wednesday.—Advanced the study of Mr. Carroll's portrait, etc.

Thursday.—Finished it—dined with them and after dinner, packed up and removed my apparatus to Robinson's . . .

27 Saturday.—Called on Chas. Carroll, Jr., Waterloo Row, and left with him a memorandum of my price for different size pictures.

Sully, "Journal," Thomas Sully Papers, AAA, roll N18, frames 296–297

_____

292 Carroll, Charles (1737–1830).

Of Carrollton. American patriot and signer of the Declaration of Independence. Painted as a study for the whole length for the Marquis of Wellesley [husband of Carroll's granddaughter], begun May 22nd, 1826, finished May 25th, 1826. Bust.

Price, $40.00

Sully, "List of Paintings," in Edward Biddle and Mantle Fielding, *The Life and Works of Thomas Sully* (1921; New York: Da Capo Press, for Kennedy Graphics, 1970), p. 117

Provenance
The artist, Philadelphia, to at least 1836 (on basis of copy by his daughter Ellen of that year)

Thomas B. Carroll (1817–1894), Troy and Saratoga Lake, N.Y.

Descended in family

[M. Knoedler & Co., New York, 1965]

John D. Rockefeller 3rd and Blanchette Hooker Rockefeller,

New York, 1965–1979

FAMSF, 1979.7.94

Exhibition History
The Baltimore Museum of Art, *Anywhere So Long as There Be Freedom: Charles Carroll of Carrollton, His Family and His Maryland*, 1975, exh. no. 32

San Francisco 1976, exh. no. 28

Selected Reference
Edward Biddle and Mantle Field-

ing, *The Life and Works of Thomas Sully* (1921; New York: Da Capo Press, for Kennedy Graphics, 1970), cat. no. 292

Related Works
Charles Carroll of Carrollton, 1827
Oil on canvas, 81⅛ x 51¼ in.
The Thomas Gilcrease Institute of American History and Art, Tulsa, Okla.

Charles Carroll of Carrollton, 1827
Oil on canvas, 30 x 25 in.
Mr. and Mrs. Henderson Supplee, Jr., as of 1972

Ellen Sully (American, 1816–1896)
After *Charles Carroll of Carrollton*, 1836
Oil on academy board, 24 x 20 in.
The Historical Society of Pennsylvania, Philadelphia

_____

32 VIEW NEAR THE VILLAGE OF CATSKILL, 1827

Oil on wood panel, 24½ x 35 in.
Signed and dated lower left: *T. Cole/1827*

THOMAS COLE

b. Bolton-le-Moor, Lancashire, England 1801
d. Catskill, N.Y. 1848

Thomas Cole, the son of a woollen manufacturer of Lancashire, was born at Bolton le Moor, England, on the first of February, 1801. Deriving through his imaginative tendency a vivid and somewhat romantic idea of America, he was glad to accompany his father's large family thither in 1819. Steubenville, Ohio, was the place chosen for their residence. The scenery of that picturesque State developed his native love of beauty; but his early years were marked by more than the usual vicissitude and privation attending the pursuit, not only of knowledge but of subsistence, in a new country by a youth of great sensibility and high aspirations. . . . Obliged to take likenesses for support, his sympathies were all with landscape art; his first attempts were crude, but his observation and love of nature were instinctive and habitual; and at length in Philadelphia he met with recognition and encouragement. The impression Cole made on the public was novel and auspicious. To him may be directly traced the primal success of landscape painting as a national art in the New World.

Henry T. Tuckerman, *Book of the Artists: American Artist Life* (1867; New York: James F. Carr, 1966), pp. 224–225

_____

As mountains are the most conspicuous objects in landscape, they will take the precedence in what I may say on the elements of American scenery.

It is true that in the eastern part of this continent there are no mountains that vie in altitude with the snow-crowned Alps—that the Alleghanies and the Catskills are in no point higher than five thousand feet. . . . [T]he Catskills, although not broken into abrupt angles like the most picturesque mountains of Italy, have varied, undulating, and exceedingly beautiful outlines—they heave from the valley of the Hudson like the subsiding billows of the ocean after a storm. . . .

I will now speak of another component of scenery, without which every landscape is defective—it is water. Like the eye in the human countenance, it is a most expressive feature. . . .

. . . The Hudson for natural magnificence is unsurpassed. . . . [W]here can be found scenes more enchanting? The lofty Catskills stand afar off—the green hills gently rising from the flood, recede like steps by which we may ascend to a great temple, whose pillars are those everlasting hills, and whose dome is the blue boundless vault of heaven. . . .

. . . But American associations are not so much of the past as of the present and the future. Seated on a pleasant knoll, look down into the bosom of that secluded valley, begirt with wooded hills—through those enamelled meadows and wide waving fields of grain, a silver stream winds lingeringly along—here, seeking the green shade of trees—there, glancing in the sunshine: on its banks are rural dwellings shaded by elms and garlanded by flowers—from yonder dark mass of foliage the village spire beams like a star. You see no ruined tower to tell of outrage—no gorgeous temple to speak of ostentation; but freedom's offspring—peace, security, and happiness, dwell there, the spirits of the scene. . . . [T]hose neat dwellings, unpretending to magnificence, are the abodes of plenty, virtue, and refinement.

Thomas Cole, "Essay on American Scenery," *The American Monthly Magazine* 7 (January 1836): 5, 6, 8, 11–12

In the summer of 1827, Cole took a studio in Catskill, in sight of his beloved mountain. He was like a lover who could not stay away from the beloved. Daily he went forth to gaze on their beautiful brows, and to kneel at their feet. Daily he walked in their midst, and in their sacred presence held counsel with nature and God.

E. Anna Lewis, "Art and Artists of America: Thomas Cole, N.A.," *Graham's Magazine* 46, no. 4 (April 1855): 334

Cole first sketched this scene [speaking of *View near the Village of Catskill*] in the late summer of 1825 and continued to make new drawings and paintings from near this spot well into the 1840s. The prominent mountains are Kaaterskill High Peak and Round Top, while the famous Mountain House is seen against the slope of South Mountain at the upper right.

Howard S. Merritt, *Thomas Cole*, exh. cat. (Rochester, N.Y.: Memorial Art Gallery of the University of Rochester, 1969), p. 23

Rockefeller is aware that paintings do not often reveal their full content at once. In his private office hangs an early painting by Thomas Cole, *View Near Catskill Village*, a quiet painting that somehow mingles Claude Lorrain and the American landscape. At first he was not especially taken with the painting, he admits, but now it has a place of honor, satisfying by the subtlety with which it presents its half-concealed beauties.

Joshua Taylor, "A Personal and Distinctive Collection of American Art Makes Its Debut," *Smithsonian Magazine*, April 1976, p. 46

Provenance
Lawrence A. Fleischman (b. 1925) and Barbara Greenberg Fleischman (b. 1924), Detroit, by 1962–1965

[Kennedy Galleries, New York, 1965–1966]

John D. Rockefeller 3rd and Blanchette Hooker Rockefeller, New York, 1966–1993

FAMSF, 1993.35.7

Exhibition History
New York, National Academy of Design, *Second Annual Exhibition*, 1827, exh. no. 35

The Detroit Institute of Arts, *American Paintings and Drawings from Michigan Collections*, 1962, exh. no. 29

Tucson, University of Arizona Art Gallery, *American Painting, 1765–1963: Selections from the Lawrence A. and Barbara Fleischman Collection of American Art*, 1964, exh. no. 18

Rochester, N.Y., Memorial Art Gallery of the University of Rochester, *Thomas Cole*, 1969, exh. no. 10

San Francisco 1976, exh. no. 34

Poughkeepsie, N.Y., Vassar College Art Gallery, *The Hudson River School: The Vassar College Collection and Loans*, 1979, no publ.

Tokyo 1982, exh. no. 19

Selected Reference
Ellwood C. Parry III, *The Art of Thomas Cole: Ambition and Imagination* (Newark: University of Delaware Press, 1988), pp. 40, 51, 381 n. 51

Related Works
In the Catskills, 1837
Oil on canvas, 39 x 63 in.
The Metropolitan Museum of Art, New York

River in the Catskills, 1843
Oil on canvas, 28¼ x 41¼ in.
Museum of Fine Arts, Boston

Catskill Creek, New York, 1845
Oil on canvas, 26½ x 36 in.
The New-York Historical Society, New York

Oil on canvas, 20¼ x 16 in.
Signed and dated lower right: *J.N. 1834*

JOHN NEAGLE
b. Boston, Mass. 1796
d. Philadelphia, Pa. 1865

John Neagle, the son-in-law of [Thomas] Sully, was born in Boston, while his parents, who were Philadelphians, were on a visit to that city. . . . He had a quarter's instruction in drawing from Pietro Amora [*sic*—Pietro Ancora, act. ca. 1800–1843]; and probably from his enjoyment of vivid colors, like several embryo painters mentioned in this work, when obliged to become a tradesman's apprentice, selected coach-painting as an employment. His master studied with a limner [Bass Otis], with a view to the ornamental part of his business, and young Neagle was frequently employed to carry palette, colors, and brushes, from factory to atelier; in this way, he soon grew familiar with the processes and materials of Art, and encouraged by Wilson, Peale [Charles Willson Peale] and Sully, in 1818, began practice in Philadelphia. Thence he went to Lexington, Ky., and experienced much privation and discouragement, until the fortunate accidental sitter appeared; and his fame, after a successful sojourn at New Orleans, grew rapidly, until we find him married [he married Mary Chester Sully in 1826], and busy in his old home, in 1820. Six years after, the full-length, stalwart and vigorous figure of Patrick Lyon, the blacksmith, at his forge, gained him wide reputation. . . . Neagle was a great admirer of Stuart, and some of his portraits have a strength and vividness akin to that master. . . . Some years before his death he became paralyzed. . . . In his prime he was a remarkably genial companion, and devoted to active life. For eight years he was president of the Artists' Fund Society of Philadelphia.

Henry T. Tuckerman, *Book of the Artists: American Artist Life* (1867; New York: James F. Carr, 1966), pp. 65–66

Mr. Neagle was ever kind and considerate to young artists. He answered their questions frankly, and gave them advice freely when they sought it. His candor amounted nearly to a fault, but none who knew him took offence at it. If pressed to give an opinion, he kindly but unreservedly pronounced it, however sorely it might grate upon the ear. But he had the rare merit of telling a young artist how he might improve his pictures. No man could talk more simply and plainly upon art. He could always give a satisfactory reason for everything he did. . . .

None but a man of good common sense, said Neagle, ever becomes a good painter. The reason is obvious: every picture is an argument, and if it is well stated on canvas, it carries conviction with it. Every good picture is a compromise, in which secondary objects are sacrificed to the leading points. . . .

In his prime he was about five feet eight inches in height. He was erect in his carriage, courteous in manners, always smartly dressed, prepossessing in appearance, and a strict observer of the etiquette of life. He had a swarthy complexion, keen black eyes, black straight hair, and a somewhat Indian-like expression of face. His conversation was intelligent and interesting. With literature, science and music he was well acquainted, and on all subjects connected with his art he had a large store of information and anecdote. His individuality was remarkable. I knew of no man who resembled him.

Thomas Fitzgerald, "John Neagle, the Artist," *Lippincott's Magazine* 1 (May 1868): 489–490, 491

It is at all times & under any circumstances, an unpleasant task to paint from the dead human Subject, but I have taken a violent cold by working in a cold room upon the post mortem portrait of Mr. Hildeburn's Son. This boy was about 10 years old; had been only two months before, sent to be educated in Massachusetts. He there died Suddenly, perhaps from want of good nursing; was buried, and in eleven days was brought on here and reinterred in Philadᵃ. I wished merely to take a mask in plaster and make a few memorandums for my recollection

but Mr. H insisted I sh^d *paint*. So I stood the coffin on the foot & at night by Candles on a stick to slide as the height was required I painted many hours that night—took a cast of the face in plaster— & next morning early resumed my labours at the easel for so great a length of time that I now feel the effects of my long exposure, without exercise, in the cold. I have been disabled from painting since 30th Jany. but have employed my time in arranging papers & reading on the arts. I am never alone when I have a good book, or a sheet of paper to scribble upon, or am engaged in the study & contemplation of my art. I often hear people complain of a dull day, when they cannot gossip, of feeling of loneliness. I never knew, from that cause, what such a feeling is. I am never happy, if I cannot claim a portion of every day to my own quiet study & contemplation. When the rain or hail is beating against the windows of my Studio, and I alone, if my room within is to my liking, I am content; and yet I enjoy greatly a tramp in the rain or Snow Storm and am very fond of such company as can converse upon the subjects that interest me. I am fond of company of a certain kind when there is no restraint.

Neagle, "Blotter," 4 February 1835, John Neagle Papers, AAA, roll 3656, frame 1160

The following is an interesting comparison of his earliest prices with those at the height of his career.

"March 7, 1832. Found a torn card in the cockloft containing a list of my first prices"

Bust 7 x 9″	$9.00	Hands and heads	25.00
Bust 8 x 10″	10.00	¾ length	50.00
Bust 18 x 15″	15.00	Full length	100.00

Price List of September 1836.

Head 17 x 20″	$80.00	Small half length	250.00
Bust 21½ x 26″	100.00	Bishop's length	300.00
¾ Bust 25 x 30″	150.00	¾ length	400.00
Kit Kat	200.00	Whole length	600.00

Marguerite Lynch, "John Neagle's 'Diary,'" *Art in America* 37, no. 2 (April 1949): 87

Provenance
Presumably Helmuth family

[Kennedy Galleries, New York, 1965–1966]

John D. Rockefeller 3rd and Blanchette Hooker Rockefeller, New York, 1966–1979

FAMSF, 1979.7.76

Exhibition History
New York, Kennedy Galleries, *Past and Present: Two Hundred Years of American Painting, Part One: Eighteenth and Nineteenth Centuries*, 1966, exh. no. 149

34 LUMAN REED, CA. 1836

Oil on canvas (now mounted on hardboard), 30⅜ x 25⅜ in.

ASHER B. DURAND

b. Jefferson Village (now Maplewood), N.J. 1796
d. Maplewood, N.J. 1886

Credited with having made native art fashionable, Luman Reed (1785–1836) must be numbered among the great patrons of American art during the nineteenth century. Reed started his career as a clerk in a country store near Albany and advanced, by the age of twenty-eight, to become a partner in a wholesale grocery house in New York City. With business activity stimulated by the opening of the Erie Canal, Reed accumulated a substantial fortune between 1815 and 1832. He built a large mansion in lower Manhattan. . . . After making his first purchases [of contemporary American art] at the 1834 exhibition of the National Academy of Design, he embarked on a career of artistic patronage unprecedented in New York, showing particular interest in the works of Asher B. Durand, Thomas Cole, William S. Mount, and George Flagg. . . . Reed quickly assembled an impressive collection, and soon turned the third floor of his home into a picture gallery, which he opened to visitors one day a week.

Reed died prematurely in 1836. As a testimonial, a group of merchant-collectors who had been inspired by his example subscribed funds to buy his collection, and in 1844–1845 the New York Gallery of Fine Arts was established. After being shown in various places, including Vanderlyn's Rotunda, the collection was deposited with the New-York Historical Society in 1858.

Albert Ten Eyck Gardner and Stuart P. Feld, *American Paintings: A Catalogue of the Collection of the Metropolitan Museum of Art*, vol. 1, *Painters Born by 1815* (New York: The Metropolitan Museum of Art, 1965), p. 209

I cannot yet tell you how long I shall be obliged to stay nor what I shall have to do [in Boston], but I expect to do considerable and I am ready to do all that I can do, and only regret that I am not able to do much more & better for the generous & excellent man, at whose request and in whose company, I am come here. His Kindness & Liberality towards me are without limit—the more I see of him, the more I esteem & admire him and am the more willing to submit cheerfully to any inconvenience. . . . So I need scarcely tell you that the only regret that I feel in serving M^r. Reed is that I am obliged to remain so long absent.

Durand to Mary Frank Durand, 3 June 1835, Asher B. Durand Papers, AAA, roll N19, frame 923

Since the departure of M^r. Reed which was on Wednesday last, I am somewhat lonesome. his kindness and liberality towards me are without bounds, he is determined to make something of me, (I much regret that he has not a better material to work on) and if ever I attain to any excellence in painting it will be more owing to him than any other cause. More than words are wanted by me to express the feeling that his interest in me has excited.

Durand to John W. Casilear, 14 June 1835, Asher B. Durand Papers, AAA, roll N19, frame 930

———

I am quite happy in being identified with you in your Boston visit & I hope we may often be identified together if my being so with you may be the means of promoting your interest & success in this "naughty world."

Luman Reed to Durand, 18 June 1835, Asher B. Durand Papers, AAA, roll N19, frame 941

———

My dear son[,] I write to you on a subject of the highest importance to you & to me. You have already been informed by Caroline that you would probably go with M^r. Reed in the Spring, and such is the agreement between M^r. Reed & myself. So as soon as the River opens you will prepare for the business. M^r. R. has just taken two of his young Men into the Firm, and will in consequence have an opening for one like yourself in the Store, early in the Spring, and he has accordingly applied to me on the subject.

I cannot tell you how much pleasure this proposition gives me & I hope it will not be less gratifying to yourself. You may not be able to perceive at once all the advantages of a bringing up under the charge of such a man, but you must see at once, that to be connected with the first in the U.S. in that line of business, is no trifling matter. . . . I need not tell you that independent of this favour I am already indebted to M^r. Reed for services that have placed me in more favourable circumstances by far, . . . & that I feel my utmost exertions & capacity inadequate to repay his kindness, and I therefore hope & believe that you will do all in your power without complaint, towards the fulfilment of his designs in regard to us both, and, to show him that you are grateful for the kindness he has shown your Father as well as the great advantages which he offers to you. I would say much on this subject, for it is one most deeply interesting to me but I have but little time to write. I have been at M^r. Reed's house for more than two weeks, painting the doors of his gallery, and shall be there again after some few weeks. I am now painting his portrait again.

> Durand to John Durand, 14 February 1836, Asher B. Durand Papers, AAA, roll N19, frames 983–984

The fatal hour has come. Our dear friend [Luman Reed] is dead. The funeral will take place on Thursday afternoon. Come and look for the last time on the man whose equal we never shall see again.

I can say no more.

> Durand to Thomas Cole, 7 June 1836, Asher B. Durand Papers, AAA, roll N19, frame 1036

I have nearly finished another portrait of our dear departed Friend [Luman Reed] which satisfies me better than any other attempt.

> Durand to Thomas Cole, 7 July 1836, Asher B. Durand Papers, AAA, roll N19, frame 1062

Provenance
Descended in family of sitter to C. G. H. Mulford, Hopewell, N.Y., by 1937

[Scott & Fowles, New York, ca. 1940]

Lawrence A. Fleischman (b. 1925) and Barbara Greenberg Fleischman (b. 1924), Detroit, by 1964–1966

[Kennedy Galleries, New York, 1966–1967]

John D. Rockefeller 3rd and Blanchette Hooker Rockefeller, New York, 1967–1979

FAMSF, 1979.7.35

Exhibition History
Tucson, University of Arizona Art Gallery, *American Painting, 1765–1963: Selections from the Lawrence A. and Barbara Fleischman Collection of American Art*, 1964, not in publ.

San Francisco 1976, exh. no. 35

Selected Reference
Frederick Baekeland, "Collectors of American Painting, 1813 to 1913," *American Art Review* 3, no. 6 (November–December 1976): 124

Related Works
Luman Reed, 1835
Oil on canvas, 30 x 25 in.
Private collection

Luman Reed, ca. 1835
Oil on canvas, 30⅛ x 25⅜ in.
The Metropolitan Museum of Art, New York

Luman Reed, ca. 1835
Oil on canvas, 36 x 27 in.
National Portrait Gallery, Washington, D.C.

Luman Reed, ca. 1844
Oil on canvas, 30 x 25 in.
The New-York Historical Society, New York

35   VIEW OF THE CITY OF NEW YORK FROM HOBOKEN, 1839

Opaque watercolor on paper, mounted on canvas, 16¼ x 23⅜ in.
Signed, dated, and inscribed lower left (on painted crate): *N.N. CALYO/Drawn on the spot/1839.* and
V.D./New York; inscribed on label on reverse: *View of the City of New York Taken from Hoboken drawn on
the spot by N: Calyo*.

36   NEW YORK FROM WILLIAMSBURGH, CA. 1839

Opaque watercolor on paper, mounted on canvas, 16⅜ x 23¼ in.
Inscribed on label on reverse: *New York/taken from Williamsburgh/Dessinée d'apres nature par/
Nicolino Calyo*

NICOLINO CALYO

b. Naples, Italy 1799
d. New York, N.Y. 1884

Born in Naples in 1799, Nicolino was the son of Giuseppe Calyo, who is said to have been a colonel in the Neapolitan army. Nicolino studied art at the Naples Academy, and as a young man allied himself with the popular movement against King Ferdinand IV. After the insurrectionary movements of 1820 and 1821, Nicolino was forced to flee along with many other Neapolitans, including the poet Dante Gabriel Rossetti [*sic*—Gabriele Pasquale, Dante Gabriel's father]. Calyo spent the next eight years traveling in Europe and studying art. In 1829 he was among the Italian exiles living in Malta. From Malta he appears to have gone to Spain. . . . At the beginning of the Carlist War in Spain, Calyo left for America and is first heard of in Baltimore in August 1834. . . . On July 17, 1835, he left Baltimore for Philadelphia, and by the end of 1835 he was in New York, where he painted his well-known scenes of the Great Fire of December 16–17, 1835. Calyo first appears in the New York City directory in 1836–37 as a professor of painting. Among the artist's works are a number of city views and a series of characterizations called "Cries of New York." . . . In 1847 he exhibited a diorama of the Mexican War and in 1848 began a panorama of the Connecticut River, which was exhibited in 1850. He was also involved in scenic painting and set design with two of his sons, John (1829–93) and Hannibal (1835–83). . . . Calyo also painted portraits and is especially noted for his works in gouache.

"Nicolino Calyo," in Richard J. Koke, comp., *American Landscape and Genre Paintings in the New-York Historical Society*, 3 vols. (Boston: G. K. Hall & Co., in association with the New-York Historical Society, 1982), 1:129

The author knows no man more competent to judge the authenticity of paintings, by what masters they were executed and to restore them when injured than my friend Nicolino Calyo, an accomplished scholar, a true artist, a true connoisseur . . . and an honest man.

Shearjashub Spooner, *A Biographical History of the Fine Arts*, 1867, quoted in Margaret Sloane Patterson, "Nicolino Calyo and His Paintings of the Great Fire of New York, December 16th and 17th, 1835," *The American Art Journal* 14, no. 2 (Spring 1982): 22

It is . . . as a painter in gouache that Calyo is best known and most appreciated today. His handling of this medium reached its climax in his views of the Great Fire of New York and in other views of the harbor, which he produced at the same time. Although . . . he subsequently turned to other subjects and media, his work in gouache remains the best evidence of his talent.

Margaret Sloane Patterson, "Nicolino Calyo and His Paintings of the Great Fire of New York, December 16th and 17th, 1835," *The American Art Journal* 14, no. 2 (Spring 1982): 22

———

The cityscape was an attractive and prominent form of painting all through the eighteenth and early nineteenth century. In North America it commonly took the form of engraved views. Paintings are quite rare and eagerly sought after.

. . . [Calyo's] best works are those done from nature, rather than repetitions from his sketches. Yours are done from nature . . . and are delightful examples of this form of landscape art.

E. P. Richardson to John D. Rockefeller 3rd, 19 December 1977, copy in FAMSF departmental files

Provenance
John D. Rockefeller 3rd and Blanchette Hooker Rockefeller, New York, unknown date of acquisition–1979

FAMSF, 1979.7.22 (*Hoboken*), 1979.7.23 (*Williamsburgh*)

Related Works
New York from Williamsburgh, 1838
Gouache on paper
Hirschl & Adler Galleries, New York, before 1982

New York from Williamsburgh, possibly 1838
Gouache on paper, mounted on canvas, 20 x 29 in.
The New-York Historical Society, New York

New York from Hoboken
Gouache on paper, mounted on canvas, 23¾ x 32 in.
The New-York Historical Society, New York

---

37 ALFRED SULLY, 1839

Oil on paperboard (now mounted on laminate board), 24 x 20 in.
Signed and dated on reverse, in chalk (visible before lining): *T.S. 1839*

THOMAS SULLY
b. Horncastle, Lincolnshire, England 1783
d. Philadelphia, Pa. 1872

The subject, Alfred Sully, wears the gray and black uniform of a West Point Cadet of the Period. He was born in Philadelphia, 1821, died in Fort Vancouver, Washington Territory, April 17, 1879, and was a son of Thomas Sully, the artist (1783–1872) and Sarah (Annis) Sully (1779–1867). He was graduated from West Point in 1841, and was assigned to the Second Infantry during the war with the Seminole Indians. Later, in 1849, he was promoted to the rank of Captain. In 1853 he took part in the operations against the Rogue River Indians and in December of that year, while on his way to New York, he was wrecked off the coast of California and was six days on a desert island. In 1860–1861 he took part against the Cheyenne Indians. During the Civil War he served in the defense of Washington till March 4, 1862, when he was made Colonel of the Third Minnesota regiment, and later was brevetted Lieutenant-Colonel, U.S. Army, for gallantry at Fair Oaks, and Colonel for Malvern Hill. He engaged in the Virginia and Maryland campaigns, and led a brigade at Chancellorsville. At the close of the war he was given the brevet of Major-General of volunteers, and that of Brigadier-General in the regular army. He became Lieutenant-Colonel, July 28, 1866, and Colonel of the 10th Infantry, December 10, 1872. Heitman's *Historical Register of the United States Army* gives the date of the subject's death as April 27, 1879, and lists him as Colonel of the 21st Infantry in 1873.

A Loan Exhibition of Portraits of Soldiers and Sailors in American Wars, exh. cat. (New York: Duveen Galleries, 1945), pp. 60–61

———

Begun	Size	For whom painted	Price	Finished
July 18	Head	Alfred Sully for his mother	150	July 20th

Sully, "Account of Pictures Painted by Thomas Sully," Thomas Sully Papers, AAA, roll N18, frame 44

Provenance

The artist and Sarah Annis Sully (1779–1867), Philadelphia, 1839–1872

Descended in family to Virginia Sully (Mrs. Clarence) Booth (1905–1989), Long Island, N.Y., 1947–1970

[Hirschl & Adler Galleries, New York, 1970]

John D. Rockefeller 3rd and Blanchette Hooker Rockefeller, New York, 1970–1993

FAMSF, 1993.35.26

Exhibition History

The Brooklyn Museum, *Exhibition of Portraits, Miniatures, Color Sketches, and Drawings by Thomas Sully*, 1921, exh. no. 3

Philadelphia, Pennsylvania Academy of the Fine Arts, *Memorial Exhibition of Portraits by Thomas Sully*, 1922, exh. no. 91

New York, Duveen Galleries, *A Loan Exhibition of Portraits of Soldiers and Sailors in American Wars*, 1945, exh. no. 34

New York, Hirschl & Adler Galleries, *Forty Masterworks of American Art*, 1970, exh. no. 14a

San Francisco 1976, exh. no. 29

Tokyo 1982, exh. no. 20

Washington, D.C., National Portrait Gallery, *Mr. Sully, Portrait Painter: The Works of Thomas Sully, 1783–1872*, 1983, exh. no. 60

Selected Reference

Edward Biddle and Mantle Fielding, *The Life and Works of Thomas Sully, 1783–1872* (1921; New York: Da Capo Press, for Kennedy Graphics, 1970), cat. no. 1, 683

Related Work

Alfred Sully, ca. 1839
Watercolor and gouache on ivory, diameter 2⅜ in.
Richard and Gloria Manney, New York, as of 1990

Oil on paper, mounted on canvas, 10⅞ x 14¾ in.
Inscribed on back of mounting canvas: *W. Page./1845* [*sic*]

WILLIAM PAGE
b. Albany, N.Y. 1811
d. Tottenville, N.Y. 1885

Of all American portrait-painters William Page is the most originally experimental: he has studied his art in theory as well as practice; he has indulged in a wide range of speculation as regards the processes, the methods, and the principles of adepts therein: not satisfied with admiring and emulating Titian and Paul Veronese, he has sought to wrest from their works the secret of that magical color which dazzles and defies the modern painter. At different times Page has painted in different ways—seeking truth by experiment, and in so doing, at one period, achieving a marvellous success, and, at another, ending with a lamentable failure. We doubt if in the range of modern art there can be found from the same hand so great a variety of triumphs and of crudities; the works of Page justify the highest eulogiums of his admirers, and the severest protests of his critics. . . . He seems to unite the conservative instincts of an old-world artist with the bold, experimental ambition of our Young Republic.

> Henry T. Tuckerman, *Book of the Artists: American Artist Life* (1867; New York: James F. Carr, 1966), p. 295

————

I am just finishing a small picture of Cupid and Psyche from the cast you may remember to have seen in my room—kissing in a wood—I would like you to see it, but you can't.

> Page to James Russell Lowell, 21 March 1843, quoted in Joshua Taylor, *William Page: The American Titian* (Chicago: University of Chicago Press, 1957), p. 48

————

The eighteenth annual exhibition of the National Academy is now open to the public, and, judging from a hasty glance through the rooms, we are disposed to credit the report of artists that it contains an unusual number of good pictures. But it is not our purpose, at this time, to criticise any of the performances on the walls of the Academy; we shall confine our remarks entirely to a picture that we were surprised not to find there, and were still more surprised to learn that the "Council" had excluded on the score of indecency. And what will the visitors to the Academy think of the character of a picture that could compel the council to so harsh a sentence, when they have seen some of the gross and disgusting things that have found a place there? Will they not justly think that it must have been unfit for a brothel?

But what will they think of the Pecksniffian morality of these "council"-men, all of them professed artists, when they are informed that the excluded painting was a small cabinet picture by one of the best artists in the country, who has been placed by common consent at the very head of his profession—a gentleman of unexceptionable private character, who has never been guilty of a violation of any of the proprieties of society, and whose pure imagination has always been manifest in the productions of his pencil; and that the subject of the painting was neither more nor less than a simple study from one of the most refined and spiritual groups of the antique—the Cupid and Psyche—and that it was handled in the most delicate and least offensive manner possible. . . .

. . . Of what use are life schools and casts from the antique, if artists are not to be allowed the privilege of exhibiting paintings which represent the human form? if they are to waste their talents and narrow down the conceptions of their genius to the productions of the mantua-maker and the tailor! . . .

We are extremely loth to believe, that the artists composing the "Council" of the Academy could be influenced by any paltry feelings of jealousy toward one of their own associates; but we are compelled to the conclusion that some such feeling must have operated upon the minds of these gentlemen, when they refused to place in this exhibition the painting alluded to.

> H. F. [Charles F. Briggs], "The Rejected Picture," *The New World* 6, no. 18 (6 May 1843): 545–546

————

It is for refusing to place upon the walls of their saloon a copy of a subject so hackneyed, that even the newsboys could scarcely give it away, that the liberal and high-minded gentlemen of the Committee of Arrangements are bespattered with the refined filth of this scavenger critic. . . .

    . . . And now as to the character of "the rejected picture" as a work of art, (since criticism is provoked,) in what class of art is it to be ranked? Grant that its technical merits were unexceptionable, which is far from being the fact, no artist who valued his standing among his professional brethren, more than the ephemeral flatteries of dubious friends, would plume himself on *colored copies of antique statues*; his ability to originate would justly be called in question. . . . Granting, then, that the "rejected picture" was excluded for its indelicacy, (which we have only the doubtful authority of H. F. for supposing,) we applaud the motives that determined the committee to exclude it. They deserve all praise from the guardians of the public morals for doing it. They show by that very act that they are worthy of the high trust to which their brethren in the Arts have appointed them, and herein we have a guarantee that the National Academy of Design while directed by men of their character, will not be prostituted to please the "salacious" cravings of libertine fancies.

    N. T. M., "The Rejected Picture," *The New World* 6, no. 19 (13 May 1843): 577

––––––––––

If the picture of Cupid and Psyche was rejected in conformity with a fundamental rule of the Academy acted upon for 18 years [against exhibiting copies], it strikes us [as] a singular fact that the artist, who was a student of the Academy, a pupil of the President, formerly of the council himself, and upwards of seven years an academician, should have been so ignorant of it as to have painted a picture expressly for exhibition, which the youngest student of the Academy must have known would be rejected. The truth is, the picture was no copy at all. . . . The figures were encompassed in a delightful bit of cool and refreshing landscape, which, although intended for a subordinate effect, might well have been considered as a principal, and the figures as accessories. The artist gave his figures the form of a well known group, to preserve a sentiment of purity; but all the merit of color, of expression, and light and shadow, and the beauty of the landscape were his own, and made the picture original in all the essentials of a painting.

    H. F. [Charles F. Briggs], "The National Academy," *The New World* 6, no. 20 (20 May 1843): 604

––––––––––

There, too [in the Boston Athenaeum exhibition], is the Cupid and Psyche of Page, which so shocked the delicacy of your citizens, when exhibited in New York. The people of Boston are either less refined or less squeamish, for it does not seem to have given any offence here.

L. O. S., "Matters and Things in Boston," *Brother Jonathan* 6, no. 4 (23 September 1843): 101

Provenance
Descended in artist's family to Pauline Page (Mrs. Lesslie Stockton) Howell, Philadelphia and West Palm Beach, Fla., 1952–1959

Lawrence A. Fleischman (b. 1925) and Barbara Greenberg Fleischman (b. 1924), Detroit, 1959–1966

[Kennedy Galleries, New York, 1966]

John D. Rockefeller 3rd and Blanchette Hooker Rockefeller, New York, 1966–1979

FAMSF, 1979.7.77

Exhibition History
Boston Athenaeum, *Seventeenth Exhibition of Paintings and the Fifth Exhibition of Sculpture*, 1843, not in publ.

The Detroit Institute of Arts, *Travelers in Arcadia: American Artists in Italy, 1830–1875*, 1951, exh. no. 78

New York, American Academy of Arts and Letters, 1954, exh. no. 109

Palm Beach, Fla., Norton Gallery of Art, 1959

Milwaukee Art Center, *American Painting, 1760–1960: A Selection of 125 Paintings from the Collection of Mr. and Mrs. Lawrence A. Fleischman, Detroit*, 1960, no exh. no.

Tucson, University of Arizona Art Gallery, *Selections from the Lawrence A. and Barbara Fleischman Collection of American Art*, 1964, exh. no. 74

New York, The Metropolitan Museum of Art, *Nineteenth-Century America: Paintings and Sculpture*, 1970, exh. no. 70

New York, Whitney Museum of American Art, *Eighteenth- and Nineteenth-Century American Art from Private Collections*, 1972, exh. no. 48

San Francisco 1976, exh. no. 51

Selected References
Joshua C. Taylor, *William Page: The American Titian* (Chicago: University of Chicago Press, 1957), pp. 46–50, 53, 60, 62–63, 145, cat. no. 16

William H. Gerdts, *The Great American Nude: A History in Art* (New York: Praeger, 1974), pp. 77–78, 203, 206

Abraham A. Davidson, *The Eccentrics and Other American Visionary Painters* (New York: E. P. Dutton, 1978), pp. 53, 100–102

The American Canvas, pp. 74–75, 235

---

39 DOUGLASS' SQUIRREL, CA. 1843

Watercolor, ink, graphite, and glaze on wove paper, 12¼ x 9½ in.
Inscribed in graphite lower left: *Douglass' Squirrel*

JOHN JAMES AUDUBON

b. Les Cayes, Saint-Dominique (now Haiti) 1785
d. New York, N.Y. 1851

In presenting the following pages to the public, the authors desire to say a few words explanatory of the subject on which they have written. The difficulties they have attempted to surmount, and the labour attending their investigations, have far exceeded their first anticipations. . . .

A considerable portion of the country to which our attention has been directed, is at the present period an uncultivated and almost unexplored wild, roamed over by ferocious beasts and warlike tribes of Indians.

The objects of our search, Quadrupeds, are far less numerous than birds at all times, and are, moreover, generally nocturnal in their habits, and consequently obtained with far greater difficulty than the latter. . . .

We have had our labours lightened, however, by many excellent friends and gentlemen in different portions of the country, who have, at great trouble to themselves, procured and sent us various animals—forwarded to us notes upon the habits of different species, procured works on the subject otherwise beyond our reach, and in many ways excited our warmest feelings of gratitude. Mr. J. K. TOWNSEND, of Philadelphia, allowed us to use the rare and valuable collection of Quadrupeds which he obtained during his laborious researches on the western prairies, the Rocky Mountains, and in Oregon, and furnished us with his notes on their habits and geographical distribution. . . .

In our Illustrations we have endeavoured (we hope not without success,) to place before our patrons a series of plates, which are not only scientifically correct, but interesting to all, from the varied occupations, expressions, and attitudes, we have given to the different species, together with the appropriate accessories, such as trees, plants, landscapes, &c., with which the figures of the animals are relieved.

John James Audubon and the Reverend John Bachman, *The Viviparous Quadrupeds of North America*, 3 vols. text and 2 vols. plates (New York: J. J. Audubon, 1846–1853), I:v, vii, viii, xi

---

SCIURUS DOUGLASSII. — Bach.
Douglass' Squirrel.
PLATE XLVIII. — Male and Female. Natural size.

HABITS.

Our specimens of Douglass' Squirrel were procured by Mr. Townsend. He remarks in his notes:—"This is a very plentiful species, inhabits the pine trees along the shores of the Columbia River, and like our common Carolina squirrel lays in a great quantity of food for consumption during the winter months. This food consists of the cones of the pine, with a few acorns. Late in autumn it may be seen very busy in the tops of the trees, throwing down its winter-stock; after which, assisted by its mate, it gathers in and stows away its store, in readiness for its long incarceration." . . .

GEOGRAPHICAL DISTRIBUTION.

Douglass obtained his specimens of this Squirrel on the Rocky Mountains, and Townsend found it on the Columbia River. . . .

This species was found by DOUGLASS and by TOWNSEND about the same time. These gentlemen, if we have been rightly informed, met together in the Far West. We drew up a description from specimens sent us by Mr. TOWNSEND, and used the grateful privilege of a describer, in naming it (*S. Townsendii*) after the individual who we supposed had been the first discoverer. Under this name we sent our description to the Acad. of Nat. Sciences of Philadelphia, which was read Aug. 7th, 1838. After arriving in England, however, the same year, we saw a similar specimen in the Museum of the Zool. Society, and heard that it had been named by GRAY, on the 11th October, 1836, who had called it after DOUGLASS (*S. Douglassii.*) He had not, as far as we have been able to ascertain, published any description of it. . . .

We, however, supposing that he had described it, immediately changed our name to that proposed by GRAY, and in our monograph of the genus assigned to him the credit of having been the first describer, although he had, it appears, only named the animal.

> John James Audubon and the Reverend John Bachman, *The Viviparous Quadrupeds of North America*, 3 vols. text and 2 vols. plates (New York: J. J. Audubon, 1846–1853), 1:370–372

Employ yourself in drawing every quadruped you can lay your hands on. . . . Don't flatter yourself that this book is child's play—the birds are a mere trifle compared with this. I have been at it all my life . . . we all have much to learn in this matter.

> The Reverend John Bachman to Audubon, 1839, quoted in Edward H. Dwight, *Audubon Watercolors and Drawings*, exh. cat. (Utica, N.Y.: Munson-Williams-Proctor Institute, 1965), p. 50

This very enterprising ornithologist and artist has attracted great attention by undertaking to publish from drawings and writings of his own on American ornithology, the figures in which are the size of life. How much science gains by increasing the picture of a bird beyond that size necessary to display all the parts distinctly, is with me questionable; but the work of Mr. Audubon, as far as I have seen it, is honorable to his skill, perseverance and energy. It is gratifying to see the arts of design enlisted in the cause of science, and it is one of the many proofs of man's progress towards the goal intended for him. . . . In works on natural history we see the incalculable advantage of the arts of design to convey those images which words cannot present to the mind. . . .

We will now refer to Mr. Audubon's published account of himself, which I could wish had less mystification about it. . . .

Mr. Audubon tells us that "the productions of nature" became his playmates, and he soon felt that intimacy with them, "not consisting of friendship merely, but bordering on frenzy, must accompany" his "steps through life." His father encouraged and instructed him in his study of nature—when or where we are not told. When a child he "gazed with ecstasy upon the pearly and shining eggs as they lay imbedded in the softest down.". . . His father showed him pictures of birds, and he tried to copy them—"to have been torn from the study would have been death to me." "I produced hundreds of these rude sketches annually."

Notwithstanding this frenzy and ecstasy growing with his growth, we are told that he "applied patiently and with industry" to the study of drawing; and at the age of seventeen, after "many masters" had "guided his hand," he says he "returned from France, whither I had gone to receive the rudiments of my education." And then, at the age of seventeen, "my drawings had assumed some form. David had guided my hand in tracing objects of a large size."

"I returned," he proceeds, "to the woods of the new world with fresh ardor, and commenced a collection of drawings, which I henceforth continued, and which is now publishing under the title of 'The Birds of America.'"

> William Dunlap, *A History of the Rise and Progress of the Arts of Design in the United States*, 3 vols. (1834; Boston: C. E. Goodspeed & Co., 1918), 3:202, 205, 206

Provenance

Lawrence A. Fleischman (b. 1925) and Barbara Greenberg Fleischman (b. 1924), Detroit, by 1964–1966

[Kennedy Galleries, New York, 1966–1967]

John D. Rockefeller 3rd and Blanchette Hooker Rockefeller, New York, 1967–1979

FAMSF, 1979.7.5

Exhibition History

Philadelphia, Pennsylvania Academy of the Fine Arts, *Small*

Pictures of Large Import from the Collection of Lawrence A. and Barbara Fleischman of Detroit, Michigan, 1964, exh. no. 1

New York, Kennedy Galleries, *American Drawings, Pastels and Watercolors, Part One: Works of the Eighteenth and Early Nineteenth Centuries*, 1967, exh. no. 70

San Francisco 1976, exh. no. 23

FAMSF, *Selected Acquisitions, 1977–1979*, 1979, exh. no. 4

FAMSF, *Masterworks from the Achenbach Foundation for Graphic Arts*, 1981, no publ.

FAMSF, *Animals Real and Imagined*, 1981, no publ.

Tokyo 1982, exh. no. 21

FAMSF, *Master Drawings from the Achenbach Foundation for Graphic Arts*, 1985, exh. no. 89

Related Work

Douglass Squirrel, 1844, hand-colored lithograph, in John James Audubon and the Reverend John Bachman, *The Viviparous Quadrupeds of North America*, 3 vols. text and 2 vols. plates (New York: J. J. Audubon, 1846–1853), pl. 48 Inscribed lower left: *Drawn from Nature by J. J. Audubon, F.R.S. F.L.S.*; lower center: *SCIURUS DOUGLASSII, Gray/Douglass Squirrel/Natural Size/1, Male, 2, Female* [the FAMSF work shows this female]; lower right: *Lith. Printed & Col.ᵈ by J. T. Bowen, Phila. 1844*

40 GENERAL HENRY SEWALL, 1844

Black and white chalk on brown wove paper, mounted on cardboard, 21¼ x 15 in.
Signed and dated lower left: *1844 E. Johnson*; inscribed on reverse: *Genl. Henry Sewall/Aged 92—/ Augusta Me. Nov. 26 1844—/E. Johnson, del—*

EASTMAN JOHNSON
b. Lovell, Maine 1824
d. New York, N.Y. 1906

In 1845 Eastman was established in a successful practice; one of the Senate committee rooms in the Capitol was given him for a studio, and it was in this august atelier that he executed the portrait of the widow of Alexander Hamilton in 1846. . . .

John Quincy Adams also sat for him, as did General Sewell [*sic*], an old Revolutionary officer, Judges Story and McLean of the Supreme Court, some of the foreign ministers, members of Congress, etc. Professor [Samuel F. B.] Morse, who was "still esteemed as a painter," came to see him, and as he was leaving said: "Well, you can reach the top of the ladder if you wish to."

William Walton, "Eastman Johnson, Painter," *Scribner's Magazine* 40, no. 3 (September 1906): 264

The earliest extant drawings date from 1844 and reveal a twenty-year-old artist deficient in his knowledge of anatomy, but obviously talented. Johnson's early style is illustrated in two drawings at the Brooklyn Museum . . . both dated July 1844, as well as in a drawing of his maternal grandmother, *Mrs. Jeremiah Chandler* (M. Knoedler & Co., Inc., New York), not dated, and a fourth, *General Sewall*, dated November 26, 1844 (private collection [the FAMSF drawing]). In all four works there is an unidealized frankness and an emphasis on the lineaments of age, that leads us to suppose that the drawings were good likenesses, a criterion of paramount importance to Yankee patrons since the days of the early limners. The drawings show an effort to render intelligent people in the reality of their being and without any prettiness or superficial comment. They are, however, clearly by the hand of one untrained in the subtleties of academic methods. The heads are enlarged considerably when compared with the breadth of the shoulders; the hands, where shown, are disproportionately small. Mrs. Chandler's neck barely exists while the General's neck is exaggeratedly lengthened. Moreover, the chair and cane in this last portrait are rendered mechanically. Light and shadow operate not to unify the form but to clarify each individual feature. This clarity and isolation of the separate entities create an archaic effect often typical of beginning artists.

Johnson seems to have made a modest income with his crayon portraits, traveling to local towns to find commissions, and passing several months in Portland, Maine, where he allegedly drew portraits of Henry Wadsworth Longfellow's sister, Mrs. Pierce, and Longfellow's parents. But the pivotal moment in his career came sometime in late 1844 or 1845 when Johnson decided to move to Washington, D.C., in order to establish himself in the portrait

business in the nation's capital. Johnson was permitted, perhaps through his father's political connections, to occupy one of the Senate committee rooms as a studio. It was Johnson's avowed ambition to gather for himself a portfolio of drawings of eminent Americans, and to this end many of the capital's most distinguished citizens obliged him with sittings.

> Patricia Hills, *The Genre Painting of Eastman Johnson: The Sources and Development of His Style and Themes* (New York: Garland Publishing, 1977), pp. 23–24

Henry Sewall, Jr. (1752–1845), entered the army as corporal, 1775. He served at the siege of Boston, the Burgoyne and Jersey campaigns and was muster master of De Kalb's Division, 1778. He commanded a company, 1779, was aide to Gen. William Heath, 1781, and served to the close of the war. He was an original member of the Cincinnati and its vice-president when he died at Augusta. His pension in 1826 was allowed for seven years' service.

> *Lineage Book: National Society of the Daughters of the American Revolution* (Washington, D.C.: Daughters of the American Revolution, 1896), vol. 13, p. 226

Provenance
[Kennedy Galleries, New York, 1969]
John D. Rockefeller 3rd and Blanchette Hooker Rockefeller, New York, 1969–1979
FAMSF, 1979.7.68

Exhibition History
San Francisco 1976, exh. no. 78

Selected Reference
Kennedy & Company, *Exhibition of Charcoal Drawings by Eastman Johnson*, exh. cat. (New York: Kennedy & Company, 1920), p. 12

Oil on canvas, 25⅛ x 30¼ in.

**GEORGE CALEB
BINGHAM**
b. Augusta County, Va. 1811
d. Kansas City, Mo. 1879

Of Mr. Bingham himself, we would say a word. As a painter, whatever he is, he is by means of his own unassisted application, and untutored study. His boyhood was spent upon the banks of the Missouri; and never, since he reached the stature of manhood, has he been East of the Mississippi. Except those of his own execution, he never saw a portrait painted in his life. Aware of these facts, there is no one who can enter his room, without being struck with more than admiration, with the many evidences of a deep, native originality, which surround his portraits. . . .

St. Louis must continue, for a long time, the principal nursery of the fine arts, in "the far west"; and, it is hoped, that as the Metropolis of Missouri, she will take an especial pride in fostering the native genius of the State. If the West will but extend a cherishing patronage, she can rear up, from the number of her youth, sons of genius, that, like the trees of her own deep forests, will attain the largest and the stateliest growth. If the young artist, who has called forth these remarks, possesses the talents which we conceive, let them be excited and drawn out by liberality of encouragement at home, and ere long, the country shall see with delight, and hear with pleasure, the productions and the praises,—to borrow a title of Rubens—of a Western "meteor of the art."

> "The Fine Arts," *The Missouri Intelligencer*, 14 March 1835, quoted in Albert Christ-Janer, *George Caleb Bingham of Missouri: The Story of an Artist* (New York: Dodd, Mead & Company, 1940), pp. 17–18

Every lover of art should drop into Jones's, on Fourth street—102. Bingham, who with Deas is making a brilliant reputation by the delineation of western scenes, has four really capital paintings there [*Boatmen on the Missouri* among them], on their way to the exhibition at New York. There is an absolute life about them which it is refreshing to look upon.

> "Very Fine Paintings," (*St. Louis*) *Weekly Reveille*, 23 March 1846

[The American Art-Union acquired paintings for annual exhibition and distribution to its membership by lottery. *Boatmen on the Missouri* was included in the 1846 lottery.]

We, the subscribers, appointed to scrutinize the ballots of the American Art-Union for 1846, hereby certify that we have performed that duty, and find that the names on the ballots herewith submitted, correspond with the names of the subscribers on the subscription book.

JOHN P. RIDNER,
ROB'T F. FRASER.

Dated at 8 o'clock, P.M.,
   Friday, December 18th, 1846
   The Tellers then deposited the ballots containing the names of the members in one wheel, and those containing the numbers of the pictures in another, and the numbers were drawn . . . with the following result. . . .
   14 Boatmen on the Missouri, by *Geo. C. Bingham*, to J. R. Macmurdo, New Orleans, La.

> *Transactions of the American Art-Union for the Year 1846* (New York: G. F. Nesbitt, 1847), pp. 30, 31

In *Boatmen on the Missouri* . . . Bingham definitively found his heroes of Western American life: the river and its workers. Three figures, firmly and crisply silhouetted against the hazy bank of trees on the far shore, will soon be transferring wood to the steamboat which is fast approaching in the distance. By most accounts, nineteenth-century Missouri boatmen were a boisterous and a vulgar lot; here, Bingham seems to consider them as ancient river gods, relaxed and confident guardians of commerce. Imbued with classical restraint, they beckon the viewer into their world, a world not of bookish wisdom, but rather one of physical well-being, psychological balance, and practical good sense. . . .

Of the three figures in *Boatmen on the Missouri*, two return the viewer's gaze with sympathetic equanimity while the third, closing the composition, holds his head down as he works. The unblinking stare of the boatmen lock into the viewer's eyes, while the horizontally extended oars intersect with the vertical edges of the canvas to hold the composition firmly in place. . . . Now, the formal relationship of boat, oars, and the edges of the picture plane call attention to the edges of the canvas, almost in a tongue-in-cheek manner. The sharply defined image is suspended in place, for the benefit of both the viewer and the artist. The structural geometry of the river paintings elevates Bingham's work above all precedents to a new level of accomplishment and visual resolution.

Michael Edward Shapiro, "The River Paintings," in *George Caleb Bingham*, exh. cat. (Saint Louis: The Saint Louis Art Museum, in association with Harry N. Abrams, 1990), p. 151

Provenance
American Art-Union, New York, 1846 (purchased for $100)

J. R. Macmurdo, New Orleans, 1846 (by lottery)

John H. Clarke, New Orleans, by 1905

Descended in family to George R. Bergin, La Jolla, Calif., 1960–1966

[Kennedy Galleries, New York, 1966]

John D. Rockefeller 3rd and Blanchette Hooker Rockefeller, New York, 1966–1979

FAMSF, 1979.7.15

Exhibition History
St. Louis, Jones's, 1846, no publ.

New York, American Art-Union, 1846, exh. no. 14

Washington, D.C., National Collection of Fine Arts, *George Caleb Bingham 1811–1879*, 1967, exh. no. 14

San Francisco 1976, exh. no. 30

Tokyo 1982, exh. no. 23

Boston, Museum of Fine Arts, *A New World: Masterpieces of American Painting, 1760–1910*, 1983, exh. no. 55

The Saint Louis Art Museum, *George Caleb Bingham*, 1990, no exh. no.

Selected References

E. Maurice Bloch, *The Paintings of George Caleb Bingham: A Catalogue Raisonné* (Columbia: University of Missouri Press, 1986), cat. no. 174

The American Canvas, pp. 76–77, 235

Nancy Rash, *The Painting and Politics of George Caleb Bingham* (New Haven and London: Yale University Press, 1991), pp. 65–67, 81–84, 91–92

Michael Shapiro, *George Caleb Bingham* (New York: Harry N. Abrams, in association with the National Museum of American Art, 1993), pp. 51–55

Related Works

Preliminary drawings:

Boatman
Brush and black ink and wash over pencil, 9½ x 8 in.
Private collection, Scarsdale, N.Y., as of 1975

Boatman
Brush and black ink and wash over pencil, 8¹⁄₁₆ x 8¹³⁄₁₆ in.
St. Louis Mercantile Library Association

Unknown (American)
After *Boatmen on the Missouri*, ca. 1905
Oil on canvas, 25⅜ x 30¼ in.
The Henry Francis du Pont Winterthur Museum, Winterthur, Del.

---

42 THE PEACEABLE KINGDOM, CA. 1846

Oil on canvas, 25 x 28½ in.

EDWARD HICKS

b. Attleborough (now Langhorne), Pa. 1780
d. Newtown, Pa. 1849

PEACEABLE KINGDOM
Taken from the Eleventh Chapter of the Prophet Isaiah

6. The wolf also shall dwell with the lamb, and the leopard shall lie down with the kid; and the calf, and the young lion, and the fatling together; and a little child shall lead them.

7. And the cow and the bear shall feed; their young ones shall lie down together: and the lion shall eat straw with the ox.

8. And the sucking child shall play on the hole of the asp, and the weaned child shall put his hand on the cockatrice's den.

or,

6. The *wolf* shall with the *lambkin* dwell in peace,
His grim carnivorous thirst for blood shall cease,
The beauteous *leopard* with his restless eye,
Shall by the *kid* in perfect stillness lie;
The *calf*, the *fatling*, and the young *lion* wild,
Shall be led by one sweet little *child*.
7. The *cow* and *bear* shall quietly partake,
Of the rich food the ear and cornstalk make;
While each their peaceful young with joy survey,
As side by side on the green grass they lay;
While the old *lion* thwarting nature's law,
Shall eat beside the *ox* the barley straw.
8. The sucking *child* shall innocently play
On the dark hole where poisonous reptiles lay;
The crested *worm* with all its venom then,
The weaned *child* shall fasten in his den.

The illustrious *Penn* this heavenly kingdom felt,
When with Columbia's native sons he dealt;
Without an oath a lasting *Treaty* made,
In Christian *Faith* beneath the elm tree's shade.

One of these cards was given by Edward Hicks to each buyer or receiver of a "Peaceable Kingdom."

L. L. Beans, *The Life and Work of Edward Hicks* (Trenton, N.J.: L. L. Beans, 1951), p. 2

Towards the end of his life, Edward Hicks wrote, ". . . how awful the consideration: I have nothing to depend on but the mercy and forgiveness of God, for I have no works of righteousness of my own. I am nothing but a poor old worthless insignificant painter." This lamentation

came from one of the most popular and esteemed preachers of his day. Completely untutored except in the field of coachmaking, he began to create paintings in his fortieth year, copying virtually all his subjects from engravings in whatever time he could spare from his unpaid ministry and from the trade [decorative and sign painting] that supported him and his family. In his last years he produced his greatest paintings, uninhibited by the guilt he felt for the hours spent on them instead of preaching. With the passing of time, his fame as a minister has been almost forgotten, but he has come to be considered one of America's outstanding historical and allegorical painters.

Leon Anthony Arkus, *Three Self-Taught Pennsylvania Artists: Hicks—Kane—Pippin*, exh. cat. (Pittsburgh: The Museum of Art, Carnegie Institute, 1966), n.p.

————————

A famous old painting, "The Peaceable Kingdom," work of Edward Hicks, was recently located in the Gregg household at Purcellville and this week was sold by Mrs. Ruth Gregg Bowman, of Lucketts, to a New York art gallery.

It is understood that Mrs. Bowman realized a handsome price for the painting that had been done by Hicks for her great-great-grandfather, Daniel Janney (1787–1859). Mrs. Bowman, commenting on the sale, said that the painting would have required considerable art work and expense to restore it to its original condition.

The painting is an imaginative and allegorical landscape showing children mingling happily with wild and domestic animals—all living peaceably.

Hicks was an ordained Quaker minister and a descendant of Robert Hicks, who landed at Plymouth in 1621. It is said that the young artist painted "The Peaceable Kingdom" when at Lincoln, and presented it to his friend, Daniel Janney.

"New York Art Gallery Buys Painting Here," unidentified Loudoun County, Va., newspaper clipping, 25 May 1944, FAMSF departmental files

Provenance
Dr. Daniel Janney (1787–1859), Goose Creek (now Lincoln), Loudoun County, Va., ca. 1846–1859

Descended in family to Ruth Daniel Gregg (Mrs. Leonard C.) Bowman (b. 1919), Purcellville, Loudoun County, Va., 1938–1944

[The Downtown Gallery, later in the year selling a half-share to M. Knoedler & Co., New York, 1944]

Joseph Katz (1888–1958) and Kate Kropman Katz, Baltimore, 1944–1946

[M. Knoedler & Co., New York, 1946]

Martin B. Grossman (1896–1981) and Mary Jane Cooper Grossman (1914–1981), New York, 1946–1968

[Hirschl & Adler Galleries, New York, 1968]

John D. Rockefeller 3rd and Blanchette Hooker Rockefeller, New York, 1968–1993

FAMSF, 1993.35.14

Exhibition History
New York, The Downtown Gallery, *Loan Exhibition*, 1945, exh. no. 28

Williamsburg, Va., Abby Aldrich Rockefeller Folk Art Collection, *Edward Hicks, 1780–1849*, 1960, exh. no. 40

Pittsburgh, The Museum of Art, Carnegie Institute, *Three Self-Taught Pennsylvania Artists: Hicks–Kane–Pippin*, 1966, exh. no. 30

Princeton, N.J., The Art Museum, Princeton University,

European and American Art from Princeton Alumni Collections, 1972, exh. no. 34

San Francisco 1976, exh. no. 26

Tokyo 1982, exh. no. 22

Selected References
Frederic Newlin Price, *Edward Hicks, 1780–1849* (Swarthmore, Pa.: The Benjamin West Society, Swarthmore College, 1945), p. 26

Alice Ford, *Edward Hicks: Painter of the Peaceable Kingdom* (Philadelphia: University of Pennsylvania Press, 1952), pp. xv, 93, 154

Eleanore Price Mather and Dorothy Canning Miller, *Edward Hicks: His Peaceable Kingdoms and Other Paintings* (Newark: University of Delaware Press, 1983), cat. no. 49

Related Works
Of the sixty recorded Peaceable Kingdom subjects, there are four, dating ca. 1844–1846, distinctive for the "arching leopard" in the lower left foreground. These include the FAMSF picture and

Peaceable Kingdom with Arching Leopard, 1844
Oil on canvas, 24 x 31¼ in.
Abby Aldrich Rockefeller Folk Art Center, Williamsburg, Va.

Peaceable Kingdom with Arching Leopard, ca. 1844
Oil on canvas, 24 x 31¼ in.
Location unknown

Peaceable Kingdom with Arching Leopard, 1844–1846
Oil on canvas, 23⅞ x 31¼ in.
Dallas Museum of Art

---

43 COUNTRY POLITICIAN, 1849

Oil on canvas, 20⅜ x 24 in.
Signed and dated lower left: *G.C. Bingham/1849*.

GEORGE CALEB BINGHAM
b. Augusta County, Va. 1811
d. Kansas City, Mo. 1879

The Missouri Artist—Yesterday, we had the pleasure of examining three paintings by G. C. Bingham, Esq. who is better known by the sobriquet above given—albeit he is not unknown as a statesman and politician. In his peculiar line of Western characters he has added three gems to the productions of his pencil. One is a scene in a bar-room, in which the group is most perfect and life like. The jolly old landlord, smoking his pipe; a politician, most earnestly discussing to a very indifferent listening farmer the Wilmot Proviso, whilst a boy, with his coat tail turned up to the stove, is reading a show bill.

(St. Louis) Daily Missouri Republican, 17 April 1849

A clever picture by Bingham, the Missouri Artist, has been added to the purchases since our last publication. One or two other works by him will probably be upon exhibition during the present month, and attract much attention by the fidelity of their representations of Western life and manners. . . . All these works are thoroughly American in their subjects, and could never have been painted by one who was not perfectly familiar with the scenes they represent. It was this striking nationality of character, combined with considerable power in form and expression, which first interested the Art-Union in these productions. . . . His figures have some *vitality* about them. They look out of their eyes. They stand upon their legs. They

are shrewd or merry or grave or quizzical. They are not mere empty ghosts of figures—mere pictures of jackets and trousers with masks attached to them.

[Andrew Warner], *Bulletin of the American Art-Union* 2, no. 5 (August 1849): 10

As an artist, Mr. Bingham possesses decided genius. The pictures which he has painted, illustrating western life and character, are works of much merit; and, in this line, for originality and accuracy, he has no superior, perhaps, in our country. As a portrait painter, he also stands deservedly high. The evidences of his genius and skill in this respect, are to be found in private residences in many parts of Missouri, as well as in other portions of the country. Nearly all the pictures which adorn the Capitol of the State at Jefferson City, are the works of his pencil. . . .

It is not alone in his profession, that Mr. Bingham has won an enviable fame. Wherever he is known his name is held in honorable mention, as a good citizen and an honorable man. As the Treasurer of the State during the dark and trying period of the civil war, and when great opportunities were offered to make money, he discharged the duties of the office with scrupulous fidelity to his trust; coming out of it as he went in, a poor, but honest man. In the discharge of the delicate and important duties of the office which he now holds [Adjutant General of Missouri], he has acquitted himself with credit. Mr. Bingham is a man of fine intellectual powers; he has read extensively, and is a gentleman of wide intelligence. He is a terse, strong and vigorous writer.

Walter Bickford Davis and Daniel S. Durrie, *An Illustrated History of Missouri . . . Including . . . Biographical Sketches of Prominent Citizens* (St. Louis: A. J. Hall and Company; Cincinnati: Robert Clarke & Co., 1876), pp. 470–471

Provenance
American Art-Union, New York, 1849 (purchased for $200)

John Boyd, Winsted, Conn., 1849 (by lottery)

Descended in family to Russell Boyd Pratt (1891–1963) and Theodora Dunn Pratt (b. ca. 1881), Towanda, Pa., to 1970

Robert Johnson, Towanda, Pa., 1970–1971

[Vose Galleries, Boston, 1971–1972]

John D. Rockefeller 3rd and Blanchette Hooker Rockefeller, New York, 1972–1979

FAMSF, 1979.7.16

Exhibition History
Cincinnati, Western Art Union, 1849, exh. no. 151

New York, American Art-Union, 1849, exh. no. 232

San Francisco 1976, exh. no. 31

The Saint Louis Art Museum, *George Caleb Bingham*, 1990, no exh. no.

Selected References
E. Maurice Bloch, "A Bingham Discovery," *American Art Review* 1, no. 1 (September–October 1973): 22–26

Barbara S. Groseclose, "Painting, Politics, and George Caleb Bingham," *The American Art Journal* 10, no. 2 (November 1978): 5, 6, 8

E. Maurice Bloch, *The Paintings of George Caleb Bingham: A Catalogue Raisonné* (Columbia: University of Missouri Press, 1986), cat. no. 185

The American Canvas, pp. 78–79, 235

Nancy Rash, *The Painting and Politics of George Caleb Bingham* (New Haven and London: Yale University Press, 1991), pp. 93–95, 106–111, 107, 124–125

Michael Shapiro, *George Caleb Bingham* (New York: Harry N. Abrams, in association with the National Museum of American Art, 1993), pp. 75–77, 79, 81, 83, 92–93, 135

Related Works
Preparatory drawings, all in the St. Louis Mercantile Library Association:

Citizen
Ink and pencil, 9/16 x 8¹¹/16 in.

Citizen
Ink and pencil, 9½ x 9⅜ in.

Country Politician
Ink and pencil, 9⅜ x 9¼ in.

Distracted Onlooker
Ink and pencil, 9/16 x 6⅞ in.

Indifferent-looking Farmer
Ink and pencil, 9⅜ x 9³/16 in.

Jolly Old Landlord
Ink and pencil, 9⅜ x 6⅞ in.

Study of a Greatcoat
Ink and pencil, 9⅜ x 6¹⁵/16 in.

Canvassing for a Vote (Candidate Electioneering), 1851/52
Oil on canvas, 25⅛ x 30³/16 in.
Nelson-Atkins Museum of Art, Kansas City, Mo.

---

44 CAPTAIN DANIEL S. HAWKINS, 1850

Oil on wood panel, 8⅛ x 6¼ in.
Inscribed on reverse: *A sketch of/Capt. Daniel S. Hawkins/By Wᵐ S. Mount/March 12ᵗʰ 1850./taken at 50 years/of age. $100-00*

WILLIAM SIDNEY MOUNT
b. Setauket, N.Y. 1807
d. Setauket, N.Y. 1868

The paintings of W. S. Mount, one of the few American artists that deserve to be called painters, are of a strictly national character; the pride and boast, not only of his native Long Island, nor yet of the State of New-York solely, but of the whole country. . . .

The youngest of three brothers, artists, our painter, the son of a substantial Long Island farmer, was born at Setauket, Suffolk co., Nov. 26, 1807. Up to the age of seventeen he had been bred "a farmer's boy," as he himself expresses it, and which early education sufficiently explains the character of the subjects of his art—all rural scenes of a domestic character, or, as in most cases, of out-of-door scenes and occupations. At that age he came up to New-York and commenced an apprenticeship as sign and ornamental painter, to his eldest brother, Henry S. Mount. . . . Feeling no doubt an instinctive superiority to this occupation, the future artist relinquished it for a higher walk. He commenced seeking after good pictures as models, and entered a student of the National Academy of Design, 1826. . . .

In 1828, he painted his first picture, a portrait of himself. In 1829, recommenced painting, in New-York, portraits. History early fired his ambition, and he imagined himself destined to succeed in Scripture pieces. . . . But he soon found his true line. . . .

He has been so universally considered *the comic painter* of the country, that his power in portraits has been overlooked. . . .

The scenery about Stony Brook is not beautiful nor romantic, but has a certain rural charm that confirms local affection. . . . Here, in serenity, and in the enjoyment of social pleasures, practising a genial hospitality, with abundance of good-humor and native courtesy,

combining much intelligence and true natural refinement, resides a pleasant society, of which the Mount family forms the centre of attraction. Pleasant excursions, and little parties at home or in the neighborhood, relieve the toils of the studio, the farm, the manufactory; and more real happiness is found than amid the splendid luxuries of the city. . . .

The character of the artist is reflected in his works,—his sweetness of temper, purity of feeling, truthfulness, gayety of heart, humorous observation, and appreciation of homely beauties of nature that are overlooked by the common eye. . . .

In common with all members of his family, who inherit a turn for humor and vivacity of spirits, he is a lover of and skilled in music, plays with spirit on the violin, and is fond of all social and innocent pleasures.

His figure is tall and slight, but graceful; his gait buoyant and springy; his manners cordial, cheery, and full of bonhomie; with a voice uncommonly musical and insinuating.

[W. Alfred Jones], "A Sketch of the Life and Character of William S. Mount," *The American Whig Review* 14, no. 80 (August 1851): 122, 123, 124, 126, 127

Year 1849

A cabinet portrait of Capt. Shalah Hawkins, a present.

Mount, "Catalogue of Portraits and Pictures," The Museums at Stony Brook Archives, reprinted in Alfred Frankenstein, *William S. Mount* (New York: Harry N. Abrams, 1975), p. 472

This portrait of a shrewd, humorous and kindly man who seems to have stepped out of one of Mount's best genre paintings is another indication that an artist is often at his best when painting his own family. Mount's mother was a Hawkins. After the death of her husband, Thomas S. Mount of Setauket, she and her young children moved back to her father's home at Stoney [*sic*] Brook, Long Island. The Hawkins family among whom the artist thus grew up was an interesting and gifted one.

E. P. Richardson, *American Art: An Exhibition from the Collection of Mr. and Mrs. John D. Rockefeller 3rd*, exh. cat. (San Francisco: The Fine Arts Museums of San Francisco, 1976), p. 102

March 12th [1850] I finished a small cabinet portrait of Capt Hawkins—by glazing with pure color drone [drawn?] thinly. The first & second sittings were painted with an eye to the finishing tints. W. S. M.

Mount, "The Whitney Journal," The Museums at Stony Brook Archives

———

Daniel Shaler Hawkins commonly called "Capt. Shaler" was born at Setauket, Nov. 24th 1798 and in early life followed the sea. He was captain of a packet running from Stony Brook to New York which was one of the chief means of communication between these two points before the advent of the railroad. Later on he retired to his farm at Stony Brook where he died in 1868.

Charles J. Werner, comp., *Genealogies of Long Island Families* (New York: Charles J. Werner, 1919), p. 95

Provenance
Daniel Shaler Hawkins (1798–1868), Stony Brook, N.Y., 1850–1868

Louise Ockers (ca. 1888–1970), Oakdale, N.Y., by 1970

[Kennedy Galleries, New York, 1970–1971]

John D. Rockefeller 3rd and Blanchette Hooker Rockefeller, New York, 1971–1979

FAMSF, 1979.7.75

Exhibition History
New York, Kennedy Galleries, *American Masters, Eighteenth to Twentieth Centuries*, 1971, exh. no. 16

San Francisco 1976, exh. no. 39

Selected Reference
Alfred Frankenstein, *William Sidney Mount* (New York: Harry N. Abrams, 1975), p. 472

---

45 FROM THE HARZ MOUNTAINS, 1853

Oil on canvas, 24½ x 32¾ in.
Signed and dated lower left: *T. W. Whitridge 1854*

WORTHINGTON WHITTREDGE
b. Springfield, Ohio 1820
d. Summit, N.J. 1910

Whittredge is remarkably accurate in drawing—a probable result of his Düsseldorf studies; and there is sometimes not only a feeling *for* but *in* his color, which betokens no common intimacy with the picturesque and poetical side of nature. . . . There is a chastened power and faithful study in the best of this artist's works which appeal quietly, but with persuasive meaning, to the mind of every one who looks on nature with even an inkling of Wordsworth's spirit, and it has been justly said of Whittredge that his landscapes often "give the aspect of foreign scenes, treated with remarkable fidelity, and with a greater degree of repose in harmony with the sentiment of the country portrayed."

Worthington Whittredge was born in Ohio, in 1820. His father was a Massachusetts farmer, and one of the earliest emigrants to the West. . . . As soon as the future artist attained his majority he went to Cincinnati, with a view to establish himself in some kind of business. After trying several pursuits, and failing to succeed in any, he determined to follow his artistic tendencies, and at once applied himself to acquire the necessary preliminary instruction; and soon began to paint portraits. . . . His love for the country and nature, together with the enticing examples of landscape art occasionally presented to him, soon won him to a more congenial branch. For a time he devoted himself entirely to studying from nature, taking his paint-box in his hand and going into the woods, in the manner of our landscape-painters at the present time, a mode of study not so generally pursued at that period as now. He continued to paint in Cincinnati . . . until 1849, when, receiving a number of commissions from the leading men of the place, he determined to visit Europe. He first went to London, and after passing a short time in that city, proceeded to Paris, where he remained several months; visiting the Rhine on a sketching tour, he stopped at Düsseldorf, and made the acquaintance, among others, of Andreas Achenbach, who kindly offered to take him as a pupil. Not very well pleased with the general style of German art, he still held Achenbach, Lessing, and a few others, in high estimation; and this rare opportunity being offered to obtain instruction, he embraced it, and remained under the tuition of this celebrated artist

about three years. His summers were spent in making sketches on the Rhine, in Westphalia, the Harz Mountains, and in Switzerland.

. . . Nearly all Whittredge's pictures painted in Düsseldorf, as well as those afterward finished at Rome, were sent directly to his Western friends, and have never been exhibited in New York. . . .

Whittredge is a progressive artist; he acquired with the dexterity, some of the mannerism of the Düsseldorf school; but constant and loving study of nature, since his return from abroad, has modified this habitude; he is more original, and applies his skill with deeper sentiment; conscientiously devoted to his art, for manly fidelity to the simple verities of nature, no one of our painters is more consistently distinguished than Worthington Whittredge.

Henry T. Tuckerman, *Book of the Artists: American Artist Life* (1867; New York: James F. Carr, 1966), pp. 514–515, 516, 518

It was through [the artist Carl Friedrich] Lessing that [Whittredge] also became immersed in the cultural life of the city [Düsseldorf]. . . . For example, he was acquainted with all the poets and musicians in Düsseldorf, particularly Robert and Clara Schumann whom he got to know "very well.". . .

Whittredge records a trip with Lessing to Hannover, which included an excursion to the nearby Harz Mountains. The journey must have taken place in August and September of 1852, the dates on a series of drawings by Lessing (Cincinnati Art Museum) which correspond in subject and style to Whittredge's. Except for the addition of a group of riders, *From the Harz Mountains* duplicates a drawing evidently showing a view near Regenstein (formerly E. P. Richardson, Philadelphia), but the perception of daylight in the delicately shaded sketch is altered to a more Romantic atmosphere using Lessing's dark palette. The canvas may be considered Whittredge's first important essay in the mainstream of Düsseldorf landscape painting. . . .

From the Harz Mountains is probably the earliest of an important group of three paintings recorded in Whittredge's account book on April 21, 1853. . . . The chronology of these canvases is problematic. They are signed and dated 1854, but all of them must have been executed between October 1852 and April 1853. . . . Whittredge postdated two of the paintings, not to mention several others, probably to make them look like recent works to clients.

Anthony F. Janson, *Worthington Whittredge* (Cambridge and New York: Cambridge University Press, 1989), p. 41

———

Completed Commissions and other Pictures

April 21st 1852 [crossed over 1853]. [thumbnail sketch of FAMSF painting] from The Harz Mountains 33/24¾ inches. To Cincinnati for sale. Accepted by Mr. Chas. Stetson for his Commission May 6ᵗʰ 1849. $100.

Whittredge, "Account Book," p. 129, Worthington Whittredge Papers, AAA, roll D28, no frame no.

Provenance
Charles Stetson (1796–at least 1863), Cincinnati, from 1854
Mrs. Conlon, New Rochelle, N.Y., ca. 1920–ca. 1974
[Berry-Hill Galleries, New York, 1974–1975]
John D. Rockefeller 3rd and Blanchette Hooker Rockefeller, New York, 1975–1989
FAMSF, 1989.8

Exhibition History
Sarasota, Fla., John and Mable Ringling Museum of Art, *Worthington Whittredge*, 1989, no publ.

Selected References
Anthony F. Janson, "Worthington Whittredge: Two Early Landscapes," *Bulletin of the Detroit Institute of Arts* 55, no. 4 (1977): 205

Marc Simpson, "Recent Acquisition: Worthington Whittredge's *From the Harz Mountains*," *Triptych*, no. 47 (September–October 1989): 21–24

Related Works
Landscape in the Harz Mountains, 1852
Watercolor and pencil on paper, 13⁹⁄₁₆ x 19¹¹⁄₁₆ in.
Mrs. E. P. Richardson, Philadelphia

Carl Friedrich Lessing (German, 1808–1880)
Rocky Landscape in the Harz Mountains, 1852
Graphite and wash with touches of opaque white on gray paper, 11 x 19 in.
Cincinnati Art Museum

---

46 ALLEN CLAPP, 1854
_____

Oil on canvas, 30 x 25 in.
Signed and dated lower right: *M. J. Heade/1854*

MARTIN JOHNSON HEADE
b. Lumberville, Pa. 1819
d. St. Augustine, Fla. 1904

Martin Johnson Heade is being given his first one-man exhibition exactly 150 years after his birth. His reputation in his own long lifetime (1819–1904) was never more than a small one; that his art is now properly appreciated for the first time suggests that he is a modern discovery, rather than a rediscovery. . . .

Heade had the longest career (from 1840 to 1904) and produced the most varied body of work of any American artist of the nineteenth century. However his worldly failure was inevitable, since for most of his life he was out of the physical, social and artistic mainstream of America. Thus in the 1840s and '50s, when George Caleb Bingham and Frederic E. Church were celebrating the exuberance of the expanding nation in their river scenes and landscapes, Heade was struggling to perfect an already out-dated portrait style. Though he had traveled as a boy to Rome and Paris, he began in a primitive, linear style. He seems to have been a typical itinerant portraitist for these two decades, though at times he could reach a high level of characterization and painterly skill, as in the portrait of *William R.* [*sic*—Allen] *Clapp*. In this elegant study in black and white the artist already signals that his primary concern would be formal structure rather than adherence to reality.

Theodore E. Stebbins, Jr., "Introducing Martin Johnson Heade," *Art News* 68, no. 8 (December 1969): 53

———

On Friday last Allen Clapp, formerly Steward of the Pennsylvania Hospital, died at the Institution in the eighty-third year of his age. The deceased was a worthy member of the Society of Friends and highly esteemed by all who had any intercourse with him as a most amiable, benevolent and kind hearted man. His good qualities peculiarly fitted him for the post he occupied for a quarter of a century in the institution, where he had peaceably closed his long career of usefulness. He resigned the stewardship a year or two since on account of the infirmities of age and has for several months been gradually sinking.

"Death of Estimable Man," *(Philadelphia) Public Ledger*, 3 March 1851

———————

Allan, b. May 5, 1768. He lived in Westchester, N.Y., many years, thence moved to Philadelphia, where he died [1851]. He was Superintendent of the Philadelphia Hospital for 25 years. Allan Clapp was noted for his fine presence and courtly manners, and was considered the gentleman of the family, *par excellence*.

Ebenezer Clapp, comp., *The Clapp Memorial: A Record of the Clapp Family in America* (Boston: David Clapp & Son, 1876), p. 285

———————

[W]e have determined from the Minutes of the Board of Managers of Pennsylvania Hospital that Allen Clapp served as Steward of the hospital from September 27, 1830 to March 26, 1849. In fact the minutes of September 27, 1830 state that "Allen Clapp and his wife, Margaret, were hired as Steward and Matron for a joint salary of $1,000 per year". I believe they got room and board also.

Joyce K. Cooper, Assistant to the President, Pennsylvania Hospital, to Sandra K. Feldman, 26 November 1974, copy in FAMSF departmental files

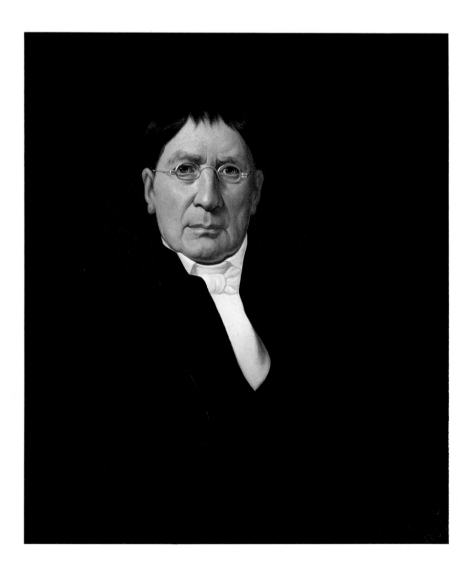

In 1850 I was a resident, as substitute, in the Pennsylvania Hospital. When writing my name in the book kept for that purpose, and writing it as I usually have done,—Walter F.,—the old steward, Friend Allen Clapp, then eighty-two years of age, said, "Thou must write thy name in full." When Franklin was written, he exclaimed, "Walter Franklin! When I was a lad I saw General Washington and Lady Washington come up the river in a boat, and walk on a carpet to Walter Franklin's house, where they were to stay, in New York." My mother was the daughter of Walter Franklin.

> Dr. Walter Franklin Atlee to *The Times*, 20 February 1889, extracted in "Notes and Queries: Washington in 1789," *The Pennsylvania Magazine of History and Biography* 13 (1889): 115

I give and bequeath the Portrait of my father to John Clapp Junior, son of John Clapp, deceased, of the City of New York.

> William R. Clapp's Will, File 3596K, Estate of William R. Clapp, Mercer County, Archives Division, New Jersey Department of State, Archives and Record Management, Trenton

Provenance
William R. Clapp (1797–1883), the subject's son, Trenton, N.J., 1854–1883
Descended in family
[Kennedy Galleries, New York, by 1962]
Dr. Irving F. Burton and Shirley Burton, Huntington Woods, Mich., 1962–1972

[Auction sale, Sotheby Parke-Bernet, New York, 18 October 1972, lot no. 3, sold for $8,000]
[Kennedy Galleries, New York, 1972]
Howard Garfinkle, New York, 1972–1973
[Kennedy Galleries, New York, 1973–1974]

John D. Rockefeller 3rd and Blanchette Hooker Rockefeller, New York, 1974–1979
FAMSF, 1979.7.50

Exhibition History
New York, National Academy of Design, *Thirty-fourth Annual Exhibition*, 1859, exh. no. 510
College Park, University of Maryland Art Gallery, *Martin Johnson Heade*, 1969, exh. no. 3

Selected References
Robert G. McIntyre, *Martin Johnson Heade, 1819–1904* (New York: Pantheon Press, 1948), p. 21
Theodore E. Stebbins, Jr., *The Life and Works of Martin Johnson Heade* (New Haven and London: Yale University Press, 1975), pp. 16, 124, 206
The American Canvas, pp. 90–91, 236

---

47 SEATED MAN, 1856

Black crayon on brown wove paper, 14 x 11⅛ in.
Signed and dated bottom center: *W. Rimmer Dec. 17/1856*

WILLIAM RIMMER
b. Liverpool, England 1816
d. South Milford, Mass. 1879

Dr. William Rimmer . . . was well known in art circles in Boston for the eighteen years preceding his death in 1879, as a remarkable lecturer upon art anatomy, a skilful delineator of its forms, as the sculptor of several statues and busts, and as a man who had painted much without establishing a reputation as a painter. For four years, included in this period, he was also known in New York as the director of the School of Design for Women at the Cooper Institute.

Of his origin nothing whatever was learned, either by his friends or the public; and outside of his family-circle little was known of his life or his struggles, even by his immediate friends. . . .

In May, 1880, an exhibition of Dr. Rimmer's works, consisting of sculptures, paintings, and drawings, was opened at the Boston Art Museum. Many even among his pupils were astonished at the variety and imaginative character of this collection. Such fertility, such rare and profound intuitive knowledge, so great comprehension of composition, had never before been seen in the works of an American artist.

> Truman H. Bartlett, *The Art Life of William Rimmer: Sculptor, Painter, and Physician* (1890; New York: Da Capo Press, for Kennedy Graphics, 1970), pp. v–vi

---

Depictions of Rimmer's family represent a significant portion of his *oeuvre*, especially in the graphic medium. The majority of these drawings represent family members during quiet

moments. The sitter here [referring to the FAMSF work] may be one of the artist's brothers, either Thomas Rimmer, Jr., or George Rimmer.

Jeffrey Weidman, in Jeffrey Weidman et al., *William Rimmer: A Yankee Michelangelo*, exh. cat. (Hanover and London: University Press of New England, for the Brockton Art Museum/Fuller Memorial, 1985), p. 43

———————

William Rimmer as a doctor was wise and able, if economically unsuccessful and often preoccupied with other concerns. Had he become a teacher of medical anatomy, he might have been a superb one in the great Boston tradition of the Warrens and Oliver Wendell Holmes. Instead, he ultimately was able to devote his full intellect, talent, and energy to his great love: art and art anatomy. What medicine lost, art gained.

Philip Cash, "American Medicine in the Time of William Rimmer," in Jeffrey Weidman et al., *William Rimmer: A Yankee Michelangelo*, exh. cat. (Hanover and London: University Press of New England, for the Brockton Art Museum/Fuller Memorial, 1985), p. 25

———————

Draw according to feeling. Feel how a woman or a man looks. . . .

Draw men, not women: you will weaken your artistic power if you do otherwise. . . .

In the female head, passions are intensified by a display of the sensibilities: in the male head, the passions are intensified by a display of the physical energies. . . .

The hair and beard relate to the physical constitution (suppositional). The eye relates to the intellect. The mouth relates to the animal passions and the appetites. . . .

The beard may hide the features, but can never dominate in the expression of an intellectual head.

William Rimmer, quoted in Truman H. Bartlett, *The Art Life of William Rimmer: Sculptor, Painter, and Physician* (1890; New York: Da Capo Press, for Kennedy Graphics, 1970), pp. 103, 104, 105

---

48 TOM WALKER'S FLIGHT, CA. 1856

Oil on canvas, 26¾ x 33¾ in.

JOHN QUIDOR

b. Tappan, N.Y. 1801
d. Jersey City, N.J. 1881

M r. Quidor was a pupil of John Wesley Jarvis. He had painted several fancy subjects with cleverness. His picture of Rip Van Winkle has merit of no ordinary kind. His principal employment in New York, has been painting devices for fire engines, and work of that description.

William Dunlap, *A History of the Rise and Progress of the Arts of Design in the United States*, 3 vols. (1834; Boston: C. E. Goodspeed & Co., 1918), 3:87

The first of the painters to turn inward upon his own imagination for his art was one of the most individual of artists. Scarcely known during his lifetime, his work is still generally ignored. . . . But the vital fact is that John Quidor, born in 1800, found in Washington Irving's books a source of phantasy which transmuted jolly stories into highly intensified and poetic genre. . . . At a time when sentiment was becoming increasingly essential to sensitive painters, he was caricaturing and relishing in a Flemish spirit the uncouth, vivid Ichabod Crane. Technically he was far ahead of his time, painting in rough, misty, glittering touches, something like Monticelli's in effect. But Monticelli was of a later generation, and Quidor was apparently unique. . . . Unlike William S. Mount, his contemporary, Quidor evolved his compositions out of an idea, not from an observation of nature. He did not hesitate to embower the festivities on the Battery, for instance, in a Watteau-like design. . . . *Anthony van Corlear Brought into the Presence of Peter Stuyvesant* [Munson-Williams-Proctor Institute, Utica, N.Y.] recalls Rowlandson and Hogarth in a remote and non-imitative way. The chief point is that Quidor loved the characters he portrayed even as he was laughing at them and lolling Falstaff-like in his imaginative cups.

> Alan Burroughs, *Limners and Likenesses: Three Centuries of American Painting* (Cambridge, Mass.: Harvard University Press, 1936), pp. 153–154

———

On one hot afternoon in the dog days, just as a terrible black thundergust was coming up, Tom sat in his counting house in his white linen cap and India silk morning gown. He was on the point of foreclosing a mortgage. . . .

Tom lost his patience and his piety—"The devil take me," said he, "if I have made a farthing!"

Just then there were three loud knocks at the street door. He stepped out to see who was there. A black man was holding a black horse which neighed and stamped with impatience.

"Tom, you're come for!" said the black fellow, gruffly. Tom shrunk back, but too late. He had left his little bible at the bottom of his coat pocket, and his big bible on the desk buried under the mortgage he was about to foreclose: never was sinner taken more unawares. The black man whisked him like a child astride the horse and away he galloped in the midst of a thunder storm. The clerks stuck their pens behind their ears and stared after him from the windows. Away went Tom Walker, dashing down the streets; his white cap bobbing up and down; his morning gown fluttering in the wind, and his steed striking fire out of the pavement at every bound. When the clerks turned to look for the black man he had disappeared.

> Washington Irving, "The Devil and Tom Walker," in *Tales of a Traveller, Part 4* (Philadelphia: H. C. Carey and I. Lea, 1824), pp. 46–47

Provenance
Bell collection, Paris

Lawrence A. Fleischman (b. 1925) and Barbara Greenberg Fleischman (b. 1924), Detroit, by 1955–1960

[Kennedy Galleries, New York, 1960–1966]

Private collection, N.H., 1966–1977

[Kennedy Galleries, New York, 1977]

John D. Rockefeller 3rd and Blanchette Hooker Rockefeller, New York, 1977–1979

FAMSF, 1979.7.84

Exhibition History
The Detroit Institute of Arts, *Collection in Progress: Selections from the Lawrence and Barbara Fleischman Collection of American Art*, 1955, exh. no. 7

Milwaukee Art Center, *American Painting, 1760–1960: A Selection of 125 Paintings from the Collection of Mr. and Mrs. Lawrence A. Fleischman, Detroit*, 1960, no exh. no.

Utica, N.Y., Munson-Williams-Proctor Institute, *John Quidor*, 1965, exh. no. 14

Cambridge, Mass., Fogg Art Museum, Harvard University, *Nineteenth-Century American Art*, 1976, no publ.

Selected References
David M. Sokol, "The Art of John Quidor," *American Art Review* 1, no. 4 (May–June 1974): 68, 70

Christopher Kent Wilson, "The Life and Work of John Quidor" (Ph.D. diss., Yale University, 1982), pp. 172, 174–176, 290

The American Canvas, pp. 68–69, 234

Related Work
The Devil and Tom Walker, 1856
Oil on canvas, 27 x 34 in.
The Cleveland Museum of Art

49 RIVER SCENE, 1858

Oil on paperboard, 5½ x 9¼ in.
Signed and dated lower left: *AB /1858*. (initials in monogram)

ALBERT BIERSTADT

b. Solingen, Germany 1830
d. New York, N.Y. 1902

Among the German emigrants who have settled in New England, within the last fifty years, is a family, the head of which was by profession a soldier, who had seen hard service during the Peninsular War. Two years before he arrived in the United States, his son Albert was born at Düsseldorf. This family, whose name is Bierstadt, have resided for many years at New Bedford, in Massachusetts. There this son, now so well-known as a landscape painter, received his school education, and subsequently engaged in various employments, always with a predilection for art, however, which he casually indulged from his earliest years. . . . Those interested in his welfare discouraged his ambition, or rather his love of art as a profession, because they knew how precarious it often proves as an exclusive resource, and because the youth had not given evidence of any remarkable talent; while his probity, application, and mastery of practical affairs gave them reason to believe in his future success in more remunerative and less ideal occupations. . . . [I]t was not until 1851, when he was in his twenty-third year, that he began to paint in oils, and determined to earn the means of visiting his native city, Düsseldorf. . . . As an academic disciple, however, Bierstadt gave no striking proof of individual merit. . . . In this, as in so many other instances, a true direction and development in landscape art was gained away from the studio, by the personal and independent study of Nature herself. . . .

The same careful finish of details, skilful management of light, and eye for picturesque possibilities, which make Bierstadt's Old World subjects so impressive and suggestive, have rendered many of his studies of American scenery full of bold and true significance. He passed part of a summer, after his return from Europe [i.e., the summer of 1858], among the White Mountains, and besides the materials for a typical landscape of that romantic region, he gained some special studies full of character and masterly effects.

Henry T. Tuckerman, *Book of the Artists: American Artist Life* (1867; New York: James F. Carr, 1966), pp. 387–388, 389

Now in drawing landscape, neither Mr. [Thomas] Hill nor Bierstadt draw correctly. They get the character only. I have sat down many a time beside Bierstadt, and his drawing was not half as correct as mine, but he had a better *tout ensemble* than I.

Virgil Williams, "Virgil Williams' Art Notes to a Deaf-Mute Pupil," *The Overland Monthly* 2d ser., 9, no. 51 (March 1887): 288

—————

And yet, Bierstadt was gifted with another kind of talent, an aspect of aesthetic that bore little resemblance to the qualities found in the gigantic, flamboyant stretches of canvas which graced every rich man's parlor and drawing room at the end of the Victorian era. . . .

Startlingly modern in terms of our present understanding of aesthetics and techniques, these were small studies, details of natural phenomena, containing within their almost minuscule scale, a vastness and depth that carried the eye great distances, recreating the essential character of mountains, trees, mist, clouds, and atmosphere. In them he not only abstracted from the particular scenery before him, but treated the subject in so simplified a manner as to become truly abstract in the final result. . . .

Like handwriting, these studies become the core of the artist's personality. They are not merely swift sketches, mental notes to be carried out later in larger works in his studio. Each little painting constitutes a study in the fullest meaning of the term.

Florence Lewison, "The Uniqueness of Albert Bierstadt," *American Artist* 28, no. 7 (September 1964): 33, 72

—————

Bierstadt is also represented [in the Rockefeller Collection] by the tiny (5½-by-9¼-inch) and exquisite *River Scene*, 1858, from the period before he went West with General Lander's expedition and was awe-struck. Three men in a rowboat are locked for all eternity in a perfectly quiet body of water—they neither glide nor battle the elements. God/nature's benevolence towards these Americans comes through the transfiguring light, and the reciprocity of the reflections in the water emphasizes the harmony.

Amy Newman, "Striving for the Equipoise between Man and Nature," *Art News* 75, no. 9 (November 1976): 77

Provenance
[Auction sale, Parke-Bernet, New York, 22 October 1969, lot no. 49]
[Hirschl & Adler Galleries, New York, 1969–1970]

John D. Rockefeller 3rd and Blanchette Hooker Rockefeller, New York, 1970–1979
FAMSF, 1979.7.14

Exhibition History
San Francisco 1976, exh. no. 41
FAMSF, *Albert Bierstadt: An Observer of Air, Light and the Feeling of a Place*, 1985, no exh. no.

Selected Reference
Martha Hutson, "Mr. and Mrs. John D. Rockefeller, 3rd: Collection of American Art," *American Art Review* 3, no. 4 (July–August 1976): 82

---

50 ROMAN FISH MARKET. ARCH OF OCTAVIUS, 1858

Oil on canvas, 27⅜ x 37⅜ in.
Signed and dated lower right: *ABierstadt/1858* (initials in monogram)

ALBERT BIERSTADT
b. Solingen, Germany 1830
d. New York, N.Y. 1902

This painting shows only a small part of the remaining ruins of the portico built by Augustus in honour of his sister but reconstructed after a fire in the reign of Septimius Severus (A.D. 193–211). A medieval brick arch replaces two of the portico's Corinthian columns. The artist painted this view inside the portico, then used as a fish market, his back toward the church of Sant'Angelo in Pescheria, looking toward the old Ghetto down a vista of narrow streets long since cleared away. The fish market was removed and some excavation done in the 1870s, but the present tidy appearance of the portico is of more recent date. [William Wetmore] Story described this portico in 1862 [in his *Roba di Roma*]:

Stone slabs, broken and grappled by iron hooks, stretch out on either side into the street, and usurp it so as to leave no carriageable way between them. If it be market-

day you will see them covered with every kind of fishes. Green crusty lobsters, squirming crawfish all alive, heaps of red mullet, baskets of little shining sardines. . . . Great dark holes open into the houses behind, begrimed with dirt and smoke. Above stretches an arch supported by black beams, over which is reared a series of chambers; here juts out on its iron arm the lantern which illuminates feebly the street at night; and here, in a grimed corner, is placed a Madonna shrine with an onion-shaped lamp burning before it.

This photograph [Scherer's figure 48, from a photograph before 1870] testifies to the literal exactness of Bierstadt's painting. The view is nearly the same as that in his picture, except that it begins a little closer to the outer arch. About the time the photograph was taken Jean Jacques Ampère wrote of the portico [in *L'Empire Romain à la Rome*, 1867]:

It is one of the most remarkable ruins of Rome; it offers one of those piquant contrasts between the past and the present that are a perpetual delight to the imagination in this city of contrasts. The Portico of Octavius is today a fish market. Its columns and pediment rise in the middle of the dirtiest place in Rome. Their effect is rendered even more picturesque, perhaps, by their setting. The site is made for a water colour. When bright sunshine lights up the ancient debris, the sombre old walls, and the narrow streets where fish are sold from straw mats spread across white marble slabs, you have, besides the Roman monument, the spectacle of a medieval market place and even something like the memory of an Oriental bazaar.

Margaret R. Scherer, *Marvels of Ancient Rome* (New York and London: Phaidon Press, for the Metropolitan Museum of Art, 1956), repr. no. 47

———

This, Bierstadt's only urban scene, was the first finished composition to result from his travels to Italy. Painted after he returned to New Bedford, Massachusetts, it was exhibited in 1858 at the Boston Athenaeum, which quickly purchased it. . . . With the meticulous handling Bierstadt had mastered in Düsseldorf, it presents a tableau of life at the fish market on the ruins of Rome's Portico of Octavia, where local folk haggle, loiter, and guard their wares, seemingly oblivious to the surviving remnants of ancient Roman glory that surrounds them.

Near the Tiber's sharp bend Caesar Augustus erected a spacious portico of 270 columns, which he named for his sister Octavia. . . . The surrounding area, graced by temples and libraries in ancient times, became Rome's Ghetto, the walled city within a city where Jews were confined until 1870 by papal decree.

This site allowed Bierstadt to depict an aspect of Rome that frequently dismayed mid-nineteenth century tourists. . . .

At the picture's right, a hapless tourist couple—the gentleman clutching Murray's red guidebook, the lady brushing off a beggar—are bewildered by the condition of the place they have ventured through labyrinthine streets to see.

. . . [Bierstadt] makes a wry comment on the devaluation of Rome's ancient grandeur, summed up by the fallen capital in the foreground, now merely a surface for cutting fish. At the right, two demigods of the classical world, the *Barberini Faun* (Glyptothek, Munich) and the *Sleeping Endymion* (Capitoline Museum, Rome), have become a worker dozing beside his broom and a dirty, barefoot fisherman asleep on the pavement.

> Diana Strazdes, "The Arch of Octavius," in Theodore E. Stebbins, Jr., *The Lure of Italy: American Artists and the Italian Experience, 1760–1914*, exh. cat. (Boston: Museum of Fine Arts, in association with Harry N. Abrams, 1992), p. 214

Dear Mr. Bolton

I trust the Athenaeum will not deliver the painting to Mr. Bierstadt. —He asks for it because he has never of late done work equal to this early specimen.

This is a question of 20 years standing. More than once he has come to me about it & I have referred him to the Trustees of the Athenaeum. Once they appointed a Comt^{ee} to look into the matter. Mr. J. Elliot Cabot examined the picture & reported that an exchange was inadvisable. He was of the opinion that Mr. Bierstadt's later work had not the quality of this early piece.

> Charles G. Loring to Charles K. Bolton, 21 November 1901, in response to Bierstadt's proposal that the Athenaeum exchange *Roman Fish Market* for a later landscape, Athenaeum records

Provenance
Boston Athenaeum, purchased from the artist for $400, 1858–1976

[Hirschl & Adler Galleries, New York, 1976]

John D. Rockefeller 3rd and Blanchette Hooker Rockefeller, New York, 1976–1979

FAMSF, 1979.7.12

Exhibition History
New Bedford, Mass., *New-Bedford Art Exhibition*, 1858, exh. no. 50

Boston Athenaeum, *Exhibitions of Paintings and Statuary, at the Athenaeum Gallery*, 1858, exh. no. 315; 1859, exh. no. 212; 1860, exh. no. 112 (1st ed.), exh. no. 125 (2d ed.); 1861, exh. no. 91; 1862, exh. no. 91; 1863, exh. no. 60; 1864, exh. no. 58; 1866, exh. no. 299; 1868, exh. no. 206; 1869, exh. no. 200; 1870, exh. no. 53; 1871, exh. no. 42; 1871–1872, exh. no. 43; 1872, exh. no. 217; 1873, exh. no. 128

New York, National Academy of Design, *Thirty-fourth Annual Exhibition*, 1859, exh. no. 757

Possibly Buffalo Fine Arts Academy, 1865

Boston, Museum of Fine Arts, extended loan, 1876–1976

Boston, Museum of Fine Arts, *Contemporary Art*, 1879, exh. no. 156

The Detroit Institute of Arts, *The World of the Romantic Artist: A Survey of American Culture from 1800 to 1875*, 1944, exh. no. 88

Norton, Mass., Library Art Gallery, Wheaton College, *American Paintings*, 1945, exh. no. 6

The Detroit Institute of Arts, *Travelers in Arcadia: American Artists in Italy, 1830–1875*, 1951, exh. no. 4

New York, The American Academy of Arts and Letters and The National Institute of Arts and Letters, *The Great Decade in American Writing, 1850–1860*, 1954, exh. no. 102

The Newark Museum, *Of Other Days: Scenes of Everyday Life*, 1957, no exh. no.

New York, Grolier Club, *The Italian Influence on American Literature*, 1961, exh. no. 240

Wilmington, Delaware Art Center, Wilmington Society of Fine Arts, *American Painting, 1857–1869*, 1962, exh. no. 5

Santa Barbara, Calif., Santa Barbara Museum of Art, *Albert Bierstadt, 1830–1902: A Retrospective Exhibition*, 1964, exh. no. 8

Possibly Manchester, Mass., Essex County Club, 1969

Fort Worth, Amon Carter Museum, *A Bierstadt*, 1972, exh. no. 10

New York, Hirschl & Adler Galleries, *The American Experience*, 1976, exh. no. 34

FAMSF, *Albert Bierstadt: An Observer of Air, Light and the Feeling of a Place*, 1985, no exh. no.

The Brooklyn Museum, *Albert Bierstadt: Art and Enterprise*, 1991, exh. no. 11

Boston, Museum of Fine Arts, *The Lure of Italy: American Artists and the Italian Experience, 1760–1914*, 1992, exh. no. 28

Selected References

"Exhibition of Paintings," *The (New Bedford, Mass.) Evening Standard*, 8 July 1858

Henry T. Tuckerman, "Albert Bierstadt," *The Galaxy* I (15 August 1866): 679

G. W. Sheldon, *American Painters: With One Hundred and Four Examples of Their Work Engraved on Wood* (1881; New York: Benjamin Blom, 1972), p. 147

Gordon Hendricks, *Albert Bierstadt: Painter of the American West* (New York: Harry N. Abrams, in association with the Amon Carter Museum of Western Art, [1974]), pp. 54, 55, 57–58, 60, 64, 90, 94, 317, 320

Matthew Baigell, *Albert Bierstadt* (New York: Watson-Guptill Publications, 1981), pp. 18–19

51 TWILIGHT, 1858

Oil on canvas (now mounted on hardboard), 23⅞ x 35⅞ in.
Signed and dated lower left: *F. E. CHURCH/58*

FREDERIC EDWIN CHURCH

b. Hartford, Conn. 1826
d. New York, N.Y. 1900

It was by a gradual transition that Church advanced from the faithful rendition of details, to a comprehensive realism in general effect, as a comparison of his early with his recent pictures demonstrates; but from the first, an attempt to transcend the most common and familiar, and to represent the most impressive phases and phenomena, is apparent. . . . The sky was the field of his earliest triumphs; some of its most remarkable and least delineated phases in the western hemisphere, he boldly and truly transferred to canvas. Few artists have so profoundly and habitually studied sunshine and atmosphere. It has long been his daily custom to ascend a hill, near his country home, to observe the sunset; and in his landscapes "the earth is always painted with reference to the skies," which is one reason of their truth to nature. A want of softness, or rather too great emphasis, in his conceptions, was deemed his great fault; but this is mainly owing to his choice of subjects. As an orator seeks a theme fitted to give ample scope to rhetoric, an artist of scientific eloquence naturally inclines to the phenomenal and the characteristic, not so much for the love of effect, as from an instinctive interest in such scenes and objects in nature as are exceptional and impressive. . . .

Time was when a landscape was painted by a kind of mathematical formula; rules of composition, far more than observation of fact, formed the basis of the work. . . . And it was long deemed essential to an American student that he should go abroad and learn tricks of light, and how to manage color for effect. But here is a painter who has never been in Europe, and who, having acquired the requisite dexterity in the use of the pencil, went confidently to nature herself, using his eyes and his intelligence, and striving to reproduce what he saw, knew, and felt. . . .

While thus initiating a high executive standard, few have contributed more toward making landscape art popular than Church.

Henry T. Tuckerman, *Book of the Artists: American Artist Life* (1867; New York: James C. Carr, 1966), pp. 371, 372, 373

———

Twilight was derived from an oil sketch, now at Olana [Church's home on the Hudson River, a historic site administered by the New York State Office of Parks, Recreation and Historic Preservation], that depicts precisely the same cloud patterns and a similar hilly site. . . .

The close association between the painting and the preliminary oil sketch provides an excellent opportunity for a few observations on Church's working methods in this period.

The sketch, which was certainly executed on the spot (although just where is unknown), is primarily an attempt to record the color and shape of the cloud formations and the general configurations of the land below. It is very broadly and freely brushed, no doubt the result of fifteen or twenty minutes of careful observation and work. Owing to its free handling and roughly textured pigment, the sketch gives little illusion of depth to the sky or mass to the clouds. However, in the finished oil, Church, although adhering closely to the general scheme of the sketch, transformed the sky and clouds. The clouds seem soft, vaporous, and suffused with light, and the pigment has been skillfully manipulated to leave little trace of brushstroke that would interfere with the illusion. Clearly Church had learned through long study exactly how to capture such evanescent effects. As John Ruskin would comment some years later, "He can draw clouds as few men can."

Franklin Kelly, *Frederic Edwin Church and the National Landscape* (Washington, D.C.: Smithsonian Institution Press, 1988), pp. 85–86

Church also continued in these years [the later 1850s] to explore the North American wilderness, with a corresponding shift away from the pastoral viewpoint. . . . In *Twilight (Sunset)* [Albany Institute of History and Art], painted early in 1856, the presence of a substantial house in what is seemingly a wilderness area suggests an uncertain and perhaps uneasy relationship between American nature and American civilization. In a closely related painting, also known as *Twilight* [the FAMSF painting], however, Church introduced only a lonely trapper's hut into the otherwise unspoiled wilderness. One of Church's most mysterious and evocative works, *Twilight* is also one of his most beautifully painted, with softly glowing colors and a convincing sense of light and atmosphere.

Franklin Kelly, "A Passion for Landscape: The Paintings of Frederic Edwin Church," in *Frederic Edwin Church*, exh. cat. (Washington, D.C.: National Gallery of Art, 1989), p. 53

Provenance

[Harry Shaw Newman Gallery/ The Old Print Shop, New York, by 1953]

O. W. June, New York, by 1960

Lawrence A. Fleischman (b. 1925) and Barbara Greenberg Fleischman (b. 1924), Detroit, 1960–1965

[Kennedy Galleries, New York, 1965–1966]

John D. Rockefeller 3rd and Blanchette Hooker Rockefeller, New York, 1966–1993

FAMSF, 1993.35.6

Exhibition History

Indianapolis, John Herron Art Museum, *Romantic America*, 1961, exh. no. 8

The Detroit Institute of Arts, *American Paintings and Drawings from Michigan Collections*, 1962, exh. no. 55

Tucson, University of Arizona Art Gallery, *American Painting, 1765–1963: Selections from the Lawrence A. and Barbara Fleischman Collection of American Art*, 1964, exh. no. 17

New York, Kennedy Galleries, *Past and Present: Two Hundred Years of American Painting, Part One: Eighteenth and Nineteenth Centuries*, 1966, no exh. no.

San Francisco 1976, exh. no. 45

Washington, D.C., National Gallery of Art, *American Light: The Luminist Movement, 1850–1875*, 1980, no exh. no.

FAMSF, *Director's Choice: Twenty Years of Collecting*, 1987, no publ.

Washington, D.C., National Gallery of Art, *Frederic Edwin Church*, 1989, exh. no. 31

Selected Reference

David Huntington, "Frederic Edwin Church, 1826–1900: Painter of the Adamic New World Myth" (Ph.D. diss., Yale University, 1960), pp. 70–71, Appendix, cat. no. 42

Related Works

Twilight, Short Arbiter 'Twixt Day and Night, 1850
Oil on canvas, 32 x 48 in.
The Newark Museum

Sunset, 1856
Oil on canvas, 24 x 36 in.
Munson-Williams-Proctor Institute, Utica, New York

Twilight (Sunset), 1856
Oil on canvas, 16¼ x 24¼ in.
Albany Institute of History and Art

Study for "Twilight," ca. 1856
Oil on paper, 12 x 18 in.
New York State, Office of Parks, Recreation and Historic Preservation, Olana State Historic Site

The Evening Star, 1858
Oil on canvas, 7¾ x 10½ in.
Jamee and Marshall Field, Chicago, as of 1988

Twilight in the Wilderness, 1860
Oil on canvas, 40 x 64 in.
The Cleveland Museum of Art

52 A RIVER LANDSCAPE, 1858

Oil on canvas, 32 x 48 in.
Signed and dated lower right: *A B Durand/1858*

ASHER B. DURAND

b. Jefferson Village (now Maplewood), N.J. 1796
d. Maplewood, N.J. 1886

I was born on the 21st day of August, 1796, at a small village in the township of Springfield, county of Essex, state of New Jersey. My father was a watchmaker and silversmith by profession. . . . A more industrious man never lived. Yet with all his industry and resources he was unable to amass anything beyond the means for a comfortable living, owing chiefly to extremely moderate charges for his labour and the maintenance of a large family of children. . . .

. . . I am the sixth of seven brothers, and, if I may judge by earliest recollections, the feebleness of my constitution was in proportion to the order of succession. I remember a keen sense of insignificance compared with the rest of my brothers. I was, indeed, a delicate child. . . .

My father and two of my elder brothers were accustomed to engrave monograms and other devices on the various articles manufactured by them, and in this art I was early initiated. But I was not content with this, having shown some skill in drawing animals as well as the human figure. . . . [J]ust entering my seventeenth year, I took my seat in his [Peter Maverick's] engraving-room, regularly apprenticed to him for a term of five years. . . .

My career as engraver thus commenced in October 1812. . . . My progress was rapid. I soon surpassed my shopmates, and became the chief assistant of my master.

Durand, "Autobiographical Fragment," in John Durand, *The Life and Times of A. B. Durand* (1894; New York: Da Capo Press, for Kennedy Graphics, 1970), pp. 18–24

———

After ten years of prosperous labor upon small figures and portraits [engraving banknotes and copying others' works], Durand, partly through the liberal encouragement of his friend, Luman Reed, in 1835 abandoned engraving for portrait and landscape-painting; . . . for landscape art he had always cherished a fondness, having its source in the earnest love of nature which has ever characterized his works. The honesty of his purpose and fidelity of his habits, increased by so long a practice in the imitation and minute labors of an engraver, were carried into his new vocation; and with these technical facilities, a scope and sentiment

which redeemed them from mere mechanical excellence; elaborated with care, they were not less idylic in spirit than faithful in detail. . . . [T]he full power of his taste and talent, and especially his feeling for nature found memorable expression in a series of American Landscapes. . . .

His brother-artists testified their respect for his character and admiration of his talent by electing him President of the National Academy of Design, an office he held several years. . . . Seldom has an honor been more justly awarded. . . . His reverence—a sentiment essential to the pure interpretation of nature—is manifest in his style and tone of painting.

Henry T. Tuckerman, *Book of the Artists: American Artist Life* (1867; New York: James F. Carr, 1966), pp. 188–189, 196

———

Yes! go first to Nature to learn to paint landscape, and when you shall have learnt to imitate her, you may then study the pictures of great artists with benefit. . . . I would urge on any young student in landscape painting, the importance of painting direct from Nature as soon as he shall have acquired the first rudiments of Art.

A. B. Durand, "Letters on Landscape Painting: Letter 1," *The Crayon* 1, no. 1 (3 January 1855): 2

———

Go not abroad then in search of material for the exercise of your pencil, while the virgin charms of our native land have claims on your deepest affections. Many are the flowers in our untrodden wilds that have blushed too long unseen, and their original freshness will reward your research with a higher and purer satisfaction, than appertains to the display of the most brilliant exotic. The "lone and tranquil" lakes embosomed in ancient forests, that abound in our wild districts, the unshorn mountains surrounding them with their richly-textured covering, the ocean prairies of the West, and many other forms of Nature yet spared from the pollutions of civilization, afford a guarantee for a reputation of originality that you may elsewhere long seek and find not.

A. B. Durand, "Letters on Landscape Painting: Letter 2," *The Crayon* 1, no. 3 (17 January 1855): 34–35

Provenance
Possibly Lewis M. Rutherford (1816–1892), New York, or L. R. Menger, or Benjamin N. Huntington (ca. 1816–1882), Rome, N.Y., 1858

[Harvey Additon, Boston, ca. 1910]

Winthrop Coffin (ca. 1863–1938), Brookline, Mass., ca. 1910–1938

Richard S. Halfyard (1901–1988)

and Eliza Halfyard (1906–1984), Belmont, Mass., ca. 1938–1971

[Vose Galleries, Boston, 1971–1972]

John D. Rockefeller 3rd and Blanchette Hooker Rockefeller, New York, 1972–1993

FAMSF, 1993.35.8

Exhibition History
Possibly New York, National Academy of Design, *Thirty-third Annual Exhibition*, 1858, exh. no. 492 (*Landscape*, lent by L. M. Rutherford) or exh. no. 585 (*In New Hampshire*, lent by L. R. Menger)

San Francisco 1976, exh. no. 36

Tokyo 1982, exh. no. 27

Selected References
Possibly John Durand, *The Life and Times of A . B . Durand* (1894; New York: Da Capo Press, for Kennedy Graphics, 1970), p. 176

David B. Lawall, *Asher B . Durand: A Documentary Catalogue of the Narrative and Landscape Paintings* (New York and London: Garland Publishing, 1978), cat. no. 226

Related Work
A Pastoral Scene, 1858
Oil on canvas, 21⅞ x 32⅜ in.
National Gallery of Art, Washington, D.C.

53 SUNRISE AMONG THE ROCKS OF PARADISE AT NEWPORT, 1859

Oil on canvas, 18 x 30 in.
Signed and dated lower left: *JF.K . 59* (*J* and *F* in monogram)

JOHN F. KENSETT
b. Cheshire, Conn. 1816
d. New York, N.Y. 1872

Like Durand, Kensett was initiated into the practice of landscape art through engraving; and to this may be ascribed somewhat of the careful work so manifest in his pictures. He studied engraving with his uncle, Alfred Daggett, who, for several years, was noted for the excellence of his bank-note vignettes. While thus occupied in the fine execution incident to this art, he turned to painting as a recreation; and his love therefor, as well as his progressive taste and ability therein, led him in 1845 to abandon the burin for the pencil. . . .

While in Europe in 1840 with Durand, [John] Casilear, and [Thomas] Rossiter, he studied the antique and practised in oil. It was amid the gracious scene of Pope's juvenile rhymes, that Kensett first enjoyed the delight of successfully representing nature: "My real life commenced there," he writes, "in the study of the stately woods of Windsor, and the famous beeches of Burnham, and the lovely and fascinating landscape that surrounds them.". . .

. . . He passed seven years abroad, constantly improving in execution and enlarging his knowledge of scenery. Upon his return to his native land, he commenced a series of careful studies of our mountain, lake, forest, and coast landscape; and in his delineation of rocks, trees, and water, attained a wide and permanent celebrity. . . . Since 1848 he has been connected with the National Academy, and his studio has been one of the attractions in New York to all lovers of art and scenery. . . .

. . . Careful observation is the source of Kensett's eminent success. He gives the form and superficial traits of land and water so exactly as to stamp on the most hasty sketch a local character indicative of similitude. His landscapes would charm even a man of science, so loyal to natural peculiarities are his touch and eye. . . .

There is one obstacle to impartiality in estimating Kensett, as an artist, to one who knows him well; and that is the personal confidence and sympathy he inspires. Of all our artists, he has the most thoroughly amiable disposition, is wholly superior to envy, and pursues his vocation in such a spirit of love and kindliness, that a critic must be made of very hard material who can find it in his heart to say a severe, inconsiderate, or careless word about John F. Kensett.

Henry T. Tuckerman, *Book of the Artists: American Artist Life* (1867; New York: James F. Carr, 1966), pp. 510, 511, 513, 514

———

Jan. 25 [1859]
    pd. Sunrise among the Rocks of Paradise at Newport—Wynans—300

    "A List of All Paintings Sold with Prices and to whom Sold, Years 1848 to Year of Kensett's Death Dec/1872," John F. Kensett Papers, AAA, roll N68–85, frame 479

———

Paradise Rocks, the rough landscape immediately behind Sachuest Beach in Middletown, was painted by Kensett in 1859. This particular view is just to the west of Hanging Rock, looking northeast across the marsh between Hanging Rock Ridge and "second ridge," now identified with Red Fox Trail in the Norman Bird Sanctuary. The rocks to the right of the canvas extend out to form Hanging Rock. . . .

This rough and barren landscape is not as remote as it might at first appear, for it is only a few yards from the road that connected the beaches of Middletown with Newport. It was a popular afternoon ride from the town, where "hanging rocks, showing their dark sides and surmounted with stunted spruce and fir trees" contrasted with the sands of Sachuest Beach "whitened by the breakers." For Kensett's wealthy patrons . . . , these scenes provided a souvenir of their Newport summer retreat which hung in their urban winter homes.

> Robert Workman, "Among the Rocks of Great Waters at Newport, Rhode Island," *The Eden of America: Rhode Island Landscapes, 1820–1920*, exh. cat. (Providence: Museum of Art, Rhode Island School of Design, 1986), p. 28

Provenance
Unidentified member of the Wynans family, from 1859

[David David, Philadelphia, by 1967]

[Kennedy Galleries, New York, 1967–1968]

Lawrence A. Groo, Jr., New York, 1968–1969

[Kennedy Galleries, New York, 1969]

John D. Rockefeller 3rd and Blanchette Hooker Rockefeller, New York, 1969–1979

FAMSF, 1979.7.69

Exhibition History
New York, The American Federation of Arts, *John Frederick Kensett, 1816–1872*, 1968, exh. no. 31 (as *Among the Rocks of Great Waters at Newport*)

Providence, Museum of Art, Rhode Island School of Design, *The Eden of America: Rhode Island Landscapes, 1820–1920*, 1986, exh. no. 9 (as *Among the Rocks of Great Waters at Newport, Rhode Island*)

Newport, R.I., Newport Art Museum, *The Lost Landscape: The Romantic Vision*, 1991, no publ.

Selected References
John Howat, "John F. Kensett, 1816–1872," *The Magazine Antiques* 96, no. 3 (September 1969): 399 (as *Among the Rocks of Great Waters at Newport*)

The American Canvas, pp. 84–85, 235

Related Works
Paradise Rocks, Newport, ca. 1859
Oil on canvas, 18⅛ x 29⅞ in.
The Newark Museum

John H. B. Latrobe (American, 1803–1891)
American Scene, 1861
Oil on canvas, 20 x 32 in. (sight)
Maryland Historical Society, Baltimore

Oil on canvas, 36 x 71⅜ in.

WILLIAM PAGE
b. Albany, N.Y. 1811
d. Tottenville, N.Y. 1885

Now when Jesus was born in Bethlehem of Judea, in the days of Herod the king, behold, wise men from the east came to Jerusalem, saying, "Where is he who has been born king of the Jews? For we have seen his star in the East, and have come to worship him." When Herod the king heard this, he was troubled, and all Jerusalem with him. . . . And being warned in a dream not to return to Herod, they [the wise men] departed to their own country by another way. Now when they had departed, behold, an angel of the Lord appeared to Joseph in a dream and said, "Rise, take the child and his mother, and flee to Egypt, and remain there till I tell you; for Herod is about to search for the child, to destroy him." And he rose and took the child and his mother by night, and departed to Egypt.

The Bible, Revised Standard Version, Matthew 2:1–3, 12–14

My dear Mr. Ruskin:

We send to you every now and then somebody hungry for a touch from your hand; we who are famished for it ourselves. But this time we send you a man whom you will value perfectly for himself and be kind to from yourself, quite spontaneously. He is the American artist, Page, an earnest, simple, noble artist and man, who carries his Christianity down from his deep heart to the point of his brush. Draw him out to talk to you, and you will find it worth while. He has learnt much from Swedenborg, and used it in his views upon art.

Elizabeth Barrett Browning to John Ruskin, 3 June 1859, quoted in E. P. Richardson and Otto Wittmann, *Travelers in Arcadia: American Artists in Italy, 1830–1875*, exh. cat. (Detroit: The Detroit Institute of Arts, 1951), pp. 53–54

I am now just finishing a "Flight into Egypt" six feet long, which is to be sent to London to Mr Henry Stevens my wifes brother there to be sold if possible.

Page to Frank G. and Sarah Shaw, 14 May 1859, Houghton Library, Harvard University (bMS Am 765 [619])

The first version of the "Flight into Egypt" was lost at sea, but Page had retained a tracing of the composition and executed another, larger than the first, which was finished only in 1859. It is an unusual painting with its quiet, somber mood, evoking a sense of expectation at the same time it establishes a feeling of tranquillity. "Who of those who were so fortunate as to see this work of Mr. Page will ever forget the solemn, yet radiant tone pervading the landscape of sad Egypt, along which went the fugitives?" wrote [Paul] Akers [in 1861].

The effect of the picture is dependent to a large degree on a compositional organization quite remarkable for its time. . . . The color intensifies the effect of space and the mood of quiet. . . .

If one were moved to discuss paintings in terms of music and poetry, this would be a most provocative subject. Like the Venus [one version now at the National Museum of American Art, Washington, D.C.], this painting, too, had its poetical meter for Page. In wishing to express "the hot desert and the long weary journey," Browning's "Childe Roland to the Dark Tower Came" rose repeatedly to his lips.

And just as far as ever from the end:
Naught in the distance but the evening, naught
To point my footsteps farther!

These poetic associations he considered "a mere rhythmic sensation which seemed to keep time to the subject." A startled Italian model who noticed Page's habit of mumbling verse furtively informed a visitor of his opinion—"mezzo matto!" But the rhythm, Page felt, dominated every stroke of the brush and helped imbue the very painterly means themselves with a poetic consistency. "Every picture," he said, "requires the hum of verses."

One surprising aspect of the painting is the appearance of Joseph. Instead of the traditional elder in flowing robes, he is a vigorous, muscular figure, suggesting in his alert stance the Vatican's standing discus-thrower which Page had studied with such care. It is Joseph who braves the barren expanse of new country while Mary docilely follows.

Joshua Taylor, *William Page: The American Titian* (Chicago: University of Chicago Press, 1957), pp. 152–153

Provenance
Descended in artist's family to Pauline Page (Mrs. Lesslie Stockton) Howell, Philadelphia and West Palm Beach, Fla., 1952–1964

[Kennedy Galleries, New York, 1964–1974]

John D. Rockefeller 3rd and Blanchette Hooker Rockefeller, New York, 1974–1979

FAMSF, 1979.7.78

Exhibition History
The Detroit Institute of Arts, *Travelers in Arcadia: American Artists in Italy, 1830–1875*, 1951, exh. no. 79

Staten Island Institute of Art and Sciences, New York, *Staten Island and Its Artistic Heritage*, 1967, no publ.

New York, Kennedy Galleries, *American Masters, Eighteenth to Twentieth Centuries*, 1971, exh. no. 20

New York, Kennedy Galleries, *American Masters, Eighteenth to Twentieth Centuries*, 1972, exh. no. 45

Berkeley, Calif., University Art Museum, *The Hand and the Spirit: Religious Art in America, 1700–1900*, 1972, exh. no. 28

San Francisco 1976, exh. no. 52

Selected References
E. P. Richardson, "Two Portraits by William Page," *The Art Quarterly* I, no. 2 (Spring 1938): 95, 103

Joshua Taylor, *William Page: The American Titian* (Chicago: University of Chicago Press, 1957), pp. 152–153, 216, cat. no. 35

Joshua Taylor, "The Fascinating Mrs. Page," *The Art Quarterly* 20, no. 4 (Winter 1957): 358, 362

Related Work
Flight into Egypt, ca. 1856 Owned by a Mr. Field and lost at sea before 1860

Oil on canvas, 11⅝ x 9½ in.
Signed lower left: *EVEDDER* (initials in monogram)

ELIHU VEDDER
b. New York, N.Y. 1836
d. Rome, Italy 1923

Elihu Vedder was born in the city of New York, February, 1836. His father, a dentist, was then in practice there; but soon after went to Cuba, where he still resides. Both the parents of the artist are of the old Dutch stock of the Mohawk Valley, and came from the vicinity of Schenectady. As a child, the little Elihu would chew sticks into brushes, and invest his money in cheap paints. . . . Ardent in temperament, and diligent in pursuit of art, he was also eminently social, and had a keen appreciation of humor. His original attempts were timid; . . . it was only by degrees . . . that he exhibited that fertility of imagination and vigor of handling, which have since characterized his works. . . .

Of all our *genre* painters, Elihu Vedder is the most individual and independent. A scion of the old Knickerbocker stock, and but now in his prime, he has pursued his artistic way with singular self-reliance, freedom, and faith. Whatever defects there may be in his pictures, they are never uninteresting, rarely unimpressive; and this is because his mood and manner are his own; he follows out a weird, fantastic, or ideal vein, which is the reverse of the conventional and familiar, and yet is too genuine to be grotesque. Perhaps no one of our artists has excited greater expectations. We instinctively imagine him about to surprise or enchant us, so many hints of the strange, the psychological, and the poetically suggestive, are given by his compositions. He passed several years in Italy, then opened a studio in New York, his native city, and has again gone abroad.

Henry T. Tuckerman, *Book of the Artists: American Artist Life* (1867; New York: James F. Carr, 1966), pp. 453, 451

Another picture we remember [looking back over Vedder's early career to the National Academy of Design exhibition of 1862]—"Dominican Monks in the Convent Garden"—a little canvas, but painted with mingled sweetness and power by a man who, it was plain, saw things with his own eyes, and not according to rule. He loved this Italian sky, these cypresses, this golden light; he looked at them, not as botanist, not as philosopher, but as passionate lover, and painted them from his dream, to feed his dream. There was no carelessness in this little work; no carelessness but earnest care to record a happy memory, sun-steeped in golden dew; no denying of Nature to gain a so-called miscalled ideal; the ideal was evidently being sought where alone it is to be found, in faithfulness to Nature, in loyalty to her truth. It was singular work. People pored over it, wondered at it, left it—came back to it. The best of his pictures, hung high as it was, out of reach, in the dark, had power in it to draw curious eyes, which studied and remembered it. Mr. Vedder had conquered his place; his place could not conquer him.

Clarence Cook, "National Academy of Design," *New-York Daily Tribune*, 4 June 1864

It was here [at the foot of the long ascent to Fiesole] I painted two of my best studies, and also a little picture I always thought highly of. . . .

The little picture was really a sketch I made on a dark stormy day, of Fiesole with the road and cypresses coming down from it, into the foreground of which I had painted three Dominican friars, whose black and white garments carried out the feeling seen in hillside and sky. This little picture must have perished in a Loan Exhibition held in Madison Square Garden, when part of the building collapsed. The memory of its loss is one of my pet griefs to this day. . . .

The little picture of the monks was bought by Mrs. Laura Curtis Bullard. She also bought the "Lost Mind." She was from the beginning, and always remained, my good friend.

Elihu Vedder, *The Digressions of V.* (London: Constable & Co.; Boston and New York: Houghton Mifflin Company, 1911), pp. 164–165, 166

Reading with pleasure again your kind letter I noticed that I did not give you enough details concerning Miss Lisie Potter as asked. Will say that I firmly believe now that she never bought the precious little painting though she knew much about your fame & your great works.

All the Potter family is now dead & she sold me the picture few months before her end; The Potters never spoke to neighbors about paintings they probably had none. The last twenty or thirty years an old lady & her son Henry E. Coddington came to live with Miss Lisie Potter they probably brought your painting the three Monks of Fiesola there. Where did they get it? no one will ever know as they are all dead without any relatifs to be found. I have been able to hear at last of a nephew of the Coddingtons, but he is in France fighting with the British army. It is very likely as Mrs. Bullard's son thinks, that the painting was either stolen, or overlooked in the ruins & afterwards picked up by a workingman.

Anyway after all, it has been found & will be hanging again with the other pictures in Mr. Bullard's residence after things will be straightened out with the insurance Co. which we have not been able to find yet.

Prosper Guerry to Vedder, 20 April 1915, Elihu Vedder Papers, AAA, roll 524, frame 202

Provenance

Laura Curtis Bullard (d. 1912), Brooklyn, purchased for $75, ca. 1862–1880

Retrieved by unknown person from Madison Square Garden collapse, 21 April 1880

Probably Henry E. Coddington, New York

Lisie Potter (d. ca. 1905), New York, by ca. 1905

Prosper Guerry, New York and Elizabeth, N.J., ca. 1905–1915

Harold Curtis Bullard (ca. 1880–1949), New York and Fairfield, Conn., 1915–before 1919

Elihu Vedder, by 1919–1923

Descended in artist's family

[Danenberg Galleries, New York, by 1973]

John D. Rockefeller 3rd and Blanchette Hooker Rockefeller, New York, 1973–1979

FAMSF, 1979.7.101

Exhibition History

New York, National Academy of Design, *Thirty-seventh Annual Exhibition*, 1862, exh. no. 474

New York, Madison Square Garden, *Loan Exhibition*, 1880

Washington, D.C., The Corcoran Gallery of Art, *Seventh Exhibition of Oil Paintings by Contemporary American Artists*, 1919, exh. no. 46 (as *The Three Monks at Fiesole*)

San Francisco 1976, exh. no. 93 (as *Three Monks Walking in a Garden at Fiesole*)

Washington, D.C., National Collection of Fine Arts, *Perceptions and Evocations: The Art of Elihu Vedder*, 1978, exh. no. 7

Selected References

Art Interchange 4, no. 9 (28 April 1880): 76

Regina Soria, *Elihu Vedder: American Visionary Artist in Rome, 1836–1923* (Rutherford, N.J.: Fairleigh Dickinson University Press, 1970), pp. 28–29, cat. no. 25

Martha Hutson, "Mr. and Mrs. John D. Rockefeller, 3rd: Collection of American Art," *American Art Review* 3, no. 4 (July–August 1976): 84

Related Works

Fiesole, 1859
Oil on canvas, 15 x 29½ in.
The Detroit Institute of Arts

Drawing of a Monk, ca. 1859
Pencil on paper, 5⅜ x 3⅛ in.
Harold O. Love Family Collection, Detroit, as of 1979

The Monk's Walk: In a Garden near Florence, 1863
Location unknown

Monks on the Appian Way, ca. 1865
Oil on canvas, 3¼ x 5 in.
National Museum of American Art, Washington, D.C.

56 WINDSOR CASTLE, 1860

Oil on canvas, 17¾ x 29⅞ in.
Signed and dated lower left: *S R Gifford 1860*

SANFORD R. GIFFORD

b. Greenfield, N.Y. 1823
d. New York, N.Y. 1880

My acquaintance with Gifford began twenty-five years ago [i.e., ca. 1855], or soon after he commenced his career as an artist. Of his boyhood or college days [at Brown University, in Providence, R.I.] I know but little. I once asked him how it happened that he chose the study of art instead of choosing some other occupation. He replied in his characteristic way, "I don't know; it happened so," and this was as far as I could get.

Gifford lived in Rome in the most unostentatious manner. Abundantly able to provide elegant apartments for himself with separate studio, he preferred to hunt Rome over to find a single room where he could overlook the city and look out upon the evening sky. . . .

But it is here at home in his little old studio in the Tenth St. studio building where we knew him best. . . . [T]hough ordinarily no great talker, he conversed readily when art was the subject. He held broad views and had few prejudices. His language was extremely clear and forcible, and when speaking of painting he used no foreign terms. . . .

When sketching he preferred to look about for the fleeting effects of nature. He would frequently stop in his tracks to make slight sketches in pencil in a small book which he always carried in his pocket and then pass on, always suspicious that if he stopped too long to look in one direction the most beautiful thing of all might pass him by at his back.

Worthington Whittredge, *The Autobiography of Worthington Whittredge, 1820–1910*, ed. John I. H. Baur (1942; New York: Arno Press, 1969), pp. 55, 57, 59

This artist loved the light. His finest impressions were those derived from the landscape when the air is charged with an effulgence of irruptive and glowing light. . . .

His pictures manifest a lucid spontaneity that is perhaps their greatest charm. They are the free expression of the higher and more poetic qualities of landscape. They are not the merely literal rendering of the facts of nature with prosaic precision. They are, rather, a lucid reminiscence, a passional and poetic form of art that kindles emotion, or moves one to reverie.

John F. Weir, "Sanford R. Gifford: Artist and Man," *New-York Daily Tribune*, 12 September 1880

On the 9th [July 1855] . . . I shouldered my haversack and umbrella case and said good bye
to London for a while. I had the curiosity to put my haversack on the scales of a weigher who
has his station here, as I crossed Waterloo Bridge to the Windsor Station, and who for a
penny tells your weight. The weight of my bag and its contents was fifteen pounds. In it I
have three shirts, one pair of socks, sketch box & extra colors, writing portfolio, ink, two
sketch books, one block for oil sketches, maps, Black's Tourist, two thin books for journal,
notes and expenses, tobacco & pipe, a few cigars, an extra haversack, matches, fish line and
hooks, tooth brush, sewing apparatus, handkerchiefs, and a few other little things. I have
only the gray woolen suit that I stand in—no overcoat. I would have been glad to take a black
coat for social purposes, but that would double the bulk of my luggage, and so I preferred to
deprive myself of what a black coat might possibly bring me. . . .

It was four o'clock when I reached Windsor. . . .

In the evening I made a sketch of the castle from "Datchett Mead" in the home park.
"Datchett Mead" you remember was the place where the Merry Wives of Windsor got Fall-
staff [sic] a ducking. It was quite light while I was sketching, viz, 9 o'c. Twilight does not
entirely fade till 10, or later.

July 10th. My birthday. I celebrated it by doing a good many things—first by making a
sketch of the castle from the Thames, which here winds about very much and bears (according
to a history of the town I picked up here) the name of Windsor—from the Saxon Wyndesor,
Wyndeshore [this is probably the sketch on which the FAMSF painting is based]. . . .

11th. A rainy day which I occupied in writing letters. In the evening we had a fine
sunset, and I enjoyed a walk up the Thames. . . . There was a fine "effect" on the castle just
before sunset. It crowns a bluff, and at this time its regal towers and battlements were relieved in the warm sunlight against the dark sullen gray of the clouds behind them: high over
them arched a brilliant rainbow.

Gifford, "European Letters," vol. 1, Sanford R. Gifford papers, AAA, roll D21, letter no. 5

———————

241. WINDSOR CASTLE. Size, 16 x 30. Sold in 1861 to H. W. Rogers, Buffalo, N.Y. . . .

253. SUNRISE AT WINDSOR CASTLE, A SKETCH. Not dated. Size, 4 x 6. Owned by Miss Bertha E. Davy [probably the sketch on which the FAMSF painting is based, no. 241].

John F. Weir, *A Memorial Catalogue of the Paintings of Sanford Robinson Gifford, N.A.* (1881; New York: Olana Gallery, 1974), pp. 23–24

Provenance
H. W. Rogers, Buffalo, from 1861

[Hirschl & Adler Galleries, New York, 1969–1971]

John D. Rockefeller 3rd and Blanchette Hooker Rockefeller, New York, 1971–1979

FAMSF, 1979.7.44

Exhibition History
New York, Hirschl & Adler Galleries, *The American Scene: A Survey of the Life and Landscape of the Nineteenth Century*, 1969, exh. no. 30

Austin, The University of Texas Art Museum, *Sanford Robinson Gifford*, 1970, exh. no. 18

Selected References
Ila Weiss, *Poetic Landscape: The Art and Experience of Sanford R. Gifford* (Newark: University of Delaware Press, 1987), p. 10

The American Canvas, pp. 104–105, 237

Related Works
Windsor Castle, 1855
Oil on wood, mounted on canvas, 4¼ x 7¼ in.
Museum of Art, Rhode Island School of Design, Providence

Sunrise at Windsor Castle, a Sketch, ca. 1855
Oil on board (?), 4 x 6 in.
Miss Bertha E. Davy, as of 1881

Windsor Castle, ca. 1855
Oil on canvas, 16¼ x 25¼ in.
The Cooley Gallery, Old Lyme, Conn., as of 1988

Windsor Castle, 1859
Oil on canvas, 10½ x 19½ in.
George Walter Vincent Smith Art Museum, Springfield, Mass.

57 JUSTICE, CA. 1860

Oil on canvas, 20⅛ x 24⅛ in.
Signed lower right: *Blythe*

DAVID GILMOUR BLYTHE

b. East Liverpool, Ohio 1815
d. Pittsburgh, Pa. 1865

In 1856 David Gilmour Blythe was at the pivotal point of his artistic career. He had just moved to Pittsburgh, Pennsylvania, from East Liverpool, Ohio, his hometown, to which he had returned but two years earlier after several years of wandering in the Midwest in search of a place where he might peacefully settle. His need for a haven was acute, for in the years between 1850 and 1852 he had been buffeted by the deaths of his wife and father, and the dismal failure of an ambitious moving panorama on which he had staked both his financial security and his professional reputation. Embittered by his losses and by what he felt was pervasive social and political corruption, Blythe had by 1856 begun to turn away from the portraiture on which he had survived for the previous sixteen years, and had started instead to focus on images that satirized the folly and turpitude of mankind. . . .

While journalists, editors, and the clergy were also objects of Blythe's verbal attacks, his most sardonic jibes were aimed at the American system of legal justice and its various professional servants.

> Our courts with few exceptions
> Are fit subjects for like objections.
> Public opinion first, Blackstone second.
> Justice, now here's the way law is reckoned
> Now-a-days. And then our juries—
> Oh! if there are such things as Furies
> Why don't they "pitch in"? Curious,
> Just imagine twelve ignoramuses
> With flat heads and red "wammuses"
> Sitting in judgment on an intricate
> Case of law. Beautiful, isn't it?

. . . There is also support in the provenance of a number of paintings for extended visits to Baltimore and Philadelphia in 1859. . . .

Blythe was a satirist, or had become one, and as such was concerned that his genuine contempt and outrage—no less than his equally genuine laughter at the passing spectacle of less consequential vanities—be communicated directly and efficiently to his viewers; that is, to the very public whose corruption and folly he abhorred. To accomplish this, his art had to be obviously satire, for which it drew upon familiar examples of caricature. Yet it also had to possess the formal order and painterly means to give it the pictorial authority it was not likely to possess as graphic art. . . .

In other courtroom scenes, Blythe's interest is not so much in the faults of solicitor and judge but rather in the ridiculousness of those who are called before the court for judgment. *The First Mayor of Pittsburgh* [The Museum of Art, Carnegie Institute, Pittsburgh] and *Justice* both represent municipal courts, charged with enforcement of local statutes of misdemeanor. Such courts accumulated the victims of the previous night's constabulary sweep. . . .

In both of these paintings two of Blythe's later trademarks appear: the classical portrait bust (or its proxy, the American eagle), . . . and the diminutive and stogie-chomping newsboy. . . . At such times Blythe almost seems to be creating a form of stock company theater in which certain characters recur in specific roles, providing witness if not also commentary. The heroic American (or classical) past and the less heroic but vital contemporary press remain critical observers of the present.

Bruce W. Chambers, *The World of David Gilmour Blythe, 1815–1865*, exh. cat. (Washington, D.C.: National Collection of Fine Arts, 1980), pp. 11, 37, 40, 65, 71–72

————

The Plug Uglies, Rip Raps, and Blood Tubs [inscribed on the poster attached to the judge's bench] were ruffian street gangs of the 1850s and early 1860s who were anti-foreign and pro-slavery in sentiment. The Know Nothing party was originally a secret society calling itself

the Order of the Star-Spangled Banner whose members, if questioned about the organization, were commanded to answer that they "know nothing." Founded in New York City, the party exploited a growing anti-foreign, anti-Catholic sentiment in the United States in the 1850s, and for a time, threatened to become one of the two major political parties.

"Sidelights: A Report from Baltimore," *Maryland Historical Magazine* 64 (1969): 285

———

Perhaps the most useful Know-Nothing symbol was that of Sam [*SAM!* is inscribed on the poster attached to the judge's bench]—the mysterious nickname often used by Marylanders to refer to the party, but understood "only by his friends." "Have you seen Sam" echoed through Maryland during the 1850s—in conversation, newspapers, and formal speeches. . . . To outsiders the cognomen came to stand for the Know-Nothing party.

Jean H. Baker, *Ambivalent Americans: The Know-Nothing Party in Maryland* (Baltimore: The Johns Hopkins University Press, 1977), p. 37

Provenance
Possibly Alexander Nimick, Pittsburgh, Pa., by 1879
[Hirschl & Adler Galleries, New York, 1969]
John D. Rockefeller 3rd and Blanchette Hooker Rockefeller, New York, 1969–1979
FAMSF, 1979.7.18

Exhibition History
Possibly Pittsburgh, Mercantile Library Association, *Pittsburgh Library Loan Exhibition*, 1879, exh. no. 34 (as *Calculating the Chances*, lent by Alexander Nimick)
San Francisco 1976, exh. no. 32
Washington, D.C., National Collection of Fine Arts, *The World of David Gilmour Blythe, 1815–1865*, 1981, exh. no. 37, cat. no. 186
Tokyo 1982, exh. no. 26
Washington, D.C., National Portrait Gallery, *Portraits of the American Law*, 1989, not in publ.

Selected Reference
Mahonri Sharp Young, "Letter from the U.S.A.: A Rockefeller Collection of American Art," *Apollo* 103, no. 172 (June 1976): 513

Related Work
The First Mayor of Pittsburgh, ca. 1860–1863
Oil on academy board, 23⅜ x 19⅜ in.
The Museum of Art, Carnegie Institute, Pittsburgh

---

58 **SUNLIGHT AND SHADOW, 1862**

Oil on canvas, 39 x 32½ in.
Signed and dated lower right: *ABierstadt./1862.* (initials in monogram)

ALBERT BIERSTADT
b. Solingen, Germany 1830
d. New York, N.Y. 1902

His next tour, the following year [1855], was through Hesse-Cassel; and, while there, he was much struck, one afternoon, with a beautiful effect of light and shade, on the mossy, massive front and low arched door of a quaint mediæval church [the Löwenburg Chapel at Castle Wilhelmshöhe was built 1793–1800 in imitation of the Gothic], with a wide-spreading venerable tree beside the wall, and an old woman seated under the gateway. The whole scene was full of mellow, time-hallowed, and consecrated repose. Bierstadt caught, with singular vividness and truth, the details and expression of the scene, so familiar in its materials, yet so eloquent in its "Sunshine and Shadow"—and by this appropriate name he called the picture which he subsequently elaborated from it, and which first made him generally and favorably known in art. It was so suggestive of the peaceful and picturesque old towns of Europe, that scores of travellers desired to possess it; while the agreeable surprise at so effective and real a picture, whose subject was so unpretending, added to his popularity, and to the merit of the artist as a fond and faithful student of nature.

. . . [T]he "Sunshine and Shadow" has been exhibited repeatedly, and before his Rocky Mountain landscape appeared, was the best known of Bierstadt's pictures.

Henry T. Tuckerman, *Book of the Artists: American Artist Life* (1867; New York: James F. Carr, 1966), p. 388

———

No. 34, Sunlight and Shadow, by A. Bierstadt, is an effect of sunshine upon the stone wall and balustrade of an old church, and is more perfectly painted than any sunshine we ever saw. Look through your closed hand at it from a little distance. See how the light glances along the top of the balustrade, flecking the posts beneath, and how kind and placid and warm it lies upon the wall itself of the church. Inside the door the sunshine never comes, only the light. It is cool, and odorous, and still within. There are gorgeous gleams on the high painted windows, but far up in the vaulting nave and around the altar there is grave shade always, and a few cloaked solitary figures are silently kneeling. You do not see all this in the picture; oh no, but it is there, in the church. This is the court where the wicked cease from troubling, the pasture where the weary are at rest. And the sunlight, dropping through masses of leaves, rests like a benediction. This picture, too, is a poem.

"The Lounger: The National Academy, No. II," *Harper's Weekly* 6, no. 280 (10 May 1862): 290

Among the younger landscape painters of the day, few occupy a better position in the world of art, than Albert Bierstadt. . . . This mood [a predilection for strong contrasts of light and shade] is especially noticeable in his "Sunlight and Shadow," a picture first exhibited in the Academy last year, and now holding a place in the just opened gallery of the Fine Arts Academy in Buffalo. It represents the entrance of an old stone church, across the front of which a gnarled oak throws its twisted boughs, wearing their midsummer robes. Ivy clings to its rough bark, the deep green of the leaves of which contrasts finely with the lighter ones of the oak. Through the foliage the sunlight sifts, lighting up the sober gray of the church walls, or casting upon it the dark and flickering shadows of dancing leaves. Seated near the gateway is an old woman, poverty-stricken and ill, bearing a child in her arms. She, in another sense than that generally recognized by those who gaze on the picture, illustrates one of its titles, the "Shadow;" while in the richly clad man seen leaning against a marble column within the edifice, we find another example of the "Sunlight." The management of the lights and shades in this picture is remarkable, and the effect produced extremely pleasing.

Barry Gray, "Bierstadt, the Artist," *New York Leader*, 17 January 1863

———

Bierstadt's . . . "Sunshine and Shadow" has just been forwarded to Boston. . . . Bierstadt has refused $3,500 for this work. The chromo-lithographs of it, just published, are, with the exception of their being on a reduced scale, almost fac-similes.

"Fine Art Items," *Watson's Weekly Art Journal* 2, no. 1 (5 November 1864): 20

Provenance
Eliza Bierstadt (1833–1896), New Bedford, Mass., and Niagara Falls, N.Y., by 1867–1896

Mrs. Stevenson, Niagara Falls, N.Y., by ca. 1958

[Argosy Gallery, New York, ca. 1958–1973]

John D. Rockefeller 3rd and Blanchette Hooker Rockefeller, New York, 1973–1979

FAMSF, 1979.7.10

Exhibition History
Brooklyn Art Association, *The Third Exhibition of the Brooklyn Art Association*, 1862, exh. no. 175 (as *Light and Shadow*, listed for sale)

New York, National Academy of Design, *Thirty-seventh Annual Exhibition*, 1862, exh. no. 34 (listed for sale)

Buffalo Fine Arts Academy, 1863

Boston Athenaeum, *Paintings and Statuary Exhibited for the Benefit of the National Sailors' Fair*, 1864, exh. no. 339 (as *Light and Shade*)

New York, Mutual Art Association, 1865

New Haven, Conn., Yale School of the Fine Arts, *First Annual Exhibition of the Yale School of the Fine Arts*, 1867, exh. no. 34

Buffalo Fine Arts Academy, *Works of Art on Exhibition at the Gallery of the Buffalo Fine Arts Academy*, 1869, exh. no. 79

Buffalo Fine Arts Academy, *Works of Art on Exhibition at the Gallery of the Buffalo Fine Arts Academy*, 1870, exh. no. 78

New York, The Century Association, 1876, exh. no. 6 (as *Sunlight and Shade*)

New York, The National Academy of Design and the Metropolitan Museum of Art, *New York Centennial Loan Exhibition of Paintings, Selected from the Private Art Galleries*, 1876, exh. no. 395 (as *Light and Shade*)

New York, The Metropolitan Museum of Art, *Loan Exhibition of Paintings*, 1880, exh. no. 29

London, *American Exhibition, London*, 1887, exh. no. 1385 (as *Sunshine and Shade*, lent by the artist)

Fort Worth, Amon Carter Museum, *A Bierstadt*, 1972, exh. no. 32

San Francisco 1976, exh. no. 40

Kunstmuseum Düsseldorf, *Die Düsseldorfer Malerschule*, 1979, exh. no. 30

Tokyo 1982, exh. no. 31

FAMSF, *Albert Bierstadt: An Observer of Air, Light and the Feeling of a Place*, 1985, no exh. no.

The Brooklyn Museum, *Albert Bierstadt: Art and Enterprise*, 1991, exh. no. 29

Selected References
"Albert Bierstadt," *California Art Gallery* 1, no. 4 (April 1873): 49

Worthington Whittredge, *The Autobiography of Worthington Whittredge, 1820–1910*, ed. John I. H. Baur (1942; New York: Arno Press, 1969), p. 27

Gordon Hendricks, *Albert Bierstadt: Painter of the American West* (New York: Harry N. Abrams, in association with the Amon Carter Museum of Western Art, [1974]), pp. 26, 104, 106, 110, 113, 140, 144, 155, 173, 229, 250, 321

The American Canvas, pp. 120–121, 238

Related Works
Sunlight and Shadow: Study, 1855
Oil on paper, 18½ x 13 in.
The Newark Museum

Sunlight and Shadow,
19 June 1862
Pencil on paper, 5 x 5 in.
The Whaling Museum, New Bedford, Mass.

After *Sunlight and Shadow*, 1864
Chromolithograph, 22 x 18¾ in.
Published by Emil Seitz, printed by Storch and Kramer, Berlin

Oil on canvas, 20 x 36 in.
Signed and dated lower left: *MJ Heade 1863*

MARTIN JOHNSON HEADE

b. Lumberville, Pa. 1819
d. St. Augustine, Fla. 1904

Heade's seascapes are never joyous; more than his other paintings, they express the loneliness of the man. No less originally conceived than his marsh scenes or still lifes, they show Heade as part of the continuous mystical tradition in American painting, as a successor to Washington Allston and a predecessor of Albert Ryder.

. . . When he painted the sea, he painted it as disquieting, with harsh, cold light, and should an occasional figure be depicted, it is infinitesimally small and powerless.

Only about thirty seascapes survive, as against perhaps four times that many marsh scenes, and a good number of them are concentrated in the early 1860s. . . . [A]t their best, they are among the most intense of American paintings. . . .

Among the numerous marine views painted in 1863, Heade's most productive year, is *Twilight, Spouting Rock Beach* [the FAMSF painting]. (Interestingly enough, Vose sold Heade a frame exactly the size of this painting, 20″ x 36″, on April 28, 1863; the price was $20.) . . . No longer simply a pleasant view of the shore, his subject now is quite clearly the single wave which breaks up out of the calm water. Man's presence is barely visible. . . . The time is twilight, and a cool raspberry-colored horizon lies between a gray-green sky and a gray sea.

Theodore E. Stebbins, Jr., *The Life and Works of Martin Johnson Heade* (New Haven and London: Yale University Press, 1975), pp. 67–73

Seascape offered our artists a challenge to individual expressiveness and a shape for their feelings about their location in the physical universe and its relation to our metaphysical quest for ultimate meaning. It offered the American people a mirror of their experience and put them in touch with the largest rhythms of the natural world, with their historic past, and

with their personal experience. It imaged their commercial and national aspirations, their sense of dislocation in the universe, and their hopes of spiritual succor.

Roger B. Stein, *Seascape and the American Imagination* (New York: Clarkson N. Potter, 1975), p. 130

This 1863 sunset scene has long been thought to depict Spouting Rock Beach near Newport, Rhode Island, but now is known to be a view from Singing Beach at Manchester, Massachusetts. In Heade's time Manchester was one of several popular seaside resorts just to the north of Boston, and its picturesque coastline attracted a number of artists. In the left foreground is the rocky tip of Eagle Head and in the center is visible the long, slightly sloping Great Egg Rock. Heade has taken some liberties with the geography at the right, however. The large rock is Rock Dundy, which is in fact located to the far right of Heade's vantage point on Singing Beach. He must have been so attracted to the distinctive profile of Rock Dundy that he decided to paint it in place of the less articulated and smaller Little Salt Rocks, located straight off the beach. Such a composite view was in keeping with Heade's approach to creating some of his other paintings.

Heade depicted the site in at least three other paintings in the years between 1861 and 1863, one of them matching the de Young view almost exactly (1861, collection Henry Melville Fuller). These two paintings relate closely to a sketch of the site Heade probably made in the summer of 1860 (Spanierman Gallery, New York).

Sarah Cash, Assistant Curator, Amon Carter Museum, 9 March 1994, FAMSF departmental files

Provenance
Gustav D. Klimann (1915–1982), Boston, by 1965

[Vose Galleries, Boston, 1965]

Theodore E. Stebbins, Jr. (b. 1938), Cambridge, Mass., 1965–1966

[Hirschl & Adler Galleries, New York, 1966–1967]

John D. Rockefeller 3rd and Blanchette Hooker Rockefeller, New York, 1967–1993

FAMSF, 1993.35.12

Exhibition History
Cambridge, Mass., Fogg Art Museum, *Luminous Landscape: The American Study of Light, 1860–1875,* 1966, exh. no. 18 (as *Breaking Wave, Newport*)

College Park, University of Maryland Art Gallery, *Martin Johnson Heade,* 1969, exh. no. 17 (as *Twilight, Spouting Rock Beach*)

San Francisco 1976, exh. no. 48

Tokyo 1982, exh. no. 34

FAMSF, *Director's Choice: Twenty Years of Collecting,* 1987, no publ.

Selected References
William S. Talbot, "Landscape and Light," *The Bulletin of the Cleveland Museum of Art* 60, no. 1 (January 1973): 16

Theodore E. Stebbins, Jr., *The Life and Works of Martin Johnson Heade* (New Haven and London: Yale University Press, 1975), pp. 71, 73, cat. no. 58 (as *Twilight, Spouting Rock Beach*)

Related Works
View from Singing Beach Including Eagle Head, ca. 1860

Pencil on paper, 6⅜ x 10 in. Spanierman Gallery, New York, as of 1994

Spouting Rock Beach, Newport, Rhode Island, 1861
Oil on canvas, 11½ x 25 in. Henry Melville Fuller, New York and New Hampshire, as of 1969

Dawn, 1862
Oil on canvas, 12¼ x 24¼ in. Museum of Fine Arts, Boston

Spouting Rock, Newport, 1862
Oil on canvas, 25 x 50 in. Thyssen-Bornemisza Collection, Lugano and Madrid

---

60 BED OF THE TORRENT MUGNONE, NEAR FLORENCE, 1864

Oil on hardboard, 6⅝ x 16¼ in.
Inscribed and dated on reverse: BED OF THE TORRENT MUGNONE/NEAR FLORENCE/*1864*; *Painted for Mrs. R. W. Sanford/by Elihu Vedder 64*; [drawn design for frame]

ELIHU VEDDER
b. New York, N.Y. 1836
d. Rome, Italy 1923

The banks of the Mugnone torrent, which runs around a part of Florence past the Porta San Gallo, used to be a favourite walk of the frequenters of the Caffè Michelangelo [an artists' gathering place in Florence]. . . . On the high banks of this stream, overlooking the country bounded by the great bare hills from which in winter came those icy blasts that gave us all sore eyes (the eyes having been previously prepared in the acrid tobacco-smoke of the caffè during the long winter evenings, or strained, painting by the little smoky, dim oil-lamps of the Accademia Galli), we walked and settled all the great questions of the day. Following

up the stream, you finally reached the spot where it passes under a bridge at the foot of the long ascent which leads to Fiesole. It was here I painted two of my best studies.

> Elihu Vedder, *The Digressions of V.* (London: Constable & Co.; Boston and New York: Houghton Mifflin Company, 1911), pp. 163, 164

Mrs. Milton Sanford N.Y.
　View near Florence. Bed of the Mugnone Torrent ---
　The autumn leaf? ---
　Monk　　　　3 pictures—　　　　　$200.00

> Vedder, "List of Works Sold since 1856," Elihu Vedder Papers, AAA, roll 528, frame 854

From the few landscapes that can be attributed securely to Vedder's first stay in Florence, it is clear that he was much impressed by the idea of catching the effect of nature with a relatively few simple shapes. . . . In the long horizontal format preferred also by Vedder's Italian colleagues, it [*Italian Landscape with Sheep and Florentine Well*, Museum of Fine Arts, Boston] creates its effect with a few strongly silhouetted forms. As so often in the landscapes of [the Italian landscape painter Giovanni] Costa, it moves through a series of horizontal striations with none of the usual *repoussoirs* common to classical landscape painting. The painting's charm is in its pattern of rather shaggy shapes, not in the character or detail of its objects. Unlike American painters who earlier sought dramatic views of classical sites around Rome, in his small landscapes Vedder seemed to prefer unspectacular subjects and well-worn forms, whose muted rhythms provide the theme of the picture. Instead of recording the well-known monuments of Florence or trying to capture the spectacular panorama of the city from the hills as had many of his predecessors, he joined his Italian friends in searching out more humble areas that revealed the age-old quiet of the Tuscan countryside.

> Joshua Taylor, "Perceptions and Digressions," *Perceptions and Evocations: The Art of Elihu Vedder*, exh. cat. (Washington, D.C.: National Collection of Fine Arts, 1979), pp. 38, 40

Provenance
Probably Mrs. Milton Sanford, New York, from 1864

Lawrence A. Fleischman (b. 1925) and Barbara Greenberg Fleischman (b. 1924), Detroit, by 1955–1966

[Kennedy Galleries, New York, 1966–1968]

John D. Rockefeller 3rd and Blanchette Hooker Rockefeller, New York, 1968–1979

FAMSF, 1979.7.100

Exhibition History
New York, National Academy of Design, *Forty-first Annual Exhibition*, 1866, exh. no. 288 (as *Paysage Fiesole, near Florence*, lent by Milton H. Sanford)

The Detroit Institute of Arts, *Collection in Progress: Selections from the Lawrence and Barbara Fleischman Collection of American Art*, 1955, exh. no. 22

Washington, D.C., United States Information Service, *Nine Gener-ations of American Painting: A Loan Exhibition from the Detroit Institute of Arts and the Lawrence A. Fleischman Collection*, 1958 (organized for travel to South America, Greece, and Israel), Israel cat., exh. no. 25

Milwaukee Art Center, *American Painting, 1760–1960: A Selection* of *125 Paintings from the Collection of Mr. and Mrs. Lawrence A. Fleischman, Detroit*, 1960, no exh. no.

Wilmington, Delaware Arts Center, *American Painting, 1857–1869*, 1962, exh. no. 84

Washington, D.C., Smithsonian Institution Traveling Exhibition

Service, *Paintings and Drawings by Elihu Vedder*, 1966, exh. no. 8

New York, Kennedy Galleries, *The American Artist Abroad*, 1968, no exh. no.

San Francisco 1976, exh. no. 94

Washington, D.C., National Collection of Fine Arts, *Perceptions and Evocations: The Art of Elihu Vedder*, 1978, exh. no. 9

Tokyo 1982, exh. no. 37

Selected Reference

Regina Soria, *Elihu Vedder: American Visionary Artist in Rome, 1836–1923* (Rutherford, N.J.: Fairleigh Dickinson University Press, 1970), pp. 28–29, cat. no. 33

Related Works

Study of Rocks, Bed of Torrente Mugnone, near Florence, 1858–1860
Oil on canvas, 10½ x 15 in.
Davison Art Center, Wesleyan University, Middletown, Conn.

Fiesole, 1859
Oil on canvas, 15 x 29¼ in.
The Detroit Institute of Arts

---

61   THE BRIGHT SIDE, 1865

Oil on canvas, 12¾ x 17 in.
Signed, dated, and inscribed lower left: *Winslow Homer NY 65*

WINSLOW HOMER
b. Boston, Mass. 1836
d. Prout's Neck, Maine 1910

It is invigorating to find boldness and truth amid the trivial and false. In the works of Winslow Homer we have a direct style and faithful observation of nature. The best example of Mr. Homer's talent is that called "Bright Side," a picture hanging in the north gallery, representing a group of negro mule-drivers dozing on the sunny side of an army-tent. There is in this work a dry, latent humor, and vigorous emphasis of character; and the episode of camp-life is told in a manly way. The painting throughout is intelligent and not labored, frank in its characteristics, and happily fitted to express the subject. . . . Mr. Homer is a young painter, but he has the manner of a practised hand, if we except refinement. We greet him as one of the most healthful among figure painters, and who brings to art just what redeems it from weakness and morbidness. Welcome this hearty energy of life; and if the painter shows that he observes more than he reflects, we will forget the limitation and take his work as we take nature, which, if it does not think is yet the cause of thought in us.

"National Academy of Design: Fortieth Annual Exhibition. Concluding Article," *(New York) Evening Post*, 31 May 1865

Mr. Winslow Homer's "Light and Shade" is a right sterling piece of work, most satisfactory and encouraging. It is altogether the best thing he has painted, and that is saying much, for, in many qualities, he is not excelled by any man among us. If he shall paint every picture with the loyalty to nature and the faithful study that marks this little square of canvas, he will become one of the men we must have crowned when the Academy gets officers that have a right to bestow crowns. Meanwhile, the public crowns the best chronicler of the war, so far, with smiling eye and silent applause.

"National Academy of Design: Fortieth Annual Exhibition. Sixth Article," *New-York Daily Tribune*, 3 July 1865

Provenance

William H. Hamilton, New York, 1865–at least 1868

Thomas B. Clarke (1848–1931), New York, by 1886–1899

[Auction sale, American Art Association, Chickering Hall, New York, 15–18 February 1899, lot no. 123, sold for $525]

Samuel P. Avery, Jr. (d. 1920), New York, from 1899

William A. White, Brooklyn, by 1911–1917

[Macbeth Galleries, New York, 1917–1918, sold for $500]

Julia E. Peck (1875–1971), New York and Port Huron, Mich., 1918–1971

Mrs. Richard Andrae, Port Huron, Mich., 1971

[Auction sale, Du Mouchelle Art Galleries, Detroit, 22 October 1971]

[Schweitzer Gallery, New York, 1971–1972]

John D. Rockefeller 3rd and Blanchette Hooker Rockefeller, New York, 1972–1979

FAMSF, 1979.7.56

Exhibition History

Brooklyn Art Association, *Spring [Ninth] Exhibition at the Academy of Music, Brooklyn*, 1865, exh. no. 129

New York, National Academy of Design, *Fortieth Annual Exhibition*, 1865, exh. no. 190

Paris, *Exposition Universelle*, 1867, exh. no. 27 (as *Le Côté clair*)

New York, National Academy of Design, *First Winter Exhibition*, 1867, exh. no. 673

Munich, Glaspalaste, *Internationalen Kunstausstellung*, 1883, exh. no. 916 (as *Armee-Fuhrleute*)

New York, Union League Club, *Illuminated Books and Manuscripts, Old Masters and Modern Paintings: Loan Collection*, 1890, exh. no. 38 (as *The Sunny Side*)

Philadelphia, Pennsylvania Academy of the Fine Arts, *Thomas B. Clarke Collection of American Pictures*, 1891, exh. no. 94

New York, Union League Club, *The Paintings of Two Americans: George Inness, Winslow Homer*, 1898, exh. no. 32

New York, The Metropolitan Museum of Art, *Winslow Homer Memorial Exhibition*, 1911, exh. no. 1

New York, Maynard Walker Gallery, *Paintings by Six Americans*, 1935, exh. no. 6

Pittsburgh, The Carnegie Institute, *An Exhibition of American Genre Paintings*, 1936, exh. no. 48

New York, Whitney Museum of American Art, *Winslow Homer Centenary Exhibition*, 1937, exh. no. 2

New York, The Metropolitan Museum of Art, *Life in America: A Special Loan Exhibition of Paintings Held during the Period of the New York World's Fair*, 1939, exh. no. 195

New York, Whitney Museum of American Art, *Winslow Homer*, 1973, exh. no. 5

San Francisco 1976, exh. no. 69

Baltimore, Walters Art Gallery, *African Image: Representations of the Black throughout History*, 1980, no publ.

Tokyo 1982, exh. no. 52

FAMSF, *Winslow Homer Wood Engravings: Visions and Revisions*, 1983, no publ.

FAMSF, *Winslow Homer: Paintings of the Civil War*, 1988, exh. no. 13

Houston, The Menil Collection, *Winslow Homer's Images of Blacks: The Civil War and Reconstruction Years* (shown only at Raleigh, North Carolina Museum of Art, 1989), no exh. no.

Selected References

William Howe Downes, *The Life and Works of Winslow Homer* (Boston and New York: Houghton Mifflin Company, 1911), pp. 51, 53, 54, 57, 58

Lloyd Goodrich, *Winslow Homer* (New York: The Macmillan Co. and the Whitney Museum of American Art, 1945), pp. 20, 39

Albert Ten Eyck Gardner, *Winslow Homer, American Artist: His World and His Work* (New York: Bramhall House, 1961), pp. 126, 129, 237–239

The American Canvas, pp. 136–137, 239–240

Related Works

Study for "The Bright Side," 1864
Oil on paper, 6½ x 8¼ in.
J. Nicholson, as of 1988

Sketch for "The Bright Side," ca. 1864
Pencil and wash on paper, 6⅜ x 9¾ in.
Private collection, as of 1990

Army Teamsters, 1866
Oil on canvas, 17½ x 28¼ in.
Mr. and Mrs. Paul Mellon, Upperville, Va., as of 1993

The Bright Side, 1866
Wood engraving, 2¾ x 3⅜ in.
Published in *Our Young Folks* (July 1866)

After *Army Teamsters*, 1889
Chromolithograph, 17 x 25½ in.
Colby College Museum of Art, Waterville, Maine

Oil on canvas, 14¼ x 19¼ in.
Signed lower right: *ABierstadt* (initials in monogram)

ALBERT BIERSTADT
b. Solingen, Germany 1830
d. New York, N.Y. 1902

And Niagara! that wonder of the world!—where the sublime and beautiful are bound together in an indissoluble chain. In gazing on it we feel as though a great void had been filled in our minds—our conceptions expand—we become a part of what we behold! At our feet the floods of a thousand rivers are poured out—the contents of vast inland seas. In its volume we conceive immensity; in its course, everlasting duration; in its impetuosity, uncontrollable power. These are the elements of its sublimity. Its beauty is garlanded around in the varied hues of the water, in the spray that ascends the sky, and in that unrivalled bow which forms a complete cincture round the unresting floods.

Thomas Cole, "Essay on American Scenery," *The American Monthly Magazine* 7 (January 1836): 8

———

Niagara Falls

This great Mecca of the world's worshippers of landscape beauty, the mighty wonder of Niagara, is on its namesake river, a strait connecting the flood of Lakes Erie and Ontario, and dividing a portion of the State of New York on the west from the Provinces of Canada. . . .

The Horse-Shoe Fall, which leads the host of astonishments in this astonishing place, is the connecting link between the scenes of the American and of the Canadian sides of the river, always marvellous from whatever position it is viewed. This mighty cataract is 144 rods across, and, it is said by Prof. Lyell, that fifteen hundred millions of cubic feet of water pass over its ledges every hour.

Appletons' Illustrated Hand-Book of American Travel (New York: D. Appleton & Co., 1857), pp. 161, 164

———

Mr. Bierstadt is studying Niagara, and Mr. Beard is doing likewise with the Western prairies.

"Art Notes," *The Round Table* n.s. 1, no. 1 (9 September 1865): 7

———

[Frederic] Church's great rival in the 1860s and 1870s, Albert Bierstadt (1830–1902), was also greatly attracted to the subject of Niagara Falls. He first visited the site in the summer of 1869 [more likely 1865], staying with his famous photographer-brother Charles who lived and worked in Niagara Falls, and returned on several occasions. Bierstadt painted numerous Niagaras—the exact number is unknown, but there are at least a dozen extant canvases.

Few landscapists after the Civil War were to represent the Falls and their setting so variously. Some pictures were dramatic close-ups; others, distant views; some epic visions; others, unaffected glimpses. Charles Bierstadt's Niagara photographs may well have influenced his brother's paintings. . . . None of Bierstadt's Niagaras contain extra-aesthetic meanings: they remain visually interesting and often novel views of a much-painted scene.

Jeremy Elwell Adamson, *Niagara: Two Centuries of Changing Attitudes, 1697–1901*, exh. cat. (Washington, D.C.: The Corcoran Gallery of Art, 1985), pp. 70–71

Provenance
Roland J. McKinney (1897–1971), Los Angeles and New York, by 1949

[M. Knoedler & Co., New York, 1949–1969]

John D. Rockefeller 3rd and Blanchette Hooker Rockefeller, New York, 1969–1979

FAMSF, 1979.7.13

Exhibition History
New York, M. Knoedler & Co., *American Paintings, 1750–1950*, 1969, exh. no. 55

San Francisco 1976, exh. no. 43

FAMSF, *Albert Bierstadt: An Observer of Air, Light and the Feeling of a Place*, 1985, no exh. no.

Stockholm, Nationalmuseum, *En Ny Värld: Amerikanskt landskapsmåleri, 1830–1900*, 1986, exh. no. 4

Selected References
Martha Hutson, "Mr. and Mrs. John D. Rockefeller, 3rd: Collection of American Art," *American Art Review* 3, no. 4 (July–August 1976): 83

Kynaston McShine, ed., *The Natural Paradise: Painting in America, 1800–1950*, exh. cat. (New York: The Museum of Modern Art), p. 100

Kevin Starr, "Albert Bierstadt: The Civilizing Eye," *Sierra: The Sierra Club Bulletin* 62, no. 9 (November–December 1977): 27

Related Work
Home of the Rainbow, Horseshoe Fall, Niagara, ca. 1869
Oil on canvas, 16½ x 22 in.
Mr. and Mrs. George Strichman, as of 1985

63 CHRISTMAS SPORTS IN AMERICA—SHOOTING TURKEYS, CA. 1865

Watercolor over graphite on wove paper, 10⅞ x 13¾ in.
Signed lower left: *F.O.C. Darley-fecit*; inscribed bottom: *Christmas sports in America—Shooting turkeys—*

FELIX O. C. DARLEY
b. Philadelphia, Pa. 1822
d. Claymont, Del. 1888

Felix Octavius Carr Darley, was born in Philadelphia, June 23, 1822, of English parents. . . . His artistic tastes showed themselves in boyhood, but at the age of fourteen he was placed in a mercantile house, and never received any regular education in art. He, however, spent his leisure hours in drawing, and some of his humorous sketches attracting attention, he was paid a handsome sum by the publisher of the "Saturday Museum" [a popular journal] for a few designs. This encouragement decided him to abandon a commercial life, and he thenceforth devoted his talents to art. For several years he was employed by large Philadelphia publishers and produced, with other work, a series of drawings for the Library of Humorous American Works. In 1848, Darley removed to New York, and executed a number of illustrations for the "Sketch Book," and "Knickerbocker's History of New York," and others of Irving's writings. This year also saw the publication of his outline drawings to "Rip Van Winkle," made for the American Art Union, and in 1849 appeared a similar series of designs to the "Legend of Sleepy Hollow," likewise issued under the auspices of that institution. . . . He painted at times in oil and water-colors (he was one of the early members of the American Society of Painters in Water-Colors), made innumerable illustrations for books and periodicals, including five hundred sketches for Benson J. Lossing's "Our Country," and illustrated, among other works, Dickens, Shakspeare, Longfellow's "Evangeline," and Hawthorne's "Scarlet Letter." . . . Darley died very suddenly on March 27, 1888, at the age of sixty-five, being then engaged on a second set of drawings illustrating Dickens's works. This seems but a bare outline of a life, but to use his own words, "I have neither met with accident nor adventure of any kind; mine has been neither a strange nor eventful history," and the full record of his existence will be found in his works.

Walter Montgomery, ed., *American Art and American Art Collections*, 2 vols. (1889; New York and London: Garland Publishing, 1978), 1:385–386

————

Connected by birth with a family not only eminent but endeared for dramatic talent, and related to the favorite portrait-painter of the day—Thomas Sully—the young man had a legitimate claim to find subsistence and satisfaction in rendering the comedy of life into artistic significance. His love for the pursuit was instinctive; but he possessed also two special endowments therefor—facile power and an original and vivid sense of the humorous. Fortunately, just at this time, that peculiar vein of humorous writing which, from its local interest and character, deserved its name of "American," had become a recognized element of popular literature—the attraction of which could be indefinitely enhanced by skilful and suggestive illustration. . . .

It is well to consider if there be anything ridiculous in one's manner or appearance, before coming within the scope of Darley's vision. If your nose is *retrousez* or pointed, your figure dumpy, or the way in which you try to be agreeable slightly exaggerated, the quick perception and ready crayon of Darley may transform you into such a nasal individuality,

such an incarnated dump, or absurd exquisite, that whoever once beholds the sketch, will ever after involuntarily laugh at the sight of you, even at a funeral. . . . Two or three lines suffice Darley to metamorphose his fellow-creatures, while he preserves their identity. . . . It is easy to imagine the result when this facility and characteristic limning is applied to illustrate graphic, verbal description. The artist not only reproduces, but often transcends or satirizes the author's conception. It is no wonder that so clever and prolific a draughtsman is beset by the publishers; his free, significant, and original sketches will give a zest to any book. He makes one realize how ironical, acute, observant, and natural it is possible to be with no instrument but a lead-pencil; he tells a story with a dash, reveals a character by a curve, and embodies an expression with two or three dots. It is better than a comedy to look over his sketch-book.

> Henry T. Tuckerman, *Book of the Artists: American Artist Life* (1867; New York: James F. Carr, 1966), pp. 471–472, 475–476

Provenance
[Hirschl & Adler Galleries, New York, 1967–1968]

John D. Rockefeller 3rd and Blanchette Hooker Rockefeller, New York, 1968–1979

FAMSF, 1979.7.33

Exhibition History
New York, Hirschl & Adler Galleries, *American Paintings for Public and Private Collections*, 1967, exh. no. 44

---

64 NEW YORK HARBOR FROM HOBOKEN, CA. 1865

Transparent and opaque watercolor over graphite on wove paper, 13½ x 19½ in.

JOHN WILLIAM HILL
b. London, England 1812
d. West Nyack, N.Y. 1879

John William Hill was the son of the famous engraver John Hill. At the age of seven he emigrated to the United States with his mother and sisters, joining the elder Hill in Philadelphia. . . . In 1822 the family moved to New York City, and shortly thereafter Hill was apprenticed to his father for seven years. During this time, Hill may have assisted his father in executing the engravings for the *Hudson River Portfolio*, for by the time he left the elder Hill's employ he was working in the same vein. . . . Hill was introduced to John Ruskin's *Modern Painters* while in Maine on a sketching trip for the Smith Brothers [publishing firm], a book that greatly influenced his later work. . . . Within four or five years he was devoting himself almost entirely to painting directly from nature. . . . Increasingly involved in the work of the close-knit Society for the Advancement of Truth in Art—an American offshoot of the English Pre-Raphaelite group, Hill was acknowledged the senior member of the group in 1863 when it published its little periodical called *The New Path*. In later years, he devoted more and more time to his watercolor views of local New York scenery.

> "John William Hill," in Richard J. Koke, comp., *American Landscape and Genre Paintings in the New-York Historical Society*, 3 vols. (Boston: G. K. Hall & Co., in association with the New-York Historical Society, 1982), 2:134–135

On the evening of the twenty-seventh of January in the present year, a number of persons met at 32 Waverly Place, in the city of New York. Believing in the overwhelming power of the Truth, especially in Art, they had for some time seen the necessity of a united effort to revive true Art in America, and had assembled at this time to take counsel together, and if thought proper to organize an Association for the better promotion of the end just stated. . . .

"We hold that the primary object of Art is to observe and record truth, whether of the visible universe or of emotion. All great Art results from an earnest love of the beauty and perfectness of God's creation, and is the attempt to tell the truth about it. . . .

"Therefore, that the right course for young Artists is faithful and loving representations

of Nature, 'selecting nothing and rejecting nothing,' seeking only to express the greatest amount of fact. It is, moreover, their duty to strive for the greatest attainable power of drawing."

"Association for the Advancement of Truth in Art," *The New Path* 1, no. 1 (May 1863): 11

———

The artist is a telescope—very marvelous in himself, as an instrument. . . . And the best artist is he who has the clearest lens, and so makes you forget every now and then that you are looking through him.

M., "The Office of Imagination," *The New Path* 1, no. 7 (November 1863): 78

———

The American Pre-Raphaelites loved watercolor. Their special affection for this medium sets them apart from the English Pre-Raphaelite Brotherhood, whose members only occasionally worked in watercolor; it also distinguishes them from the ranks of the Hudson River School, whose adherents, by 1860, rarely used watercolor at all. In conjunction with a detailed, naturalistic style, a predilection for watercolor marks the truly radical Ruskinian painter in America. Every artist-member of the Pre-Raphaelite Association for the Advancement of Truth in Art produced elaborate, finished watercolors for exhibition. Most of the painters in the larger group known as the American Pre-Raphaelites worked frequently in watercolor, and some never worked in oils at all. Together, their efforts in watercolor made an enduring contribution to American art, for they lent critical support to the first exhibitions of the American Watercolor Society and so laid the foundation of the medium's lasting popularity in the United States.

Kathleen A. Foster, "The Pre-Raphaelite Medium: Ruskin, Turner, and American Watercolor," in Linda S. Ferber and William H. Gerdts, *The New Path: Ruskin and the American Pre-Raphaelites*, exh. cat. (Brooklyn: The Brooklyn Museum, 1985), p. 79

Provenance
[Kennedy Galleries, New York, by 1968]

John D. Rockefeller 3rd and Blanchette Hooker Rockefeller, New York, 1968–1979

FAMSF, 1979.7.52

Exhibition History
New York, Kennedy Galleries, *American Drawings, Pastels and Watercolors, Part Two: The Nineteenth Century, 1825–1890*, 1968, exh. no. 40

Oil on paperboard, 12⅛ x 15⅛ in.
Signed lower right: *E. Johnson*.

EASTMAN JOHNSON
b. Lovell, Maine 1824
d. New York, N.Y. 1906

In all his works we find vital expression, sometimes *naïve*, at others earnest, and invariably characteristic; trained in the technicalities of his art, keen in his observation, and natural in his feeling, we have a *genre* painter in Eastman Johnson who has elevated and widened its naturalistic scope and its national significance. His pictures are in constant demand, and purchased before they leave the easel.

Henry T. Tuckerman, *Book of the Artists: American Artist Life* (1867; New York: James F. Carr, 1966), pp. 469–470

When Mr. Johnson paints children his subject is common only in the sense that the daisy of the field is common. All the tenderness, all the sympathy of the man is expressed. I will say more, all the poetry of the man is expressed. In those sad and luminous faces of children we see that life is serious to the American from his childhood. In New England his chief object is to keep warm and to "get on."

Eugene Benson, "Eastman Johnson," *The Galaxy* 6, no. 1 (July 1868): 111

[Referring to the FAMSF painting:] Very popular during the nineteenth century, these small anecdotal genre scenes constituted a substantial part of Johnson's output. Related as much to the theater as to painting conventions, they often, as in this case, invoked the presence and

collaboration of the audience (by means of a clue in the title) to complete the meaning of the mime.

Here we see two boys, comfortably ensconced in a discarded barrel playing cards. Unbeknownst to them but clear to us, a girl, passing by, has become an eavesdropper, overhearing the privacy of their conversation. This triangular relationship between a group of characters, a hidden eavesdropping actor, and ourselves, has a centuries-old pedigree on the stage, especially in comedy, but it enjoyed its period of greatest popularity in painting during the nineteenth century.

Implying no profound meaning, the artist simply presents the small situation for our pleasure. Painted in a richly layered manner, the painting evokes the rough texture of a wintry forest and focuses our interest on this minor human incident.

> Margaretta M. Lovell, *American Painting, 1730–1960: A Selection from the Collection of Mr. and Mrs. John D. Rockefeller 3rd*, exh. cat. (Tokyo: National Museum of Western Art, 1982), exh. no. 51 (printed text in Japanese; English original in FAMSF departmental files)

Provenance
Miss Dunham, Greenwich, Conn., to 1944

Private collection, 1944–1969

[Newhouse Galleries, New York, 1969–1970]

John D. Rockefeller 3rd and Blanchette Hooker Rockefeller, New York, 1970–1979

FAMSF, 1979.7.65

Exhibition History
FAMSF, *Eastman Johnson: Seven Paintings by the Highly Regarded Nineteenth-Century American Artist*, 1979, no publ.

Tokyo 1982, exh. no. 51

---

66 SUGARING OFF, CA. 1865

Oil on canvas, 16⅞ x 32 in.
Signed lower left: *E. J.*

EASTMAN JOHNSON
b. Lovell, Maine 1824
d. New York, N.Y. 1906

Eastman Johnson has been passing a pleasant summer in Freyburg [*sic*], Me., making careful studies for a picture of a New England "sugaring off" in the maple districts.

> "Art Notes," *The Round Table* n.s. 1, no. 1 (9 September 1865): 7

One of the latest subjects which have occupied his [Johnson's] pencil is drawn from his own childhood's reminiscences of the scenes amid which he was born. In Maine, of old, no rustic festival equalled in merriment and local interest the "boiling-day" in the sugar-camp. The woods of maple glow with fire; picturesque groups of farmers and gudewives, and maidens and children animate the forest; a gossip lays down the law here; a political quidnunc comments on a stale newspaper there; old people smoke pipes on a mossy bank; young ones whisper love by the thicket. There is usually a fiddler, an ancient negro, and an improvised feast; and all these elements, with the woods for a background, and characteristic dresses, faces, and groups, combine to form rare materials for a scene quite peculiar to this country; yet becoming more rare and less picturesque as locomotive facilities reduce costume, dress, speech, and even faces, to a monotonous uniformity.

> Henry T. Tuckerman, *Book of the Artists: American Artist Life* (1867; New York: James F. Carr, 1966), p. 471

This is a festival in a sugar camp on the occasion of sugaring off. Mr. Johnson was very much interested in the operation of sugar making, and found in the camps a large number of picturesque motives for his brush. He spent three months yearly for five seasons in studying the life of the camps, and has recorded types and customs which are fast disappearing. The incidents represented in this picture are the dancing and merrymaking at the time of sugar-

ing off, and a large party of men and women are enjoying themselves, some dancing to the playing of fiddlers perched on a woodpile, others love-making and others gossiping.

The Works of the Late Eastman Johnson, N.A., sale cat. (New York: American Art Galleries, 1907), lot no. 135

One hundred and fifty-one paintings by the late Eastman Johnson were sold at the American Art Galleries Tuesday and Wednesday nights by Thomas E. Kirby for a total of $5,857.50 [*sic* —over $12,000 was raised, according to the list of recorded bids]. . . . The list of principal pictures sold follows: . . .

"A Different Sugaring Off," Andrew C. Zabriskie 175

"Eastman Johnson Sale," *American Art News* 5, no. 20 (2 March 1907)

It is difficult, therefore, to date with precision, from internal evidence, one of the most important of Johnson's genre scenes which was done at about this time. This is the group of scenes depicting the making of maple sugar with its attendant social festivities in the woods near Fryeburg, Maine, where he had spent his early youth. . . .

One thing seems clear, namely, that Johnson himself was unusually absorbed in this series and hoped some day to weld his many studies into a single large picture. [William] Walton has calculated that he did some forty maple sugar scenes in all and says, in regard to his projected large version, that, "This he hoped some day to carry to completion as his masterpiece, and on one or two occasions made definite attempts to secure the commission from some wealthy patron of the arts." As far as is known, he did not succeed, and the picture never was painted.

In spite of this, the series illuminates remarkably well Johnson's approach to genre when he was seriously interested. The paintings fall into two distinct classes, the "finished studies", as he called them, of individual incidents at the sugar camp and, secondly, the larger studies for the panoramic view toward which he was working.

John I. H. Baur, *Eastman Johnson, 1824–1906: An American Genre Painter*, exh. cat. (Brooklyn: Brooklyn Museum, Brooklyn Institute of Arts and Sciences, 1940), pp. 20–21

Provenance

The artist, ca. 1865–1906

[Auction sale, American Art Galleries, New York, 26–27 February 1907, lot no. 135, sold for $175]

Andrew C. Zabriskie (1852–1916), New York and Barrytown Corners, N.Y., 1907–1916

Descended in family to his son, Christian A. Zabriskie (d. ca. 1970), Barrytown Corners, N.Y., by 1935–1970

Yale University Art Gallery, New Haven, Conn., 1970

[Kennedy Galleries, New York, 1970–1971]

John D. Rockefeller 3rd and Blanchette Hooker Rockefeller, New York, 1971–1979

FAMSF, 1979.7.63

Exhibition History

New York, Whitney Museum of American Art, *American Genre: The Social Scene in Paintings and Prints*, 1935, exh. no. 65

New York, Kennedy Galleries, *American Masters, Eighteenth to Twentieth Centuries*, 1971, exh. no. 19

New York, Whitney Museum of American Art, *Eastman Johnson Retrospective Exhibition*, 1972, exh. no. 36

San Francisco 1976, exh. no. 82

FAMSF, *Eastman Johnson: Seven Paintings by the Highly Regarded Nineteenth-Century American Artist*, 1979, no publ.

Selected References

Patricia C. F. Mandel, "Selection VII: American Paintings from the Museum's Collection, c. 1800–1930," *Bulletin of the Rhode Island School of Design: Museum Notes* (April 1977): 158, 161 n. 7

Joseph S. Czestochowski, *The American Landscape Tradition: A Study and Gallery of Paintings* (New York: E. P. Dutton, 1982), p. 114

Related Works

Sugaring Off, ca. 1861–1866
Oil on canvas, 52¾ x 96½ in.
Museum of Art, Rhode Island School of Design, Providence

Sugaring Off, ca. 1861–1866
Oil on canvas, 33½ x 53½ in.
The Huntington, San Marino, Calif.

The Maple Sugar Camp: Turning Off, ca. 1865–1873
Oil on wood, 10⅛ x 22⅜ in.
Thyssen-Bornemisza Collection, Lugano and Madrid

67 ON THE HUDSON, 1867

Oil on canvas, 39 x 72 in.
Signed, dated, and inscribed lower left: *J.G. Brown./NY 1867*

JOHN GEORGE BROWN

b. Durham, England 1831
d. New York, N.Y. 1913

J. G. Brown was trained in England in the trade of glass working as well as in painting. By 1853 he had settled in Brooklyn, where he pursued the former occupation. Around 1855, however, with the encouragement of fellow Brooklyn residents, collector-dealer Samuel P. Avery and Régis Gignoux, Brown set himself up as a portrait painter. His particular adeptness with children stimulated the artist to develop . . . small-scale, or cabinet-size, genre subjects, in Tuckerman's words, "of a juvenile and sportive kind." Success prompted a move in 1860 to the Tenth Street Studio Building in New York, where Brown discovered what was to be an even more popular theme in "types of child-life in the streets of the great metropolis," the bootblacks and newspaper boys for which he is known today. . . .

In fact, in the 1860s and 1870s, Brown's range as a painter was considerably wider than is generally acknowledged. That he was extremely adept at pure landscape is established without a doubt by his brilliant painting of 1867, *View of the Palisades, Snead's Landing* [the FAMSF painting]. In this large work, effects of light and color are handled with a conviction born of regular outdoor study.

Linda S. Ferber, "Ripe for Revival: Forgotten American Artists," *Art News* 79, no. 10 (December 1980): 72

We hear from day to day of our artists seeking the spoils of nature in distant fields, where the labor of study may be relieved by the excitement of the hunt or the dreamy repose of the angler's toil, or the more questionable allurements of fashionable society. But why will not some earnest student, some enthusiast in art, devote his summer to the palisades of our noble Hudson, those breastworks which nature herself threw up in the old Titanic days, when element warred with element. The palisades, viewed from a distance, present a somewhat monotonous outline, unattractive to the lovers of the picturesque; but when seen near by, from the water's edge, and thus in parts, they offer peculiar and highly interesting studies of rock and tree. . . . [I]f any scenery in the United States clothes itself with the mour[n]ful interest that attaches to old-world ruins, it is surely the Palisades of the Hudson. These perpendicular, buttressed walls, rising originally straight from the river's edge, were built, one might think, by some primeval race—some Titan brood, warring against a later dynasty. . . . But a new power has entered, stealthily at first, low down the mountain sides, but it soon closes in deadly embrace with the rocky heights—the power of organic life—and the battle

still wages. We know of no places more suggestive of this contest than the Palisades. The perpendicularity of the rock, its columnar formation, the deep recesses of shadow in its sides, the ruin at its base—all this on the one side, and on the other the vigorous, yet unequal growth of vegetation. . . . For ages yet this contest will continue to wage—on the one hand a slow but remorseless advance, on the other a stern, defiant, yet mournful resistance—a contest typical of the yet grander conflict in the arena of human development, in which the organizing principles of freedom and brotherhood contend with the brute elemental forces of human nature.

Who of our artists, we ask again, will make a close study of these Palisades, and represent for us some portion or portions in a manner which shall awaken all the suggestions of the original?

"The Palisades," *Watson's Weekly Art Journal* 3, no. 12 (15 July 1865): 179, 180

—————

In conducting further research on your painting . . . I find the village is not Sneden's [L]anding, but Fort Lee, New Jersey. This has been determined through the identification of the boat in the foreground and through the use of top[o]graphical maps.

The "Thomas E. Hulse", a 314 ton sidewheel steamboat, was built in 1851, in Jersey City, New Jersey, on March 30, 1875, it was sunk by ice. This boat, and another, the "Edwin Hulse" served the commuters from Jersey communities along the Hudson. The boats left from Spring Street, New York and stopped at Weehawken, Guttenberg, Bull Ferry, Edgewater, Pleasant Valley and Fort Lee. The trip one-way took an hour.

The ferry landing is a little south of the present George Washington bridge. The point where the bridge is located is in the cleft in the Palisades directly above the "Hulse's" smokestack. Part of the old wharf may still be seen. . . .

The large boat near the "Hulse" is the "Cayuga", built in New York, in 1845, and abandoned in 1889.

Robert P. Arzberger, Vice President, Tracy, Kent & Co., Advertising, to James Graham, Graham Gallery, New York, 22 November 1967, FAMSF departmental files

—————

No. 176, Fort Lee, N.J., by J. G. Brown. Very truthfully done, pleasant in color, and good manipulation.

"The National Academy of Design," *Watson's Art Journal* 8, no. 6 (30 November 1867): 90

No. 8 *Fort Lee, New Jersey—Steamboat "Thomas E. Hulse" in the Distance* Height, 11 inches; length, 20 inches

The Palisades are aglow in the rich coloring of early fall, their tall cliffs throwing shadows down their banks under a westering sun. Scattered houses appear on the gentler slopes; and on the blue Hudson—its surface mirroring foliage and skies—is the ancient commuters' steamboat of the title (with other craft). Signed at the lower left: *J. G. Brown, 1865*

Catalogue of the Finished Pictures and Studies Left by the Well-known American Artist the Late J. G. Brown, N.A., sale cat. (New York: American Art Association, 1914), lot no. 8 [describing the study for the FAMSF painting]

Provenance
Lewis Gouverneur Morris (1883–1967) and Alletta Nathalie Lorillard Bailey Morris (ca. 1885–1935), New York and Newport, R.I., ca. 1933–ca. 1964
[Graham Gallery, New York, ca. 1964–1967]
John D. Rockefeller 3rd and Blanchette Hooker Rockefeller, New York, 1967–1979
FAMSF, 1979.7.19

Exhibition History
New Haven, Conn., Yale School of the Fine Arts, *First Annual Exhibition,* 1867, exh. no. 112
New York, National Academy of Design, *First Winter Exhibition,* 1867, exh. no. 176 (as *Fort Lee, N.J.*)
New York, The Union Club, extended loan, ca. 1935–ca. 1964
San Francisco 1976, exh. no. 57

Tokyo 1982, exh. no. 30
Springfield, Mass., George Walter Vincent Smith Art Museum, *Country Paths and City Sidewalks: The Art of J. G. Brown,* 1989, exh. no. 48
Santa Barbara, Calif., Santa Barbara Museum of Art, *America in Art: Fifty Great Paintings Celebrating Fifty Years,* 1991, no exh. no.

Selected References
John K. Howat, *The Hudson River and Its Painters* (New York: The Viking Press, 1972), p. 136
The American Canvas, pp. 128–129, 239

Related Work
Fort Lee, New Jersey—Steamboat "Thomas E. Hulse" in the Distance
Oil on canvas, 11 x 20 in.
Auction sale, American Art Association, 1914, lot no. 8 [study for the FAMSF painting]

---

68 THE GREAT SWAMP, 1868

Oil on canvas, 14⅞ x 30⅛ in.
Signed and dated lower left: *M. J Heade. 68.*

MARTIN JOHNSON HEADE
b. Lumberville, Pa. 1819
d. St. Augustine, Fla. 1904

Cropsey, Sontag, Gi[g]noux, Heade, and G. L. Brown, are names also in good standing as American landscapists, of something more than local reputation. All are realistic to a disagreeable degree, Heade only by color affording any sensuous gratification or relief from the dreary, mechanical intellectuality of the others. His speciality is meadows and coast-views, in wearisome horizontal lines and perspective, with a profuse supply of hay-ricks to vary the monotony of flatness, but flooded with rich sun-glow and sense of summer warmth.

James Jackson Jarves, *The Art-Idea* (1864; Cambridge, Mass.: Harvard University Press, Belknap Press, 1960), p. 193

[Heade] has been very successful in his views of the Hoboken and Newburyport meadows, for which the demand has been so great that he has probably painted more of them than of any other class of subjects.

Clara Erskine Clement and Laurence Hutton, *Artists of the Nineteenth Century and Their Works: A Handbook,* 6th ed. (1879; Boston: Houghton, Mifflin and Company, 1893), p. 340

Heade's marsh represents neither wilderness nor society, but for him possessed the best qualities of each, for it gave man the opportunity to make the most of the earth, yet do it no harm. The farmer who sought forage in the marsh had to be a jack-of-all-trades, for he

"engaged in salt haying—yes—but along with it went the teaching of fishing, hunting, and seamanship as well, if 'down meadow gundalowing' could be called that." He was not working at cultivation in the normal sense, for "salt haying was really harvesting a wild crop rather than planting and tilling the soil." This is not to say that no labor was involved; quite the contrary: skill, good timing of the tides, and many strong hands were needed to cut the hay, to stack and trim it skillfully, so that all but the outer layer remained dry, and then to take it off by cart or boat (the "gundalow"). . . .

Given the marsh pictures dating up to 1866, and aware of the slow, general decline in the quality of Heade's painting—the looser brushwork and diminished tautness of composition—evident as early as 1871, one can fairly consider Heade's great series of marshes as having been done during the late 1860s. This was certainly his most creative period as an artist—a time during which he was based in New York, between his second and third trips to South America, and one that inspired his most powerful paintings of the sea . . . and his most sensitive interior landscapes.

Theodore E. Stebbins, Jr., *The Life and Works of Martin Johnson Heade* (New Haven and London: Yale University Press, 1975), pp. 52, 53

———

The often repeated theme of sunrise or sunset over wide-spreading salt marshes appealed to two sides of Heade's nature. The poetry of light and space and solitude meant a great deal to him. But he was also a sportsman, with a life-long passion for shore bird shooting. To the gunner, dawn and sunset are the best moments of the day. Perhaps the double inspiration may explain why he could paint the subject so frequently with undiminished pleasure. This example belongs to the years 1867–68, which his latest biographer believes saw his highest achievements in landscape. Although it is hazardous to select one moment from so long a career, especially from one devoted to painting the same favorite themes again and again, certainly Heade never painted light and silence in a more moving way.

E. P. Richardson, *American Art: An Exhibition from the Collection of Mr. and Mrs. John D. Rockefeller 3rd*, exh. cat. (San Francisco: The Fine Arts Museums of San Francisco, 1976), p. 124

Provenance
[Snedecor, New York]

Possibly Henry Morrison Flagler (1830–1913), New York,

St. Augustine, and Palm Beach, Fla.

[Sloan & Roman, New York, ca. 1968–1970]

John D. Rockefeller 3rd and Blanchette Hooker Rockefeller, New York, 1970–1993

FAMSF, 1993.35.11

Exhibition History
Unidentified exhibition, early twentieth century, exh. no. 47 (as *Great Marshes*)

San Francisco 1976, exh. no. 49

Oil on canvas, 11¾ x 17½ in.
Signed and dated lower right: *G. Inness 1869*

GEORGE INNESS
b. Newburgh, N.Y. 1825
d. Bridge of Allan, Scotland 1894

More vigorous and suggestive, but less equable, are the landscapes of George Inness, some of which are among the most remarkable works of the kind produced among us. Inness, in his best moods, is effective through his freedom and boldness, whereby he often grasps the truth with refreshing power. . . . He paints, at times, with haste and carelessness; he does not always do himself justice. Yet rarely do we see one of his landscapes without finding therein a picturesque effect, or a subtle meaning, indicative of the rarest skill and the most absolute genius; if limited in scope, yet actual and true.

George Inness has been singularly loyal to his French ideal in landscape; he is an admirer of [Théodore] Rousseau, and reproduces his manner perfectly. There is great strength in his limning of trees, great effect in his treatment of light. His best landscapes have the mellow, shadowy tone of the old world. . . .

George Inness was born at Newburgh, Orange county, N.Y., on the 1st of May, 1825. When an infant he was removed to New York, and thence, after a few years, to Newark, N.J., where his parents established their home. As early as the age of thirteen the boy's love of drawing was such that a master was allowed him; he was an old gentleman named Baker; the pupil soon learned to make good copies in oil of his teacher's pictures; but, at this time, he was attacked with epilepsy, to which painful malady he has been liable ever since, to the great detriment of consecutive and sustained artistic work. At the age of sixteen Inness went to New York, and attempted to learn engraving with a view of making it a profession; but ill-health obliged him to return home, where, from time to time, he painted and sketched, and, at the age of twenty, passed a month in [Régis-François] Gignoux's studio, and then fairly embarked in landscape art. He has visited Europe twice, but never studied with any one, or copied a picture. . . .

It accords with the imaginative scope and spiritual instinct of Inness, that he should incline to the doctrines of Swedenborg; his appearance, temperament, and character belong to that phase of artist-life where insight and enthusiasm, the unpractical and the sensitive elements, predominate. Inness is, as we have said, unequal in his artistic efforts, but he is also sometimes unequalled; and his foreign proclivities and his suggestive method offer a not undesirable contrast to those wherein merely imitative skill and local fidelity are exhibited, —thus adding another element to the delightful variety of taste and talent that belongs to American landscape art, and attests its honest individuality.

> Henry T. Tuckerman, *Book of the Artists: American Artist Life* (1867; New York: James F. Carr, 1966), pp. 527, 532

––––––––

In 1860 he [Inness] was settled in the simple country scenery of Medfield, Massachusetts, where he painted some of his best pictures. . . . After four years he left Medfield for Eaglewood, near Perth Amboy, New Jersey. . . .

In the same conversation, Mr. Inness expressed himself as follows concerning the true purpose of the painter: This purpose is "simply to reproduce in other minds the impression which a scene has made upon him. A work of art does not appeal to the intellect. It does not appeal to the moral sense. Its aim is not to instruct, not to edify, but to awaken an emotion. This emotion may be one of love, of pity, of veneration, of hate, of pleasure, or of pain; but it must be a single emotion, if the work has unity, as every work should have, and the true beauty of the work consists in the beauty of the sentiment or emotion which it inspires. Its real greatness consists in the quality and the force of this emotion. Details in the picture must be elaborated only enough fully to reproduce the impression that the artist wishes to reproduce."

> G. W. Sheldon, *American Painters* (1878; New York: Benjamin Blom, 1972), pp. 30, 32

––––––––

Burnt sienna is a most valuable color. George Inness used to call it the Jesus Christ of colors.

Virgil Williams, "Virgil Williams' Art Notes to a Deaf-Mute Pupil," *The Overland Monthly* 2d ser., 9, no. 51 (March 1887): 290

————

More interesting even than these early paintings are several rapid studies and sketches for compositions, in which the painter has shaken himself free from conventions, which had never had but a very slight hold upon him, and in which his aim appears to have been that of the Impressionists—to attain as close a rendering as possible of some fleeting effect in nature. His unfailing sense of balance, his aptitude for composition, has made of every one of these studies a finished picture to all intents and purposes, while the momentary aspect of clouds, waves, rain, or wind-swept foliage is usually very happily expressed. It is noticeable that there are few sunset studies of this character, and that the few that exist are quiet in color. . . . There must be a considerable number of these studies in existence, and they are among the best things that Inness has produced.

"The Inness Paintings," *The Art Amateur* 32, no. 3 (February 1895): 77

————

Dear Abe:

It was good of you to send me a copy of the beautifully illustrated catalogue of your current exhibition of fine American paintings [New York, Hirschl & Adler Galleries, *American Paintings for Public and Private Collections*, 1967], and a photograph of the Inness, "Evening at Medfield, Mass.", illustrated in the catalogue.

This painting will be recorded and reproduced in a supplement [to Ireland's catalogue raisonné on George Inness's work], for which I am gathering material.

LeRoy Ireland to A. M. Adler, 12 December 1967, LeRoy Ireland Papers, AAA, roll 994, frame 387

Provenance
Sobin family (reportedly relatives of the artist), Derby, Conn., to ca. 1966

[Florene Maine, Ridgefield, Conn., by 1966]

[Hirschl & Adler Galleries, New York, 1966–1968]

John D. Rockefeller 3rd and Blanchette Hooker Rockefeller, New York, 1968–1993

FAMSF, 1993.35.19

Exhibition History
New York, Hirschl & Adler Galleries, *A Salute to the Whitney Museum: An Exhibition of 250 Years of American Art, 1690–1940*, 1966, exh. no. 16 (as *Medfield, Massachusetts*)

New York, Hirschl & Adler Galleries, *American Paintings for Public and Private Collections*, 1967, exh. no. 57

Related Works
Massachusetts Landscape, 1865
Oil on canvas, 24 x 36 in.
David Findlay, Jr., New York, as of 1984

A Breezy Autumn, 1887
Oil on canvas, 30 x 50 in.
Private collection, as of 1985

Oil on canvas, 38½ x 32⅜ in.
Signed and dated lower right: *E. Johnson./1869.*

EASTMAN JOHNSON

b. Lovell, Maine 1824
d. New York, N.Y. 1906

Johnson was one of the ablest practitioners of the "portrait interior," which derived from the eighteenth-century conversation piece and enjoyed a great vogue in the prosperous decade following the Civil War. In this example James Brown [1791–1877], eminent banker, railway and shipping magnate, is shown with his wife, Eliza Coe Brown [1803–1890], and their grandson, William Adams Brown [1865–1943], in the parlor of their house on University Place. This room was completely redecorated after 1846 in the Renaissance revival style by the French cabinetmaker and interior furnisher Leon Marcotte . . . , whose fashionable establishment was patronized by New York society in the third quarter of the nineteenth century. Considered one of his masterpieces, the room was dismantled in 1869, when Brown moved uptown to Park Avenue, and some of the decorations were installed in the new drawing room. Brown apparently commissioned this painting [it was commissioned by John Crosby Brown, whose parents and son are depicted] as a memento of his old home. It is possibly based in part on a photograph of the Browns in their parlor taken by Matthew [*sic*] Brady in the late 1850s, in which Mrs. Brown is shown in very much the same pose. The

painting offers a superlative rendering of the rich brilliant colors of the room, its elegant proportions and opulent decor, and fine lifelike portraits of the Browns.

> *Nineteenth-Century America: Paintings and Sculpture*, exh. cat. (New York: The Metropolitan Museum of Art, 1970), exh. no. 143

A work by Eastman Johnson, No. 196, in the East Room attracts great attention for its admirable qualities of drawing, composition and color. The figures of the elder persons are somewhat constrained, but nothing could be more natural than the action of the little child, laying its hand on grandpapa's arm, to attract his attention from the newspaper. The accessories are painted with realistic fidelity and scrupulous devotion to truth of detail.

> "Fine Arts: The National Academy of Design," *New-York Times*, 30 April 1869

[I]s it possible that an artist could have invented or chosen this dreadful room? We cannot believe that Mr. Johnson would do either. . . . But he has gone to his task in a noble spirit of self-sacrifice, determined to do even if he had to die. What conscience has been expended on the chandelier. It looks as if made up of the artist's crystallized tears of vexation at having to waste his time over the tasteless thing. What quiet skill has given us the mantelpiece, though it must have hung like a millstone round his neck in the doing. And how skillfully he has wrought the whole discordant upholstery mess into a harmony which, while it allows nothing to escape, makes it easy to forget all the incongruous detail.

> "The Fine Arts: The National Academy of Design," *New-York Daily Tribune*, 22 May 1869

Mr. Eastman Johnson is much more intelligible in No. 196. His "Portraits" are portraits of mirrors, curtains, carpet, mantel-piece, and upholstery in general, with, incidently, an old gentleman, a lady, and a tiny child, the last being on tiptoe and in blue velvet, and busily whispering in the old gentleman's ear. What the little urchin says may be read in the listener's wincing and astonished expression. It can be nothing else than the question: "Have a weed, Grandpa?"

> "National Academy of Design," *Appleton's Journal of Popular Literature, Science, and Art* 1, no. 10 (5 June 1869): 309

My Dear James

You will receive in Liverpool through B S & Co. . . . a box from New York containing as a Xmas gift to yourself and your good wife from your grandparents [i.e., the sitters, James and Eliza Brown], a picture [the version of the FAMSF painting now in the National Gallery of Art, Washington, D.C.] the history of which is curious, as it owes its existence to a combination of misunderstandings which I will tell you about when we meet. To make a long story short I will simply say in this present note, that it is Eastman Johnson's handiwork, and considered as a specimen of his workmanship very good. It is in reality a copy of a portion of the picture he painted for me [the FAMSF painting], the crayon drawing of which your mother has, and is really a very good likeness of your grandfather, with a poor one of your grandmother.

. . . Your grandfather felt that you, as the bearer of his name, . . . would not object to have a likeness of himself in his old age, the last one probably for which he will ever sit.

> John Crosby Brown, to James Clifton Brown, 22 December 1870, copy in the E. P. Richardson Collection, National Museum of American Art/National Portrait Gallery Library

---

I am so happy to have it [*The Brown Family*] go into the right hands. I think that the Rockefeller tradition is such that ultimately the picture may well end in the public trust.

> Margaret C. (Mrs. John Crosby II) Brown to Hirschl & Adler Galleries, New York, ca. May 1972, FAMSF departmental files

Provenance

John Crosby Brown (1838–1909) and Mary Adams Brown (d. 1918), New York, 1869–1918

Descended in family to John Crosby Brown II (ca. 1892–1950) and Margaret Courtwright Brown (b. 1904), New York and Old Lyme, Conn., ca. 1943–1971

[Hirschl & Adler Galleries, New York, 1971–1972]

John D. Rockefeller 3rd and Blanchette Hooker Rockefeller, New York, 1972–1979

FAMSF, 1979.7.67

Exhibition History

New York, National Academy of Design, *Forty-fourth Annual Exhibition*, 1869, exh. no. 196 (as *Portraits*)

New York, The Metropolitan Museum of Art, *Nineteenth-Century America: Paintings and Sculpture*, 1970, exh. no. 143

New York, Hirschl & Adler Galleries, New York, *Faces and Places: Changing Images of Nineteenth-Century America*, 1972, exh. no. 51

San Francisco 1976, exh. no. 79

FAMSF, *Eastman Johnson: Seven Paintings by the Highly Regarded Nineteenth-Century American Artist*, 1979, no publ.

Tokyo 1982, exh. no. 50

Selected References

William Adams Brown, *A Teacher and His Times: A Story of Two Worlds* (New York and London: Charles Scribner's Sons, 1940), p. 41

Patricia Hills, *The Genre Painting of Eastman Johnson: The Sources and Development of His Style and*

Themes (New York: Garland Publishing, 1977), pp. xiv, 112, 118–121, 122, 164

The American Canvas, pp. 112–113, 238

Related Works

The Brown Family, 1869
Oil on paper, mounted on canvas, 23⅜ x 28½ in.
National Gallery of Art, Washington, D.C.

The Brown Family
Crayon drawing
Location unknown

---

71 THE DYING CENTAUR, 1869

Bronze, 21½ x 25½ x 20 in. (cast 1967 by Joseph Ternbach for Kennedy Galleries)
Signed on top front of base: *W Rimmer*; inscribed on left side: © *by Kennedy Galleries Inc. 1967 #1/15*

WILLIAM RIMMER
b. Liverpool, England 1816
d. South Milford, Mass. 1879

The Annual exhibition of the Cooper Union School of Design for Women in New York took place on Thursday evening [May 27], and was an occasion of great interest. The institution is under the direction of Dr. Rimmer, an artist well known in Boston. A Correspondent who was present writes us: "Several of the Doctor's works were on exhibition with those of his pupils, both in sculpture and painting, . . . and his latest work, the 'Centaur,' in which the Doctor shows his thorough knowledge of the animal as well as the human figure, to say nothing of the difficult combination of horse and man."

> *Boston Daily Evening Transcript*, 2 June 1869, quoted in Jeffrey Weidman, "William Rimmer: Critical Catalogue Raisonné," 7 vols. (Ph.D. diss., Indiana University, 1981), 1:307–308

Dr. Rimmer was as successful in the expression of animal nature as in any thing. His conception of the brute was superb. It was, doubtless, not the thing of which he approved as an ideal, nor what he considered the best object of his thoughts and study. It was nevertheless just the thing in which his imagination found itself most unprejudiced, and the least trammelled by theory. . . . The doctor's centaur is quite unique, and without a peer. The doubling-back of the horse, the terrible writhing of the animal part, has never been expressed in any such way before. To be sure, the torso is mannered to a certain degree; but its attachment to the horse is extraordinarily clever, and its ideal character only serves to contrast it the more perfectly with the beast,—to which it is welded.

> Quoted in Truman H. Bartlett, *The Art Life of William Rimmer: Sculptor, Painter, and Physician* (1890; New York: Da Capo Press, for Kennedy Graphics, 1970), p. 136

The *Dying Centaur* was the first sculpture by William Rimmer to be cast in bronze under the auspices of the Rimmer Memorial Committee, formed in 1905 by William R. Ware, Daniel Chester French, and Edward R. Smith. . . . The relationship of Rimmer's original plaster cast of the *Dying Centaur* to the subsequent twentieth century plasters and bronzes is complex. . . .

The original plaster's surface was marked by blow-holes in the face and chest. The need arose, therefore, in the bronze casting for the creation of a plaster cast of the *Centaur* in which the blow-holes had been corrected. . . . From my study of the extant documentation, I have concluded that the plaster cast of the *Dying Centaur* which is now owned by the Yale University Art Gallery was made in 1905, presumably at the Gorham Foundry in Providence,

from the original plaster cast, correcting the blow-holes in the original, for without their correction (elimination), these blow-holes would have appeared in the bronze cast. . . .

. . . This plaster cast was raised from relative obscurity when Kennedy Galleries purchased it from Lincoln Borglum [son of Gutzon Borglum, involved with the 1905 casting], using it in 1967 to copyright an edition of fifteen numbered bronze casts.

Jeffrey Weidman, "William Rimmer: Critical Catalogue Raisonné," 7 vols. (Ph.D. diss., Indiana University, 1982), 1:312, 313, 315–316

Provenance
[Kennedy Galleries, New York, 1967]

John D. Rockefeller 3rd and Blanchette Hooker Rockefeller, New York, 1967–1979

FAMSF, 1979.7.86

Exhibition History
New York, Whitney Museum of American Art, extended loan, 1967–1968

San Francisco 1976, exh. no. 53

FAMSF, *American Sculpture: The Collection of The Fine Arts*

Museums of San Francisco, 1982, exh. no. 3

Selected Reference
Jeffrey Weidman, "William Rimmer: Critical Catalogue Raisonné," 7 vols. (Ph.D. diss., Indiana University, 1981), 1: cat. no. 39B (Sculpture)

Related Works
Dying Centaur, 1869
Plaster, 21½ x 26¼ x 22 in.
Museum of Fine Arts, Boston

Dying Centaur, 1905
Plaster moulage after 1869 original plaster, 21½ x 26½ x 22 in.
Yale University Art Gallery, New Haven, Conn.

Oil on canvas, 12 x 45⅜ in.
Signed and dated lower left: *18V69* (in monogram); signed, dated, and inscribed on reverse, center stretcher
brace: *Elihu Vedder fecit Rome 1868 New York—69*

ELIHU VEDDER

b. New York, N.Y. 1836
d. Rome, Italy 1923

Now Adam knew Eve his wife, and she conceived and bore Cain, saying "I have gotten a man with the help of the Lord." And again, she bore his brother Abel. Now Abel was a keeper of sheep, and Cain a tiller of the ground. In the course of time Cain brought to the Lord an offering of the fruit of the ground, and Abel brought of the firstlings of his flock and of their fat portions. And the Lord had regard for Abel and his offering, but for Cain and his offering he had no regard. So Cain was very angry, and his countenance fell. The Lord said to Cain, "Why are you angry, and why has your countenance fallen? If you do well, will not you be accepted? And if you do not do well, sin is couching at the door; its desire is for you, but you must master it." Cain said to Abel his brother, "Let us go out to the field." And when they were in the field, Cain rose up against his brother Abel, and killed him. Then the Lord said to Cain, "Where is Abel your brother?" He said, "I do not know; am I my brother's keeper?" And the Lord said, "What have you done? The voice of your brother's blood is crying to me from the ground. And now you are cursed from the ground, which has opened its mouth to receive your brother's blood from your hand."

The Bible, Revised Standard Version, Genesis 4:1–12

———

A northern land would not supply, unless in exceptional cases, elements of pathetic expressions which are at once so sad and sweet, so dignified and so severe, as those of Mr. Vedder's *Dead Abel* (No. 34). The long vista of a sandy hollow in what appears to be a hilltop among many hills, the summits of which show to right and left, and are, like those nearer to us, covered with dark, almost bronze-hued herbage. The atmosphere is still as death; for the smoke of an altar rises and drifts not at all: at the foot of the altar lies a corpse; by its side is a fireless pile and a rejected offering; shadows are spread in the valley, and the summits are seen in a light which, however lovely, seems, Medusa-like, to be growing paler and paler with a horror that transcends fear. The pathos of this work is monumental.

William Davies, "Winter Exhibition at the Dudley Gallery," *The Athenaeum*, no. 2245 (5 November 1870): 598

———

Mr. Vedder, in spite of his array of figure pictures, . . . is most powerful, most unconscious, most himself, in purely landscape work, or those pictures which have landscape for a chief part of the composition.

Examine, for instance, the landscape in "The Lost Mind," and notice how much effect is produced by the background. . . . [I]n "The Dead Abel" it holds a larger place than the figure of the slain man—which might be that of a sleeper as well as anything more tragic. The land-

scape is as striking in all these pictures as the figure itself; in some cases it is more original and effective.

"Elihu Vedder," *Scribner's Monthly* 21, no. 1 (November 1880): 115

Characteristic of the melancholy turn of Vedder's imagination as a young man is his account of painting *The Plague in Florence*. According to his story, wanting to paint a study of an arm, he decided to use the blank foreground area of a painting with houses and a sunset. "No sooner had I painted in this arm lying stretched on the ground," he wrote, "than I foresaw the picture." He added the half-burned rags and a group of monks, partially covered the head, identified the skyline with the silhouette of the campanile in Florence, and he had his grim picture of the plague. Actually the painting he was working on at the time, for which he was making a study of the arm, was not much less melancholy. It was the depiction of *The Dead Abel*, the lifeless body stretched out in the foreground of a characteristically gloomy and resistant landscape.

Joshua Taylor, "Perceptions and Digressions," *Perceptions and Evocations: The Art of Elihu Vedder*, exh. cat. (Washington, D.C.: National Collection of Fine Arts, 1979), pp. 99–100

Provenance

Francis Lee Higginson (1841–1925), Boston, 1871–1925 (purchased for $700)

Descended in family to F. Lee H. Wendell, Chicago, by 1976

[Vose Galleries, Boston, 1976–1977]

John D. Rockefeller 3rd and Blanchette Hooker Rockefeller, New York, 1977–1979

FAMSF, 1979.7.103

Exhibition History

New York, National Academy of Design, *Third Winter Exhibition*, 1869, exh. no. 169

London, England, Dudley Gallery, *Winter Exhibition of Cabinet Pictures in Oil*, 1870, exh. no. 34 (as *Dead Abel*)

Boston, Museum of Fine Arts, *Exhibition of Contemporary Art*, 1879, exh. no. 382

Washington, D.C., National Collection of Fine Arts, *Perceptions and Evocations: The Art of Elihu Vedder*, 1978, exh. no. 113

Selected References

S. G. W. Benjamin, *Art in America* (1880; New York and London: Garland Publishing, 1976), p. 94

W. H. Bishop, "Elihu Vedder," *The American Art Review* 1, no. 9 (July 1880): 371

Ernest Radford, "Elihu Vedder," *The Art Journal* (London) 51 (April 1899): 102

Regina Soria, "Elihu Vedder's Mythical Creatures," *The Art Quarterly* 26, no. 2 (Summer 1963): 191

Regina Soria, *Elihu Vedder: American Visionary Artist in Rome, 1836–1923* (Rutherford, N.J.: Fairleigh Dickinson University Press, 1970), pp. 58, 60, 72, 93, 257 n. 6, cat. no. 174

Related Works

The Plague in Florence, ca. 1867
Oil on canvas, 8½ x 11½ in.
Lee B. Anderson, New York, as of 1970

Adam and Eve Mourning the Death of Abel, 1911
Oil on canvas, 14¼ x 47½ in.
The Newark Museum

---

73 THE MOTHER, CA. 1870

Oil on paperboard, 15½ x 13 in.
Signed lower right: *E. Johnson*.

EASTMAN JOHNSON
b. Lovell, Maine 1824
d. New York, N.Y. 1906

An artist of original style and considerable reserve power is found represented in the canvases of Mr. Eastman Johnson, who has deservedly won an excellent reputation for the vigorous and natural treatment of genre drawn from American domestic life. It is difficult to see why these homely but thoroughly artistic compositions are not as strong and true as those painted by artists of high repute in Europe. Mr. Johnson does not, however, confine himself altogether to genre, but has also done some excellent work in compositions wholly ideal, showing fine fancy and sentiment, and rich, careful color.

S. G. W. Benjamin, "Present Tendencies of American Art," *Harper's New Monthly Magazine* 58, no. 346 (March 1879): 491 [text accompanying reproduction after the crayon drawing of *The Mother* on p. 487]

Perhaps it is my bias as a historian that leads me to be glad you have decided to keep the Eastman Johnson [*The Mother*]. I have a theory, however, that much of the best American genre painting in the 19th century was inspired by (not imitated from) the Dutch 17th century painters: as this Eastman Johnson certainly was. It is both like and unlike the painting by Pieter de Hooch or Metsu: and as an American treatment of an ancient and timeless theme, your picture pleased and interested me.

E. P. Richardson to John D. Rockefeller 3rd, 2 June 1965, FAMSF departmental files

During the 1870s, Eastman Johnson painted numerous domestic scenes of mothers and their children, perhaps a reflection of his own domestic happiness (he married in June 1869) and growing family. Certainly Johnson was aware of the long pictorial tradition behind the mother and child motif, and with his constant emphasis on the inherent dignity of images of everyday life, his *Mother and Child* readily suggests a secular variation on a familiar religious subject. . . . Johnson has pared his composition down to the barest necessities; the close-up viewpoint creates an intimate and deeply personal interpretation of the Victorian ideal of motherhood. The dramatic lighting—the dark background contrasting with the brightness striking the mother's face and the body of her nursing child—heightens the mood of sanctity and divinity.

Lee M. Edwards, *Domestic Bliss: Family Life in American Painting, 1840–1910*, exh. cat. (Yonkers, N.Y.: The Hudson River Museum, 1986), p. 90

Provenance
[Wildenstein, New York, 1946–1965]

John D. Rockefeller 3rd and Blanchette Hooker Rockefeller, New York, 1965–1979

FAMSF, 1979.7.66

Exhibition History
Possibly New York, National Academy of Design, American Society of Painters in Water Colors,
Sixth Annual Exhibition, 1873, exh. no. 320

New York, Wildenstein, *Eastman Johnson, 1824–1906*, 1948, exh. no. 8 (as *Mother Feeding Her Child*)

Los Angeles County Museum of History, Science and Art, *Winslow Homer, 1836–1910; Eastman Johnson, 1824–1906*, 1949, exh. no. 9 (as *Mother Feeding Her Child*)

FAMSF, *Eastman Johnson: Seven Paintings by the Highly Regarded Nineteenth-Century American Artist*, 1979, no publ.

Yonkers, N.Y., The Hudson River Museum, *Domestic Bliss: Family Life in American Painting, 1840–1910*, 1986, exh. no. 37 (as *Mother and Child*)

Selected Reference
Patricia Hills, *The Genre Painting of Eastman Johnson: The Sources and Development of His Style and Themes* (New York: Garland Publishing, 1977), p. 97

Related Works
Mother and Child
Crayon heightened with white on brown paper, 16½ x 13¼ in. Private collection, Vt., as of 1987

Nantucket Mother and Child
Oil on paperboard, 15 x 12½ in. M. Knoedler & Co., New York, as of 1975

74 FIRE IN A MISSOURI MEADOW AND A PARTY OF SIOUX INDIANS ESCAPING FROM IT, UPPER MISSOURI 1832, 1871

Oil on paperboard, mounted on paperboard, 18 x 24¼ in.
Signed and dated lower left: *G. Catlin. 1871.*; inscribed on paper label on reverse: *Fire in a Missouri Meadow,/and a party of Sioux In-/-dians escaping from it./Upper Missouri./1832./Painted by George Catlin.*

GEORGE CATLIN
b. Wilkes-Barre, Pa. 1796
d. Jersey City, N.J. 1872

But there is yet another character of burning prairies, that requires another Letter, and a different pen to describe—the war, or hell of fires! where the grass is seven or eight feet high, as is often the case for many miles together, on the Missouri bottoms; and the flames are driven forward by the hurricanes, which often sweep over the vast prairies of this denuded country. There are many of these meadows on the Missouri, the Platte, and the Arkansas, of many miles in breadth, which are perfectly level, with a waving grass, so high, that we are obliged to stand erect in our stirrups, in order to look over its waving tops, as we are riding through it. The fire in these, before such a wind, travels at an immense and frightful rate, and often destroys, on their fleetest horses, parties of Indians, who are so unlucky as to be overtaken by it; not that it travels as fast as a horse at full speed, but that the high grass is filled with wild pea-vines and other impediments, which render it necessary for the rider to guide his horse in the zig-zag paths of the deer and buffaloes, retarding his progress, until he is overtaken by the dense column of smoke that is swept before the fire—alarming the horse, which stops and stands terrified and immutable, till the burning grass which is wafted in the wind, falls about him, kindling up in a moment a thousand new fires, which are instantly wrapped in the swelling flood of smoke that is moving on like a black thunder-cloud, rolling on the earth, with its lightning's glare and its thunder rumbling as it goes.

> George Catlin, *Letters and Notes on the Manners, Customs, and Conditions of the North American Indians*, 2 vols. (London: the author, 1841), 2:17

———

I wish to inform the visitors to my Gallery that, having some years since become fully convinced of the rapid decline and certain extinction of the numerous tribes of the North American Indians; and seeing also the vast importance and value which a full *pictorial history* of these interesting but dying people might be to future ages—I sat out alone, unaided and unadvised, resolved, (if my life should be spared), by the aid of my brush and my pen, to rescue from oblivion so much of their primitive looks and customs as the industry and ardent enthusiasm of one lifetime could accomplish, and set them up in a *Gallery unique and imperishable*, for the use and benefit of future ages.

I have already devoted more than seven years of my life exclusively to the accomplishment of my design, and that with more than expected success.

I have visited with great difficulty, and some hazard to life, forty-eight tribes, (residing within the United States, and British and Mexican Territories;) containing about 300,000

souls. I have seen them in their own villages, have carried my canvass and colours the whole way, and painted my portraits, &c. from the life, as they now stand and are seen in the Gallery.

The collection contains (besides an immense number of costumes and other manufactures) 310 *Portraits* of distinguished men and women of the different tribes, and 200 *other Paintings*, descriptive of *Indian Countries*, their *Villages*, *Games* and *Customs*; containing in all above 3000 figures.

As this immense collection has been gathered, and *every painting has been made from nature*, BY MY OWN HAND—and that too, when I have been paddling my canoe, or leading my pack-horse over and through trackless wilds, at the hazard of my life;—the world will surely be kind and indulgent enough to receive and estimate them, as they have been intended, as *true and fac-simile traces of individual and historical facts*; and forgive me for their present unfinished and unstudied condition, as works of art.

George Catlin, *A Descriptive Catalogue of Catlin's Indian Gallery . . . Now exhibiting in the Egyptian Hall, Piccadilly, London* (London: C. Adlard, 1840), n.p.

Provenance
Gratiot Washburne (b. ca. 1850), Washington, D.C.

[Graham Gallery, New York, by 1966]

John D. Rockefeller 3rd and Blanchette Hooker Rockefeller, New York, 1966–1979

FAMSF, 1979.7.24

Exhibition History
San Francisco 1976, exh. no. 25

Selected References
William H. Truettner, *A Study of*

Catlin's Indian Gallery (Washington, D.C.: Smithsonian Institution Press, in cooperation with the Amon Carter Museum of Western Art and the National Collection of Fine Arts, 1979), p. 248

The American Canvas, pp. 66–67, 234

Related Works
Prairie Meadows Burning, 1832
Oil on canvas, 11 x 14⅛ in.
National Museum of American Art, Washington, D.C.

Engraved replica of 1832 original oil in George Catlin, *Letters and Notes on the Manners, Customs, and Conditions of the North American Indians . . . with Four Hundred Illustrations, Carefully Engraved from His Original Paintings, and Coloured after Nature, in Two Volumes* (London: the author, 1841), 2: pl. 128

After *Prairie Meadows Burning*, ca. 1853
Watercolor, 11 x 14 in.

Thomas Gilcrease Institute of American History and Art, Tulsa, Okla.

After the 1841 engraving, ca. 1859
Pen and ink, 9 x 14 in.
Thomas Gilcrease Institute of American History and Art, Tulsa, Okla.

Prairies Burning, Upper Missouri, Prairie Meadow, ca. 1855–1870
Oil on paperboard, 18⅛ x 24½ in.
Buffalo Bill Historical Center, Cody, Wyo.

Oil on canvas, 25 x 39 in.
Signed and dated lower left: *WMH./74.* (initials in monogram)

WILLIAM MORRIS HUNT

b. Brattleboro, Vt. 1824
d. Appledore, N.H. 1879

Hunt's first serious essay in landscape painting was probably made in the spring of 1874, when he visited Florida in pursuit of recreation and health. . . .

While in Florida he was the guest of his friend, Hon. John M. Forbes of Milton, Mass., and many beautiful charcoal drawings were the result of this trip. He was especially successful in catching the spirit of the dreamy landscape of that region. His paintings of the St. John's River and of several of the Florida creeks were exquisite in color and sentiment, and found ready purchasers. . . .

No painter had ever seen Florida as Hunt saw it, and the cordial reception given to his work in Boston aroused in him a new interest and enthusiasm. He felt that the spring and summer season need not always be spent in a city studio; that there was a new book to be opened, a new song to be sung,—the praise of out-of-door life.

> Helen M. Knowlton, *Art-Life of William Morris Hunt* (Boston: Little, Brown, and Company, 1900), pp. 105–106

––––––––––

We are having real summer weather here [Magnolia, Fla.]. Thermometer sometimes as high as 82°, or even higher. Alligators sunning themselves in the creeks, and the foliage now so dense that the novelty of it is passed; also that lovely contrast of the brown masses of trees with the bright, tender green. All this, with an occasional gigantic cypress reflected in the perfectly still water of the creeks, make pictures to wonder at if not to paint.

> Hunt, to unknown correspondent, 2 April 1874, quoted in Helen M. Knowlton, *Art-Life of William Morris Hunt* (Boston: Little, Brown, and Company, 1900), p. 106

––––––––––

Originally starting out for the avowed purpose of hunting the picturesque, we sailed for the mouth of the St. John's—a river that reaches into the very heart of the [Florida] peninsula, and from the ill-defined shores of which you can branch off into the very wildest of this, in one sense, desolate region. . . . Once fairly launched on the waters of the St. John's . . . we impatiently passed all intervening places until we arrived at Pilatka, a central point, from which we could easily reach the Black River, the more famous Ocklawaha, and other small streams, only navigable for boats of miniature size. . . .

. . . [T]his section of country has always been remarkable for its recuperative effects upon invalids, who, living farther north, suffer from the borean blasts of our long and dreary winters. . . . Among the especial resorts for invalids is Green Cove Springs, near Magnolia, famous for curing rheumatism and a hundred complaints, and composed of a series of warm sulphurous pools, in some places twenty-five feet deep. . . .

One of our strangest experiences in these mysterious regions was forced upon us one morning. . . . Our rude craft was in a basin, possibly a quarter of a mile in diameter, entirely surrounded by gigantic forest-trees, which repeated themselves with the most minute fidelity in the perfectly translucent water. For sixty feet downward we could look, and at this great depth see duplicated the scene of the upper world, the clearness of the water assisting rather than interfering with the vision. . . . The most novel and startling feature was when our craft came from the shade into the sunshine, for then it seemed as if we were, by some miraculous power, suspended seventy feet or more in the mid air, while down on the sanded bottom was a sharp, clear *silhouette* of man, boat, and paddle.

"St. John's and Ocklawaha Rivers, Florida," in William Cullen Bryant, ed., *Picturesque America*, 2 vols. (New York: D. Appleton & Co. 1872), 1:18, 19, 29, 30

———

For twenty years I was unable to paint a good picture. I had to make their portraits all the time . . . study the skulls like a fortune teller or phrenologist. I'll be damned if I do anything of the sort again.

Hunt, 13 January 1875, quoted in Marchal E. Landgren and Sharman Wallace McGurn, *The Late Landscapes of William Morris Hunt*, exh. cat. (College Park: University of Maryland Art Gallery, 1976), p. 70

Provenance
Peter Charndon Brooks, Jr. (1831–1920), Boston, by 1879–1920

Descended in family to Eleanor Brooks (Mrs. Richard M.) Saltonstall (1865–1961), Newton, Mass., 1920–1961

[Spanierman Gallery, New York, by 1967]

John D. Rockefeller 3rd and Blanchette Hooker Rockefeller, New York, 1967–1993

FAMSF, 1993.35.18

Exhibition History
Boston Art Club, otherwise unidentified exhibition held after 1876 and by 1879

Boston, Museum of Fine Arts, *Exhibition of the Works of William Morris Hunt*, 1879, exh. no. 30 or 111 (as *St. John's River, Florida*, lent by Peter Charndon Brooks, Jr.)

Boston, Museum of Fine Arts, *Memorial Exhibition of the Works of William Morris Hunt, 1824–1879*, 1924, exh. no. 34 or 44 (as *St. John's River, Florida*, lent by Mrs. Richard M. Saltonstall)

Possibly Buffalo Fine Arts Academy/Albright Art Gallery, 1924, exh. no. 26 (as *St. John's River, Florida*, lent by Mrs. R. M. Saltonstall)

San Francisco 1976, exh. no. 77

Tokyo 1982, exh. no. 40

Selected References
Martha A. S. Shannon, *Boston Days of William Morris Hunt* (Boston: Marshall Jones Co., 1923), pp. 129–130

William Morris Hunt: A Memorial Exhibition, exh. cat. (Boston: Museum of Fine Arts, 1979), p. 83

Sally Webster, *William Morris Hunt, 1824–1879* (Cambridge: Cambridge University Press, 1991), pp. 108–111

Related Works
Governor's Creek, Florida, 1873
Charcoal on buff paper, 8⅜ x 11⅛ in.
Museum of Fine Arts, Boston

St. Johns River, ca. 1873
Private collection, Jacksonville, Fla., as of 1994

Governor's Creek, Florida, 1873 or 1874
Oil on canvas, 10 x 16 in.
Columbus Museum, Columbus, Ga.

Oil on paperboard, 21⅞ x 16¾ in.
Signed and dated lower left: *E. Johnson/1875.*

EASTMAN JOHNSON
b. Lovell, Maine 1824
d. New York, N.Y. 1906

Eastman Johnson sends his pleasant Nantucket picture, entitled "What the Shell Says." It represents a pretty little girl applying a sea-shell to an old man's ear. The subject is cleverly composed and is richly colored. It was exhibited in the Century Gallery at the December meeting.

"Artists' Fund Society: Sixteenth Annual Exhibition," *(New York) Evening Post,* 19 January 1876

A private view of the pictures contributed to the Artists' Fund Society was afforded to artists, members of the press, and a number of leading connoisseurs at the Kurtz Gallery in Madison square last evening. The paintings are ninety in number and entirely cover the walls of the gallery. Among the most notable of them may be mentioned Mr. Eastman Johnson's "What the Shell Says." . . . This is in Mr. Johnson's happiest style, and is quite equal in breadth of touch and strength of expression to anything which he has recently executed.

"The Artists' Fund Society: Private View of the Pictures at the Kurtz Gallery," *New-York Times,* 19 January 1876

The sale by auction of pictures contributed in aid of the Artists' Fund took place . . . last evening, Mr. Robert Somerville officiating as auctioneer. The attendance was large and the bidding spirited, sharp competition occurring for the possession of Eastman Johnson's "What the Shell Says." . . .

. . . "What the Shell Says," Eastman Johnson, $725 [the highest price paid for any picture at the auction].

"The Artists' Fund: Sale of Pictures Contributed in Aid of the Fund," *New-York Times,* 26 January 1876

[A]nd whether holding a shell to the ear, chasing a butterfly, companioned by a deer or a lamb, worshipped by Magi as incarnate love and truth, sportive, tranquil, awed, elated, fond or wayward—always and everywhere the image of childhood to poet and painter, to the landscape, the household, the shrine, the temple and the grave—is a redeeming presence, a harmonizing and hopeful element, the token of what we were, and prophecy of what we may be; and therefore it is that we

    —hold it a religious duty
    To love and worship children's beauty;
    They've the least taint of earthly clod,
    They're freshest from the hand of God.

Henry T. Tuckerman, "Children," *The Galaxy* 4 (July 1867): 318

Regarded as he is, as the founder of a school of American genre of the highest order, Eastman Johnson's "What the Sea Says" is an admirable example of his art. Inspired in his choice of subjects by the largest sympathy with humanity, he gives us an interpretation of them which in its simple and unaffected eloquence has all the grandeur of great art. In "What the Sea Says" he presents to us babyhood and age, drawn together by the voice of eternity, which is no more a mystery to the babe than to the grandsire. What romances lie hidden in the sonorous shell whose murmurs sing of the great waters and their marvels in a voice time cannot silence? What secrets of the sounding deep from which it comes might it reveal if we could but translate its song? To grandfather, looking wise as he listens, it tells of wreck and horror, of long voyages when the rolling main was his pathway to fortune, of hopes and lives wrecked and washed down by the monster whose tones it echoes; to baby its chant is but one of the romances of a life that has not yet begun. . . .

. . . "What the Sea Says," being shown at the Paris Exposition in 1878, made his name one of honor in the estimation of the keenest critics of the old world, as it had already become with those of the new.

Alfred Trumble, *Representative Works of Contemporary American Artists* (1887; New York and London: Garland Publishing, 1978), n.p.

Provenance
Benjamin Hazard Field (1814–1893), New York, 1876–1893

[Graham Gallery, New York, 1961]

Private collection, 1961–1965

[Graham Gallery, New York, 1965–1966]

John D. Rockefeller 3rd and Blanchette Hooker Rockefeller, New York, 1966–1979

FAMSF, 1979.7.64

Exhibition History
New York, Century Association, December 1875, exh. no. 15 (as *The Conch Shell*)

New York, Kurtz Gallery, *Artists' Fund Society, Sixteenth Annual Exhibition*, 1876

Philadelphia, United States Centennial Commission, Art Gallery, *International Exhibition*, 1876, exh. no. 72 (as *What the Sea Says*)

Paris, *Exposition Universelle*, 1878, exh. no. 70 (as *Ce que disent les coquillages*)

New York, The Metropolitan Museum of Art, *Loan Collection of Paintings and Sculpture in the West Galleries and the Grand Hall*, 1881, exh. no. 41 (as *What the Shell is Saying*)

FAMSF, *Eastman Johnson: Seven Paintings by the Highly Regarded Nineteenth-Century American Artist*, 1979, no publ.

Selected References
United States Centennial Commission, *International Exhibition, 1876. Reports and Awards*, ed. Francis A. Walker (Washington, D.C.: Government Printing Office, 1880), 7:88, no. 415

"Two Art Exhibitions: The Metropolitan Loan—New and Notable Pictures," *The American Art Journal* 35, no. 3 (14 May 1881): 47

Related Works
What the Shell Says (Listening to the Shell), ca. 1875
Oil on board, 22 x 17¾ in.
The Thomas Gilcrease Institute of American History and Art, Tulsa, Okla.

The FAMSF composition is painted over a sketch for *The Boyhood of Lincoln*, 1868
Oil on canvas, 46 x 37 in.
University of Michigan Museum of Art

77 HORSE CHESTNUT BLOSSOM, CA. 1875

Oil on wood panel, 16¾ x 8⅞ in.

WALTER GAY
b. Hingham, Mass. 1856
d. Bréau, France 1937

When I spotted the *Horse Chestnut Blossom* painting, it seemed immediately to suggest an attribution to Walter Gay, as a work done in Boston in the mid-1870s, before he went abroad. Though I've not seen a tremendous number of his early still lifes, the ones I have examined are pretty much of a piece—vertical pictures, on panel, usually with the flowers and/or blossoms against a dark background, and featuring an unusual combination of fairly broad paint handling, sometimes rather lusciously done, with rather specific, surprisingly detailed botanical treatment. All of which are characteristic of your painting—in addition to its high quality.

William H. Gerdts, The Graduate School and University Center of the City University of New York, 27 December 1993, FAMSF departmental files

I was born January 22nd 1856 in the old house—a double one (ours was the side next the church) overlooking the square of old Elm trees diagonally opposite the Fiske House. . . . At the age of nine, my family moved, (I always thought unwisely) to Dorchester. I went later on to the Roxbury Latin School, then considered one of the best schools in the country. I fear I profited little there as my copy books attest, being covered with drawings instead of the work which I was expected to do.

At the age of 17 in 1872 a great opportunity came into my life, that of going west, at that time a wilderness, peopled by Indians, & buffalo. My uncle Charles Blake who was to start a ranch, invited me & I jumped at the chance. There I spent the year 1872–3 & had thrilling experiences. I had always wanted to paint, however, & on going back to Boston took up painting seriously, without a master. I painted flower pictures with some small success. Then in 1876 I got another opportunity. Mr. Hunt the well known artist, & my Uncle Allan, both advised me to go abroad to study. I went to France by way of England, & staid 11 years without returning to America studying in the schools, & becoming a pupil of Bonnat. . . . I began to paint interiors about 1894 & have had many exhibitions both in Paris, & of late years in America.

Gay to his brother, William Gay, 8 October 1929, Walter Gay Papers, AAA, roll 2802, frames 632–634

Walter Gay, a nephew of the distinguished landscape painter W. Allen Gay, has for some years been making a specialty of flower pieces, in which he has attained to merited distinction. While strikingly true to nature, his flower groups have an idealistic grace which commends them to amateurs. Mr. Gay, being about to sail for Europe to prosecute his studies in art, has placed some twenty of his flower pieces, with some sketches from nature and object pieces for sale at Williams & Everett's. They are well worthy of the attention of all persons friendly to art; for, if we may judge from the promise shown by Mr. Gay, they will be more valuable five years hence than they are now.

Unidentified newspaper clipping, ca. 1876, Walter Gay Papers, AAA, roll 2802, frame 642

At Williams & Everett's are some panel paintings of flowers and ferns by Walter Gay, a nephew of W. Allen Gay, the well-known landscape artist. During the past year pictures by Walter Gay have been frequently on exhibition at this gallery, and they have been much admired by visitors. At first it was a simple spray of Forget-me-not, or a few flowers of the Lily of the Valley, or a bit of the vine with leaf and flower of the Morning Glory, simply painted on black ground. . . .

. . . Mr. Gay is a young artist and one of the few who devote themselves to flower painting. His success thus far has been great, and his works give promise of good things in the future.

Unidentified newspaper clipping, ca. 1876, Walter Gay Papers, AAA, roll 2802, frame 643

———

[I]t was not as a figure or landscape painter that Gay established his early career in Boston. Instead, he supported himself as a painter of still lifes of flowers. Although the format often varied, the majority of Gay's surviving flower paintings are on narrow, vertical prepared wooden panels with smooth polished surfaces. Moreover, he appears to have concentrated exclusively on wildflowers and foliage, rather than on cultivated garden flowers or exotic greenhouse varieties. Most often, Gay's flowers are painted against a neutral black background and in a painterly style of delicate brushstrokes that define the individual petals and leaves, and the flowers are never consciously "arranged" in vases or used as part of a complex table top setting composition, but rather grouped together in small sprays or depicted as if still growing.

Gary A. Reynolds, *Walter Gay: A Retrospective*, exh. cat. (New York: Grey Art Gallery and Study Center, 1980), p. 16

Provenance
Reportedly William Morris Hunt (1824–1879), Boston, ca. 1875–1879

[Adelson Galleries, Boston, 1970]

Theodore E. Stebbins, Jr. (b. 1938), Branford, Conn., 1970–1971

[Kennedy Galleries, New York, 1971–1973]

John D. Rockefeller 3rd and Blanchette Hooker Rockefeller, New York, 1973–1979

FAMSF, 1979.7.71

Exhibition History
New York, Kennedy Galleries, *Artists' Studies: A Group Show of Seven Nineteenth- and Twentieth-Century American Painters*, 1973, exh. no. 72 (as by John La Farge)

San Francisco 1976, exh. no. 83 (as by John La Farge)

Selected Reference
Henry Adams, "John La Farge, 1830–1870: From Amateur to Artist" (Ph.D. diss., Yale University, 1980), p. 236

78 WOMAN IN WHITE DRESS, CA. 1875

Oil on paperboard, 22⅜ x 14 in.
Signed lower right: *E.J.*

EASTMAN JOHNSON
b. Lovell, Maine 1824
d. New York, N.Y. 1906

In the 1870s Johnson painted several interiors of girls and women alone, engaged in private personal activities—removed from the company of men and children. In many of these, light acts as an accent to the mood or to symbolize the presence of an outside agent [as in *Woman in White Dress*, although this work has been cut down on the left side to eliminate the figure of a child approaching the door with a bouquet of flowers]. . . . This quiet, private light also pervades *The Earring*, in which the subject is caught at the moment of fastening an earring—a small moment but one requiring her total absorption. In *Not at Home* the light shining through the parlor suggests the movement of the woman who flees up the darkened stairs. In this painting, as in many seventeenth-century Dutch interiors, there is a suggestion of other rooms, of spaces beyond the confines of the canvas.

> Patricia Hills, *Eastman Johnson*, exh. cat. (New York: Clarkson N. Potter, in association with the Whitney Museum of American Art, 1972), pp. 82, 83

Paintings of ladies in elegant interiors were not Johnson's specialty. Henry James, reviewing Johnson's pictures in 1875 for *The Galaxy*, disagreed with the art critic . . . who had praised Johnson's "happy talent to render familiar scenes with elegance of style." James said of *The Earring*:

> For [Johnson's] lady in a black velvet dressing-gown, fastening in an earring, we did not greatly care, in spite of the desirable mahogany buffet against which she is leaning. Mr. Johnson will never be an elegant painter—or at least a painter of elegance. He is essentially homely.

Johnson, himself, would probably have concurred with James, for the largest part of his oeuvre has rural or rustic settings. . . .

. . . [B]y the 1870s the sketch was recognized as a fully acceptable work of "art", although not to the liking of everyone. . . .

We have evidence that Johnson, too, was fond of such first sketches. An obituary of the artist by a writer claiming to have been Johnson's friend stated that "He liked to keep his sketches, and knew they were better." Moreover, photographs of Johnson's studio prove that Johnson kept his many sketches for his own delectation.

> Patricia Hills, *The Genre Painting of Eastman Johnson: The Sources and Development of His Style and Themes* (New York: Garland Publishing, 1977), pp. 142, 133

Provenance

The artist, ca. 1875–1906

Descended in family to Baron M. L. Reigersberg Versluys, by 1977

[Hirschl & Adler Galleries, New York, 1977]

John D. Rockefeller 3rd and Blanchette Hooker Rockefeller, New York, 1977–1979

FAMSF, 1979.7.62

Exhibition History

New York, Hirschl & Adler Galleries, *A Gallery Collects*, 1977, exh. no. 35

FAMSF, *Eastman Johnson: Seven Paintings by the Highly Regarded Nineteenth-Century American Artist*, 1979, no publ.

Related Works

Not at Home, ca. 1872–1880

Oil on academy board, 26½ x 22¼ in.

The Brooklyn Museum

The Earring, 1873
Oil on academy board, 26 x 22 in.
The Corcoran Gallery of Art, Washington, D.C.

Watercolor over charcoal on wove paper, 17¾ x 22¼ in
Signed and dated left center: *HOMER/1877* (in japanesque format)

WINSLOW HOMER

b. Boston, Mass. 1836
d. Prout's Neck, Maine 1910

At the head of these pictures [in the annual exhibition of the Society of Painters in Water Colors], which are inspiriting to those who have watched our Art-progress are the works of Mr. Winslow Homer, who has been a favorite for many years in his out-door scenes, his animated figures, and the vivacity of his dramatic situations. . . . [T]his year we wandered in the rooms of the Water Colour Exhibition, and, as we went along, we observed the yellow-grey hue of the walls, which gave delicacy and lightness to the scene, [and] we analysed the impression received from the pure and pale backgrounds of many of the works. . . . But suddenly our eye was caught and held by studies of such remarkable force and precision of tones, and subtlety of hues, that we involuntarily exclaimed to ourselves that some new artist had dawned upon the French or the Roman world. The contrasts were so peculiar and so delicate, and the tints so full of texture, that for the first glance we had not the thought even to observe the form of the objects they composed. The perfectly free and precise handling, too, was in entire accord with the methods of the best of the foreign aquarellists, and it was entirely distinct from any suspicion of "niggling," or of an inexperienced hand.

"The Tenth New York Water-Colour Exhibition," *The Art Journal* (New York) 3 (March 1877): 95

C.A. 3867

Mr. Winslow Homer is fond of experiment, and is nothing if not Mr. Winslow Homer. Four out of his five pictures are figures of young women, and we notice that the hands and feet are enormous and coarse, and that three of the faces display large, sickly, dirty, faint green patches. No other young women in the room (nor any old women either) have such patches. As for ourselves, we never saw the like of them either on canvas or on epidermis.

(New York) Evening Post, 13 February 1877, quoted in Gordon Hendricks, *The Life and Work of Winslow Homer* (New York: Harry N. Abrams, 1979), p. 130

It was while Homer was occupying his studio in the old studio building in West Tenth Street that he became acquainted with John La Farge, who had a studio in the same building. . . . La Farge relates the following incident of those days:—

"I met him [Homer] on the stairs as I was going up, and I knew by his gesture that he was coming to me. We went up to his room without a word, and he pointed to a picture he had just painted. It was that of a girl who had hurt her hand, and the expression of the face was what in my Newport language I know as 'pitying herself.' This was as delicate an expression as it is possible to conceive. The painter of the surf and the fisherman and the sailor and the hunter and every active and fierce edge of the sea was here touching one of the most impossible things to render. He said nothing; he pointed; I understood. He wished to show me that he, too, could paint otherwise, and we went downstairs together without a word."

William Howe Downes, *The Life and Works of Winslow Homer* (Boston and New York: Houghton Mifflin Company, 1911), pp. 83–84

Provenance
[Possibly auction sale, Charles F. Libbie Gallery, Boston, 29 May 1878, no publ.]

William S. Eaton, Boston, possibly 1878–ca. 1926

Descended in family to his son, Francis S. Eaton, Boston and Tucson, by 1926–1943

[Macbeth Galleries, New York, 1940–1943 (unsold)]

[Babcock Galleries, New York; Macbeth Galleries, New York; and Milch Gallery, New York, 1943–1946]

[Milch Gallery, New York, 1946]

Charles D. Lang, Baltimore, 1946–1954

[Milch Gallery, New York, 1954–1956]

Mr. and Mrs. William J. Poplack, Detroit, 1956–1959

[Hirschl & Adler Galleries, New York, 1959–1960]

John D. Rockefeller 3rd and Blanchette Hooker Rockefeller, New York, 1960–1993

FAMSF, 1993.35.15

Exhibition History
New York, National Academy of Design, American Society of Painters in Water Colors, *Tenth Annual Exhibition*, 1877, exh. no. 396 (for sale, $250)

New York, The Century Association, 2 June 1877, exh. no. 35

Boston, Museum of Fine Arts, extended loan, 1926–1940

Andover, Mass., Addison Gallery of American Art, Phillips Academy, *Winslow Homer: Water Colors, Prints and Drawings*, 1936, no exh. no. (as *Afternoon Chat*)

New York, Brearley School, *Art in the United States, Part II*, 1964, no publ.

San Francisco 1976, exh. no. 70

Selected References
Gordon Hendricks, *The Life and Work of Winslow Homer* (New York: Harry N. Abrams, 1979), pp. 129–130, 281

Nicolai Cikovsky, Jr., *Winslow Homer* (New York: Harry N. Abrams, in association with the National Museum of American Art, 1990), p. 61

Nicolai Cikovsky, Jr., "Winslow Homer's National Style," in *American Icons: Transatlantic Perspectives on Eighteenth- and Nineteenth-Century American Art*, Issues and Debates, no. 2 (Santa Monica, Calif.: The Getty Center for the History of Art and the Humanities, 1992), pp. 260–261

Object record, manuscript catalogue raisonné of the works of Winslow Homer, by Lloyd Goodrich, courtesy of the City University of New York, Lloyd Goodrich and Edith Havens Goodrich, Whitney Museum of American Art Record of the Works of Winslow Homer

80 A DAY DREAM, 1877

Oil on paperboard, 24 x 12 in.
Signed and dated lower left: *E. Johnson/–77*; inscribed on reverse (twice): *A Day Dream*

EASTMAN JOHNSON
b. Lovell, Maine 1824
d. New York, N.Y. 1906

Almost from the start his [Johnson's] pictures have been widely appreciated, and have brought him annually a handsome financial return. Many of them, perhaps the best of them, have the simple, tender characterization, the sweet, serene inspiration, that make Edouard Frère's *genre* works so pleasing; and almost all of them display a real original power that penetrates and discloses the newness and freshness of common scenes. Mr. Johnson's subjects are taken from American life. . . . His pictures are presentations of national types.

G. W. Sheldon, *American Painters* (New York: D. Appleton and Company, 1881), p. 167

More pensive and inscrutable is the young woman in *Day Dreams* of 1877, who gazes out the window at the falling snow. Here one is tempted to see the window as a symbol of a world beyond the kitchen, the sewing room, and the nursery, inaccessible to the young woman. But even if the window does not function as a metaphor, it functions as it always has in European art, as a transmitter of outside light into an interior. The window also justifies Johnson's technique of combining cool lights along with warm lights against a warm background of transparent shadows.

> Patricia Hills, *The Genre Painting of Eastman Johnson: The Source and Development of His Style and Themes* (New York: Garland Publishing, 1977), p. 142

It is the magic of painting to catch a fleeting moment and make it timeless. In this [*A Day Dream*] . . . Johnson has preserved for us a single, graceful gesture. He surprises and touches us by his unsentimental tenderness toward life.

> E. P. Richardson, *American Art: An Exhibition from the Collection of Mr. and Mrs. John D. Rockefeller 3rd*, exh. cat. (San Francisco: The Fine Arts Museums of San Francisco, 1976), p. 190

Day Dreams
A young girl stands in a pensive attitude leaning against the corner of a window, her head turned over her left shoulder, her right arm akimbo and her left hand held to her belt. She wears a dark gray jacket, trimmed with red, and a blue-striped skirt. Signed at the lower left, *E.J.* Height 12 inches; length, 24 inches. [inscribed: *Bernet-agent 130*]

> *The Works of the Late Eastman Johnson, N.A.*, sale cat. (New York: American Art Galleries, 1907), lot no. 102 [apparently, given the described signature and orientation, referring not to the FAMSF painting but to a closely related, currently unlocated work]

Provenance
Rose A. Durfee, late 19th or early 20th century
[Victor Spark, New York, by 1968]
John D. Rockefeller 3rd and

Blanchette Hooker Rockefeller, New York, 1968–1993
FAMSF, 1993.35.20

Exhibition History
New York, Whitney Museum of American Art, *Eastman Johnson:*

Retrospective Exhibition, 1972, exh. no. 92
San Francisco 1976, exh. no. 81

Related Works
Woman at a Window, 1872
Oil on academy board, 9 x 12 in.

Carmine Dalesio, New York, as of 1940
The Long, Long Weary Day, 1873
Oil on academy board, 22½ x 12 in.
Vose Galleries, Boston, as of 1974

---

81 FLOWER STUDY, 1877

Oil on canvas, 27⅛ x 20 in.
Signed and dated lower right: *Geo. C. Lambdin/77*

GEORGE COCHRAN LAMBDIN
b. Pittsburgh, Pa. 1830
d. Philadelphia, Pa. 1896

Roses were Lambdin's favorite blooms, and he went on to develop one of the best-known of the many famous flower gardens in Germantown, outside of Philadelphia. This garden was the basis for a series of rose garden pictures that he painted once he turned more and more to still-life specialization, after about 1870. Lambdin painted many beautiful flower still lifes in a conventional format of a bouquet in a vase upon a tabletop, but more innovative was his . . . depiction of growing flowers usually silhouetted against a slightly textured wall of stucco or plaster. In these pictures, the flowers are usually shown in a seemingly informal setting and arrangement, but actually beautifully arranged in sinuous arabesques of stems and blooms, wherein the natural life cycle of bud to full flower to ageing bloom is well observed and delineated. . . .

. . . [T]he basic format, the informal setting and arrangement, and the depiction of a natural growth cycle are derived from [John] Ruskin and reflect the impact of the writings of Charles Darwin. This is a form of painting in the gray area between landscape and still life:

more than nature studies, but distinctively removed from the traditional floral still life in which Lambdin was also a specialist of the first rank.

William H. Gerdts, *Down Garden Paths: The Floral Environment in American Art* (Rutherford, N.J.: Fairleigh Dickinson University Press; London and Toronto: Associated University Presses, 1983), pp. 19, 20, 21

———

I believe the most beautiful position in which flowers can possibly be seen is precisely their most natural one—low flowers relieved by grass or moss, and tree blossoms relieved against the sky. How it happens that no flower-painter has yet been moved to draw a cluster of boughs of peach blossom, or cherry blossom, or apple blossom just as they grow . . . is more than I can understand.

John Ruskin, 1857, quoted in Ruth Irwin Weidner, *George Cochran Lambdin, 1830–1896*, exh. cat. (Chadds Ford, Pa.: Brandywine River Museum, 1986), p. 32

———

It is difficult to conceive of anything which could afford a more delicate and sensitive medium for the expression of the tender and subtle sentiments than is offered by the floral kingdom. To ascribe to a gift of flowers some special significance beyond that included in the simple giving of a gift is so natural that the construction of a flower language has been much less strained and artificial than might be at first supposed.

The use of this delicate code has increased in favor with polite society and is employed to no small extent by those whose taste and refinement are sufficiently cultured and acute to permit its use. . . .

Chrysanthemum, Red,   . . . I love.
Chrysanthemum, White,   . . . Truth.
Chrysanthemum, Yellow,   . . . Slighted love.

Correct Form in the Etiquette of Cards and Stationery to Which Is Appended the Sentiments of Flowers and Jewels (Chicago: The Inland Printer Company, 1894), pp. 39, 51

82 THE SPHINX OF THE SEASHORE, 1879

Oil on canvas, 16 x 27⅞ in.
Signed and inscribed lower right: *EV.ROMA / Copyright 1899 by E. Vedder* (initials and *R* in monogram)

ELIHU VEDDER
b. New York, N.Y. 1836
d. Rome, Italy 1923

*T*he Sea-Sphinx seems to epitomize the problem of ruin. It asks why ships go down, why the hard earnings of toil are scattered to the winds, why sailors drown and leave their bones to whiten on alien shores. It points the old, baffling inquiry as to the need in the economy of things of the wholesale devastation, involving guilty and innocent alike, which we observe in continual progress. Expression for this is sought in a shape resembling the mythical Sphinx of Œdipus, sent to ravage the territory of Thebes. It is squatted, with a bleached human skull between its paws, on a vast quicksand, bristling with cable-rings, anchor-flukes, and other appurtenances of vessels which have been swallowed up in it. The head and breast are those of an imperious, beautiful woman, whose dishevelled hair merges with the mane of the lion's body constituting the lower portion. The shore is a dark, repellent mud rather than sand, and on its edges are drawn—a detail for which the painter has shown in other works an especial fondness—the curves of thin, shallow waves which have run far up upon it. A spectral light broods over the whole. The red of a faint after-glow touches some distant sand dunes, and the rising moon is seen between bars of leaden and purplish cloud.

W. A. Bishop, "Elihu Vedder," *The American Art Review* 1, no. 8 (June 1880): 326

My dear Mr. Vedder:

I am going to do a thing I have never in my whole life done before, namely this, to ask for an autograph, yours, if you please, that I may put it beneath a photograph of that splendid stormy sea shore sphinx. I was so fortunate as to secure one today, & I want your name to put to it. I always have sworn that if the Angel Gabriel came to town I wouldn't ask for his autograph—pride is said to go before a fall, & I wish so much for this that I really am a little amused at my own enthusiasm. Be good enough to write it on a slip of paper that I may put the finishing touch to my treasure. I never take any notice of such requests unless the petitioner sends an envelope to save me all trouble. I will treat you like wise. I have never once done this thing before, but your work is so wonderful & so takes possession of my imagination that I want the signature of the hand that did it all.

Celia Thaxter to Vedder, 2 April 1880, Elihu Vedder Papers, AAA, roll 2323, frames 164–165

In *The Sphinx of the Seashore* there is, if we may so express it, a glow of darkness. It is, perhaps, his most unique painting, a subject conceived as only Vedder can conceive one: in the middle distance of a sombre landscape, a chimera-like figure with a woman's head, her

mouth open, the white teeth gleaming through the gloom—a conception of a scourge teeming with purport.

"American Studio Talk," *International Studio* 10, no. 37 (March 1900): suppl., ii

———

Sphinx of the Seashore 28″ x 16″ $1500//Given Mr. Sargent

Vedder, "Pictures I have painted: Mr. Wllm Macbeth" [in reference to 1912 exhibition at Macbeth Galleries], Elihu Vedder Papers, AAA, roll 528, frame 910

———

The Sphinx of the Seashore is related to a drawing Vedder used in his major illustration project—Omar Khayyám's *Rubáiyát* [Boston: Houghton Mifflin and Co., 1884]. That drawing, called by Vedder *The Inevitable Fate*, accompanied verses of the twelfth-century Persian mathematician-astronomer's poems on the mysteries of life and death:

> (55)
> Would you that spangle of Existence spend
> About The Secret—quick about it Friend!
> A Hair perhaps divides the False and True—
> And upon what, prithee, does Life depend?

> ———

> (58)
> A moment guess'd—then back behind the Fold
> Immerst of Darkness round the Dramma roll'd
> Which for the Pastime of Eternity,
> He does Himself contrive, enact, behold.

Vedder considered the question of human existence in his own writings. On the sphinx of the seashore he wrote:

> The Philosopher [Omar Khayyám] had evidently pondered on the fact of the disappearance of so many forms of life and the certainty that in time even man himself with all his inventions must disappear from the face of the earth. What

wonder that he calls the brief moment of existence between two eternities a spangle or that the artist should represent this idea under the form of the all devouring Sphinx. [Elihu Vedder Papers, American Academy and National Institute of Arts and Letters, New York]

Jennifer Saville, in *The American Canvas: Paintings from the Collection of The Fine Arts Museums of San Francisco* (New York: Hudson Hills Press, in association with The Fine Arts Museums of San Francisco, 1989), p. 138

Provenance

The artist, 1879–1912

Porter E. Sargent (1872–1951), Boston, 1912–1951

Descended in family to F. Porter Sargent (1915–1975), Boston, 1951–ca. 1955

Lawrence A. Fleischman (b. 1925) and Barbara Greenberg Fleischman (b. 1924), Detroit, by 1955–1966

[Kennedy Galleries, New York, 1966–1968]

John D. Rockefeller 3rd and Blanchette Hooker Rockefeller, New York, 1968–1979

FAMSF, 1979.7.102

Exhibition History

New York, The Century Association, 1880, exh. no. 1

New York, Vedder's Union Square Studio, 1880

Possibly Boston Art Club, *Twenty-second Exhibition of Paintings*, 1880, not in publ.

Boston, Williams and Everett's Gallery, *Pictures, Sketches of Pic-*

tures and Studies, by Elihu Vedder, 1880, exh. no. 6

London, England, Dowdeswell Galleries, *Exhibition of Oil Paintings, Sketches, and Drawings by Elihu Vedder*, 1899

Boston, Williams and Everett's Gallery, *Exhibition of Works by Elihu Vedder*, 1900, exh. no. 9

New York, Avery Art Galleries, *Exhibition of Works by Elihu Vedder*, 1900, exh. no. 9

Washington, D.C., Fischer Galleries, *Exhibition of Works by Elihu Vedder*, 1901, exh. no. 7

Pittsburgh, The Carnegie Institute, *Exhibition of Works by Elihu Vedder*, 1901, exh. no. 14

The Art Institute of Chicago, *Work of Elihu Vedder*, 1901, exh. no. 14

New York, Macbeth Galleries, *Exhibition of Paintings by Elihu Vedder*, 1912, exh. no. 42

Boston, Doll and Richards, *Elihu Vedder: Exhibition and Private*

Sale of His Oil Paintings and Drawings, 1912, exh. no. 31

New York, American Academy of Arts and Letters, *Exhibition of the Works of Elihu Vedder*, 1937, exh. no. 18

The Detroit Institute of Arts, *Collection in Progress: Selections from the Lawrence and Barbara Fleischman Collection of American Art*, 1955, exh. no. 23

Washington, D.C., United States Information Service, *Nine Generations of American Painting: A Loan Exhibition from the Detroit Institute of Arts and the Lawrence A. Fleischman Collection*, 1958 (organized for travel to South America, Greece, and Israel), Israel cat., exh. no. 24

Indianapolis, John Herron Art Museum, *Romantic America*, 1961, exh. no. 37

Washington, D.C., Smithsonian Institution Traveling Exhibition Service, *Paintings and Drawings by Elihu Vedder*, 1966, exh. no. 79

New York, Kennedy Galleries,

The American Artist Abroad, 1968, no exh. no.

Washington, D.C., National Collection of Fine Arts, *Perceptions and Evocations: The Art of Elihu Vedder*, 1978, exh. no. 116

Tokyo 1982, exh. no. 38

Selected References

F. D. Millet, "Elihu Vedder's Pictures," *Atlantic Monthly* 45, no. 272 (June 1880): 846

Regina Soria, *Elihu Vedder: American Visionary Artist in Rome, 1836–1923* (Rutherford, N.J.: Fairleigh Dickinson University Press, 1970), pp. 16, 200, cat. no. 379

Carter Ratcliff, "The Gender of Mystery: Elihu Vedder," *Art in America* 67, no. 7 (November 1979): 84–85, 91

The American Canvas, pp. 138–139, 240

Related Work

The Inevitable Fate, in *Rubáiyát of Omar Khayyám* (Boston: Houghton Mifflin and Co., 1884), stanzas 55 and 58

---

83 THE IRONWORKERS' NOONTIME, 1880

Oil on canvas, 17 x 23⅞ in.
Signed lower left: *Thos. Anshutz*.

THOMAS POLLOCK ANSHUTZ

b. Newport, Ky. 1851
d. Fort Washington, Pa. 1912

Equally home-born and bred, with high anatomic truths expressed in most familiar scenes, is Mr. Anshutz's "Dinner Time." The crowded courtyard of one of our monstrous American foundries is observed filled with the muscular forms of workmen nude to the waist, clustering round the pump or the trough, opening their unattractive cold dinners, gathering in clusters for intelligent political debate; in fine, doing all the most trivial actions of their moments of leisure with sledge-hammer gestures of prodigious arms and grips of powerful fingers that are used to bending metal. The tone of all this nudity seen in shade is well caught by the artist, the mystery and shadow that will not define too much are very eloquently chosen, and indicate a feeling for suggestiveness and local color; the picture, by its very dimness, impels to investigation; Mr. Anshutz evidently is fully equipped for any of the more thrilling and more telling chronicles of labor he may select for illustration. . . . It will not be surprising if Mr. Anshutz should soon be constructing admirable stories of the Life of Toil, reinforced by all the knowledge and accuracy acquired at an excellent anatomical school.

"The Philadelphia Society of Artists: Third Annual Exhibition," *The Art Amateur* 6, no. 2 (January 1882): 26

––––––––––

The exhibition, some ten years since, in New York city, of a picture called "The Ironworker's Noon," gave a new name its place of note in American art. . . . The art critics exhausted their vocabulary in praise of this work, which deserved all the commendation it received. It was admirably engraved on wood and published as a representative American Art work of the year in our leading illustrated journal. Rarely had a new star risen over the horizon of our art with such brilliancy. The artist, Thomas P. Anshütz, is a native of Kentucky. He was born in 1851, of a family of German origin, related by ties of distant kinship to the great Munich painter, Professor Herman Anshütz. He grounded himself in his art at the Pennsylvania Acad[e]my of the Fine Arts, and formed one of the remarkable group of pupils, whom Mr. Thomas Eakins developed. The sterling quality of his art has rendered him one of the most competent of instructors, as well as a subject painter of power. He has his studio in Philadelphia, and is connected with the schools of the Pennsylvania Academy.

At the stroke of noon the toilers at forges and furnaces emerge into the cinderous outer precincts of the foundry, for a brief respite from labor, and refreshment against labor yet to come. Utter weariness and the robust strength of abundant manhood are seen in contrast. One young giant stretches his powerful limbs, as if shaking off his chains. Others exhaust their superfluous vitality in a mock battle. Some seek refreshment in drenching their hot and grimy bodies with water, and others sink listlessly into supine repose. The shadow of a cloudy day rests upon the scene and softens the severity of its naturally harsh outlines and vast and ponderous massiveness, while investing the figures, which animate it, with a certain seriousness and dignity of color in keeping with the spirit of the subject.

Catalogue of the Thomas B. Clarke Collection of American Pictures, exh. cat. (Philadelphia: Pennsylvania Academy of the Fine Arts, 1891), pp. 7–8

Provenance
Thomas B. Clarke (1849–1931), New York, 1883–1899

[Auction sale, American Art Association, New York, 14–17 February 1899, lot no. 56, sold for $150]

Alfred Steckler (1856–1929), New York, 1899–1929

[Mary McShane, New York and Brooklyn, ca. 1930–1939]

[Macbeth Galleries, New York, 1939, sold for $110]

Stephen Carlton Clark (1882–1960), New York, 1939–1944

[Macbeth Galleries, New York, 1944]

[John Levy Galleries, New York, 1944]

Joseph A. Katz (1888–1958), Baltimore, 1944–after 1947

[Victor Spark, New York, by 1950]

Walter Steumpfig (1914–1970), Sherman, Conn., after 1950–before 1953

Lawrence A. Fleischman (b. 1925) and Barbara Greenberg Fleisch-

man (b. 1924), Detroit, by 1953–ca. 1965

Dr. Irving F. Burton and Shirley Burton, Huntington Woods, Mich., ca. 1965–1972

[Auction sale, Sotheby Parke-Bernet, New York, 18 October 1972, lot no. 14, sold for $250,000]

Mr. and Mrs. Howard N. Garfinkle, New York, 1972–1973

[Kennedy Galleries, New York, 1973]

John D. Rockefeller 3rd and Blanchette Hooker Rockefeller, New York, 1973–1979

FAMSF, 1979.7.4

Exhibition History
Philadelphia Sketch Club, *Annual "Best Finished Sketch" Competition*, 1881 (as *The Iron Workers*, awarded top prize)

Philadelphia Society of Artists, *Third Annual Exhibition*, 1881

New York, American Art Gallery, *The Private Collection of Thomas B. Clarke of New York*, 1883, exh.

no. 3 (as *Ironworkers' Noontime*)

Philadelphia, Pennsylvania Academy of the Fine Arts, *The Thomas B. Clarke Collection of American Pictures*, 1891, exh. no. 3

Washington, D.C., Smithsonian Institution, *First Loan Exhibition of the National Art Association*, 1892, exh. no. 1

New York, Fifth Avenue Art Galleries, under the management of the Art House, *Second Annual Summer Exhibition of American Paintings and Antique Art Objects from China and Greece*, 1894, exh. no. 2

New York, The Metropolitan Museum of Art, *Life in America: A Special Loan Exhibition of Paintings Held during the Period of the New York World's Fair*, 1939, exh. no. 271

The Baltimore Museum of Art, extended loan, 1944–1947

Washington, D.C., The Corcoran Gallery of Art, *American Processional, 1492–1900: The Story of*

Our Country, 1950, exh. no. 295

The Denver Museum of Art, *Man at Work*, 1952, no exh. no.

Ann Arbor, University of Michigan Museum of Art, *Mr. and Mrs. Lawrence A. Fleischman Collection of American Paintings*, 1953, exh. no. 2

Philadelphia, Pennsylvania Academy of the Fine Arts, *The One Hundred Fiftieth Anniversary Exhibition of the Pennsylvania Academy of the Fine Arts*, 1955, exh. no. 170 (European tour, exh. no. 58)

Washington, D.C., United States Information Service, *Nine Generations of American Painting: A Loan Exhibition from the Detroit Institute of Arts and the Lawrence A. Fleischman Collection*, 1958 (organized for travel to South America, Greece, and Israel), Israel cat., exh. no. 20

Greensburg, Pa., The Westmoreland County Museum of Art,

Thos. Anshutz

Two Hundred and Fifty Years of Art in Pennsylvania, exh. no. 5

Milwaukee Art Center, *American Painting, 1760–1960: A Selection of 125 Paintings from the Collection of Mr. and Mrs. Lawrence A. Fleischman, Detroit*, 1960, no exh. no.

The Art Gallery of Toronto, Canada, *American Painting, 1865–1905*, 1961, exh. no. 2

Tucson, University of Arizona Art Gallery, *American Painting, 1765–1963: Selections from the Lawrence A. and Barbara Fleischman Collection of American Art*, 1964, exh. no. 3

Philadelphia, Pennsylvania Academy of the Fine Arts, *Small Paintings of Large Import from the Collection of Lawrence A. and Barbara Fleischman of Detroit, Michigan*, 1964, exh. no. 2

New York, The Metropolitan Museum of Art, *Nineteenth-Century America: Paintings and Sculpture*, 1970, exh. no. 179

Philadelphia, Pennsylvania Academy of the Fine Arts, *Thomas P. Anshutz, 1851–1912*, 1973, exh. no. 8

Allentown Art Museum, Pa., *The City in American Painting*, 1973, no exh. no.

San Francisco 1976, exh. no. 55

Washington, D.C., National Gallery of Art, *Post-Impressionism: Cross-Currents in European and American Painting, 1880–1906*, 1980, exh. no. 263

Tokyo 1982, exh. no. 55

FAMSF, *The Director's Choice: Twenty Years of Collecting*, no publ.

FAMSF, *Viewpoints VI: The Studied Figure: Tradition and Innovation in American Art Academies, 1865–1915*, 1989, no exh. no.

Selected References

Francis J. Ziegler, "An Unassuming Painter: Thomas P. Anshutz," *Brush and Pencil* 4, no. 6 (September 1899): 279–283

Sandra Lee Denney, "Thomas Anshutz: His Life, Art, and Teaching" (master's thesis, University of Delaware, 1969), pp. 24–27, 42, 106, 119

Ruth Bowman, "Nature, The Photograph and Thomas Anshutz," *Art Journal* 33, no. 1 (Fall 1973): 32–40

Frank H. Goodyear, Jr., "Ironworkers: Noontime," *American Art Review* 1, no. 2 (January–February 1974): 39–46

Thomas H. Pauly, "American Art and Labor: The Case of Anshutz's *The Ironworkers' Noontime*," *American Quarterly* 40, no. 3 (September 1988): 333–358

The American Canvas, pp. 13, 160–161, 241

Randall C. Griffin, "Thomas Anshutz's *The Ironworker's Noontime*: Remythologizing the Industrial Worker," *Smithsonian Studies in American Art* 4, nos. 3–4 (Summer–Fall 1990): 129–143

Related Works

Boy in Brown: Study for "The Ironworkers' Noontime," 1880
Oil on canvas, 13 x 8 in.
Private collection, as of 1986

Factory Study for "The Ironworkers' Noontime," 1880
Oil on paperboard, 8½ x 13 in.
Hirshhorn Museum and Sculpture Garden, Washington, D.C.

Figure and Perspectival Studies for "The Ironworkers' Noontime" (8 numbered studies in sketchbook), 1880
Pencil on paper, 4⅝ x 8¼ in.
Pennsylvania Academy of the Fine Arts, Philadelphia

Frederick Juengling (American, 1846–1889)
After *The Iron-Workers' Noontime*
Wood engraving
Harper's Weekly 28, no. 1445 (30 August 1884): 570

Oil on canvas, 13 x 10 in.
Signed lower left: *A . P. Ryder*

ALBERT PINKHAM RYDER

b. New Bedford, Mass. 1847
d. Elmhurst, N.Y. 1917

Some years ago, when Mr. Ryder had but lately graduated from the schools of the Academy, he was passing through the street with a little panel in his hand. Suddenly a man stopped him. He was clad in a long Oriental gown, slippers on his feet, a fez on the back of his head. Apologizing in very fair English, he asked the young artist if the picture he had in his hand was not Persian. Very much surprised, Mr. Ryder handed it to him. The Persian examined it with great interest and explained that the color and drawing—it showed a horse and rider—was extraordinarily like those in pictures among his own countrymen. Ryder has indeed the sense for color which the subjects of the Shah used to have when they manufactured the priceless rugs and carpets of bygone reigns. And in oils at that time his drawing was as naïf as Persian. The Orient attracted him from the first. I remember a desert scene with a walled town on the horizon and in the middle distance a small Arab rider with lance. . . . Another, much richer, is an oblong panel showing horses tethered near a long white wall in which is the arch to a garden. . . . After the hackneyed pictures of the Orient this charming mosaic of colors had a most original effect.

For the most part they [his pictures] are creations of his own fancy. They have wings; they hardly touch earth at all. For Mr. Ryder is that rarest and at present most scorned artist, an idealist; not in the same sense as the painter of an "ideal head," but in a much higher and more difficult way. Before his pictures we find ourselves suddenly invited to enter fairyland. His color is an enchantress. We follow her lead and presently discover a new country, like earth and of it, but not earth exactly, in which the fancy can travel uncontrolled. In the truest sense of the word Mr. Ryder is a poet in paint.

Henry Eckford [Charles de Kay], "A Modern Colorist: Albert Pinkham Ryder," *The Century Magazine* 40, no. 2 (June 1890): 255, 254

According to his own statement, Mr. Ryder uses no sketches from nature, but lays the picture in according to what he feels to be its needs. Then follows a process of small or large changes that frequently extends over a period of years. The position of clouds in a sky, the contour of a hill, or the movement of a figure undergoes infinite modifications until the stability and harmony of masses is attained that the artist's astonishing sense of their beauty demands. "I work altogether from my feeling for these things, I have no rule. And I think it is better to get the design first before I try for the color. It would be wasted, much of the time, when I have to change things about."

Walter Pach, "On Albert P. Ryder," *Scribner's Magazine* 49, no. 1 (January 1911): 126–127

Art is long. The artist must buckle himself with infinite patience. His ears must be deaf to the clamor of insistent friends who would quicken his pace. His eyes must see naught but the vision beyond. He must await the season of fruitage without haste, without worldly ambitions, without vexation of spirit. An inspiration is no more than a seed that must be planted and nourished.

The canvas I began ten years ago I shall perhaps complete today or to-morrow. It has been ripening under the sunlight of the years that come and go. . . . It is a wise artist who knows when to cry "halt" in his composition, but it should be pondered over in his heart and worked out with prayer and fasting.

Ryder, in "Paragraphs from the Studio of a Recluse," *Broadway Magazine*, September 1905, quoted in Lloyd Goodrich, *Albert P. Ryder* (New York: George Braziller, 1959), p. 22

Provenance
Whitman W. Kenyon (d. 1926), Smithtown, N.Y., to 1926

[Auction sale, The Anderson Galleries, New York, 14–15 December 1926, lot no. 45, sold for $150, buyer identified only as R. T.]

[Babcock Galleries, New York, by 1947]

Dr. T. Edward Hanley (1894–1969) and Tullah Hanley (ca. 1922–1992), Bradford, Pa., by 1959–1967

[Robert M. Light, Boston, 1967]

[Vose Galleries, Boston, 1967]

John D. Rockefeller 3rd and Blanchette Hooker Rockefeller, New York, 1967–1979

FAMSF, 1979.7.88

Exhibition History
Washington, D.C., The Corcoran Gallery of Art, *Albert Pinkham Ryder*, 1961, exh. no. 19

New York, Whitney Museum of American Art, *Eighteenth- and Nineteenth-Century American Art from Private Collections*, 1972, exh. no. 63

Washington, D.C., National Museum of American Art, *Albert Pinkham Ryder*, 1990, exh. no. 31

Selected References
Lloyd Goodrich, *Albert P. Ryder* (New York: George Braziller, 1959), p. 114

The American Canvas, pp. 152–153, 241

Related Work
Sketch of horse and rider on reverse of *Near Litchfield, Connecticut*, 1876
Pencil on composition board, 9⅝ x 9⅛ in.
Robin B. Martin, Washington, D.C., as of 1990

Oil on canvas, 42 x 30 in.
Signed lower left: *G. Fuller*

GEORGE FULLER
b. Deerfield, Mass. 1822
d. Brookline, Mass. 1884

The exhibition is not materially different from others made by the [Boston Art] club in late years so far as regards quality, but the pictures are seen to much better advantage in the new gallery. By far the best showing is made by the portrait and figure painters, if we may assume that the latter form a class. Easily first among these is George Fuller, now the bright particular star among Boston artists, and whose apparent mannerism serves but as the medium employed to best convey the beautiful and tender poems in form and color of which he alone holds the secret. He is represented by three works in this collection. The portrait of a young woman at the head of the gallery opposite the entrance has all of the most charming characteristics of Mr. Fuller's paintings—a sweet and wholesome individuality which appeals strongly to the fancy and dwells pleasantly in the memory. You do not care to ask nor know the methods by which this artist achieves the effect, nor indeed do you trouble yourself as to whether he has any method at all: the result is there, and that satisfies. It is felt that he mixes his colors "with brains, sir." How pure and sweet and lovable is his "Maidenhood," what a refreshing presence in the room!

"The Art Club: Opening of Its General Exhibition," unidentified Boston newspaper clipping, ca. 8–10 February 1882, George Fuller Papers, AAA, roll 610, frame 1507

In his studies of girlhood Fuller has fixed the expressions as lovely of innocence and happiness as ever have been put on canvas. In his idealized heads he has created a type of beauty thoroughly natural in its character and individual in its style, and one which will live as a representative impression of the feminine beauty of the present day. In this type he has combined the choice elements of innocence and simplicity of character, and has given us a refined and sweet country maiden, full of health and youthful vigor, and rich in the promise of perfect womanhood.

F. D. Millet, "An Estimate of Fuller's Genius," in Josiah Millet, ed., *George Fuller, His Life and Works: A Memorial Volume* (Boston and New York: Houghton, Mifflin and Company, 1886), pp. 59–60

His pictures all had something to say, and like all great pictures could speak clearly to the least technically instructed. Even I could not go into that little gallery of Doll's, on Tremont Street, and find myself amid the delicate glow of the canvases with which he had hung it round, and not feel their exquisite, their authentic and singular charm. The pictures were the slowly ripened fruit of fifteen years, and they recorded not only the beloved faces of his own household, but the scarcely less beloved features of his Deerfield landscape and his happy memories of Italian travel.

Their success was no *furore*,—the furore is not the Boston way,—but it was unmistakable; and from that time it meant full recognition and generous reward. Fuller came down from Deerfield that winter and opened a studio at 12 West Street, removing a year or two later to 149A Tremont, where he painted orders for portraits, and the ideal pictures which he loved better. But in fact the portraits were ideal pictures, too, and they were the finer portraits the more freely he allowed himself to escape from uncommon places of fact. That is to say, his pictures were all poems, and I had the same pleasure in them that poetry gives.

W. D. Howells, "Sketch of George Fuller's Life," in Josiah Millet, ed., *George Fuller, His Life and Works: A Memorial Volume* (Boston and New York: Houghton, Mifflin and Company, 1886), pp. 48–49

Mrs. Elizabeth L. MacMahon of Arlington Heights [Mass.], inspiration for "Maidenhood," a life-size, three-quarter length canvas by George Fuller which recently brought more than $40,000 at a public sale in the John Levy Galleries, New York, told a Herald reporter of

events in her life since the time, when, as Miss Elizabeth L. Bradley, 21, she posed for the work in 1882 [*sic*]. . . .

"It is considered a very hard thing to photograph his work successfully," she said, "due to that very wonderful and exquisite haze. I have watched him many times, and he did it with the handle of his brush, drawing it through the wet paint, freshly laid, with a rapid, nervous, zig-zag sort of motion. He would repeat the operation, laying on more paint with a very light touch, until he had achieved the desired effect."

Mrs. MacMahon started out to be an artist herself, her acquaintance with Fuller being due to that fact. After passing many years in private schools in and around Boston, she went to Paris to complete her education, and on her return to this country continued her studies in art in Boston under the guidance of Miss Millicent Jarvis, who had a studio on Tremont street in the same building with George Fuller.

Many times Mr. Fuller requested her to pose for him, but she as many times declined the honor. He saw in her a type of the highly educated American girl, not so common then as now. . . .

Mrs. William F. Matchett, who up to the time of her death lived at Beacon and Exeter streets, a close friend, many times asked Miss Bradley for a portrait painted by a Boston artist. Finally she gave consent on the condition that the commission be given Mr. Fuller, that she might, at one stroke, please both friend and artist. . . .

The same year that the picture was made, she met William MacMahon . . . and in December, 1882, she became Mrs. William MacMahon. . . .

Mrs. MacMahon was born in Augusta, Me., 61 years ago [i.e., 1861], a daughter of the Rev. Gordon M. Bradley, who later became rector of the old St. Stephen's Church of Lynn. From the point of years in attendance, she is the oldest parishioner of Trinity Church, Boston, having made her initial appearance there in Sunday school in 1868.

"Arlington Woman Who Posed in 1882 for $40,000 Canvas Keeps Active," *Boston Herald*, November 1922, George Fuller Papers, AAA, roll 610, frame 1530

Provenance
Mr. and Mrs. William F. Matchett, Boston, 1882–ca. 1922, bought for $500

[Copley Galleries, Boston, 1922]

[John Levy Galleries, New York, 1922, sold "for more than $40,000"]

J. K. Newman, New York, 1922–1935

[Auction sale, American Art Association, Anderson Galleries, New York, 6 December 1935, lot no. 28, sold for $700]

[J. H. Weitzner, New York, 1935]

[Milch Gallery, New York, by 1960]

[Vose Galleries, Boston, 1960–1967]

[Castellane Gallery, New York, 1967]

[Hirschl & Adler Galleries, New York, 1967]

John D. Rockefeller 3rd and Blanchette Hooker Rockefeller, New York, 1967–1993

FAMSF, 1993.35.10

Exhibition History
Boston Art Club, *Twenty-fifth Exhibition of the Boston Art Club*, 1882, exh. no. 108

Boston, Museum of Fine Arts, *Memorial Exhibition of the Works of George Fuller*, 1884, exh. no. 148

New York, The Metropolitan Museum of Art, *Centennial Exhibition of the Works of George Fuller*, 1923, exh. no. 14 (as *Maidenhood—Miss Bradley*)

Selected Reference
Josiah Millet, ed., *George Fuller, His Life and Works: A Memorial Volume* (Boston and New York: Houghton, Mifflin and Company, 1886), p. 92

Related Work
Maidenhood [a head and bust portrait]
Reproduced in William Howe Downes, "George Fuller's Pictures," *International Studio* 75, no. 302 (July 1922): 206

---

86 THE OLD VERSION, 1881

Oil on canvas, 24 x 19 in.
Signed and dated lower right: *THovenden 1881* (initials in monogram)

THOMAS HOVENDEN
b. Dunmanway, County Cork, Ireland 1840
d. Norristown, Pa. 1895

In the Academy's Autumn Exhibition, just closed, there was a small painting by Hovenden, considerably more of a social study than the usual *genre*, or familiar picture. It showed a corner of a plain room, clock and pictures on the wall, and its figures were a middle-aged American husband and wife. . . . A benevolent and gentle-featured American mechanic, sitting in his shirt sleeves of a Sunday afternoon and reading the "Old Version" to his partner, that was all the title conveyed. The woman was one of the shrewd, level-headed American wives who wear their calico gowns always with a collar, who are neat as a new pin and as ready for use. She was the sort of woman to be sure that the stove-dampers were right and every crumb of dinner set away, dishes washed and all tins hung straight on the wall before she settled down to listen, with her steel spectacles on, to mark her fifty years. . . . About the whole picture was an air of steadfastness, of loyal marriage, that one rarely sees put into colors now-a-days. . . .

. . . If the Academy could buy it and hang it on the walls for all Sunday afternoon visitors to see, free of charge, they would put a better sermon in the galleries than is preached from many a pulpit the year round. As a work of art-technique it may be of slight value. But as saying what it sets out to say, it is in precisely the right key. We do need to be reminded of the "Old Version" of a loyal marriage, when the staple of theatrical plots, that many novels, and much society gossip furnishes the unpleasantness of the new version brought to light every day. The old standards are in hundreds of thousands of homes yet, but they are not made conspicuous at this time as they should be. Particularly does this seem true of Philadelphia lately.

"The Household—The Old Version—Marriage in 1882—Dainty Dishes," unidentified Philadelphia newspaper clipping, probably January 1882, Thomas Hovenden Papers, AAA, roll P13, frame 27

The next year 1881, Thomas Hovenden was elected an Associate of the New York National Academy of Design. It was in this year on June 9th that he married Miss Helen Corson of Plymouth Meeting [Pennsylvania]. . . . In the barn on the Corson property he fitted out a studio. . . . This barn had been used as a meeting place by members of a group of Abolitionists in pre–Civil War days. . . .

This same year produced "THE OLD VERSION" exhibited in New York and reproduced in the April 1882 issue of *Harper's* magazine. The models for the two figures were Mark Jones [who had earlier posed for Hovenden as a blacksmith] and Mary Yetter, who was the toll-gate keeper on the Conshohocken Pike at the township line.

Helen Corson Livezey, "Life and Works of Thomas Hovenden, N.A.," *Germantowne Crier* 8, no. 2 (May 1956): 8–9

———————

Mr. Hovenden's paintings were devoted largely to depicting homely sentiments and feelings, but those of so pure and noble a character that they found a universal response in the heart of all observers.

"The Death of Thomas Hovenden," *Topeka (Kansas) Capital*, 16 August 1895, quoted in Lee Edwards, "Noble Domesticity: The Paintings of Thomas Hovenden," *The American Art Journal* 19, no. 1 (1987): 5

———————

The Revision of the New Testament was published on May 20, 1881, and two hundred thousand copies were sold in New York on that day. In their Sunday issues of May 22 the Chicago *Times* and the Chicago *Tribune* printed the entire text. The *Times* received the four Gospels, the Acts of the Apostles, and the Epistle to the Romans by telegraph from

New York to make this publication possible; and it stated with pardonable pride that "this portion of the New Testament contains about one hundred and eighteen thousand words, and constitutes by manifold the largest despatch ever sent over the wires.". . .

The Revised Version was disappointing to many. Partisans found old proof-texts upset, conservatives thought that the revisers had made too many changes, and liberals that they had made too few. The great mass of common folk were disturbed by it, and preferred to keep on reading "the Old Version" in family worship and in private devotions.

> Luther A. Weigle, *The Pageant of America: American Idealism* (New Haven: Yale University Press; Toronto and Glasgow: Brook & Co.; London: Oxford University Press, 1928), pp. 222–223

Provenance
Lawrence A. Fleischman (b. 1925) and Barbara Greenberg Fleischman (b. 1924), Detroit, by 1960–1966

[Kennedy Galleries, New York, 1966]

[Hirschl & Adler Galleries, New York, by 1969]

John D. Rockefeller 3rd and Blanchette Hooker Rockefeller, New York, 1969–1993

FAMSF, 1993.35.17

Exhibition History
Philadelphia, Pennsylvania Academy of the Fine Arts, *Special Exhibition of Paintings by American Artists at Home and in Europe*, 1881, exh. no. 300

New York, Sherwood Building Studio Reception, early 1882

New York, National Academy of Design, *Fifty-seventh Annual Exhibition*, 1882, exh. no. 116 (as *Sunday Afternoon*, for sale, $1000)

Milwaukee Art Center, *American Painting, 1760–1960: A Selection of 125 Paintings from the Collection of Mr. and Mrs. Lawrence A. Fleischman, Detroit*, 1960, no exh. no.

Tucson, University of Arizona Art Gallery, *1765–1963: Selections from the Lawrence A. and Barbara Fleischman Collection of American Art*, 1964, exh. no. 49

San Francisco 1976, exh. no. 74

Selected Reference
Sarah Burns, *Pastoral Inventions: Rural Life in Nineteenth-Century American Art and Culture* (Philadelphia: Temple University Press, 1988), pp. 198, 268

Related Works
The Revised Version, 1881
Oil on canvas, 20 x 12¼ in.
National Academy of Design, New York

After *The Old Version*
Wood engraving
Harper's Weekly 26, no. 1319 (1 April 1882): cover

---

87 AN ARCADIAN, 1883; CAST 1930

Bronze, 8 x 5 in. (irregular)
Signed by founder lower right: *THOMAS EAKINS*; founder's mark lower left: *ROMAN BRONZE WORKS N.Y.*

THOMAS EAKINS
b. Philadelphia, Pa. 1844
d. Philadelphia, Pa. 1916

Mr. Eakins' theory and practice were to work from the living model. . . .
It was a great adventure to have the privilege of entering and working from the nude model in the life classes, and to have the advice of Mr. Eakins. It was stimulating and encouraging. However, it was not long before we heard rumors and whisperings about Eakins because he was having male and female models pose for some of the life classes. This he did in order that the student would get a better understanding, by comparison, of the construction and movement of spine and pelvis in walking. This was a good and perfectly right thing to do, as what he wished to demonstrate for the benefit of the students could not have been successfully demonstrated in any other way.

But to take so radical and unheard of a step in Philadelphia at that time—it was in the middle 'eighties—resulted in Mr. Eakins' motives being very much misunderstood; abuse and slander of all kinds were heaped upon him. However, has it not been ever thus? It's the price the innovator pays who dares to separate himself from the crowd. It would have crushed a weaker man, but Eakins was made of sturdier stuff, being intellectually the superior of his critics. It ended in his resigning from the professorship of the Pennsylvania Academy of the Fine Arts.

> Charles Bregler, "Thomas Eakins as a Teacher," *The Arts* 17, no. 6 (March 1931): 380

"I don't like a long study of casts," he said, "even of the best Greek period. At best, they are only imitations, and an imitation of imitations cannot have so much life as an imitation of nature itself. The Greeks did not study the antique: the 'Theseus' and 'Ilyssus,' and the draped figures in the Parthenon pediment were modeled from life, undoubtedly. And nature is just as varied and just as beautiful in our day as she was in the time of Phidias."

> Eakins, quoted by W. C. Brownell, "The Art Schools of Philadelphia," *Scribner's Monthly* 18, no. 5 (September 1879): 742

———

Relief work too has always been considered the most difficult composition and the one requiring the most learning. The mere geometrical construction of the accessories in a perspective which is not projected on a single plane but in a variable third dimension, is a puzzle beyond the sculptors whom I know.

> Eakins, 1882, quoted in Lloyd Goodrich, *Thomas Eakins: His Life and Work* (New York: Whitney Museum of American Art, 1933), p. 64

———

The simple processions of the Greeks viewed in profile or nearly so are exactly suited to reproduction in relief sculpture. . . . There is a limit in relief; if you keep inside of it, it is a powerful instrument to work with.

> Eakins, lecture manuscript on the laws of sculptured relief, ca. 1884, Philadelphia Museum of Art

Provenance

Susan Macdowell (Mrs. Thomas) Eakins (1851–1938), Philadelphia, 1930–1938

[Babcock Galleries, New York, 1938–after 1944]

Lawrence A. Fleischman (b. 1925) and Barbara Greenberg Fleischman (b. 1924), Detroit, by 1955–ca. 1966

Joseph Hirshhorn (1899–1981), Greenwich, Conn., ca. 1966

Leonard Baskin (b. 1922) and Lisa Baskin, Northampton, Mass., before 1971

[Kennedy Galleries, New York, 1971]

John D. Rockefeller 3rd and Blanchette Hooker Rockefeller, New York, 1971–1979

FAMSF, 1979.7.36

Exhibition History

Possibly New York, Babcock Galleries, *Exhibition of Sketches, Studies and Intimate Paintings by Thomas Eakins*, 1939, no exh. no. ("Group of Bronzes," from the estate of Mrs. Thomas Eakins)

New York, M. Knoedler & Co., *A Loan Exhibition of the Works of Thomas Eakins, 1844–1944, Commemorating the Centennial of His Birth*, 1944, exh. no. 88

The Detroit Institute of Arts, *Collection in Progress: Selections from the Lawrence and Barbara Fleischman Collection of American Art*, 1955, exh. no. 62

New York, Kennedy Galleries, *American Masters, Eighteenth to Twentieth Centuries*, 1971, exh. no. 30

San Francisco 1976, exh. no. 64

FAMSF, *American Sculpture: The Collection of The Fine Arts Museums of San Francisco*, 1982, exh. no. 13

Selected References

Lloyd Goodrich, *Thomas Eakins: His Life and Work* (New York: Whitney Museum of American Art, 1933), cat. no. 507

Moussa M. Domit, *The Sculpture of Thomas Eakins*, exh. cat. (Washington, D.C.: The Corcoran Gallery of Art, 1969), p. 26

Theodor Siegl, *The Thomas Eakins Collection* (Philadelphia: Philadelphia Museum of Art, 1978), p. 75

Lloyd Goodrich, *Thomas Eakins*, 2 vols. (Cambridge, Mass., and London: Harvard University Press, for the National Gallery of Art, 1982), 1:233, 235; 2:127

Marc Simpson, "Thomas Eakins and His Arcadian Works," *Smithsonian Studies in American Art* 1, no. 2 (Fall 1987): 83

Related Works

An Arcadian, 1883
Plaster relief, 8¼ x 5 in. Pennsylvania Academy of the Fine Arts, Philadelphia, Charles Bregler's Thomas Eakins Collection

Arcadia, 1883
Plaster relief, 11¾ x 24 x 2³⁄₁₆ in. Philadelphia Museum of Art, and at least three other versions in plaster

Arcadia, 1883; cast 1930
Bronze relief, 12½ x 25 in. Private collection, as of 1977

---

88 A SWELL OF THE OCEAN, 1883

Watercolor over graphite on wove paper, 15 x 21½ in.
Signed and dated lower left: *Winslow Homer/1883*

WINSLOW HOMER
b. Boston, Mass. 1836
d. Prout's Neck, Maine 1910

It is said that Mr. Winslow Homer, whose strong and original water-colors have been so much admired, has had so little financial encouragement in New York that he proposes to leave the city. He will have a studio-dwelling not far from Portland [Maine], where he will paint to please himself, expecting to give exhibitions of his works occasionally in Boston, his native city.

Boston Globe, 1 July 1883

———

To-day a special exhibition of the water-colors of Winslow Homer will be opened in Doll & Richards's Gallery, Park Street, to continue until December 15. . . . Mr. Homer, as was stated last spring, has left New York and retired to a secluded country home on the coast of Maine, a locality excellently adapted to the practice of his art. He is the painter *par excellence* of the life of those who go down to the sea in ships.

Unidentified newspaper review, 1 December 1883

———

Mr. Homer has got beyond expending himself in mere technique, though his technique is bold, original and powerful enough to form a merit and a study in itself. He is now evidently bent most upon expressing something, and treats his art (as the generality of our younger artists do not) as the mere medium for conveying something of social or human interest. Mr. Homer is both the historian and poet of the sea and seacoast life, somewhat as [Jean-François] Millet was of the farm and farm life.

Review, Doll and Richards Gallery exhibition, *Boston Evening Transcript*, 6 December 1883

———

Remembering that Mr. Homer, not many months ago, declared in disgust that he would show no more pictures in collective exhibitions, because the public is unappreciative, it is very gratifying to see so many of these pictures ticketed "sold."

> Review, Doll and Richards Gallery exhibition, *Boston Globe*, 9 December 1883; *all the above reviews quoted in Nicolai Cikovsky, Jr., Winslow Homer Watercolors* (New York: Hugh Lauter Levin Associates, 1991), p. 116

————————

The whole gamut of watercolor power, from the richness of elemental life depth and vividness to the density of storm darkness and human woe, and thence again to life light, joyousness, delicacy, and subtle glow, is here run with a strength and accuracy that few not seeing will believe it capable of. Indeed it seems to proclaim its capacity to be perhaps the most artistic of all art mediums when adequately handled.

> Review, Doll and Richards Gallery exhibition, *Boston Evening Transcript*, 6 December 1883, quoted in Helen Cooper, *Winslow Homer Watercolors*, exh. cat. (New Haven and London: Yale University Press, 1986), p. 119

————————

Although Homer returned from England in 1882, we shall see the Tynemouth *mise-en-scène* reappearing from time to time in his later works. . . . The picturesque phases of the life of the fishing community,—the fishermen, the fishwives, the coastguardsmen—are set forth with the intimate actuality that we always find in Homer's work, so that Tynemouth and its people will always be associated with his name and fame.

> William Howe Downes, *The Life and Works of Winslow Homer* (Boston and New York: Houghton Mifflin Company, 1911), p. 107

89 MOMENT MUSICALE, 1883

Oil on wood panel, 15¾ x 20 in.
Signed and dated lower left: *C. F. Ulrich A.N.A./1883*

CHARLES FREDERIC ULRICH

b. New York, N.Y. 1858
d. Berlin, Germany 1908

At the spring exhibition of the Academy of Design in 1880 appeared for the first time a young New Yorker, a painter of modern genre works of a singular brightness and elegance of execution, named Charles F. Ulrich. He was the son of a German photographer, who had himself practiced painting in former years, and was born in New York in 1858. Young Ulrich was taught drawing by Professor Venino, a well-known master in his day, studied in the National Academy schools, and in 1873 went abroad, where he remained for eight years. He studied at Munich . . . and exhibited his first pictures in German exhibitions.

. . . His cabinet pieces, full of character, minute in execution, and brilliant with their rendition of light, were entirely new to our art, and may be said to have marked a new departure in it. Without being in any sense imitations, they showed that the artist had been a close student of the old Dutch detail painters. . . . His manner and matter were, however, entirely modern. . . . Mr. Ulrich was elected an Associate of the National Academy in 1883, and was one of the founders of the Pastel Club. Some years ago he returned to Europe, and now has his studio in Venice.

Catalogue of the Private Art Collection of Thomas B. Clarke, New York, sale cat. (New York: American Art Association, 1899), pp. 110–111

With technical progress and growing prosperity in America, pianos became less expensive and could be found in nearly every respectable parlor. The favorite, the upright, was considered to have the best tone. . . .

. . . Its appearance could easily be improved if its top was used for the display of fine porcelain and other decorative wares, and its simple presence could be enhanced if it was surrounded by Oriental vases and other objets d'art, which also served as further evidence of affluence and culture.

Ronald G. Pisano, *Idle Hours: Americans at Leisure, 1865–1914* (Boston, Toronto, London: Little, Brown and Company, New York Graphic Society, 1988), p. 34

Provenance
[Auction sale, Parke-Bernet, New York, 3–4 June 1959, lot no. 206 (as *The Piano Sonata*)]

[Coe Kerr Gallery, New York, by 1970]

John D. Rockefeller 3rd and Blanchette Hooker Rockefeller, New York, 1970–1979

FAMSF, 1979.7.99

Exhibition History
San Francisco 1976, exh. no. 92

Selected Reference
The American Canvas, pp. 180–181, 243

---

90 NEW YORK FROM THE BAY, CA. 1883

Transparent and opaque watercolor, brown ink, and graphite on wove paper, 10¼ x 17 in.
Signed lower left: *TM*. (in monogram); inscribed lower right: *New York. from the Bay*

THOMAS MORAN

b. Bolton, Lancashire, England 1837
d. Santa Barbara, Calif. 1926

When Thomas Moran was seven years of age his parents crossed the Atlantic and settled in Philadelphia. He received a fair education at school, and was then placed with a wood-engraver, with whom he remained two years, and acquired a good knowledge of the art. This has undoubtedly been of the greatest service to him, for it gave him firmness and steadiness of touch, together with accuracy and persistent effort. It may be said to constitute all the direct art-education Mr. Moran has ever received. . . .

. . . On his return to America [from England], Mr. Moran's remarkable fertility of fancy, aided by his great technical skill and rapidity of execution, brought numerous demands on his pencil, and he soon acquired repute as an illustrator of books and magazines. It was this which eventually led him to settle in New York; *Scribner's Monthly* gave him so many commissions that in order to be near the publishers he removed to that city. As a proof of his readiness and popularity, it may be stated that during the last eight years, in addition to the large number of paintings and etchings he has produced, he has designed over 2,000 illustrations. . . .

His versatility appears again in the representation of quiet woodland scenes about home, or oozy flats near Brooklyn, above which loom, half hidden in mist, the warehouses and wharves of a great city on a sullen, melancholy day in October. Few artists, again, have

undertaken to paint so many varieties of cloud-scenery. Indeed, there is scarcely an effect of nature which Mr. Moran has not represented, and generally with excellent success.

S. G. W. Benjamin, "A Pioneer of the Palette: Thomas Moran," *The Magazine of Art* 5 (February 1882): 90, 90–91, 92

Through the Narrows opens the Inner Bay; and, as we swiftly cut through the crisp and ever-fretted waters, New York rises before us from the sea, in the centre of the picture; the city of Brooklyn, on Long Island, to the right, spreads a far and measureless sea of roofs, with endless, sky-aspiring spires; the shores of New Jersey extend along the far western border. . . . The picture cannot easily be excelled for beauty; but one or two bays in the world are finer, and none are more animated with stirring and picturesque life. Here are the tall, white-sailed ships; the swift, black-funnelled steamers; the stately steam-boats from the Hudson or the Sound; the graceful, winged pleasure-yachts; the snorting, bull-dog tugs; the quaint, tall-masted, and broad-sailed schooners; the flotilla of barges and canal-boats; the crab-shaped but swift-motioned ferry-boats, all coming, going, swiftly or slowly, amid fleets of anchored ships, from whose gaffs fly the flags of far-off nations. New-York Bay, when the air is crisp and bright, the sky brilliant with summer blue, the swelling shores clear and distinct in their wooded hills and clustering villages, the waters dancing in white-crested waves in the glaring sun, affords a picture that can scarcely be equalled.

William Cullen Bryant, ed., *Picturesque America; or, the Land We Live In*, 2 vols. (New York: D. Appleton and Company, 1872), 2:547

Provenance
[Graham Gallery, New York, by 1973]
John D. Rockefeller 3rd and Blanchette Hooker Rockefeller, New York, 1973–1979
FAMSF, 1979.7.74

Exhibition History
San Francisco 1976, exh. no. 87
FAMSF, *Master Drawings from the Achenbach Foundation for Graphic Arts*, 1985, exh. no. 97

Charcoal and white chalk on blue-gray laid paper, discolored to brown, mounted on paperboard, 17¾ x 23⅝ in.
Signed and dated lower left: *Winslow Homer/1884*

WINSLOW HOMER

b. Boston, Mass. 1836
d. Prout's Neck, Maine 1910

This morning an exhibition of special interest to artists and amateurs opens in Doll & Richards's gallery, to remain for one week only. It is an exhibition of studies in black and white by Mr. Winslow Homer, who is at present in Boston, but who expects to leave in a few days for Bermuda, where he will spend most of the winter. He has placed on the walls about 80 studies, executed with a great variety of materials—charcoal, crayon, lead pencil, chalk, India ink and watercolor—on paper of various tints. He desires it to be understood that these are in no sense to be regarded as pictures, but as studies, which are of the nature of memoranda, and form simply one of the steps in the process of making a picture. Some of them, to be sure, are carried to a very satisfactory degree of finish, but the majority are simple and broadly handled effects of masses and light and shade, made for use. The employment of white chalk for putting in the lights in charcoal studies on tinted paper is remarkably effective. Many familiar figures are to be seen in this collection, which have appeared in water colors made from them—the women knitting stockings as they pace the English seashore; the men of the life-saving service at their arduous, heroic work in stormy times; the fishermen, and other characters with which Mr. Homer has made us acquainted in his delightful pictures shown at the same place a year ago. His knowledge in the drawing of the figure is exemplified in such studies as . . . No. 57, "A Little More Yarn," . . . worthy of study. . . .

the figure itself, that the work of Mr. Homer commends itself for excellence. . . . He manifests an intimacy with and appreciation for the sea which enter into almost all that he does, and this feeling lends a certain largeness to his way of seeing things, which is a trait of great artists and a supreme merit.

"Mr. Homer's Black and White," *Boston Advertiser*, 29 November 1884

––––––––

In 1881 a happy chance directed the steps of the painter to the east coast of England, where he worked with his customary zeal for two entire seasons at Tynemouth, in Northumberland-shire, a well-known watering-place, with a fine beach, overlooked by picturesque cliffs. Tynemouth is also a seaport and fishing-town with a population of more than fifty thousand; and a better place for Homer's purposes could hardly have been found in all England. In a suburb called Cullercoates he was fortunate enough to find a dwelling which just suited him. . . . The works that he produced there sounded a deeper, stronger, more serious note than any that had preceded them. The sea, and the lives of those who go down to the sea in ships, became, from this time, his one great theme. . . .

Although Homer returned from England in 1882, we shall see the Tynemouth *mise-en-scène* reappearing from time to time in his later works, with those sturdy and supple figures of the English fishwives which fit in so well with the genius of the locality. . . . His slightest crayon studies of figures have the pictorial distinction, the fine sense of movement, and the singular beauty of design, which belong only to the great masters.

William Howe Downes, *The Life and Works of Winslow Homer* (Boston and New York: Houghton Mifflin Company, 1911), pp. 99, 107

––––––––

Years ago he gave us realistic—often very ugly but always impressive—studies of local types and characters. Then one year he sent a dozen splendid little marine views—totally unnatural to the average eye, but imposing almost in their strength and originality and fervid, half-infernal poetry. Now he gives us some large drawings of English fisherwomen—which are no longer studies, or character sketches, or *genre* pictures, but which touch a far higher plane. They are pictures in the fullest sense, and to characterize them properly one must fall back on an old-time expression, which, once worked to death, has gone out of vogue of late. They are works of High Art. That is to say, they have an ideal element which lifts them above the cleverest things that are mere prosaic transcripts of reality.

New York World, 27 January 1883, quoted in Nicolai Cikovsky, Jr., *Winslow Homer Watercolors* (New York: Hugh Lauter Levin Associates, 1991), p. 115

Provenance
[Doll and Richards Gallery, Boston, 1884]

Dr. Robert W. Hooper, Boston, from 1884

Descended in family to Louisa Chapin Hooper (Mrs. Ward) Thoron (1874–1975), Boston, to 1977

[Hirschl & Adler Galleries, New York, 1977–1978]

John D. Rockefeller 3rd and Blanchette Hooker Rockefeller, New York, 1978–1993

FAMSF, 1993.35.16

Exhibition History
Boston, Doll and Richards Gallery, *Studies in Black and White by Winslow Homer*, 1884, exh. no. 57

Boston, Museum of Fine Arts, *Winslow Homer: A Retrospective Exhibition*, 1959, exh. no. 162 (as *Fisher Girl Knitting*)

New York, Hirschl & Adler Galleries, *American Genre Painting in the Victorian Era*, 1978, exh. no. 38 (as *Fisher Girl Knitting*)

Selected Reference
Object record, manuscript catalogue raisonné of the works of Winslow Homer, by Lloyd Goodrich, courtesy of the City University of New York, Lloyd Goodrich and Edith Havens Goodrich, Whitney Museum of American Art Record of the Works of Winslow Homer

Oil on canvas, 62⅞ x 41⅜ in.
Signed and dated upper left: *John S. Sargent 1884*

JOHN SINGER
SARGENT

b. Florence, Italy 1856
d. London, England 1925

Cosmopolitanism has been one of the keynotes of Sargent's life. "An American, born in Italy, educated in France, who looks like a German, speaks like an Englishman, and paints like a Spaniard," is a phrase that largely sums him up.

> William Starkweather, "John Singer Sargent, Master Portrait Painter," *The Mentor* 12, no. 9 (October 1924): 4

———

It sounds like a paradox, but it is a very simple truth, that when to-day we look for "American art" we find it mainly in Paris. When we find it out of Paris, we at least find a great deal of Paris in it. Mr. Sargent came up to the irresistible city in his twentieth year, from Florence, where in 1856 he had been born of American parents and where his fortunate youth had been spent. He entered immediately the studio of Carolus Duran, and revealed himself in 1877, at the age of twenty-two, in the portrait of that master—a fine model in more than one sense of the word [Sterling and Francine Clark Art Institute, Williamstown, Mass.]. He was already in possession of a style; and if this style has gained both in finish and in assurance, it has not otherwise varied. . . .

Those who have appreciated his work most up to the present time articulate no wish for a change, so completely does that work seem to them, in its kind, the exact translation of his thought, the exact "fit" of his artistic temperament. . . . In an altogether exceptional degree does he give us the sense that the intention and the art of carrying it out are for him one and the same thing. . . . It is likewise so, of course, with many another genuine painter; but in Sargent's case the process by which the object seen resolves itself into the object pictured is extraordinarily immediate. It is as if painting were pure tact of vision, a simple manner of feeling. . . .

. . . These things possess, largely, the quality which makes Mr. Sargent so happy as a painter of women—a quality which can best be expressed by a reference to what it is not, to the curiously literal, prosaic, sexless treatment to which, in the commonplace work that looks down at us from the walls of almost all exhibitions, delicate feminine elements have evidently so often been sacrificed. Mr. Sargent handles these elements with a special feeling for them, and they borrow a kind of noble intensity from his brush.

> Henry James, "John S. Sargent," *Picture and Text* (1887; New York: Harper and Brothers, 1893), pp. 93–94, 112

———

There are subjects, of course, which appear to act as a direct nervous stimulus to the painter. For in each fresh portrait Mr. John Sargent would seem to see the great inexorable riddle. It is in suggesting the potentialities of his sitter that the artist differs so widely from the portrait-painters of the last century. . . . In the eighteenth century, no doubt, Romney and Reynolds were fully able to realise the dashing and buxom young matrons who came to pose to them as Hebe or Flora, but it is useless to suppose that the tense, "prickly," and complex woman of our present era could be summarised in any such off-hand way. Ladies no longer play at being goddesses; they have, possibly, even a sense of remoteness from the gods. A thousand perplexities and anxieties loom up before the contemporary man and woman, and, be sure of it, every man and woman bears something of the uneasy presage in his or her face. And this clearly Mr. Sargent has realised. A student of character, he remains a modern of moderns. With all his affiliation to the Great Masters, he reveals himself the sharpest, the most precise instrument the century has forged. We may congratulate ourselves that it is so. Every age has its characteristics, special, subtle, and intangible; lucky is the age that has also its painter, for it is he who is left to settle the visible terms by which his century shall hereafter make itself known.

> Marion Hepworth Dixon, "Mr. John S. Sargent as a Portrait-Painter," *The Magazine of Art* 23 (January 1899): 119

Provenance
Caroline de Bassano, Marquise d'Espeuilles (1847–1938), Paris and Nièvre, France, 1884–1938

Descended in family to Marquis de Casteja, 1938–1972

[Auction sale, Christie's, London, 27 June 1972, lot no. 52, sold for $35,280]

[Loeb, Paris, 1972]

[Philippe Rheims, Paris and Tokyo, 1973]

[Bernard Danenberg Galleries, New York, 1973]

[Maxwell Davidson, New York, 1973–1975]

[Hirschl & Adler Galleries, New York, 1975]

John D. Rockefeller 3rd and Blanchette Hooker Rockefeller, New York, 1975–1979

FAMSF, 1979.7.90

Exhibition History
San Francisco 1976, exh. no. 91

Tokyo 1982, exh. no. 61

Selected Reference
The American Canvas, pp. 174–175, 243

Oil on canvas, 46⅛ x 38⅛ in.

THOMAS HOVENDEN

b. Dunmanway, County Cork,
    Ireland 1840
d. Norristown, Pa. 1895

John Brown of Ossawatomie spake on his dying day:
"I will not have to shrive my soul a priest in Slavery's pay.
But let some poor slave-mother whom I have striven to free,
With her children, from the gallows-stair put up a prayer for me!"

John Brown of Ossawatomie, they led him out to die;
And lo! a poor slave-mother with her little child pressed nigh.
Then the bold, blue eye grew tender, and the old harsh face grew mild,
As he stooped between the jeering ranks and kissed the negro's child!

The shadows of his stormy life that moment fell apart;
And they who blamed the bloody hand forgave the loving heart.
That kiss, from all its guilty means redeemed the good intent,
And round the grisly fighter's hair the martyr's aureole bent!

Perish with him the folly that seeks through evil good!
Long live the generous purpose unstained with human blood!
Not the raid of midnight terror, but the thought which underlies;
Not the borderer's pride of daring, but the Christian's sacrifice!

> John Greenleaf Whittier, from "Brown of Ossawatomie" (1859), *The Complete Poetical Works of
> John Greenleaf Whittier* (Boston: James R. Osgood & Co., 1876), p. 258

An American picture of real importance, one that stands out prominently among the
thousands of new pictures thrown upon the market or forced upon the public in exhibitions
every month, is indeed a rare thing. Such a picture must have more than the allurements of
color and of handling. It must be the embodiment of a noble thought, nobly worked out. . . .
Mr. Thomas Hovenden's painting of "The Last Moments of John Brown" comes nearer to
fulfilling these conditions than any other American picture we can think of. . . . The artist was
asked to paint it for Mr. Robbins Battell, of Norfolk, Conn., and it is evident from the choice
of subject that Mr. Battell was not merely looking about for a bit of decorative color to fill
agreeably a vacant spot on his walls. . . . He evidently felt for the subject, found in it the
expression of an ideal, and, therefore, longed to see it realized. He was fortunate in finding
an artist capable not only, but willing also to carry out his desires. . . . We have hardly as yet
spoken of the subject of the picture, as our readers, presumably, need not be told that it
represents John Brown, after his attempt to raise an insurrection among the negroes at
Harper's Ferry in 1859, stopping on his way to the gallows to kiss a negro baby held up to him
by its slave mother. . . . This picture has certainly succeeded in giving form to one of the
ideas that rule and shape the modern world—the idea of liberty and the brotherhood of man;
and it will serve to show to future generations more impressively, because more directly,
than the printed page, that even in this degenerate age there were men who went serenely
to death for what they held to be just and true. For all these reasons Mr. Hovenden's "John
Brown" will live, and will be treasured when the bits and scraps and arrangements and
symphonies and harmonies that are now lauded as the highest of high art have been turned
to the wall and utterly forgotten.

> Anonymous, *The Magazine of Art* (July 1884), writing about the first version of the painting, now in
> the Metropolitan Museum of Art, New York, quoted in *The "Last Moments of John Brown"* [print
> publication prospectus] (Philadelphia: George Gebbie, 1885), pp. 9–10

It is a creditable thing for American art that a rich New York merchant, living in Connecticut,
should have ordered of Thomas Hovenden the very important painting which he has just
finished, "Last Moments of John Brown." Mr. Robbins Battell, the fortunate possessor of the
work which has occupied Hovenden's time for a year or two, owns a fine gallery, and has had

the good sense to commission Hovenden to paint a picture which should be wholly American in its subject. John Brown seems to have taken strong hold on the mind of the artist, as this is the crowning work of several essays on the same subject. If Mr. Battell will allow the picture to be exhibited in various cities throughout the country he will not only help the artist but will be doing good service to American art. *Certainly it is the most significant and striking historical work of art ever executed in the republic.*

> R., *New York Times*, 18 May 1884, writing about the Metropolitan Museum of Art version of the painting, quoted in *The "Last Moments of John Brown"* [print publication prospectus] (Philadelphia: George Gebbie, 1885), pp. 11–12

Provenance

Albert Rosenthal (1863–1939), Philadelphia, before 1920–after 1925

[Macbeth Galleries, New York, ca. 1920; returned to Rosenthal]

[Ehrich Galleries, New York]

[Hirschl & Adler Galleries, New York]

[Graham Gallery, New York, by 1974]

John D. Rockefeller 3rd and Blanchette Hooker Rockefeller, New York, 1974–1979

FAMSF, 1979.7.60

Exhibition History

Washington, D.C., The Corcoran Gallery of Art, *Commemorative Exhibition by Members of the National Academy of Design, 1825–1925*, 1925, exh. no. 240

New York, Gainsborough Galleries, *Exhibition of Famous Men in American History by American Artists*, 1929, exh. no. 27

San Francisco 1976, exh. no. 76

Charleston, W. Va., State Capitol, Governor's Office, extended loan, 1980–1985

Philadelphia, Pennsylvania Academy of the Fine Arts, *Paris 1889: American Artists at the Universal Exposition*, 1990, exh. no. 168

New York, Fraunces Tavern Museum, *Picturing History: American Painting, 1770–1930*, 1993, no exh. no.

Selected Reference
Albert Boime, *The Art of Exclusion: Representing Blacks in the Nineteenth Century* (Washington, D.C., and London: Smithsonian Institution Press, 1990), pp. 143–144

Related Works
The Last Moments of John Brown, 1884
Oil on canvas, 77⅜ x 66¼ in.
The Metropolitan Museum of Art, New York

The Last Moments of John Brown, 1885
Etching, 31½ x 25¾ in.
Published by George Gebbie, Philadelphia (etched plate in the collection of the Pennsylvania Academy of the Fine Arts, Philadelphia)

Study for John Brown
Pencil and wash on paper, approx. 13 x 17 in.

Kennedy Galleries, New York, as of 1962

Frederick Juengling (American, 1846–1889)
After *The Last Moments of John Brown*
Wood engraving
Harper's Weekly 29, no. 1467 (31 January 1885): 72–73

94 A BOHEMIAN, 1885

Oil on canvas, 25¾ x 36 in.
Signed, dated, and inscribed on bench at lower right: *DENNIS M. BUNKER/NEW YORK 1885*

DENNIS MILLER BUNKER

b. New York, N.Y. 1861
d. Boston, Mass. 1890

Dennis Miller Bunker was born in New York, November 6, 1861, and began drawing while he was going to school in the city, entering the Academy schools afterwards as a regular pupil in 1878. He did not remain there very long, but attended the classes in drawing and painting from life at the Art Students' League, working there until the autumn of 1881, when he sailed for Paris. After spending three months at the Académie Julian and in the class of Hébert at the École des Beaux-Arts, he became a pupil of Gérôme and worked in his class at the Beaux-Arts until 1884, when he returned to New York. He has been abroad once since, having spent the summer of 1888 with John S. Sargent at Calcott, near Reading, in England, where he painted landscapes.

Mr. Bunker's first pictures were exhibited at the Academy and elsewhere several years before he went abroad. Most of these were landscapes, and while he was a student in New York he painted and sold a good many pictures, and was well known during this period as a water-color painter. The first picture he exhibited after his study in Paris was a figure of a young man in a studio playing a guitar, and was called "Bohemia." For this picture he received the third Hallgarten prize at the Academy in 1885, and he was elected a member of the Society of American Artists the same year. In 1886 he went to Boston, where he was the principal instructor in drawing and painting from life at the Cowles Art School. During his stay in Boston he painted a large number of portraits and sent two or three pictures to the New York exhibitions. He came back to New York last year, and died in Boston, December 28, 1890.

Although not lacking in refinement and delicacy, his work is essentially robust and virile.

William A. Coffin, "The Artist Bunker," *The Century Magazine* 41, no. 4 (February 1891): 638

The two men [Bunker and John Singer Sargent] certainly met frequently at the hospitable residence of the now legendary Mrs. Jack Gardner, who was a friend and patron of both. They soon became close comrades and a fellow member of the Tavern Club recalled Sargent's declaring, many years after Bunker's untimely death, "that he did not remember anyone to whom he had been more deeply attached." To another member Sargent declared that Bunker had evidenced greater innate painterly gifts than any previous American artist.

R. H. Ives Gammell, *The Boston Painters, 1900–1930* (Orleans, Mass.: Parnassus Imprints, 1986), pp. 18–20

Our old friend the Academy comes with a smiling spring face to greet a rainy April. It bears in its train allurements for the hungry artist in the shape of prizes. . . . [T]o Dennis M.

Bunker's 'Bohemian' we wish well in the competition, because of its naturalness, ease of pose, and good painting on the odds and ends of the bachelor apartment.

"The Sixtieth Academy," *The Critic*, n.s. 3, no. 67 (11 April 1885): 174

———

I have only been able to work twice since my sickness. A great part of the time I play on my guitar and sing, and lead a foolish, harmless kind of life. I begin to feel so strongly that one's own approbation is the only reward ever to be had for one's work that the opinion of the world as to what I am doing becomes more and more indifferent to me.

Bunker to Anne Page, 1 September 1886, Dennis Miller Bunker Papers, AAA, roll 1201, frame 735

———

Reacting against the excesses of the Romantic era, the later nineteenth century nevertheless incorporated many of its assumptions, including such an antimaterialistic stance as the asceticism of the creative life, a concept Dennis Miller Bunker's (1861–1890) *The Guitar Player*, 1885 wonderfully illustrates.

Also known at the time as *Bohemia*, the painting pithily conveys the neo-Romantic, bohemian ethos of living only for Art, of being able to sustain oneself solely on such spiritual nourishment as art, music, or literature, of sacrificing material rewards for creative ones. In this self-portrait of the artist as impecunious musician, Bunker is seated in his spare, unpre-possessing studio, strumming a guitar and professing, through his pose and surroundings, the superiority of artistic experience over external circumstance. Played by a young, "artistic" man, the Spanish guitar suggests a subtle defiance of convention; it smacks of exotic foreign airs and sensual Mediterranean abandon. . . .

Unlike the luxurious, grandiose, and overstuffed type of studio introduced by William Merritt Chase in the 1870s, and thereafter the staple of art press and fiction alike, Bunker's picture eschews the image of prop room and treasure trove for an ambience that proclaims the purity of art, whether it be painting or the music-making Bunker has chosen to identify with it. The purpose of the chiaroscuro scene and the silent music that is a part of it is to evoke an atmosphere. Music and art join forces to express a mood of creativity.

Celia Betsky, "American Musical Paintings, 1865–1910," in *The Art of Music: American Paintings and Musical Instruments, 1770–1910*, exh. cat. (Clinton, N.Y.: Fred L. Emerson Gallery, Hamilton College, 1984), p. 64

Provenance
S. H. Blain, from 1885

[Hirschl & Adler Galleries, New York, 1971]

John D. Rockefeller 3rd and Blanchette Hooker Rockefeller, New York, 1971–1993

FAMSF, 1993.35.1

Exhibition History
New York, National Academy of Design, *Sixtieth Spring Exhibition*, 1885, exh. no. 587 (for sale, $250; won 3rd Hallgarten Prize)

Boston, Noyes & Blakeslee Gallery, *Exhibition of Paintings by*

Dennis M. Bunker, exh. no. 2 (as *Bohemian*)

San Francisco 1976, exh. no. 59 (as *The Guitar Player*)

New Britain, Conn., New Britain Museum of American Art, *Dennis Miller Bunker (1861–1890) Rediscovered*, 1978, not in publ. (shown only in New York venue at Davis & Long Gallery)

Tokyo 1982, exh. no. 57

Clinton, N.Y., Fred L. Emerson Gallery of Hamilton College, *The Art of Music: American Paintings and Musical Instruments, 1770–1910*, 1984, exh. no. 18 (as *The Guitar Player*)

FAMSF, *Director's Choice: Twenty Years of Collecting*, 1987, no publ.

Selected References
Charles M. Kurtz, *National Academy Notes and Complete Catalogue: Sixtieth Spring Exhibition, National Academy of Design, New York* (New York: Cassell & Co., 1885), pp. 47–48

"Fine Arts: Sixtieth Exhibition of the National Academy of Design. Prize Pictures?" unidentified newspaper clipping, 4 April 1885, Thomas Hovenden Papers, AAA, roll P13, frame 26

Montezuma [Montague Marks], "My Note Book," *The Art Amateur* 13, no. 1 (June 1885): 2

George William Sheldon, *Recent Ideals of American Art* (1888; New York: D. Appleton and Co., 1890), p. 40

Jared I. Edwards, "Dennis Miller Bunker (1861–90) Rediscovered," *Nineteenth Century* 4, no. 1 (Spring 1978): 74

Ronald Pisano, *Idle Hours: Americans at Leisure, 1865–1914* (Boston, Toronto, London: Little, Brown and Company, New York Graphic Society, 1988), pp. 33, 39

---

95 OLD WASHINGTON MARKET, NEW YORK CITY, 1885

Transparent and opaque watercolor over graphite on wove paper, 21 x 29⅞ in.
Signed and dated lower right: *Hughson Hawley/1885*

HUGHSON HAWLEY
b. Stratford-on-Avon, England 1850
d. Brighton, England 1936

Born in England in 1850, Hughson Hawley began his artistic career as a scenic designer at Stratford-on-Avon, where his father was the librarian. In 1880, Hawley was brought to New York by the dramatist Steele Mackaye, whose play *Hazel Kirke*, opened on Broadway on February 4, 1880. Hawley continued to do scenic work in New York for a number of years but gave it up to devote his career to architectural drawings and watercolors. In 1880 he exhibited three of his works at the National Academy of Design. From his studio in the Lincoln Building at One Union Square, he did architectural work for the firms of McKim, Mead and White, York and Sawyer, and Cass Gilbert. Beginning in 1889, his drawings appeared in *Harper's Magazine*; in 1892, he illustrated Charles Hart's *New York Stock Exchange*. Hawley's depiction of the newly built Pennsylvania Station was published by the railroad in 1910, and it is probably his most well-known work. An active member of the Players, the Lotos Club, and the Lambs, Hawley retired to Brighton, England in 1931. He lived there with his son-in-law, the writer Jeffrey Farnol, at whose home he died on May 11, 1936.

Richard J. Koke, comp., *American Landscape and Genre Paintings in the New-York Historical Society*, 3 vols. (Boston: G. K. Hall & Co., for the New-York Historical Society, 1982), 2:117

The old Washington Market, begun in 1812, is being demolished. It is to be replaced by a new iron building.

New York Times, 25 July 1883; cited in I. N. Phelps Stokes, *The Iconography of Manhattan Island, 1498–1909*, 6 vols. (New York: Robert H. Dodd, 1926), 5:1982

Provenance

[Auction sale, Christie, Manson & Woods, London, 2 July 1968, lot no. 99, sold for $1638]

[Graham Gallery, New York, 1968]

John D. Rockefeller 3rd and Blanchette Hooker Rockefeller, New York, 1968–1979

FAMSF, 1979.7.48

Related Work

Old Washington Market, New York City, 1881
Pen and ink on illustration board, 12½ x 20½ in.
The New-York Historical Society, New York

96 TAKING HIS EASE, 1885

Oil on canvas, 15¾ x 19¾ in.
Signed right center edge (on table base): *THovenden* (initials in monogram)

THOMAS HOVENDEN

b. Dunmanway, County Cork, Ireland 1840
d. Norristown, Pa. 1895

Thomas Hovenden was born in Dunmanway, County Cork, Ireland, in 1840, and was fifty-five years old when he died, and was therefore in the maturity of his artistic powers. Showing when a child exceeding cleverness in drawing, his art education began at an early age at the Cork School of Design. Coming to the United States in 1863, he became a pupil in the National Academy of Design. At once, under new influences, the talent Hovenden showed made him many friends and secured him orders. In 1874 he was in Paris, and selecting Cabanel for master, he entered the Ecole des Beaux-Arts. His return to the country of his adoption was in 1880. In 1881 he was chosen as an associate of the National Academy of Design, and in the next year became an Academician.

. . . Among his . . . principal works are . . . "Last Moments of John Brown" [and] "Taking His Ease[.]" . . . As a painter Mr. Hovenden made a direct impress on American art. Apart from that conscientious study of detail, Thomas Hovenden had a strong and vigorous touch, and he was a colorist of distinguished merit. It was in the selection of his subjects that he was always fortunate. He never sought to convey what was the violent but the natural effect, and so his incidents, as he worked them out on the canvas, always went to the heart.

"Thomas Hovenden," *Harper's Weekly* 39, no. 2018 (24 August 1895): 39

Coming to America in 1863 when all the activities of life burned with the fire of the great social and moral problem underlying the civil war the struggles of the slaves made an impression upon Mr. Hovenden's mind never to be obliterated. On his return to New York in 1880 seeking to use the material at hand he at once turned to the homely phases of the life of the coloured people. . . .

Mr. Hovenden painted almost all of his pictures at Plymouth Meeting where he and his wife had set up their studio in an old barn that had done service in the Underground Railway. It was here the first abolition meetings were held, the Corsons [Mrs. Hovenden's family] being leaders in that movement.

Amy Seville Wolff, "Life and Work of Hovenden," *Philadelphia Times*, 18 August 1895

———

Of the wondrous skill of the artist, of his masterly use of the simplest means in the simplest ways, it needs not that we should speak again at this time. When an artist paints a human countenance, aglow with loving kindness, suffused with fond memories and tender sympathies, touched with a latent sense of native humor, and withal as true to nature as nature herself, then his works praise him beyond the power of words to tell.

Baltimore Sun, 16 May 1883, Thomas Hovenden Papers, AAA, roll P13, frame 32

———

The South Gallery contains most of the large paintings in the exhibition. . . .

On the East wall, in addition to the large paintings already referred to, . . . [is] Thomas Hovenden's "Taking his Ease" (383),—an old negro leaning back in his chair enjoying his pipe.

Charles M. Kurtz, *National Academy Notes and Complete Catalogue: Sixtieth Spring Exhibition, National Academy of Design, New York* (New York: Cassell & Co., 1885), p. 33

97 ORCHID AND HUMMINGBIRD, CA. 1885

Oil on canvas, 15 x 20⅛ in.
Signed lower right: *M. J. Heade*

**MARTIN JOHNSON
HEADE**

b. Lumberville, Pa. 1819
d. St. Augustine, Fla. 1904

J. M. [*sic*] Heade was born in Bucks county, Pa., near the home of [the celebrated man
of letters] Bayard Taylor. He began his artistic career as a portrait-painter; but the love of
travel was strong within him, and few of our artists have roved more about the world; he
passed two years in Rome, sojourned in France and England, and has visited both South and
Central America. The Emperor of Brazil was delighted with Heade's pictures, and bestowed
a decoration upon him when they were exhibited. This artist has become identified with
tropical landscapes. . . . He meditates another trip to South America.

As an accurate and graceful illustrator of natural history, Heade attained a special
reputation; his delineation of birds and flowers is remarkable for the most faithful drawing
and exquisite color. During a sojourn in South America he made a fine collection of tropical
birds and butterflies, which have served him for authentic and elaborate studies.

> Henry T. Tuckerman, *Book of the Artists: American Artist Life* (1867; New York: James C. Carr,
> 1966), p. 542

———

You some time ago requested me to contribute a chapter on hummingbirds for the natural
history department of FOREST AND STREAM. As that is a subject on which I feel quite competent
to write, I do it with pleasure in an hour snatched from business.

From early boyhood I have been almost a monomaniac on hummingbirds, and there is
probably very little regarding their habits that I do not know. . . .

Every well informed person knows that the hummingbirds are found only in the New
World and the adjacent islands. . . .

We have but one species, the ruby-throat, this side of the Rocky Mountains, and about a
dozen in the west and southwest, while South America has several hundreds already known,
and new ones are discovered every year.

> Didymus [Martin Johnson Heade], "Taming Hummingbirds," *Forest and Stream* 38, no. 15
> (14 April 1892): 348

———

Hummingbirds are generally supposed to be extremely timid and almost untamable, but
when their confidence is won, which is an easy matter to those who understand them—they
are very fearless and the loveliest little pets in the world. We tame them nearly every season,
and they come to us anywhere around the place, and when the doors are open make themselves perfectly at home, even in the house. A year or two ago I called my wife's attention to
the first one of the spring, as we were sitting on the piazza, and when I called him he came at
once and examined each of us carefully and then flew off. I saw at once that it was one of our
pets of the previous year, so I went in and prepared a small bottle of sugar and water, and it

was but a few minutes before he returned and at once took his dinner as he had been accustomed to. Unfortunately he had a mate who was bossing him and dragged him northward after he had paid us but two or three visits.

> Didymus [Martin Johnson Heade], "Florida Hummingbirds," *Forest and Stream* 36, no. 23 (25 June 1891): 455

[Theodore] Stebbins has explained how . . . the orchid, whose name is derived from the Greek word meaning testicle, carried a "dangerous aura of sexuality and was thought to be an aphrodisiac." By the same token, the hummingbird was perceived to occupy a grove in Eden, and in his South American visions Heade closely juxtaposed that bird with various orchids in compositions that were powerful still lifes grafted on to steamy jungle landscapes. Sometimes he contrasted the male and female bird, in other cases two fighting males. These sexual observations had provocative echoes in the visibly erotic shapes of the orchid's vaginal flower and phallic pistils. Heade's seductive imagery reflects the drives of species postulated by Darwin paradoxically fused with the hidden sexuality of the Victorian age.

> John Wilmerding, "The American Object: Still-Life Paintings," in *An American Perspective: Nineteenth-Century Art from the Collection of Jo Ann and Julian Ganz, Jr.*, exh. cat. (Washington, D.C.: National Gallery of Art, 1981), p. 101

Provenance
Henry Morrison Flagler (1830–1913), New York, St. Augustine, and Palm Beach, Fla., until 1913

Descended in family to Thomas Stephen Kenan III, Palm Beach, Fla., ca. 1965–1969

[Joan Washburn, New York, 1969]

John D. Rockefeller 3rd and Blanchette Hooker Rockefeller, New York, 1969–1979

FAMSF, 1979.7.49

Exhibition History
St. Augustine, Fla., Arts Club of St. Augustine (Gallery 230), 1945, exh. no. 27

College Park, University of Maryland Art Gallery, *Martin Johnson Heade*, 1969, exh. no. 48

Tokyo 1982, exh. no. 35

Selected References
Robert G. McIntyre, *Martin Johnson Heade, 1819–1904* (New York: Pantheon Press, 1948), p. 62

Theodore E. Stebbins, Jr., *The Life and Works of Martin Johnson Heade* (New Haven and London: Yale University Press, 1975), cat. no. 286

The American Canvas, pp. 92–93, 236

Oil on canvasboard (now mounted on canvas), 17 x 12 in.
Signed and dated lower left: *WMHARNETT./1886.* (initials in monogram)

WILLIAM MICHAEL HARNETT

b. Clonakilty, County Cork,
   Ireland 1848
d. New York, N.Y. 1892

In telling you how I paint pictures from still-life models, it would be well for me to give you in brief a sketch of my early career in art, for the trials and hardships that I underwent were the sole reasons for my taking up that line of art work. . . .

"When I was seventeen years old, I began to learn the engraver's trade. I worked on steel, copper and wood, and finally developed considerable skill in engraving silverware. This latter work then became my chief occupation. In 1867, when I was 19 years old, I entered the Philadelphia Academy of Fine Arts as a pupil, studying with the night class. Two years later I found work in this city [New York], and came here to study in the National Academy of Design and take advantage of the free art school in the Cooper Institute. In this way I worked for various large jewelry firms during the day and at the art schools at night until 1875, when I gave up engraving and went wholly into painting. . . .

". . . I devoted more than half my days and evenings to my art studies, only working at my trade enough to supply me with money for clothes, food, shelter, paints and canvas. Consequently I had no money to spare.

"This very poverty led to my taking up the line of painting that I have followed for the past 15 years. . . . I could not afford to hire models as the other students did, and I was forced to paint my first picture from still life models. These models were a pipe and a German beer mug. After the picture was finished I sent it to the Academy and to my intense delight it was accepted. What was more it was sold. I think it brought $50. That was the first money I ever earned with my brush and it seemed a small fortune to me. . . .

"Now, let me tell you something about the painting of pictures from still life models. . . . I endeavor to make the composition tell a story. The chief difficulty I have found has not been the grouping of my models, but their choice. To find a subject that paints well is not an easy task. As a rule, new things do not paint well. . . . I want my models to have the mellowing effect of age."

Harnett, quoted in the *New York News*, 1889 or 1890, quoted in Alfred Frankenstein, *After the Hunt: William Harnett and Other American Still Life Painters, 1870–1900*, rev. ed. (Berkeley and Los Angeles: University of California Press, 1969), pp. 29, 55

The iconography of Harnett's paintings of 1886 shows an immediate response to the American environment and one which was very much to the good. . . . [H]e has here gone back to the homeliest of the homely, the most commonplace of the commonplace, and with it achieved a new subtlety both of design and connotation.

In 1886 . . . Harnett takes an old German pipe with a meerschaum bowl, a long cherry stem and an amber bit, hangs it by a string from a nail in a door, and with it achieves a masterpiece of taut abstract pattern. There are three [*sic*—two] known versions of this picture. They are very much alike, but they are not replicas: one (New York: Martin Grossman, plate 65 [the FAMSF painting]) exhibits a newspaper clipping, while the other (Oberlin College) does not; there are also differences in the cracks, nail holes, chalk marks, and finger smudgings on the green board, and the more one studies these, the more important they become, while the fact that the two pictures represent the same pipe and piece of string forming the same design sinks into comparative insignificance. Now it becomes apparent why Harnett does not like the natural wood grain of the old tradition—he can do so many more interesting things with a painted door that has been thoroughly weathered, battered, and abused.

[In a note Frankenstein adds:] In all of these works—the horseshoes and the pipes—
Harnett continues to use his Paris trick of painting his signature as if it had been whittled into
the door. In studying the signature on the Grossman [FAMSF] picture with a magnifying
glass, I saw in the painted grooves painted splinters which were not visible to the naked eye.

Alfred Frankenstein, *After the Hunt: William Harnett and Other American Still Life Painters,
1870–1900*, rev. ed. (Berkeley and Los Angeles: University of California Press, 1969), pp. 72–73

———————

I wound up my day's labors in the apartment of Martin Grossman, Sidney Janis' brother-in-
law. His Harnett is a meerschaum hanging on a wall with a newspaper clipping below it. . . .
I think this is not only an authentic Harnett but a particularly fine one. Just the tautness and
verisimilitude of the string holding the pipe is a major achievement, and it is even more
beautiful under a magnifying glass than it is without it. (This is particularly true of the incised
signature. Under the glass you would be ready to swear that that damn thing was actually cut
in wood.)

Alfred Frankenstein to the art dealer Edith Gregor Halpert, 13 July 1947, Alfred Frankenstein
Papers, AAA, roll 1377, frames 105–106

Provenance

[Unidentified auction sale, London, before 1947]

Martin B. Grossman (1896–1981) and Mary Jane Cooper Grossman (1914–1981), New York, by 1947–1969

[Hirschl & Adler Galleries, New York, 1969–1970]

John D. Rockefeller 3rd and Blanchette Hooker Rockefeller, New York, 1970–1979

FAMSF, 1979.7.46

Exhibition History

New York, American Federation of Arts, *Harnett and His School*, 1953, exh. no. 20

La Jolla, Calif., La Jolla Museum of Art, *The Reminiscent Object: Paintings by William Michael Harnett, John Frederick Peto, and John Haberle*, 1965, exh. no. 19

San Francisco 1976, exh. no. 68

Tokyo 1982, exh. no. 45

New York, The Metropolitan Museum of Art, *William M. Harnett*, 1992, exh. no. 39

Selected Reference

Alfred Frankenstein, *After the Hunt: William Michael Harnett and other American Still Life Painters, 1870–1900*, rev. ed. (Berkeley and Los Angeles: University of California Press, 1969), cat. no. 100

Related Work

Meerschaum Pipe, 1886
Oil on canvas, 17⅝ x 12¾ in.
Allen Memorial Art Museum, Oberlin, Ohio

99 A "NORTHER," KEY WEST, 1886

Watercolor over graphite on wove paper, 14 x 20 in.
Signed and inscribed on reverse, bottom center: *Winslow Homer*; top center: *"A Norther"*

WINSLOW HOMER
b. Boston, Mass. 1836
d. Prout's Neck, Maine 1910

Despite the proverb, a change of sky does mean a change of mood to some men, and among them is the sensitive, clear-eyed artist. Soon after Homer's return from England he went to Florida and the West Indies, and again brought back rich booty of a novel sort. The very essence of the tropics breathed in these new aquarelles,—bold, dashing, vivid studies of turquoise sea and blinding sun, of bright-hued plastered houses gaudy with vines and flowers, of negro fishers for sharks and divers for sponges, of impenetrable, luscious jungles and wild, wind-tossed palms. Brighter colors than any Impressionist has found in the south of France he had found in these western isles ignored of art. . . . And with what unshrinking truth to vividness of light and hue he had painted—a colorist now to rank with the boldest and freshest of our time. . . . There was an "Approaching Tornado" in which a whole tragedy lay latent just in the way the atmosphere was painted; and a "Norther—Key West" that was tragedy made palpable through three bending, agonizing palm-trees, splendid in line, and as vital and passionate as though they had been human creatures.

[Mariana Griswold] Van Rensselaer, "Winslow Homer," in *Six Portraits* (Boston and New York: Houghton, Mifflin and Company; Cambridge, Mass.: The Riverside Press, 1889), pp. 257–259

We have Homer's tropical water colors because the good people of Scarboro found that the painter made an excellent juror. To escape this perennial duty Homer went South and wintered throughout the Caribbean. His water colors . . . gave a clear insight into the simplicity of his artistic character. An oil can be "fussed," but the water color not; and his water-color sketches are marvels of crispness and directness.

Henry Reuterdahl, "Winslow Homer, American Painter: An Appreciation from a Sea-Going Viewpoint," *The Craftsman* 20, no. 1 (April 1911): 10

So far as we can judge by his effect upon us, his contemporaries, and without waiting for the verdict of posterity, Winslow Homer was unquestionably a great artist. He has given us pleasures and sensations different in kind from those which we have received from other artists of his time and, perhaps, superior to them in degree. He has shown us things which, without his eyes, we should not have seen, and impressed us with truths which, but for him, we should not have felt. He has stirred us with tragic emotion or, in the representation of common every-day incidents, has revealed to us the innate nobility of the simple and hardy lives of hunters, fishers, and seafarers. Finally, he has realized for us, as no other artist of any time has done, the power and grandeur of the elemental forces of nature, and he has dramatized for us the conflict of water, earth, and air.

Kenyon Cox, "The Art of Winslow Homer," *Scribner's Magazine* 56, no. 3 (September 1914): 377

After settling at Prout's [N]eck, Homer held a series of exhibitions of his works in Boston. His watercolors, drawings, studies, and oil paintings were shown, year after year, at the old gallery of Doll & Richards, in Park Street, and they met with a gratifying market and liberal recognition. One of the most extensive buyers of his works was the late Edward Hooper, Treasurer of Harvard College and one of the members of the Board of Trustees of the Museum of Fine Arts. Many of his finest watercolors were included in the Hooper collection. . . . At that time Homer said that Boston was the only city in the United States that gave him any practical encouragement.

> William Howe Downes, *The Life and Works of Winslow Homer* (Boston and New York: Houghton Mifflin Company, 1911), p. 126

Provenance
Edward W. Hooper (1841–1901), Boston, by 1889–1901

Descended in family to Greely S. Curtis (ca. 1871–1947) and Fanny Hooper Curtis (d. 1963), Marblehead, Mass., before 1911–1964

[Maynard Walker Gallery, New York, 1964]

[Hirschl & Adler Galleries, New York, 1964]

John D. Rockefeller 3rd and Blanchette Hooker Rockefeller, New York, 1964–1979

FAMSF, 1979.7.54

Exhibition History
New York, National Academy of Design, American Society of Painters in Water Colors, *Twenty-first Annual Exhibition*, 1888, exh. no. 432 (for sale, $150)

Boston, St. Botolph Club, *Regular Water Color Exhibition*, 1890, exh. no. 16

Boston, Museum of Fine Arts, *Loan Exhibition of Paintings by Winslow Homer*, 1911, no publ. (as *Palms in a Storm, Key West*, 1902)

Boston, Copley Society, *Paintings in Water Color by Winslow Homer, John S. Sargent, Dodge MacKnight*, 1921, exh. no. 39

Boston, Museum of Fine Arts, *Watercolors by Winslow Homer*, 1924, no publ.

Cambridge, Mass., Fogg Art Museum, Harvard University, *Water Colors by Winslow Homer, 1836–1910*, 1932, exh. no. 2

Boston, Museum of Fine Arts, *Works by Winslow Homer and John La Farge*, 1936, no publ.

Boston, Symphony Hall, Friends of the Boston Symphony Orchestra, *Exhibition of Paintings by Winslow Homer, 1836–1910*, 1937, no publ.

New York, Wildenstein, *A Loan Exhibition of Winslow Homer, for the Benefit of the New York Botanical Garden*, 1947, exh. no. 65

Washington, D.C., National Gallery of Art, *Winslow Homer: A Retrospective Exhibition*, 1958, exh. no. 131

New York, Whitney Museum of American Art, *Winslow Homer*, 1973, exh. no. 115

San Francisco 1976, exh. no. 72

Tokyo 1982, exh. no. 54

Washington, D.C., National Gallery of Art, *Winslow Homer Watercolors*, 1986, exh. no. 147

Selected References
Nicolai Cikovsky, Jr., *Winslow Homer* (New York: Harry N. Abrams, in association with the National Museum of American Art, 1990), pp. 96–97

Object record, manuscript catalogue raisonné of the works of Winslow Homer, by Lloyd Goodrich, courtesy of the City University of New York, Lloyd Goodrich and Edith Havens Goodrich, Whitney Museum of American Art Record of the Works of Winslow Homer

Watercolor over graphite on wove paper, 16 x 19⅜ in.

JOHN LA FARGE
b. New York, N.Y. 1835
d. Providence, R.I. 1910

It is noticeable in Mr. La Farge's life that he should be, in many ways, like a painter of old time, that is, traveller, reader, collector and student; colorist and decorator; painter in large and in little. He has been a working artist for forty years, and has done many things. He has made many book illustrations. . . .

He has produced also a very great number of water-color drawings, generally small, and very commonly having for their subjects pieces of foreground detail, such as one or several blossoms in a pool of water. . . .

Again he has produced, during those years of work, a few large pictures painted in oil-color or by a process which he learned in his youth and in which painted wax has a part. . . .

He has produced, also, a few such mural paintings. . . .

About 1876 these same demands upon him for [interior] decoration led him to the careful observation of ancient stained glass, with a view to providing the modern world with something which might be to it what the windows of Reims Cathedral and Fairford Church were to the Middle Ages. . . .

We are brought naturally to a consideration of Mr. La Farge's landscape. He is not generally considered as a landscape painter; and yet he has produced a great deal of landscape in the secondary or accessory part of his work. He has also painted landscape of the first intention, so to speak, landscape which is nothing but landscape. . . . Until recent years there were only half a dozen such pictures of wide landscape, numerous as were his studies in that style. . . . During the last ten years, however, La Farge has produced an immense number of singularly effective drawings in monochrome and in color, made either on the spot in Fiji, in Japan, or elsewhere in the far East, or made after his return home, from studies carefully noted during his stay abroad.

Russell Sturgis, "John La Farge," *Scribner's Magazine* 26, no. 1 (July 1899): 3–5, 9, 18–19

———

At Omaha a young reporter got the better of us; for when in reply to his inquiry as to our purpose in visiting Japan, La Farge beamed through his spectacles the answer that we were in search of Nirwana [*sic*], the youth looked up like a meteor and rejoined: "It's out of season!"

Henry Adams to John Hay, 11 June 1886, quoted in James L. Yarnall, "John La Farge and Henry Adams in Japan," *The American Art Journal* 21, no. 1 (1989): 41

———

I would have given you a present if you could have seen us on our expedition last Friday to what the old books call the *Dye boots*. This remnant of the vanished splendor of Kamakura is about twenty miles from Yokohama . . . and as La Farge says it is the most successful colossal figure in the world, he sketched it.

Henry Adams to John Hay, serial letter of 9–16 September 1886, quoted in James L. Yarnall, "John La Farge and Henry Adams in Japan," *The American Art Journal* 21, no. 1 (1989): 59–60

———

We saw it [the great bronze statue, nearly 50 feet high] first from the side through trees, as we ran rapidly to the front, where are a temple gate, and a long courtyard still in order, that leads up to the statue. From the side one can see how it bends over, and rough as it is from behind, the impression of something real was strong as its gray form moved through the openings of the trees. The photographs must long have made you know it, and they also show the great base and the immense temple ornaments that stand upon it at the feet of the statue. They show also the little lodge at the side, where the priest in attendance lives, and

gives information, and sells photographs and takes them, and generally acts as showman. We took many photographs from new points of view, and we even removed the thatch of a penthouse so as to get nearer and under the statue to the side; and I painted also, more to get the curious gray and violet tone of the bronze than to make a faithful drawing, for that seemed impossible in the approaching afternoon. . . . Now, freed from its shrine, the figure sits in contemplation of entire nature, the whole open world that we feel about us. . . . All this world of ours, which to the contemplative mind is but a figurative fragment of the universe, lies before the mental gaze of the Buddha. Unwinking, without change of direction, he looks forever. . . .

. . . As one looks longer and longer at it, with everything around it gently changing, and the shadows shifting upon its surface, the tension of expectation rises to anxiety. The trees rustle and wave behind it, and the light dances up and down the green boughs with the wind; it must move—but there is no change, and it shall sit forever.

John La Farge, *An Artist's Letters from Japan* (1897; New York: Da Capo Press, for Kennedy Graphics, 1970), pp. 225–226, 227–228

————

For many years he has been known chiefly as a decorator, and particularly as a designer in stained glass; but few painters in water-colors have shown a greater mastery of the medium, and no one has used it to better advantage. Whether judged by his large decorative work or by these small studies, several of which are finished with the delicacy of miniatures, La Farge must be accounted a great colorist, one of the few with whom the gift is an intellectual rather than a merely sensuous endowment. The difference is of the same nature as that between a great composer and a musician capable at most of inventing an "arrangement." . . . About one fourth of the paintings shown were of Japanese subjects.

"Minor Exhibitions," *The Art Amateur* 32, no. 5 (April 1895): 133

Provenance
Ruel P. Tolman (1878–1954), Washington, D.C., to 1934

[Macbeth Galleries, New York, 1934, sold for $700]

Stephen Carlton Clark (1882–1960), New York, 1934–after 1948

[Kennedy Galleries, New York, by 1968]

John D. Rockefeller 3rd and Blanchette Hooker Rockefeller, New York, 1968–1979

FAMSF, 1979.7.70

Exhibition History
New York, Macbeth Galleries, *John LaFarge, 1835–1910: Loan Exhibition*, 1948, exh. no. 22

New York, Kennedy Galleries, *John LaFarge: Oils and Watercolors*, 1968, exh. no. 15

FAMSF, *Selected Acquisitions, 1977–1979*, 1979, exh. no. 35

Tokyo 1982, exh. no. 36

FAMSF, *Master Drawings from the Achenbach Foundation for Graphic Arts*, 1985, exh. no. 96

Yonkers, N.Y., Hudson River Museum, *John La Farge Watercolors and Drawings*, 1990, exh. no. 7

Selected Reference
James L. Yarnall, "John La Farge and Henry Adams in Japan," *The American Art Journal* 21, no. 1 (1989): 40, 42, 58–60

Related Works
The Great Statue of Amida Buddha at Kamakura, 1886
Watercolor and gouache on paper, 10¾ x 10½ in.
Private collection, as of 1989

The Great Statue of Amida Buddha at Kamakura, Known as the Daibutsu, from the Priest's Garden, 1887
Watercolor and gouache over pencil on paper, 19$\frac{5}{16}$ x 12½ in.
The Metropolitan Museum of Art, New York

101 INDIANS HUNTING BUFFALO, CA. 1888

Oil on canvas, 24¾ x 35⅞ in.
Signed lower left: *ABierstadt* (initials in monogram)

ALBERT BIERSTADT
b. Solingen, Germany 1830
d. New York, N.Y. 1902

I have endeavored to show the buffalo in all his aspects and depict the cruel slaughter of a noble animal now almost extinct. The buffalo is an ugly brute to paint, but I consider my picture [*The Last of the Buffalo*, 1888, The Corcoran Gallery of Art, Washington, D.C.] one of my very best.

Bierstadt, quoted in *New York World*, March 1889, quoted in Gordon Hendricks, *Albert Bierstadt: Painter of the American West* (New York: Harry N. Abrams, in association with the Amon Carter Museum of Western Art, [1974]), p. 291

[Bierstadt's] second western excursion in 1863 was to inspire his greatest canvases. Accompanying him was Fitz Hugh Ludlow, a hashish eater, who described the journey in *The Heart of the Continent*. Ludlow's language of description was not quite hallucinatory. . . . On the one hand he regularly specified the course of their travel as if he were reading from a map, and just as often referred to flora and fauna by Latin names; on the other hand he was equally attentive to the symbolic meaning of their experience.

For example, herds of buffalo seemed as vast and powerful to him as icebergs had to others; they represented a force of nature:

> I remember my first and my succeeding impressions of Niagara; but never did I see an incarnation of vast multitude, or resistless force, which impressed me like the main herd of buffalo.

Bierstadt made hasty sketches of these creatures, in battle, stampede, and death. Years later they formed the basis of a major canvas, *The Last of the Buffalo*, an image summarizing the artist's awareness of a breed of man and animal both vanishing. Using the strong horizontal

format favoured by Church and others, he contrasts the hulking animal forms in the foreground with the spacious open landscape in the distance. In opposition are the tension of violence and the peaceful beauty of river and far mountains. But more than a panorama of breathtaking nature, it is also one of mortality, giving us at close range the full cycle of life, dying, present and past death, and by implication rebirth in the fullness of nature and the herd beyond. As an image of indiscriminate slaughter and of plundering the land's resources, it acquires a sharpened poignance for America a century later.

John Wilmerding, American Art (Harmondsworth: Penguin Books, 1976), pp. 126–127

The hunters in the party [with Bierstadt and Ludlow in 1863] sought out a small herd of buffalo and were able to isolate a great old bull that Bierstadt wanted to sketch in action. Ludlow describes the event:

> Munger, Thompson, and I rode slowly round the bull, attracting his attention by feigned assaults, that our artist might see him in action. . . . The old giant lowered his head until his great beard swept the dust; out of his immense fell of hair his eyes glared fiercer and redder; he drew his breath with a hollow roar and a painful hiss, and charged madly at the aggressor. A mere twist of the rein threw the splendidly trained horse out of harm's way, and the bull almost went headlong with his unspent impetus. For nearly fifteen minutes, this process was continued, while the artist's hand and eye followed each other at the double-quick over the board.

Bierstadt finished the sketch quickly and asked the others to dispatch the bull. Ludlow continues:

> All of us who had weapons drew up in a line, while the artist attracted the bull's attention by a final feigned assault. We aimed right for the heart and fired. . . .

Bierstadt's interest in buffaloes as subjects for drawings and paintings continued not only throughout the rest of the journey across the plains but for many years afterwards. In later years he made numerous paintings of buffalo hunts, of buffaloes drinking at waterholes, and the like. In fact, his last major painting (it has been called his greatest) was *The Last of the Buffalo*. . . .

[Late in his career d]etractors increased in number and volume, especially after Impressionism, so drastically different from Bierstadt's style, had won over the more vocal of America's art critics. Though in the late 1880s he was widely considered the dean of American artists, the jury that selected American paintings for the Paris Exposition of 1889 rejected his last great western painting, *The Last of the Buffalo*. Bierstadt pretended to be indifferent to the slight, but it probably hurt deeply. The hurt was doubtless assuaged somewhat when the painting sold a couple of years later for a reported $50,000.

> Ralph A. Britsch, *Bierstadt and Ludlow: Painter and Writer in the West*, Charles E. Merrill Monographs, no. 5 (Salt Lake City: Brigham Young University, 1980), pp. 26–28, 62–63

Five paintings by Albert Bierstadt [in the Rockefeller collection as shown in 1976] are here an unusual example of depth in a single artist's work. . . . I thought the most exciting of them all [was] *Indians Hunting Buffalo*, ca. 1888. This latter work is a study for the central grouping —an Indian spearing a buffalo charging his rearing stallion—in the mammoth *Last of the Buffalo*, 1888, which exists in two versions (Corcoran Gallery of Art and the Whitney Museum of Western Art). If there is an American equivalent to the 17th century Flemish Peter Paul Rubens oil sketch for a large scaled work, this Bierstadt canvas is it; every brushstroke seemingly applied with great rapidity and sureness. Though a study for a larger work, it is not a small painting, and shows the strength of Bierstadt's talent at a late stage in his career when he was out of fashion with his contemporaries.

> Martha Hutson, "Mr. and Mrs. John D. Rockefeller 3rd: Collection of American Art," *American Art Review* 3, no. 4 (July–August 1976): 82, 83

Provenance
[Hirschl & Adler Galleries, New York, 1970]

John D. Rockefeller 3rd and Blanchette Hooker Rockefeller, New York, 1970–1979

FAMSF, 1979.7.11

Exhibition History
San Francisco 1976, exh. no. 44

Tokyo 1982, exh. no. 33

FAMSF, *Albert Bierstadt: An Observer of Air, Light and the Feeling of a Place*, 1985, no exh. no.

Included in the San Francisco venue of the Brooklyn Museum's *Albert Bierstadt: Art and Enterprise*, 1991, not in publ.

Related Works
Sketch for "The Last of the Buffalo," 1888
Oil on paper, 13½ x 18 in.
Buffalo Bill Historical Center, Cody, Wyo.

The Last of the Buffalo, 1888
Oil on canvas, 71¼ x 119¼ in.
The Corcoran Gallery of Art, Washington, D.C.

Indian Buffalo Hunter
Oil on canvas, 30 x 44 in.
M. Knoedler & Co., New York, as of 1956

The Last of the Buffalo
Oil on canvas, 26 x 36 in.
Auction sale, Christie's, New York, 26 May 1988, lot no. 143

---

102 THE SONATA, 1889

Oil on canvas, 44¼ x 26 in.
Signed and dated lower left: *Irving R. Wiles 1889*

IRVING RAMSAY WILES

b. Utica, N.Y. 1861
d. Peconic, N.Y. 1948

Irving R. Wiles . . . is one of the strongest of the younger American figure painters, and the son of L. M. Wiles, the landscape painter. . . .

After study with his father, Carroll Beckwith and William M. Chase, Mr. Wiles in 1882 went to Paris and studied under Carolus Duran and at Julian's school. In 1884 the artist took a studio in this city. In 1886 he carried off the third Hallgarten prize at the National Academy, and won this year the Clarke prize at the same institution, with his "Sonata."

> Unidentified New York newspaper clipping, 1890, quoting the *New York Herald* for 22 December 1889, Chapellier Gallery Papers, AAA, roll N68–101, frame 460

Irving R. Wiles had taken up music as a boy, studying with the late Henri Appi. . . . At twenty, Mr. Wiles had such command of the violin that distinction as a musician was prophesied of him. At the earnest solicitation of his father, who was a painter, he consented to study at the Art Students' League classes for one year, with the privilege, if not sufficiently interested, of following any other bent at the expiration of that time. He found in painting his life work. . . .

It is natural, therefore, perhaps, that he is versatile in his painting. He is not a man of one idea, though the one idea impelling him always is good painting. . . . Known everywhere as a portrait painter, it is not so generally known that he is also a painter of pictures. Yet in his pictures . . . there is a charm of subject and execution of color and composition which has attracted amateurs and museums, who have found in these canvases where his own fancy has absolutely free play a note of individuality that has made its way home.

Dana Carroll, "The Varied Work of Irving R. Wiles," *Arts and Decoration* 1, no. 10 (August 1911): 402–403

As a painter Mr. Wiles is greatly to the fore just at present, and his pictures are justly admired for a style that is not so much pleasing for what it accurately puts in as for what it leaves out. His art has originality, in that the situations presented are new, the attitudes possessing both the grace of naturalness and, what is not quite the same thing, the naturalness of grace. You can appreciate his work more when you understand that he believes art should present only the beautiful. He does not believe, for instance, that a picture should be interesting because it presents a moral lesson of some kind. . . . Mr. Wiles prefers the genius of Sargent, who paints no harrowing scenes, and whose pictures leave so much to the imagination. He would himself rather that his pictures attract the eye by a subtle suggestion of beauty than that they attracted attention because of a deed being enacted or the merits of a good or bad deed shown. . . .

. . . In both the pictures, entitled the one "Dreaming" and the other "The Sonata," will be found evidenced this idea of beauty alone. No craving after purpose of any sort. A mere idyll, each, and caught from out a prosaic enough reality.

Theodore Dreiser, "Art Work of Irving R. Wiles," *Metropolitan Magazine* 7 (1898): 357–359

Provenance
William T. Evans (1843–1918), Glen Ridge, N.J., 1892–1900

[Auction sale, American Art Galleries, New York, 31 January–2 February 1900, lot no. 248, sold for $525]

Joseph S. Isidor (ca. 1860–1941), New York, 1900

Estate of Alice Bernheim, New York, before 1917

Joseph Green Butler, Jr. (1840–1927), Youngstown, Ohio, 1917–1919

The Butler Institute of American Art, Youngstown, Ohio, 1919–1968

[Kennedy Galleries, New York, 1968]

John D. Rockefeller 3rd and Blanchette Hooker Rockefeller, New York, 1968–1979

Berthe Saunders, New York, 1979–1984

[Wunderlich & Co., New York, 1984–1985]

Blanchette Hooker Rockefeller, New York, 1985

FAMSF, 1985.7

Exhibition History
New York, National Academy of Design, *Sixty-fourth Annual Exhibition*, 1889, exh. no. 234 (awarded Thomas B. Clarke prize for best figurative composition; for sale, $500)

Chicago, World's Columbian Exposition, *Department of Fine Arts*, 1893, exh. no. 1125

New York, Lotos Club, *Loan Exhibition of Works by American Figure Painters*, 1894

New York, National Academy of Design, *Irving R. Wiles*, 1988, no exh. no.

Selected References
Margaretta M. Lovell and Marc Simpson, "Essay on a Painting: *The Sonata*," *Triptych* 30 (June–July 1986): 20–22

The American Canvas, pp. 192–193, 244

---

103 WELL I SHOULD NOT MURMUR, FOR GOD JUDGES BEST, CA. 1890

Oil on wood panel, 13 x 8 in.
Signed upper left: *W M Chase*

WILLIAM MERRITT CHASE

b. Williamsburg, Ind. 1849
d. New York, N.Y. 1916

It may truthfully be said that artists probably get more pleasure out of portrait painting than almost any other kind of art work. In portraiture they deal with character and individuality. Each sitter presents some new phase of personality that one has never done before. There is constant variety; constant study in the work.

Chase, quoted in Carolyn Kinder Carr, *William Merritt Chase: Portraits*, exh. cat. (Akron, Ohio: Akron Art Museum, 1982), p. 7

Mr. Chase would, every few weeks, paint a portrait before the class. Those occasions, so interesting and instructive, were indeed Red Letter days.

The model posed, he would study long, in silence, the relation of head to background—note the principal characteristics of features, and formulate well in his mind his painting as a whole—and that was one of the great principles emphasized in his class instruction, namely —that a painting well thought out is more than half finished before touching brush to canvas.

Starting with a middle toned background, he would with a few masterly strokes indicate general outline and features—would place darkest shadows under features and highest light on forehead—then after starting middle tone of flesh—would with much careful thought

before each stroke, touch from one to another the many intervening tones or planes. He would make but few strokes of the brush—perhaps only one, before walking backward across the room to note the carrying quality or right relationship of planes.

Ever mindful of the underlying construction of the head he very methodically placed the tones—keeping the whole head "going," so to speak—in a mosaic sort of way.

F. Usher De Voll, quoted in Carolyn Kinder Carr, *William Merritt Chase: Portraits*, exh. cat. (Akron, Ohio: Akron Art Museum, 1982), pp. 34–35

Financial pressures forced Chase to raise funds through a major sale at Ortgies Fifth Avenue Galleries on March 6, 1891. He offered sixty-seven items in a bad market; prices remained very low for American art, as European paintings were still in vogue. The sale process used by American artists included an open house at the gallery for several days, then an auction on the final evening. . . . Prior to the sale there was considerable favorable publicity about Chase and the paintings to be sold, but the large crowd that came to the auction did not engage in lively bidding. . . . Some pictures went to dealers such as the Montross gallery, and a few went to collectors such as W. T. Evans, but a number were puchased by fellow artists for as little as $30. *Art Amateur* called the sale "The Slaughter of Mr. Chase's Pictures."

Keith L. Bryant, Jr., *William Merritt Chase: A Genteel Bohemian* (Columbia and London: University of Missouri Press, 1991), pp. 146–147

"But joking aside, my dear Will, I can't tell you how appalled I was to get a list of the sale of your pictures" . . . [referring to the 6 March 1891 sale of Chase's work], "it wasn't only awful but shameful. If you can get any comfort from the fact I will tell you that since receiving it and when I feel blue about my work I say to myself, 'Good God, what does it all matter since nobody will care a rap whether you try or don't try' . . . A fellow works himself into a sweat and after surmounting all kinds of obstacles sees that his labor was thrown away after all. So why not take life easily and give up this damned driving after something. . . . God, I believe if such a thing were to happen to me I would give up painting. One must be pretty courageous to stand it. I can well understand how you feel about it dear boy and what a dreadful shock it must have been at first. And yet I know that in spite of all you will keep on painting as if nothing at all had happened, and God bless you for it."

> Robert Blum to Chase, 1891, quoted in Katherine Metcalf Roof, *The Life and Art of William Merritt Chase* (1917; New York: Hacker Art Books, 1975), pp. 163–164

Provenance

The artist, to 1891

[Auction sale, Ortgies & Co., at the Fifth Avenue Art Galleries, New York, 6 March 1891, lot no. 50, sold for $45]

Charles Hovey Pepper (1864–1950), Concord, Mass., 1891–1950

[Castano Galleries, Boston]

[Steven Envelis, Marblehead, Mass.]

The Burlington Trust, Lynn, Mass.

[M. Knoedler & Co., New York, 1967]

John D. Rockefeller 3rd and Blanchette Hooker Rockefeller, New York, 1967–1979

FAMSF, 1979.7.28

---

104 YELLOW DAISIES IN A BROWN BOWL, CA. 1890

Oil on burlap, 22⅛ x 15⅛ in.
Signed lower right: *M J Heade*

MARTIN JOHNSON HEADE

b. Lumberville, Pa. 1819
d. St. Augustine, Fla. 1904

April 7, 1948
Dear Mr. McIntyre,
I list below the Heades I now own or have for sale:
[he then names ten works, including]
  5. *Yellow Daisies in a Brown Bowl* on a gold colored velvet drape canvas, 22 x 15 inches—signed lower right

> Victor D. Spark to Robert G. McIntyre, 7 April 1948, Robert G. McIntyre Papers, AAA, roll 3092, frame 829

In the late years Heade painted far more still life than landscape. The decade of the nineties found him working with declining strength, as we have seen, on Florida marsh scenes and other subjects; but once again, refusing to give in either to advanced age, popular style, or the fact that he and realistic painting were more out of date than ever, he produced, with miraculous energy, a final series of flower paintings that equals anything in his œuvre. . . .

In this late search for new subjects, Heade painted many different types of flowers, apparently not repeating those which failed to satisfy him. . . . An even stranger effect was produced with the *Yellow Daisies in a Bowl* (Cat. no. 313) [not the FAMSF painting], where common field flowers (symbols of innocence) are set off against red velvet, giving them an importance that seems inappropriate; again, this experiment was not repeated.

> Theodore E. Stebbins, Jr., *The Life and Works of Martin Johnson Heade* (New Haven and London: Yale University Press, 1975), pp. 166, 167

Provenance
[Victor D. Spark Gallery, New York, by 1948–1969]

[Graham Gallery, New York, 1969–1970]

John D. Rockefeller 3rd and

Blanchette Hooker Rockefeller, New York, 1970–1979

FAMSF, 1979.7.51

Selected Reference
Robert G. McIntyre, *Martin Johnson Heade, 1819–1904* (New York: Pantheon Press, 1948), p. 60

Related Works
Yellow Daisies in a Bowl, ca. 1885–1895
Oil on canvas, 14½ x 23½ in.
Private collection, as of 1975

Golden Marguerites, ca. 1890
Oil on canvas, 24 x 15 in.
Auction sale, Skinner, Bolton, Mass., 18 November 1982, lot no. 94

---

105 ORANGES IN TISSUE PAPER, CA. 1890

Oil on canvas, 10 x 17 in.
Signed lower right: *W. J. McCloskey*

WILLIAM J. McCLOSKEY

b. Philadelphia, Pa. 1859
d. Orange County, Calif. 1941

Most prominent among the [Los Angeles] portrait painters were . . . Alberta Binford McCloskey (1863–1911), and her husband William Joseph McCloskey. The McCloskeys worked in both oil and watercolor. She had been a pupil of William Merritt Chase in New York, while her husband had studied under Christian Schussele and Thomas Eakins at the Pennsylvania Academy of the Fine Arts. By 1884 the two had opened a portrait studio in Los Angeles in Child's Grand Opera House, to which they invited the public on Wednesdays. The *Los Angeles City Directory* listed them sporadically over the next twenty

years, and they are also known to have lived in New York, England, and Paris; probably, like many nineteenth-century portraitists, they moved frequently in search of commissions.

Although they apparently lived by their portraiture, the McCloskeys seem to have excelled in still lifes and genre pieces. William McCloskey specialized in paper-wrapped fruit, a subject only two or three other still-life artists attempted.

Nancy Dustin Wall Moure, *Painting and Sculpture in Los Angeles, 1900–1945*, exh. cat. (Los Angeles: Los Angeles County Museum of Art, 1980), p. 8

What really distinguishes him from his contemporaries is the tissue paper in which some of his fruit is always wrapped. The treatment of this paper—white for wrapping oranges, pastel for lemons—is a marvel of illusionism, the thinness and transparency, the crinkly texture, the delicate coloration tinged by the orange or yellow citrus fruit within constituting the real subject of the painting. . . . "Master of the Wrapped Citrus" may seem an epithet that damns with faint praise, but such is McCloskey's distinction.

William H. Gerdts, *Painters of the Humble Truth: Masterpieces of American Still Life, 1801–1939*, exh. cat. (Columbia and London: University of Missouri Press, with the Philbrook Art Center, 1981), pp. 206–207

It is probably little more than hindsight to see in McCloskey's skill the influence of his teacher—Eakins, not Schussele. . . . [A] sense of the "real," of actual physical presence that Eakins gained from his teacher, the great French academician Jean Léon Gérôme, is present here. And the sense of "rightness," of careful balance in McCloskey's compositions bespeaks Eakins, as does the sense of drama. McCloskey's fruit is richly colored and always dramatically lighted, so that it shines out within a darkness . . . just as Eakins's figures glow radiantly from their somber surroundings. And, further, McCloskey shares with many artists of his age, including Eakins, a sense of isolation and melancholy.

McCloskey's work is without pretense, and it would probably be pretentious to look for a source of his interest in this wrapped-fruit subject matter. He probably painted it because he could, and because he knew that the illusionism involved would attract attention and patrons.

William H. Gerdts and Russell Burke, *American Still-Life Painting* (New York, Washington, London: Praeger Publishers, 1971), p. 166

Provenance
Walter Wallace, New York, by 1955

[M. Knoedler & Co., New York, 1955–1963]

Lawrence A. Fleischman (b. 1925) and Barbara Greenberg Fleischman (b. 1924), Detroit, 1963–1966

[Kennedy Galleries, New York, 1966]

John D. Rockefeller 3rd and Blanchette Hooker Rockefeller, New York, 1966–1993

FAMSF, 1993.35.21

Exhibition History
Springfield, Mass., Gill's Art Galleries, *Fourteenth Annual Exhibition of Oil Paintings by Eminent American Artists*, 1891, exh. no. 89

Tucson, University of Arizona Art Gallery, *American Painting, 1765–1963: Selections from the Lawrence A. and Barbara Fleischman Collection of American Art*, 1964, exh. no. 66

Philadelphia, Pennsylvania Academy of the Fine Arts, *Small Paintings of Large Import from the Collection of Lawrence A. and Barbara Fleischman of Detroit, Michigan*, 1964, exh. no. 29

San Francisco 1976, exh. no. 84

Tokyo 1982, exh. no. 48

FAMSF, *Director's Choice: Twenty Years of Collecting*, 1987, no publ.

---

106 STUDY FOR ''BOUGUEREAU'S ATELIER AT THE ACADÉMIE JULIAN, PARIS,'' 1891

Graphite on laid paper, 17⅜ x 14⅛ in.
Inscribed lower left: *Sketching . . . /Academy . . . /*[illegible]

JEFFERSON DAVID CHALFANT
b. Chester County, Pa. 1856
d. Wilmington, Del. 1931

Jefferson David Chalfant learned the trade of cabinetmaking from his father, with whom he worked from 1870 to 1879, finishing railroad cars and painting their interiors. Upon moving to Wilmington, Delaware, Chalfant took up landscape painting as an avocation and opened a studio in 1883. In 1886, inspired by the example of William M. Harnett, Chalfant began to paint trompe l'oeil still lifes of considerable skill and wit. In 1886 Chalfant also acquired an agent in H. Wood Sullivan, who promoted the exhibition and purchase of Chalfant's art. Sullivan introduced the artist to the prominent New York art patron Alfred Corning Clark, who sent Chalfant to Paris in 1890 to acquire the professional training he thus far lacked.

Chalfant spent two years studying at the Académie Julian under William-Adolphe Bouguereau (1825–1905) and Jules-Joseph Lefebvre (1836–1911), an experience that encouraged him to attempt more ambitious figure paintings and interior arrangements. Upon his return to Wilmington in 1892, Chalfant devoted himself to small-scale genre works, whose subjects often reflected his interests in craftsmanship. At the same time Chalfant worked on mechanical inventions and obtained several patents. After the turn of the century he turned away from genre subjects, spending the last years of his career fulfilling portrait commissions.

Sally Mills, in *The American Canvas: Paintings from the Collection of The Fine Arts Museums of San Francisco* (New York: Hudson Hills Press, in association with The Fine Arts Museums of San Francisco, 1989), p. 170

Chalfant first made exacting pencil drawings for genre subjects that are beautifully detailed and carefully composed. . . . The drawings are precise pencil renderings of the genre compositions, void of shading or gradation. Although complex, the outline drawings were an important step toward the completed oil painting. Placing charcoal on the reverse, Chalfant transferred the drawing onto canvas or panel by tracing the image, a technique which accounts for similarity in size of the drawings to the paintings. An intermediate oil study was often executed, and from that the finished painting was completed.

Joan H. Gorman, *Jefferson David Chalfant, 1856–1931*, exh. cat. (Chadds Ford, Pa.: Brandywine River Museum, 1979), p. 20

Provenance

The artist and Katherine Braunstein Chalfant (1877–1923), Wilmington, Del., 1891–1931

Descended in family to his son and daughter-in-law, J. David Chalfant, Jr. (1904–1948) and Margaret Clough Chalfant (b. 1906), Wilmington, Del., 1931–1964

[David David, Philadelphia, 1964]

[Victor Spark, New York, 1965]

Ambassador J. William Middendorf II (b. 1924) and Isabelle Middendorf, New York, by 1967–1973

[Auction sale, Sotheby Parke-Bernet, New York, 28 September 1973, lot no. 21 (lot includes related painting), sold for $14,000]

Yale Kneeland (b. 1937), New York, and George Peabody Gardner III (b. 1948), New York, 1973–1977

[William Beadleston Fine Art, New York, 1977]

John D. Rockefeller 3rd and Blanchette Hooker Rockefeller, New York, 1977–1979

FAMSF, 1979.7.27

Exhibition History

New York, The Metropolitan Museum of Art, *American Paintings and Historical Prints from the Middendorf Collection*, 1967, exh. no. 48b

Philadelphia, Pennsylvania Academy of the Fine Arts, *In This Academy: The Pennsylvania Academy of the Fine Arts, 1805–1976*, 1976, exh. no. 54

Chadds Ford, Pa., Brandywine River Museum, *Jefferson David Chalfant, 1856–1931*, 1979, exh. no. 4

Williamstown, Mass., Sterling and Francine Clark Art Institute, *In the Studio: The Making of Art in Nineteenth-Century France*, 1981, exh. no. 30

FAMSF, *The Studio of the Artist*, 1981, no publ.

FAMSF, *Viewpoints VI: The Studied Figure: Tradition and Innovation in American Art Academies, 1865–1915*, 1989, no exh. no.

Selected Reference

The American Canvas, pp. 170, 242

Related Work

Bouguereau's Atelier at the Académie Julian, Paris, 1891
Oil on wood panel, 11⅛ x 14⅜ in.
FAMSF, 1979.7.26

Oil on wood panel, 11⅛ x 14⅝ in.
Signed and dated lower left: *J. D. Chalfant/1891—*; inscribed on reverse: *Atelier de Bouguereau/à l'Académie Julian/J. D. Chalfant/ Paris.—1891—*

JEFFERSON DAVID CHALFANT

b. Chester County, Pa. 1856
d. Wilmington, Del. 1931

This city is to have a representative in the art studio of Paris during this year. J. D. Chalfant, artist, will sail about April 1 with the purpose of spending several years in study abroad. The greater portion of his time will be spent in the French capital. Chalfant has almost infinite patience and is capable of [any amount] of painstaking labor to bring his work to his own measure of perfection. He is a realistic rather than ideal painter.

Wilmington, Del., correspondent to *The Times*, 8 February 1890, clipping in Jefferson David Chalfant Papers, AAA, roll 2427, frame 571

_____

While in Paris, Mr. Chalfant received his first instruction. His studies were in the nude at the Julian Academy.

The models in the academies are not as finely formed as those who go to private studios, as they are not so well paid, and only good models can command high prices; but the work that Mr. Chalfant has done from even poor subjects is fine in modeling and excellent as to flesh tint.

Caroline Rudolph, *(Wilmington, Del.) Morning News*, 1895, clipping in Jefferson David Chalfant Papers, AAA, roll 2427, frame 575

_____

The Académie is divided into nine different "Ateliers." Of these, five are devoted to men and four to women, the ateliers for the two sexes being wholly separate. Those for men are divided among the masters as follows: Bouguereau and Fleury; Constant and Lefebvre;

Doucet; Flameng and Ferrier; Chapu. . . . Upon entering, the student is free to select for himself the masters under whom he will study, and thereupon enters the atelier presided over by them.

In each atelier two models, of different sex, pose for eight hours daily, interrupted only for a rest of ten minutes every hour and of an hour at noonday. The manner of selecting models is interesting. The candidate disrobes and mounts the pedestal, taking many different positions. The "*massier*" (a student at the head of the school), takes a vote of the pupils amid a noise and confusion that is indescribable. If the majority approve, the model is employed. If by chance several of the weaker sex come together to be judged, the decision takes on somewhat the character of a judgment of Paris, not omitting the apple of discord,. the fortunate one who is preferred being the subject of envy to those not selected. The voting over, the atelier at once resumes its former quiet.

M. Riccardo Nobili, "The Académie Julian," *The Cosmopolitan* 8, no. 6 (April 1890): 747–748

———

On Wednesdays and Saturdays, Bouguereau frequently arrived early and cloistered himself with M. Julian in order to question him about the students' work, their enthusiasm, their endeavors, the progress they had made and what advice and encouragement to give them. After that . . . Bouguereau would stop in front of each easel, criticize the drawing and adjust the palette, and never leave without a word of encouragement: "We'll see how you've done by Saturday, my friend."

Académie Julian student Alfred Nettement, 1906, quoted in *The American Canvas: Paintings from the Collection of The Fine Arts Museums of San Francisco* (New York: Hudson Hills Press, in association with The Fine Arts Museums of San Francisco, 1989), p. 170

Provenance
The artist and Katherine Braunstein Chalfant (1877–1923), Wilmington, Del., 1891–1931

Descended in family to his son and daughter-in-law, J. David Chalfant, Jr. (1904–1948) and Margaret Clough Chalfant (b. 1906), Wilmington, Del., 1931–1964

[David David, Philadelphia, 1964]

[Victor Spark, New York, 1965]

Ambassador J. William Middendorf II (b. 1924) and Isabelle Middendorf, New York, by 1967–1973

[Auction sale, Sotheby Parke-Bernet, New York, 28 September 1973, lot no. 21 (lot includes related drawing), sold for $14,000]

Yale Kneeland (b. 1937), New York, and George Peabody Gardner III (b. 1948), New York, 1973–1977

[William Beadleston Fine Art, New York, 1977]

John D. Rockefeller 3rd and Blanchette Hooker Rockefeller, New York, 1977–1979

FAMSF, 1979.7.26

Exhibition History
The Wilmington Society of the Fine Arts, Delaware Art Center, *Jefferson D. Chalfant, 1856–1931,* 1959, exh. no. 4

New York, The Metropolitan Museum of Art, *American Paintings and Historical Prints from the Middendorf Collection,* 1967, exh. no. 48a

Philadelphia, Pennsylvania Academy of the Fine Arts, *In This Academy: The Pennsylvania Academy of the Fine Arts, 1805–1976,* 1976, exh. no. 55

Chadds Ford, Pa., Brandywine River Museum, *Jefferson David Chalfant, 1856–1931,* 1979, exh. no. 5

FAMSF, *The Studio of the Artist,* 1981, no publ.

FAMSF, *Viewpoints VI: The Studied Figure: Tradition and Innovation in American Art Academies, 1865–1915,* 1989, no exh. no.

Selected References
David B. Cass, *In the Studio: The Making of Art in Nineteenth-Century France,* exh. cat. (Williamstown, Mass.: Sterling and Francine Clark Art Institute, 1981), p. 41

The American Canvas, pp. 170–171, 242

H. Barbara Weinberg, *The Lure of Paris: Nineteenth-Century American Painters and Their Teachers* (New York: Abbeville Press, 1991), p. 256

Related Work
Study for "Bouguereau's Atelier at the Académie Julian, Paris," 1891 Graphite on laid paper, 17⅜ x 14⅛ in. FAMSF, 1979.7.27

Watercolor over graphite on wove paper, 14 x 20 in.
Signed and dated lower left: *HOMER 1892*

WINSLOW HOMER

b. Boston, Mass. 1836
d. Prout's Neck, Maine 1910

He was a true citizen of the wilderness. . . . His clothes seemed to have been put on him once for all, like the bark of a tree, a long time ago. . . . This woodsman, this trapper, this hunter, this fisherman, this sitter on a log, and philosopher, was the real proprietor of the region over which he was willing to guide the stranger. . . . In all that country, he alone had noticed the sunsets, and observed the . . . season, taken pleasure in the woods for themselves, and climbed mountains solely for the sake of the prospect.

Charles Dudley Warner, describing the Adirondack guide Orson Phelps, in *In the Wilderness* (Boston, 1878), quoted in Helen Cooper, *Winslow Homer Watercolors*, exh. cat. (New Haven: Yale University Press, for the National Gallery of Art, 1986), p. 179

You will see, in the future I will live by my watercolors.

Homer to Charles R. Henschel, quoted in Lloyd Goodrich, *Winslow Homer* (New York: Macmillan Company, 1945), p. 159

We have looked over a portfolio of his watercolor sketches of the Adirondacks, where he has lately been hunting, armed with a box of water colors and those big brushes which he wields with such bewildering skill, and we are more than ever impressed by his superb breadth and mastery. He gives a wonderfully vivid idea of immense scale of things, the wildness, the grandeur, the rudeness, and almost oppressive solitude of the great Northern forest. Against

this strange and stupendous background, as is his wont, he projects the virile and sinewy figures of the hardy out-door type of fearless men—the hunters, guides and fishermen of the wilderness.

Boston Evening Transcript, 23 December 1892, quoted in Nicolai Cikovsky, Jr., *Winslow Homer Watercolors* (New York: Hugh Lauter Levin Associates, 1991), pp. 117–118

Provenance
[M. Knoedler & Co., New York, by 1908]

J. R. Andrews (d. 1915), Bath, Maine, 1908–1916

[Auction sale, American Art Association, New York, 27–28 January 1916, lot no. 108, sold for $650]

[M. Knoedler & Co., New York, 1916–1917]

Charles R. Henschel (1885–1956) and Ruth K. Henschel (1885–1974), New York, 1917–1970

[M. Knoedler & Co., New York, 1970]

John D. Rockefeller 3rd and Blanchette Hooker Rockefeller, New York, 1970–1979

FAMSF, 1979.7.55

Exhibition History
Philadelphia Watercolor Club, *Eighth Annual Exhibition*, 1910, exh. no. 110

New York, The Museum of Modern Art, *Homer, Ryder, Eakins*, 1930, exh. no. 31

The Art Institute of Chicago, *A Century of Progress: Exhibition of Paintings and Sculpture*, 1934, exh. no. 470

New York, M. Knoedler & Co., *Winslow Homer, Artist: Loan Exhibition of Water Colours*, 1936, exh. no. 18

Paris, Musée du Jeu de Paume, *Trois siècles d'art aux Etats-Unis*, 1938, exh. no. 85

Boston, Institute of Modern Art, *Watercolors and Drawings by Winslow Homer*, 1941, exh. no. 11

New York, Wildenstein, *A Loan Exhibition of Winslow Homer, for the Benefit of the New York Botanical Garden*, 1947, exh. no. 69

New York, M. Knoedler & Co., *To Honor Henry McBride*, 1949, no. 16

Washington, D.C., National Gallery of Art, *Winslow Homer: A Retrospective Exhibition*, 1958, exh. no. 145

Blue Mountain Lake, New York, The Adirondack Museum, *Winslow Homer in the Adirondacks*, 1959, exh. no. 10

Washington, D.C., National Gallery of Art, *Water Colors by Winslow Homer from the Collection of Mrs. Charles R. Henschel*, 1962, exh. no. 10

Buffalo, Albright-Knox Art Gallery, *Watercolors by Winslow Homer, 1836–1910*, 1966, exh. no. 30

New York, Whitney Museum of American Art, *Winslow Homer*, 1973, exh. no. 126

San Francisco 1976, exh. no. 73

FAMSF, *Master Drawings from the Achenbach Foundation for Graphic Arts*, 1985, exh. no. 94

Washington, D.C., National Gallery of Art, *Winslow Homer Watercolors*, 1986, exh. no. 169

Selected References
Lloyd Goodrich, "Winslow Homer, *The Arts* 6, no. 4 (October 1924): 202

Theodore Bolton, "Water Colors by Homer: Critique and Catalogue," *The Fine Arts* (April 1932): 52

"The Henschel Homers: A Collector's Picking of the Watercolors," *Art News* 40, no. 9 (July 1941): 21

Nicolai Cikovsky, Jr., *Winslow Homer Watercolors* (New York: Hugh Lauter Levin Associates, 1991), p. 76

Object record, manuscript catalogue raisonné of the works of Winslow Homer, by Lloyd Goodrich, courtesy of the City University of New York, Lloyd Goodrich and Edith Havens Goodrich, Whitney Museum of American Art Record of the Works of Winslow Homer

---

109 JOB LOT CHEAP, 1892

Oil on canvas, 29⅝ x 39¾ in.
Signed and dated lower right: *J. F. Peto/92* (date now largely abraded)

JOHN FREDERICK PETO
b. Philadelphia, Pa. 1854
d. New York, N.Y. 1907

Peto . . . was essentially discovered by the art critic Alfred Frankenstein in the late forties, when Frankenstein was researching Harnett's career and the flowering of trompe-l'oeil painting that lasted from the Gilded Age through the turn of the century (or what he called "the saloon era in American painting"). Frankenstein found that the paintings that had been thought to be by Harnett working in a painterly, brushier style—even paintings that had Harnett's monogram on the front—were actually by Peto. Thirty-five years ago, Peto was virtually unknown. Records showed that he sent a few pictures to the Pennsylvania Academy of the Fine Arts when his work was getting under way, and that when he was in his mid-thirties he moved from Philadelphia to Island Heights, New Jersey, a small river-front town. He married, and lived there with his wife and daughter in almost complete obscurity for the next two decades, dying in 1907, at the age of fifty-three. He never had a formal exhibition, he seems to have kept no records and made no statements about his pictures, and there were only a handful of accounts of him or of his work in newspapers of the time.

Sanford Schwartz, "The Art World: The Rookie," *The New Yorker*, 15 August 1983, p. 80

The strongest influence upon Peto's career, without much question, was William Michael Harnett. Harnett and Peto knew each other, apparently quite well, before Harnett left Philadelphia to go to Europe in 1880. . . .

According to Peto's daughter, her father talked about Harnett constantly, invoking his name as the standard of perfection in still life. Peto painted many mug-and-pipe pictures, many writing-table still lifes, and many still lifes of money, of books on shelves and on packing cases, of violins, guns, and plucked fowl hanging against doors. All these are eminently Harnettian motifs, and some . . . seem to be Harnettian inventions. . . .

Although he was strongly influenced by Harnett in certain matters of iconography, Peto is no mere Harnett imitator. His style—drawing, use of color, and application of paint—is poles apart from Harnett's at every point in his career, and he also had his own world of subjects which Harnett never entered. . . . To be sure, Peto, like Harnett, will often dangle a torn-off book cover, suspended precariously by a single thread, over the edge of a table top. The prototype of this device can be found in a seventeenth-century still life by the Dutch master, Hubert van Ravesteyn; its route to the nineteenth-century Philadelphians lies through entirely unknown territory.

Alfred Frankenstein, *After the Hunt: William Harnett and Other American Still Life Painters, 1870–1900*, rev. ed. (Berkeley and Los Angeles: University of California Press, 1969), p. 101

Bob Carlen turned up in town today, with the slide of the Peto. It is, as you say, a remarkable one. As you will remember, the crudely hand-lettered sign, "Job Lot Cheap," also appears, in the same place, in a Harnett of 1878. . . . I cannot read the signature and date on the slide, but you say the picture was done in 1892. This is the year Harnett died. Could it be a kind of requiem for Harnett?

> Alfred Frankenstein to E. P. Richardson, 22 June 1967, E. P. Richardson Collection,
> National Museum of American Art/National Portrait Gallery Library, Washington, D.C.

———

Peto sometimes took ideas from Harnett, as he clearly did in this case. The Harnett version [*Job Lot Cheap*, Reynolda House, Winston-Salem, N.C.] was painted in 1878. The Peto . . . belongs stylistically with the richest period of the artist's career and is therefore at least twenty years younger than the Harnett. One does not need to expatiate any longer on the radiant textures and powerful contrasts of light and shade which are so characteristic of Peto. Here he sets Harnett's books in an architectural setting worthy of Josef Albers or any other geometric-abstract painter of recent years, and gives the whole the tragic tone which is uniquely his.

> Alfred Frankenstein, *The Reality of Appearance: The Trompe l'Œil Tradition in American Painting*,
> exh. cat. (New York: The New York Graphic Society, for the University Art Museum, Berkeley,
> 1970), p. 100

———

In terms of subject alone, these experiments bring us at last to one of Peto's central and most interesting images—books. From the beginning of his career books were present as ancillary props, components in the larger context of library furnishings and the conventions of American still-life painting. But as books crowded the candlestick, mug, and inkwell off his shelves, they gained increasing attention for their own power, both as repeated shapes in a composition and as repositories of the literary arts. On a more immediate, personal level books were all about the Peto house; they were familiar parts of his interior landscape of living room and studio. Thus, his paintings of books were acts of delineating his biography by recording the contents of his life and the spaces in which he worked.

> John Wilmerding, *The Art of John F. Peto and the Idea of Still-Life Painting in Nineteenth-Century
> America*, exh. cat. (Washington, D.C.: National Gallery of Art, 1983), pp. 121–122

———

Perhaps the apotheosis of Peto in his elegiac mood is the painting . . . called "Job Lot Cheap." It shows a bookstore far gone in decay, and we can read it as an elegy for an old order that was being sold up and sold off and was in any case no longer good for much. To this visitor it seemed that the word "Job" in the title can also be read in its Biblical connotation. Be that as it may, there is a resonance to Peto's best work that puts it in the class of high art, and it is good to see that fact so ably and so thoroughly set out for all to see.

> John Russell, "An American Master Comes into His Own," *New York Times*, 30 January 1983

Provenance
The artist and Christine Pearl Smith Peto (1869–1945), Island Heights, N.J., 1892–1945

Descended in family to son-in-law and daughter, George Washington Smiley (1885–1953) and Helen Serril Peto Smiley (1893–1978), Island Heights, N.J., 1945–ca. 1967

[Carlen Galleries, Philadelphia, by 1967]

John D. Rockefeller 3rd and Blanchette Hooker Rockefeller, New York, 1967–1979

FAMSF, 1979.7.81

Exhibition History
Berkeley, Calif., University Art Museum, *The Reality of Appearance: The Trompe l'Œil Tradition in American Painting*, 1970, exh. no. 60

San Francisco 1976, exh. no. 88

Tokyo 1982, exh. no. 47

Washington, D.C., National Gallery of Art, *Important Information Inside: The Art of John F. Peto and the Idea of Still-Life Painting in Nineteenth-Century America*, 1983, no exh. no.

Selected References
Alfred Frankenstein, "Yankee Rhyparography," *Art News* 69, no. 1 (March 1970): 51

The American Canvas, pp. 18, 166–167, 242

Andrew Walker, "'Job Lot Cheap': Books, Bindings, and the Old Bookseller," in Doreen Bolger et al., *William M. Harnett*, exh. cat. (Fort Worth: Amon Carter Museum; New York: The Metropolitan Museum of Art and Harry N. Abrams, 1992), pp. 236–237

Oil on canvas, 19⅞ x 15⅞ in.
Signed and dated lower right: *TMORAN . 1893* (initials in monogram)

THOMAS MORAN

b. Bolton, Lancashire, England
 1837
d. Santa Barbara, Calif. 1926

Thomas Moran, one of the greatest of American artists, is a guest of the St. James. Mr. Moran is on his way to the Yellowstone national park. He will be accompanied on his trip by W. H. Jackson of this city and the world's fair commissioners of Wyoming, the object of the trip being to secure materials for a large picture to be exhibited at the world's fair.

"A Mountain Painter," unidentified Wyoming newspaper clipping, 15 June 1892, Thomas Moran Papers, AAA, roll NTM-4, frame 559

———————

After a day at Norris we left for the Grand Cañon where we stayed two days and made a great many photos. I saw so much to sketch that I have determined to return there myself after I have been to the Geyser Basins and the lake and spend a week at work there. It is as glorious in color as ever and I was completely carried away by its magnificence. I think I can paint a better picture of it than the old one after I have made my sketches. I will not attempt to say anything about it as no words can express the faintest notion of it. . . . I have been made much of at all the places in the park as the great and only "Moran" *the* painter of the Yellowstone and I am looked at curiously by all the people at the Hotels. . . .

I am very well satisfied with the artistic side of the trip so far and I think the financial part will pan out all right when I get some work out. Altogether this trip will prove of great advantage to me I am sure.

> Moran to Mary Nimmo Moran, Yellowstone Park, Wyoming, 26 July 1892, quoted in Amy O. Bassford and Fritiof Fryxell, eds., *Home-Thoughts, from Afar: Letters of Thomas Moran to Mary Nimmo Moran* (East Hampton, N.Y.: East Hampton Free Library, 1967), pp. 119, 121–122

I place no value upon literal transcripts from Nature. My general scope is not realistic; all my tendencies are toward idealization. Of course, all art must come through Nature: I do not mean to depreciate Nature or naturalism; but I believe that a place, as a place, has no value in itself for the artist only so far as it furnishes the material from which to construct a picture. Topography in art is valueless. The motive or incentive of my *Grand Cañon of the Yellowstone* [1872, U.S. Department of the Interior] was the gorgeous display of color that impressed itself upon me. Probably no scenery in the world presents such a combination. The forms are extremely wonderful and pictorial, and while I desired to tell truly of Nature, I did not wish to realize the scene literally, but to preserve and to convey its true impression. Every form introduced into the picture is within view from a given point, but the relations of the separate parts to one another are not always preserved. For instance, the precipitous rocks on the right were really at my back when I stood at that point, yet in their present position they are strictly true to pictorial Nature; and so correct is the whole representation that every member of the expedition with which I was connected declared, when he saw the painting, that he knew the exact spot which had been reproduced. My aim was to bring before the public the character of that region.

> Moran, quoted in Walter Montgomery, ed., *American Art and American Art Collections*, 2 vols. (1889; New York and London: Garland Publishing, 1978), 2:797

Thomas Moran's real master was J. M. W. Turner. My father traded his pictures to an old bookseller, for "The Rivers of France," the "Liber Studiorium," [*sic*] and everything that contained the work of "Turner," so that when he went to England, about 1860, he knew his master perfectly in black and white, but was stunned by the radiance of color which he had not imagined but which he, himself, found literally glowing in the "Yellowstone" country, later on in his life.

> Ruth B. Moran, "The Real Life of Thomas Moran as Known to His Daughter," *The American Magazine of Art* 17, no. 12 (December 1926): 646

Provenance

[Graham Gallery, New York, by 1969]

John D. Rockefeller 3rd and Blanchette Hooker Rockefeller, New York, 1969–1979

FAMSF, 1979.7.73

Exhibition History

San Francisco 1976, exh. no. 86

East Hampton, N.Y., Guild Hall Museum, *Thomas Moran: A Search for the Scenic*, 1981, exh. no. 4

Palm Springs, Calif., Palm Springs Desert Museum, *The West as Art: Changing Perceptions of Western Art in California Collections*, 1982, exh. no. 94

Tokyo 1982, exh. no. 4

Miami, Center for the Fine Arts, *In Quest of Excellence: Civic Pride, Patronage, Connoisseurship*, 1984, exh. no. 116

Sydney, The American-Australian Foundation for the Arts, in association with the Art Gallery of

New South Wales, *America: Art and the West*, 1986, exh. no. 29

Henry Art Gallery, University of Washington, Seattle, *Myth of the West*, 1990, no exh. no.

Related Works

The Grand Canyon of the Yellowstone, 1872

Oil on canvas, 84 x 144¼ in.

On loan to the National Museum of American Art, from the U.S. Department of the Interior, Washington, D.C.

Lower Falls, Yellowstone Park, 1893

Oil on canvas, 40½ x 60¼ in.

Thomas Gilcrease Institute of American History and Art, Tulsa, Okla.

The Grand Canyon of the Yellowstone, 1893–1901

Oil on canvas, 96½ x 168⅜ in.

National Museum of American Art, Washington, D.C.

Oil on canvas, 18⅛ x 24 in.
Signed and dated lower left: -*C-Y-TURNER-94-*

CHARLES YARDLEY TURNER

b. Baltimore, Md. 1850
d. New York, N.Y. 1918

After his graduation from the Maryland Institute in 1870, [Turner] spent several days as apprentice in the architectural office of Frank E. Davis and then set out for New York (1872). He studied for the next six years at the National Academy and at the Art Students' League, which he helped to organize, and continued to earn his living by photographic work. In 1878 he began study in Paris under Jean Paul Laurens, the mural decorator, Munkácsy, the Hungarian colorist, and Léon Bonnat, the figure painter. On his return to America he became an instructor in drawing and painting at the Art Students' League (1881–84) and a director of the Maryland Institute.

His earliest popular success was his "Grand Canal at Dordrecht" (1882), but he struck his stride as figure painter in the literary and historical field. . . . In 1886 he became an Academician. He was assistant director of decoration at the Chicago World's Fair (1893) and director of color at the Pan-American Exposition (1901) at Buffalo. Increasingly, however, his interests turned to mural painting.

W[illiam] S[ener] R[usk], "Charles Yardley Turner," *Dictionary of American Biography*, rev. ed., vol. 10, pt. I, p. 59

————

The material used in the construction of the Exposition buildings was iron, wood, glass, and what is called "staff." Thirty thousand tons or two thousand carloads of the latter material were consumed. . . . It is composed chiefly of powdered gypsum, the other constituents being alumina, glycerine, and dextrine. These are mixed with water without heat, and cast in molds in any desired shape and allowed to harden. . . . The casts are shallow, and about half an inch thick. They may be in any form—in imitation of cut stone, rock, faced stone, moldings or the most delicate designs. . . .

The ornamental work of the World's Fair grounds was planned and executed practically without regard to costs.

John J. Flinn, comp., *Official Guide to the World's Columbian Exposition* (Chicago: The Columbian Guide Company, 1893), pp. 37, 38

———————

[The photographer] C. D. Arnold scrupulously documented the construction of all the major buildings. . . . Arnold also took many shots of sculptors and painters at work on the decorative features of the Fair. Some of these photographs served as models for the paintings and chromolithographs that were created for D[aniel Hudson] Burnham and F[rancis Davis] Millet's *Book of the Builders*.

Diane Kirkpatrick, *The Fair View: Representations of the World's Columbian Exposition of 1893*, exh. cat. (Ann Arbor: University of Michigan Museum of Art, 1993), p. 24

Provenance
[Kennedy Galleries, New York, by 1973]
John D. Rockefeller 3rd and Blanchette Hooker Rockefeller, New York, 1973–1979
FAMSF, 1979.7.98

Exhibition History
New York, Kennedy Galleries, *American Masters: Eighteenth and Nineteenth Centuries*, 1973, exh. no. 60
New York, Finch College Museum of Art, *Twice as Natural: Nineteenth-Century American Genre Painting*, 1974, exh. no. 74
FAMSF, *The Studio of the Artist*, 1982, no publ.
Ann Arbor, University of Michigan Museum of Art, *The Fair View: Representations of the World's Columbian Exposition of 1893*, 1993, no exh. no.

Selected Reference
Daniel Hudson Burnham and Francis Davis Millet, *World's Columbian Exposition: The Book of the Builders* (Chicago and Springfield, Ohio: Columbian Memorial Publication Society, 1894), p. 43

Related Work
Charles Dudley Arnold, *Modeling the First Staff Ornaments*, 10 July 1891
Platinum print, plate 13 in the three-volume set of Arnold's photographs documenting construction and completion of the 1893 fair
Ryerson and Burnham Libraries, The Art Institute of Chicago

———————

112 A CORNER OF MY STUDIO, CA. 1895

Oil on canvas, 24⅛ x 36 in.
Signed lower right: *W^m. M Chase*

WILLIAM MERRITT CHASE
b. Williamsburg, Ind. 1849
d. New York, N.Y. 1916

In the summer of 1878 Mr. Chase accepted a position as a professor in the new art school of New York, called the Art Students' League. His studio is in that city, in the Tenth Street Studio Building. It is one of the most artistic in the country; for the artist brought home with him a great variety of curious and interesting objects which he picked up abroad, especially during a visit which he made to Venice. There he collected wonderful bits of old bronze and beautifully carved oaken chests, like the one in which Genevra hid herself on her bridal day when the lock sprung and the falling lid closed her in forever.

Faded tapestries that might tell strange stories, quaint decorated stools, damaskeened blades and grotesque flint-locks, and elaborately carved mugs and salvers, are picturesquely arranged around the studio with a studied carelessness, together with choice specimens of the works of several of the leading German artists of the day. It is altogether a nook rich in attractions which carry the fancy back to other climes and the romance of bygone ages.

S. G. W. Benjamin, *Our American Artists* (Boston: D. Lothrop & Co., 1879), n.p.

———————

Mr. Chase upon returning to New York virtually took the town by storm, capturing its chief artistic citadel, and the exhibition gallery of the Tenth Street Studio building became the sanctum sanctorum of the aesthetic fraternity, affording midst painting, statuary, music, flowers, and flamingoes, etc., symposia most unique and felicitous, never to be forgotten by charmed participants.

Dr. Charles Henry Miller, N.A., quoted in Katherine Metcalf Roof, *The Life and Art of William Merritt Chase* (1917; New York: Hacker Art Books, 1975), p. 56

———————

There is nothing about Chase more important than his date, and by this I mean not the year of his birth, but the time of his entrance into artistic affairs in this country. . . . [I]t is on his return from Europe in 1878 that his career becomes really interesting, and, in a serious sense, places him. He came back at a psychological moment. The American school was vaguely getting ready to emerge from a period of stagnation. . . . The painter, in our modern sense, was practically unknown to [the early-nineteenth-century art chronicler William] Dunlap. . . . Neither he nor his followers, for a long time, could see the possibilities lying in technic as technic. Chase saw them. His eyes had been opened in Munich, and it was in helping to open the eyes of the rising generation which he returned to instruct that he ranged himself.

. . . Some of his old Munich *envois* superficially indicate an intense preoccupation with the old masters. . . . But look more closely at one of them . . . and . . . you notice especially the good quality of the blacks—a quality only accessible to a man who has begun to feel the glamour of sheer pigment. That is the kind of picture that [the American painters Frank] Duveneck and [J. Frank] Currier were painting. They threw convention overboard, gave themselves up to the stimulus of brush-work as Rembrandt and Hals understood it. . . . They gave paint its chance—brought into the foreground the manipulation of it for its own sake, erected manual dexterity into a talismanic factor. Chase cultivated this point of view heart and soul, and brought to its application a trait lacked by his accomplished fellows, namely, a blither taste in color. . . .

He had boldness, vivacity, the inspiriting qualities of a dashing realist, and, above all, he had ease, cleverness, the gift for playing amusing tricks with the brush. He took charge of a painting class at the Art Students' League in 1878. He participated in the early doings of the Society of American Artists. His big studio in the old building on West Tenth Street became a rallying-ground. These things are significant. They take the memory back to a period in which American art was being made over—with Chase as one of the leaders in the transformation.

Royal Cortissoz, *American Artists* (New York and London: Charles Scribner's Sons, 1923), pp. 163–166

Provenance
Edith E. Wright

[Auction sale, Sotheby Parke-Bernet, New York, 13 September 1972, lot no. 89, sold for $17,000]

[Hirschl & Adler Galleries, New York, 1972]

Private collection, 1972

[Kennedy Galleries, New York, by 1975]

John D. Rockefeller 3rd and Blanchette Hooker Rockefeller, New York, 1975–1979

FAMSF, 1979.7.29

Exhibition History
New York, Hirschl & Adler Galleries, *Faces and Places: Changing Images of Nineteenth-Century America*, 1972, exh. no. 16

New York, M. Knoedler & Co., *William Merritt Chase, 1849–1916: A Benefit Exhibition for the Parrish Art Museum, Southampton, New York*, 1976, exh. no. 48

FAMSF, *The Studio of the Artist*, 1981, no publ.

Tokyo 1982, exh. no. 58

Selected References
Nicolai Cikovsky, Jr., "William

Merritt Chase's Tenth Street Studio," *Archives of American Art Journal* 16, no. 2 (1976): 9

Annette Blaugrund, "The Tenth Street Studio Building" (Ph.D. diss., Columbia University, 1987), p. 296

The American Canvas, pp. 158–159, 241

Related Works
The Inner Studio, Tenth Street, ca. 1878
Oil on canvas, 32⅜ x 44¼ in.
The Huntington, San Marino, Calif.

Tenth Street Studio, ca. 1885
Oil on canvas, 18 x 20 in.
George J. Arden, New York, as of 1975

Henry Grinnell Thomson (American, 1850–1937)
William Merritt Chase's Tenth Street Studio, ca. 1881
Oil on canvas, 30 x 40 in.
Mr. and Mrs. Haig Tashjian, as of 1982

Unknown American photographer
East End of Wm. M. Chase's Main Studio
The Art Interchange 36 (February 1896)

---

113 NEAR THE BEACH, SHINNECOCK, CA. 1895

Oil on wood panel, 9⅞ x 13⅞ in.
Signed lower left: *Wᵐ M Chase.*

WILLIAM MERRITT CHASE
b. Williamsburg, Ind. 1849
d. New York, N.Y. 1916

Down on the southern shore of Long Island, where heather-covered hills of sand stretch from the encroaching bays to the open sea, he [Chase] had pitched his tent, and was busy with his delightful work. His tent was not of a primitive sort, like that a nomad uses, but a charming and substantial house, designed by a brother artist, Mr. Stanford White. There, in the Shinnecock Hills, Mr. William M. Chase, president of the Society of American Artists, made his summer home and spent his summer vacation. . . .

It was not mere chance that took Mr. Chase to the Shinnecock Hills, where he has spent the last two summers, nor was it the beauty of the surrounding country, the clearness of the skies, or the opaqueness of the soft and genial air that primarily induced him to go thither, where in all probability he will be found vacation after vacation for many years to come. At Southampton, the old Puritan town whose sailors were famous whalers and fishermen in a time that is past, many of New York's fashionable folk have had summer homes for several years. . . . It was these colonists who discovered the beauties of the Shinnecock Hills, a series or cluster of sand mounds once wooded with heavy trees, but now covered with coarse grass and a bunchy growth very nearly resembling the Scotch heather that lends so much color to the Highland hill-sides. Roads were put through the hills, and presently villas were built here and there on these little knolls. Among the first to build in the Shinnecock Hills was Mrs. Hoyt, a daughter of Chief Justice Salmon P. Chase. Mrs. Hoyt, a woman of great energy and practical ability, has been prominent in the movement to make the Shinnecock Hills attractive to others. She is herself an amateur artist, and quickly perceived the great advantages of the locality for the study of nature out-of-doors. She therefore conceived the idea of establishing there a summer art school, and being ambitious, as she says, she aimed high, and invited Mr. Chase to take charge of the school. With many doubts as to the success of the undertaking, Mr. Chase accepted the invitation, and began with a class in the summer of '91. This was continued during the past summer, and now the school from very modest beginnings has become an established institution, and bids fair to be known long and favorably in the American world of art.

John Gilmer Speed, "An Artist's Summer Vacation," *Harper's New Monthly Magazine* 87, no. 517 (June 1893): 3–4

When I start to paint out of doors, I put myself in as light marching order as possible; that is, I have every thing made as portable and with as little weight as it can be. I have a light color box, and take no more colors than I think I shall be sure to need. If I am going to carry wooden panels, which I usually do, I have a neatly made frame with grooves into which I can slip two panels and carry them firmly without their touching each other when the paint is wet. . . .

I carry a comfortable stool that can be closed up in a small space, and I never use an umbrella. I want all the light I can get. When I have found the spot I like, I set up my easel, and paint the picture on the spot. I think that is the only way rightly to interpret nature. I don't believe in making pencil sketches, and then painting your landscape in your studio. You must be right out under the sky. You must try to match your colors as nearly as you can to those you see before you, and you must study the effects of light and shade on nature's own hues and tints. You must not ask me what color I should use for such an object or in such a place; I do not know till I have tried it and noted its relation to some other tint, or rather if it keeps the same relation and produces on my canvas something of the harmony which I see in nature.

Chase, quoted in A. R. Ives, "Suburban Sketching Grounds: 1. Talks with Mr. W. M. Chase, Mr. Edward Moran, Mr. William Sartain and Mr. Leonard Ochtman," *The Art Amateur* 25, no. 4 (September 1891): 80

Surrounded by bay, sweet-fern and vivid patches of butterfly-weed, Chase's house is set, as it were, in the midst of one of his own landscapes, its nearest neighbor off on a distant hilltop. On one side lies the ocean in vista, on the other Peconic Bay. The water is not near enough to be heard except in a storm; its place is decorative rather than intimate. Indeed, it would seem as if house and studio must have been designed to make pictures from within, for every window and doorway frames a composition. . . .

The sky, which so impresses itself upon the imagination in those wide Shinnecock spaces, always strongly compelled Chase's painting impulse. Some days he spent hours at his wide studio window simply painting the changing clouds, veritable sky studies.

Katherine Metcalf Roof, *The Life and Art of William Merritt Chase* (1917; New York: Hacker Art Books, 1975), p. 176

Provenance
Roland Knoedler (1856–1932), New York and Paris

Private collection, New York

[Peter Davidson, New York, by 1974]

John D. Rockefeller 3rd and Blanchette Hooker Rockefeller, New York, 1974–1993

FAMSF, 1993.35.5

Exhibition History
San Francisco 1976, exh. no. 61

Related Works
Autumn (Shinnecock), ca. 1895
Oil on panel, 12⅞ x 18⅜ in.
Taggert & Jorgensen Gallery, Washington, D.C., as of 1989

Near the Beach, Shinnecock, ca. 1895
Oil on canvas, 30 x 48 in.

The Toledo Museum of Art

Shinnecock Hills, ca. 1895
Pastel on canvas, 16 x 24 in.
Peter G. Terian, as of 1993

The Shinnecock Hills, ca. 1895
Pastel on paper, 15½ x 23½ in.
Kathleen and Charler Harper, as of 1993

---

114 DAVID, CA. 1895

Oil on canvas, 62¾ x 32¾ in.

**ATTRIBUTED
TO ABBOTT
HANDERSON
THAYER**
b. Boston, Mass. 1849
d. Dublin, N.H. 1921

On getting back to America [from study in Paris], Mr. Thayer began the New York studio years, which lasted approximately from 1879 to 1890. During this period he lived with his family at one or another country-place on the Hudson River . . . coming down to his studio in New York every day. He went to Dublin, New Hampshire, at first only for the summers; but gradually the summer cottage at Monadnock came to be the permanent home. . . . At Dublin, which he seldom leaves, his life is isolated, and he spends hours at a time alone on the mountain, or in his canoe on the lake. He lives solely for his art, with the single and unvaried thought of expressing his own ideals.

Helen M. Beatty, "Abbott H. Thayer," in *Exhibition of Paintings by Abbott H. Thayer*, exh. cat. (Pittsburgh: Carnegie Institute, 1919), pp. 17–18

Abbott Thayer has always been an idealist . . . with the noblest qualities of mind and character, and his development has been ever upward, still higher, toward more lofty thoughts and ideals. If I were to choose one word by which to describe Abbott Thayer, it would be excelsior. He has realized by his living and by his art the highest spiritual qualities.

George Gray Barnard, quoted in Helen M. Beatty, "Abbott H. Thayer," in *Exhibition of Paintings by Abbott H. Thayer*, exh. cat. (Pittsburgh: Carnegie Institute, 1919), p. 19

In his pictures, all too few, and produced at intervals all too wide for his many admirers, the keynote of the technique is simplicity, and the most striking characteristic of the subjects their deep spiritual significance. . . . [E]verything from the hand of Abbott Thayer is imbued with the dignity and simplicity of the artist's own temperament, combined with a delicacy of intuition into the inner life of humanity which wins the spectator from all thought of details or accessories, bringing him into direct touch with the very ego of the subject, whether that subject be a sleeping child, a maiden looking out from the threshold of life with the eager

innocent curiosity of the neophyte, or a fellow artist already worn with the conflict between the real and the ideal.

Mrs. Arthur Bell (N. D'Anvers), "An American Painter: Abbott H. Thayer," *International Studio* 6, no. 24 (February 1899): 248

————

To Thayer as to William Blake art was a means of conversing with Paradise. For, like Blake again, he was almost equally obsessed not merely by a vision of earthly images but by a lofty conception embodied in visual symbols which transcend the temporal.

Nelson C. White, *Abbott H. Thayer, Painter and Naturalist* (Hartford, Conn.: Connecticut Printers, 1951), p. 205

————

Thayer has been criticised, in this age of science, for being sentimental, for putting wings on his female figures. . . . [H]is entire philosophy of life underlay his judgment that the nobler aspects of humanity were more worthy of celebration and record than their opposites. He saw these where others didn't, in men and boys, in sleeping babies and in dogs. It required the poet as well as the painter to discern them.

The painter William James, quoted in Nelson C. White, *Abbott H. Thayer, Painter and Naturalist* (Hartford, Conn.: Connecticut Printers, 1951), pp. 230–231

———

The emphasis on the figure carried with it an inclination toward narrative and monumental art, which, if not wholeheartedly adopted by Americans, nonetheless sensitized them to the art of the past. Many who studied in Europe took advantage of the opportunity to study the works of the Old Masters, whose vast altarpieces, grand allegorical tableaux, courtly portraits, and magnificent sculptural and architectural monuments could everywhere be seen. While a previous generation of Americans viewed such works with a shrug of the shoulders, or perhaps a puritanical shudder, Thayer and his contemporaries . . . marveled at what they saw. And while few saw fit to mimic what they saw directly, none remained unaffected by the splendor before them. . . . [H]ere was an art that gloried in aristocratic privilege, that celebrated deeds of superhuman strength and heroism, that provided an opulent counterpart to the holy texts, ancient writings, and momentous historical events that it took for inspiration.

Ross Anderson, *Abbott Handerson Thayer*, exh. cat. (Syracuse, N.Y.: Everson Museum of Art, 1982), p. 45

Provenance
[Kennedy Galleries, New York, by 1969]

John D. Rockefeller 3rd and Blanchette Hooker Rockefeller, New York. 1969–1979

FAMSF, 1979.7.96

115 THOMAS HOVENDEN, 1896

Oil on wood panel, 10¼ x 8¼ in.
Signed and dated upper right: *W. Magrath./1896.*

WILLIAM MAGRATH
b. Cork, Ireland 1838
d. Brighton, N.Y. 1918

William Magrath belongs to a class of American artists, becoming numerous, who are better appreciated in Europe than they are in their own country. His experience has been somewhat like Mr. Boughton's. Like the latter, although known as an American, he was not born on this side of the Atlantic. As the former was brought over here from England when quite young, so young Magrath was brought from Ireland. He began life as a sign-painter . . . [as] many another eminent artist did, experiencing much hardship in his fight for recognition. Mr. Magrath studied manfully, however, working with a determination which, with the undoubted talent he had to back it, was bound to win him success. . . . Many who will remember him as the pale, slim, middle-aged man of sensitive temperament and reserved manner, who chafed greatly under the harsh treatment he experienced at the hands of some critics and lack of sympathy in his work on the part of the public, and, indeed, among brothers of the brush too, who joked him on his persistence in depicting humble life "on the old sod," will be glad to know that he has already won for himself in England the honorable

recognition which was begrudged him here. He had the true soul of the artist. The picturesqueness of Irish peasant-life opened to his mind an unfailing source of subject for the style
of genre painting in which he delights and charmingly depicts.

"William Magrath," *The Art Amateur* 7, no. 4 (September 1882): 70

———

[Hovenden's] was an interesting personality. He was of medium height; had a well-built
figure and a sunny disposition; his eyes were blue; his chin strong; his brow high and broad.
He wore a beard and had an exceptionally beautiful speaking voice. His tragic death on
August 14, 1895 near his home on Germantown Pike at a grade-crossing on the Trenton-Cut-
Off of the Pennsylvania R.R. was mourned by many thousands of persons familiar with his
famous paintings as well as by his family and many friends.

Helen Corson Livezey, "Life and Works of Thomas Hovenden, N.A.," *Germantowne Crier*
8, no. 2 (May 1956): 23

———

Away from the tramp and bustle of city life, from all sounds save the singing of birds and
whispering winds, among the trees and flowers he loved so well, Thomas Hovenden, the
American painter, was buried yesterday afternoon in the quiet Quaker graveyard at Plymouth
Meeting. By his untimely death American art experiences a loss not easy to repair and the
constant tribute paid to his memory shows the sincerity and esteem in which he was held. . . .

Among those who came to mourn the artist's death, many of whom were near acquain-
tances of his in life, were . . . John McGrath [*sic*], the water color artist, of New York. . . .

The pall-bearers were . . . all relatives of the artist; and Thomas Eakins and Mr. [Samuel]
Murray, artists of this city.

"Life and Work of Hovenden," *Philadelphia Times*, 18 August 1895

Provenance

Lawrence A. Fleischman (b. 1925) and Barbara Greenberg Fleischman (b. 1924), Detroit, ca. 1950–1966 (as Thomas Hovenden, *Self-Portrait*)

[Kennedy Galleries, New York,

1966–1967 (as Thomas Hovenden, *Self-Portrait*)]

John D. Rockefeller 3rd and Blanchette Hooker Rockefeller, New York, 1967–1979 (as Thomas Hovenden, *Self-Portrait*)

FAMSF, 1979.7.58

Selected Reference

Lee M. Edwards, "Noble Domesticity: The Paintings of Thomas Hovenden," *The American Art Journal* 19, no. 1 (1987): 4 (as Thomas Hovenden, *Self-Portrait*, ca. 1890)

Related Work

Thomas Hovenden, from His Last Photograph
Wood engraving
Philadelphia Times, 18 August 1895

116 PROFESSOR WILLIAM WOOLSEY JOHNSON, CA. 1896

Oil on canvas, 24 x 20 in.

THOMAS EAKINS
b. Philadelphia, Pa. 1844
d. Philadelphia, Pa. 1916

I was born in Philadelphia July 15th, 1844. I had many instructors, the principal ones Gérôme, Dumont (Sculptor), Bonnat. I taught in the Academy from the opening of the schools until I was turned out, a period much longer than I should have permitted myself to remain there. My honors are misunderstanding, persecution, & neglect, enhanced because unsought.

> Eakins to Harrison Morris, director of the Pennsylvania Academy of the Fine Arts, 23 April 1894, Archives, Pennsylvania Academy of the Fine Arts, Philadelphia, quoted in Elizabeth Johns, *Thomas Eakins: The Heroism of Modern Life* (Princeton, N.J.: Princeton University Press, 1983), p. 148

Beneath the rather forbidding surface of Eakins' art will be found a sense of form more fully-developed than that of perhaps any other of our painters. In all his work there is not a passage that is flat, thoughtless, or merely decorative. His forms are always solid, round, situated satisfyingly in space, convincing in their weight. Everything is logical, completely understood; nothing is slurred over or vague. Eakins himself said that a picture which left too much to the imagination was "cowardly." His form has all the hard vigor of his whole personality. It gives one the same feeling of spare, sensitive muscularity as the body of a trained athlete. There is no softening or sentimentalizing; every detail is stated with uncompromising force and saliency.

In his characteristic mixture of scientific and artistic terminology he once said: "All the sciences are done in a simple way; in mathematics the complicated things are reduced to simple things. So it is in painting. You reduce the whole thing to simple factors. . . . This will make strong work. The old masters worked this way." This was a rationalization of his own large way of looking at form, by which the whole is seen and felt as a whole, and yet each part receives its full measure of individual development. It is this powerful simplicity of his vision that makes it fitting to apply to his form the much-abused word "sculptural."

> Lloyd Goodrich, "Thomas Eakins, Realist," *The Pennsylvania Museum Bulletin* 25, no. 133 (March 1930): 15

[William Woolsey] Johnson, came of distinguished ancestry. He was a descendant of Jonathan Edwards, 1703–1758, . . . of Dr. Samuel Johnson, 1696–1772, the first president of King's College (now Columbia University), and of his son William Samuel Johnson, 1727–1819, one of the framers of the Constitution of the United States. . . . William Woolsey Johnson was graduated at Yale in 1862, at the age of twenty-one, and at once became connected with the United States Nautical Almanac office. After two years of service there he became an instructor in mathematics at the Naval Academy, Newport, R. I., and in 1865 moved with the school to Annapolis, where he remained until 1870. . . . After teaching at Kenyon College, Ohio (1870–72), and at St. John's College, Md. (1872–81), he returned to Annapolis as professor of mathematics, to remain there the rest of his active life. In 1913, through a special act of Congress, he was commissioned lieutenant in the navy, and in 1921 was retired with the rank of commodore. . . .

Johnson was one of the best-known of the expository mathematicians of his time, chiefly because of his numerous contributions to mathematical literature which helped to arouse interest in mathematical studies.

D[avid] E[ugene] S[mith], "William Woolsey Johnson," *Dictionary of American Biography,* rev. ed., vol. 5, pt. 2, p. 134

———

Eakins . . . chose with the portrait one of painting's oldest subjects. He employed traditional painting techniques. He did not wish to turn his back on the past but to extend its hierarchies into his own era and place. . . .

Eakins did disturb his audience . . . and it was not because, as the critics suggested, his work was old-fashioned or "nativist." It was because he very matter-of-factly continued to convey in his paintings of men and women . . . the best serious contemporary thinking about human life and activity. Whether it was appropriate to the traditional function of portraiture was a separate question—one that concerned him little. . . .

But Eakins had begun his career as a portraitist of a modern heroism of intellect, morality, and discipline and he continued it to the end. What this meant was that from the beginning of his career he assumed the authority to depict the highest heroic ideals, and he never surrendered that power. This was the crux of his difficulty, and this the glory of his achievement. Increasingly it became clear that what he would specify as heroic had changed: while intellectual specialization was fragmenting men one from another, at the same time the

scientific study of man himself—of his brain, of his culture—was placing all men in the same company. After 1890 Eakins painted fewer and fewer sitters with environments that defined what they "did" in order to paint them in bust form to show what they "were": physical human creatures.

Elizabeth Johns, *Thomas Eakins: The Heroism of Modern Life* (Princeton, N.J.: Princeton University Press, 1983), pp. 152–153, 157

Provenance
William Woolsey Johnson (1841–1927) and Susannah Leverett Batcheller Woolsey (married 1869), Annapolis, Md., and Baltimore, ca. 1896–1927

Descended in family to his son, Charles W. L. Johnson, Baltimore, 1927–1943

[M. Knoedler & Co., New York, 1943]

[Grand Central Galleries, New York, 1943]

International Business Machines Corporation, New York and Armonk, N.Y., by 1944–1967

[Kennedy Galleries, New York, 1967–1968]

John D. Rockefeller 3rd and Blanchette Hooker Rockefeller, New York, 1968–1993

FAMSF, 1993.35.28

Exhibition History
The Baltimore Museum of Art, *Thomas Eakins, 1844–1916*, 1936, exh. no. 24

New York, M. Knoedler & Co., *A Loan Exhibition of the Works of Thomas Eakins, 1844–1944, Commemorating the Centennial of His Birth*, 1944, exh. no. 55

Pittsburgh, Carnegie Institute, Department of Fine Arts, *Thomas*

Eakins Centennial Exhibition, 1945, exh. no. 10

Selected References
Lloyd Goodrich, *Thomas Eakins* (New York: Whitney Museum of American Art, 1933), cat. no. 295A

Margaret McHenry, *Thomas Eakins Who Painted* (Oreland, Pa.: privately printed, 1946), pp. 100–101

---

117 THE CLOCK MAKER, 1899

Oil on copper, 13⅛ x 9½ in.
Signed lower left: *J.D. Chalfant*; inscribed on reverse: *The Clock Maker/1899/J.D. Chalfant*

JEFFERSON DAVID CHALFANT
b. Chester County, Pa. 1856
d. Wilmington, Del. 1931

You exhibited at the Academy last Spring the painting "The Old Clock Maker." At what price for cash would you execute a similar subject? We could find a purchaser.

George H. Ainslie, Ainslie Brothers Modern Paintings, to Chalfant, 12 November 1898, Jefferson David Chalfant Papers, AAA, roll 2426, frame 1046

Chalfant is a painter of still life, and interior pictures. He delights in small canvasses upon which he paints figures and their belongings . . . with photographic accuracy and realistic coloring. His studio accumulations are those of antique costumes, guns, pistols, and swords. Of these there are many examples which he delights to hang about on the walls and arrange on the tables in groups indicating the recent presence of their old-time owners. . . .

. . . The artist has also a fad for antique furniture, and he has several examples of it in chairs and tables which he brought from Europe on his return from an extended tour made several years ago.

Clipping from the *(Wilmington, Del.) Morning News*, 1893, Jefferson David Chalfant Papers, AAA, roll 2427, frame 575

The most intriguing factor in the development of Chalfant's genre paintings is his use of photography as a starting point. Extraordinary photographs from Chalfant's personal collection have recently come to light and offer striking insight into the artist's compositions and, more importantly, into his creative process for genre work.

The artist did not do his own photography, but depended on a local craftsman: J. Paul Brown, a photographer in Wilmington, Delaware. Chalfant's Wilmington studio was a storehouse of props used in paintings. It was in this large studio that the artist created sets, including models, for genre compositions and, in some cases recorded scenes photographically. Although he relied on photography, the resulting genre pieces did not copy the

photographs in every detail. Chalfant turned to this tool to capture attitudes of his models or to record a complicated, cluttered interior.

> Joan H. Gorman, *Jefferson David Chalfant, 1856–1931*, exh. cat. (Chadds Ford, Pa.: Brandywine River Museum, 1979), pp. 20, 22

The clockmaker is seated at a turnbench fitted with foot treadle and large American watchmaker's lathe. The countershafting is at the back of the bench. Behind the countershafting are the plates of an astronomical regulator (probably English). In front of the regulator and countershafting is an accessory headstock for the watchmaker's lathe. To the right of the headstock is an essence jar, which would have contained alcohol. Behind the jar is just visible the top of a movement blower for getting rid of dust from cleaned clock movements. In front of the lathe is an alcohol lamp and to the right lies the pendulum of the O.G. clock (on the floor just above the artist's name). Behind the alcohol lamp is a glascow brush. At the right of the pendulum is a "rattle box" for dispensing small and even quantities of various powders. Behind that is a dark glass bottle, probably containing clock oil, and behind that is a glass cover to protect clean or delicate parts. To the right of the cover is a bench vise and in front are two tool handles (for files, screwdrivers or hammers).

What the clockmaker is doing we can only guess. In his left hand is a pair of flat-nose pliers and in his right a flat file. The clock in his lap is a two-train hour and half-hour striking cuckoo clock with the dial removed (the dial's on the floor next to the O.G. clock). He might be bending and filing a metal part of the cuckoo clock.

Observations of the clockmaker David Todd, in letter from Carlene E. Stephens, Curator, Division of Engineering and Industry, National Museum of American History, Smithsonian Institution, Washington, D.C., 24 October 1986, FAMSF departmental files

Provenance
[Commissioned by Ainslie Brothers Modern Paintings, New York, 1899]

John J. Walton (1839–1907), Brooklyn and Freeport, N.Y., 1899–1907

An unidentified member of the Osborne family

[Unidentified auction sale, 6 May 1971]

[Schweitzer Gallery, New York, 1971]

John D. Rockefeller 3rd and Blanchette Hooker Rockefeller, New York, 1971–1979

FAMSF, 1979.7.25

Exhibition History
San Francisco 1976, exh. no. 60

Chadds Ford, Pa., Brandywine River Museum, *Jefferson David Chalfant*, 1979, exh. no. 29

Selected Reference
Jonathan Fairbanks, "Craft Sources and Images; Visual

Sources for the Study of the Craftsman," *The Craftsman in Early America* (Winterthur, Del.: Winterthur Museum, 1984), pp. 325, 328–330

Related Works
The Clock Tinker, 1898
Pencil on paper, 13 x 9¾ in.
Auction sale, Sotheby's, New York, 27 May 1993, lot no. 213

The Old Clock-Maker, 1898
Oil on copper, 12¾ x 9¾ in.

Private collection, as of 1986

Study for "The Old Clock-Maker," 1898
Oil on board, 12 x 9 in.
Brandywine River Museum, Chadds Ford, Pa.

Study for "The Old Clock-Maker," ca. 1898
Pencil on paper, 12¾ x 9½ in.
William Benton Museum of Art, University of Connecticut, Storrs

---

118 FRANK JAY ST. JOHN, 1900

Oil on canvas, 23⅞ x 19⅞ in.
Signed and dated right center: *EAKINS/1900.*

THOMAS EAKINS
b. Philadelphia, Pa. 1844
d. Philadelphia, Pa. 1916

Be it known that I, Frank Jay St. John, of the city and county of Philadelphia . . . have invented an Improvement in [Fire] Grate-Bars [portions of which may be seen in the background of the FAMSF painting], of which the following is a specification. . . .

My improvement comprehends certain features in the construction of shaking grate bars adapted to steam boiler work more particularly, whereby they may be made of great length and by the impartation of a rocking motion be operated at the center as well as at the ends to secure the combined rocking and transverse shifting movement capable of breaking down the clinkers and cleaning the grate of ash and cinders. . . .

. . . I have, after a most extensive use and thorough practical test of these improved bars, found that not only do they enable a clean and bright fire to be maintained, but entail less labor on the stoker than with any bars which my experience has brought to my notice.

Frank Jay St. John, in *Specifications and Drawings of Patents Issued from the United States Patent Office for March, 1894* (Washington, D.C.: Government Printing Office, 1894), pp. 188, 189

After 1886, Eakins' focus on his role as a painter was sharpened by the elimination from his life of his teaching responsibilities, and he added breadth and depth to his portrait gallery. He painted Whitman, cowboys, and a more modern surgical clinic, more physicians and scientists—including several on the frontier of exploration, more artists, several more musicians . . . ; anthropologists—they, too, in the front of the advance of scientific knowledge, a journalist, publisher, educators, more military leaders, mathematicians, cultural leaders in Philadelphia, boxers and wrestlers; critics; collectors; curators and art dealers; business men; lawyers; actresses; prelates of the Catholic Church. . . . In its range and size this collection of portraits is an astonishing group. It is a collection of eminent Philadelphians, of eminent men

and women, that reveals the vast expansion of modern life. . . . At its center was a man remarkably sensitive to, and appreciative of, achievement in many forms.

Elizabeth Johns, *Thomas Eakins: The Heroism of Modern Life* (Princeton, N.J.: Princeton University Press, 1983), p. 150

———

His interest was in the people of his surroundings and in their work and recreations, and from these he chose his motives. His continual search was for character in all things. The purpose of his work seems at times akin to that of a scientist—of a natural historian who sets down the salient traits of the subject he is studying—but in his case the scientific point of view was directed by a keen appreciation of the pictorial and frequently of the dramatic. The technical side of his painting partook also of the scientific with stress on the studies of anatomy and perspective, which, however, were kept in due subservience by his recognition of the higher elements of art. His pictures manifest always a contained and serious outlook; they are free from all vagueness in thought or form.

Bryson Burroughs, introduction to *Thomas Eakins Memorial Exhibition*, exh. cat. (New York: The Metropolitan Museum of Art, 1917), p. vi

Provenance

Frank Jay St. John (d. 1900), Philadelphia

Descended in family to Caroline Chappelle, before 1960

Lawrence A. Fleischman (b. 1925) and Barbara Greenberg Fleischman (b. 1924), Detroit, ca. 1960–1966

[Kennedy Galleries, New York, 1966]

John D. Rockefeller 3rd and Blanchette Hooker Rockefeller, New York, 1966–1979

FAMSF, 1979.7.37

Exhibition History

Milwaukee Art Center, *American Painting, 1760–1960: A Selection of 125 Paintings from the Collection of Mr. and Mrs. Lawrence A. Fleischman, Detroit*, 1960, no exh. no.

Washington, D.C., National Gallery of Art, *Thomas Eakins: A Retrospective Exhibition*, 1961, exh. no. 82

The Detroit Institute of Arts, *American Paintings and Drawings from Michigan Collections*, 1962, exh. no. 81

Tucson, University of Arizona Art Gallery, *American Painting, 1765–1963: Selections from the Lawrence A. and Barbara Fleischman Collection of American Art*, 1964, exh. no. 30

Philadelphia, Pennsylvania Academy of the Fine Arts, *Small Paintings of Large Import from the Collection of Lawrence and Barbara Fleischman of Detroit, Michigan*, 1964, exh. no. 14

New York, Whitney Museum of American Art, *Thomas Eakins:*

Retrospective Exhibition, 1970, exh. no. 79

San Francisco 1976, exh. no. 65

Tokyo 1982, exh. no. 60

Selected References

Henri Gabriel Marceau, "Catalogue of the Works of Thomas Eakins," *The Pennsylvania Museum Bulletin* 25, no. 133 (March 1930): 26

Lloyd Goodrich, *Thomas Eakins: His Life and Work* (New York: Whitney Museum of American Art, 1933), cat. no. 337

Gordon Hendricks, *Thomas Eakins: His Photographic Works* (Philadelphia: Pennsylvania Academy of the Fine Arts, 1969), pp. 45, 48, 75

Gordon Hendricks, *The Life and Work of Thomas Eakins* (New

York: Grossman Publishers, 1974), p. 248

Lloyd Goodrich, *Thomas Eakins*, 2 vols. (Cambridge, Mass., and London: Harvard University Press, for the National Gallery of Art, 1982), 2:103

Michael Fried, *Realism, Writing, Disfiguration: On Thomas Eakins and Stephen Crane* (Chicago: University of Chicago Press, 1987), pp. 27, 32

The American Canvas, pp. 146–147, 240

Related Work

Possibly Samuel Murray (American, 1869–1941)
Eakins Painting "Portrait of Frank St. John," 1900
Photograph, 3¾ x 4⅜ in.
Hirshhorn Museum and Sculpture Garden, Smithsonian Institution, Washington, D.C.

---

119 LITTLE LAMERCHE, CA. 1900

Oil on canvas, 24 x 19 in.
Signed and inscribed upper right: *To my friend Anne D. Blake/Cecilia Beaux*.

CECILIA BEAUX
b. Philadelphia, Pa. 1855
d. Gloucester, Mass. 1942

Cecilia Beaux, whose mother died twelve days after Beaux's birth and whose French father lived principally in Europe, was raised by maternal relatives in Philadelphia. In 1872 or 1873 Beaux studied art at the Van der Whelen School in that city and a decade later worked with William Sartain (1843–1924). She apparently entered the classes of the Pennsylvania Academy of the Fine Arts in 1877, although she later denied this. She began exhibiting at the academy in 1879, where from 1885 on her portraits won considerable acclaim. In 1888 and 1889 Beaux traveled throughout Europe, studying in Paris both privately and at the Académie Julian, as well as taking evening classes at the Atelier Colarossi. She spent the summer of 1888 at the artists' colony of Concarneau in Brittany.

After her return to the United States in 1889, Beaux exhibited paintings, primarily portraits, in both Philadelphia and New York; earning medals and critical attention from 1893 to 1898 with a series of works that are among her strongest. In 1895 she joined the faculty of the Pennsylvania Academy, where she taught through 1915, although after around 1900 she spent most of her time in New York or at her summer home in Gloucester, Massachusetts. Until the early 1920s Beaux exhibited widely, continuing to win medals and important portrait commissions, including appointment to the U.S. War Portraits Commission after the

First World War. Beaux was a fluent practitioner of the international style of late-nineteenth-century portraiture. . . . A broken hip in 1924 forced a sharp reduction in her painting activities. She published her detailed memoirs, *Background with Figures*, in 1930.

Marc Simpson, in *The American Canvas: Paintings from the Collection of The Fine Arts Museums of San Francisco* (New York: Hudson Hills Press, in association with The Fine Arts Museums of San Francisco, 1989), p. 168

————

The young Breton girls [the FAMSF painting has at times been identified as being of a young woman from Brittany] have faces whose forms have as good a reason for being what they are as has the modelling of the perfect wild creature of unmixed strain. Beauty is an unpopular word now, but a face that halts the passing stranger, by its pure cool perfection of line and proportion, its color and texture like the inward slope of a seashell—well—if "beauty" will not do, what will? She is *paysanne*—where did she get those facial lines that mean high race in the selective sense of the word?

> Cecilia Beaux, *Background with Figures* (Boston and New York: Houghton Mifflin Company, 1930), pp. 145–146

————

Miss Beaux is not only the greatest living woman painter, but the best that has ever lived. Miss Beaux has done away entirely with the idea of sex in art.

> William Merritt Chase, quoted in "Greatest Woman Painter," *Philadelphia Public Ledger*, 3 November 1899

————

The critics are very enthusiastic. Berenson, Mrs. Coates tells me, stood in front of the portraits—Miss Beaux's three—and wagged his head. "Ah, yes, I see! Some Sargents. The ordinary ones are signed John Sargent, the best are signed Cecilia Beaux," which is, of course, nonsense in more ways than one, but it is part of the general chorus of praise.

> Maria Lansdale, extract from letter of February 1904, transcription in Cecilia Beaux Papers, AAA, roll 426, frame 1677

————

The mood of the painter who undertakes to deal with a living soul must indeed be poised and alive at every point. He must feel in the depths of his own nature the shadow of a shade of change—of expansion or contraction, that passes over the being before him, and must do this when he does not seem to be looking. He must see and feel it with the almost tender insight of sympathy—while at the same time in another chamber of his mind he coolly decides whether he does or does not want it in the picture—whether it will or will not further his scheme—whether it can best be accomplished by the tiniest lift in the eyebrow—and whether the paint on the forehead is wet enough or dry enough to serve for so subtle and delicate a change—and whether it had best be done today or tomorrow. In the midst of these calculations the sitter moves her arm,—and a wondrous fold appears in a scarf heretofore uninteresting—in arrangement. A wave of beauty and recognition passes over him, without in the least disturbing method and calculation—and it may be that a sharp upward stroke in the background, or the enforcing of an upward line in the head will serve and be the result of the soul touching soul of the moment before.

> Cecilia Beaux, "Portraiture," lecture at Simmons College, 14 May 1907, quoted in Henry S. Drinker, *The Paintings and Drawings of Cecilia Beaux* (Philadelphia: Pennsylvania Academy of the Fine Arts, 1955), pp. 117–118

Provenance
Anne Dehon Blake, Boston, ca. 1900–ca. 1917

[Frank W. Bayley, Boston, ca. 1917–1919]

Rhode Island School of Design, Providence, 1919–1945

[Auction sale at exhibition *Old and New England*, Rhode Island School of Design, Providence, R.I., 1945]

Godfrey Simonds (1904–1952), Providence, R.I., from 1945

Mr. and Mrs. Edward M. Payne, Rowayton, Conn., by ca. 1976

Private collection, ca. 1976

[Schweitzer Gallery, New York, 1976–1977]

John D. Rockefeller 3rd and Blanchette Hooker Rockefeller, New York, 1977–1979

FAMSF, 1979.7.7

Exhibition History
New York, Durand-Ruel Galleries, *Exhibition of Paintings by Cecilia Beaux*, 1903, no exh. no.

Boston, Horticultural Hall, *Loan Exhibition: Paintings*, 1906, exh. no. 23 (as *Head of a Dutch Girl*)

Cincinnati Art Museum, *Twenty-first Annual Exhibition of American Art*, 1914, exh. no. 4 (as *Head of a Young Dutch Girl*)

New York, Galleries of the American Fine Arts Society, *Sixth Annual Circuit Exhibition of the National Association of Portrait Painters*, 1916, exh. no. 1 (as "*Lammerche*")

FAMSF, *Viewpoints IX: Views of Brittany*, 1989, no exh. no. (as *Young Brittany Woman*, "*Lammerche*")

Selected Reference
The American Canvas, pp. 168–169, 242 (as *Young Brittany Woman*, "*Lammerche*")

Related Work
Vermeer, "*Little Lammerche*," 1889
Oil on canvas, 16½ x 14 in.
Mrs. Samuel L. M. Barlow, Gloucester, Mass., as of 1955

Oil on canvas and wood boards with brass plate, 25½ x 21½ in.
Labeled with brass plate top center: *JOHN F. PETO*

JOHN FREDERICK PETO

b. Philadelphia, Pa. 1854
d. New York, N.Y. 1907

Harnett, as has been shown, often went in for "objects of intrinsic beauty"; that is one of the main reasons for his success in his lifetime, although today it is regarded as his principal shortcoming. Peto clung to his "banal" subjects throughout his span as an artist, and that is one of the main reasons for his failure to attract buyers while he was alive, but today it is regarded as one of his major virtues. Modern painters like Kurt Schwitters and Robert Rauschenberg have taught us the fantasticality of the commonplace and the pathos of the discarded, and Peto is one of the great masters in this realm of artistic expression. . . .

It does not take a Freudian psychologist to perceive that Peto's concern with used-up, discarded, and rejected things parallels his own life. This has gently poetic implications.

Alfred Frankenstein, *After the Hunt: William Harnett and Other American Still Life Painters, 1870–1900*, rev. ed. (Berkeley and Los Angeles: University of California Press, 1969), pp. 103, 107

The cup in high relief contrasts with the cracks behind cut into the wood surface, just as the incised letters below differ from the nameplate above. Peto adds further visual ambiguity in his painted frame around the central panel and in the title's play on words. Together in the middle are the painted cup and the written noun, while the last symbol can be read as the numeral *4* or as a rebus suggesting the preposition *for*. . . . Verbally, the phrase evokes nostalgia for a lost frontier past: in a sophisticated urban age the simple tin cup is a relic to dream on. It may also represent the drink Peto's neighbors sought despite local Methodist prohibitions. Whatever the overlay of meanings in this deceptively plain work, Peto is at his best here in delighting both the eye and the mind.

> John Wilmerding, *Important Information Inside: The Art of John F. Peto and the Idea of Still-Life Painting in Nineteenth-Century America*, exh. cat. (Washington, D.C.: National Gallery of Art, 1983), pp. 164, 166

[Peto's] carefully lidded anger, his frustration, and his ambition are all packed into "The Cup We All Race 4," which was made a few years before his death. The painting shows a little tin cup hanging on a hook on a cracked old green wood wall. Gouged in the wood, in capital letters that slant this way and that and are themselves a feat of realist painting, are the words and the numeral that give the painting its title. . . . "The Cup We All Race 4," which must be one of the earliest paintings, American or European, to make use of a graffito, has the presence, and something of the funny belligerence, of a heraldic shield.

. . . The phrase and the cup also might be an ironic reference to the sailing meets along the Toms River, which Peto could see from his house, and in nearby Barnegat Bay. In the face of a great number of his pictures, though, these aren't the first interpretations that come to mind. At the exhibition [at the National Gallery of Art], which was an echo chamber of the history of art, and showed one man's single-minded pursuit of the laurels of his profession, there was little doubt about who was racing and what he was racing for.

> Sanford Schwartz, "The Art World: The Rookie," *The New Yorker*, 15 August 1983, pp. 86–87

Provenance
The artist and Christine Pearl Smith Peto (1869–1945), Island Heights, N.J., ca. 1900–1945

Descended in family to son-in-law and daughter, George Washington Smiley (1885–1953) and Helen Serril Peto Smiley (1893–1978), Island Heights, N.J., 1945–1950

Nelson Rockefeller (1908–1979), New York, 1950–ca. 1970

[Kennedy Galleries, New York, by 1970]

John D. Rockefeller 3rd and Blanchette Hooker Rockefeller, New York, 1970–1979

FAMSF, 1979.7.80

Exhibition History
The Brooklyn Museum, *John F. Peto*, 1950, exh. no. 48

Cincinnati, The Contemporary Arts Center, Cincinnati Art Museum, *An American Viewpoint: Realism in Twentieth-Century American Painting*, 1957, no exh. no.

La Jolla, Calif., La Jolla Museum of Art, *The Reminiscent Object: Paintings by William Michael Harnett, John Frederick Peto, John Haberle*, 1965, exh. no. 50

San Francisco 1976, exh. no. 89

Tokyo 1982, exh. no. 46

Washington, D.C., National Gallery of Art, *Important Information Inside: The Art of John F. Peto and the Idea of Still-Life Painting in Nineteenth-Century America*, 1983, no exh. no.

Selected References
John I. H. Baur, "Peto and the American Trompe l'Oeil Tradition," *The Magazine of Art* 43, no. 5 (May 1950): 183, 185

M. L. d'Otrange Mastai, *Illusion in Art: Trompe l'Oeil, A History of Pictorial Illusionism* (New York: Abaris Books, 1975), p. 301

The American Canvas, pp. 18, 164–165, 242

Watercolor over graphite on wove paper, 12⅜ x 19⅜ in.
Signed lower left: *P Prndergast*

**MAURICE BRAZIL
PRENDERGAST**

b. St. John's, Newfoundland 1858
d. New York, N.Y. 1924

Prendergast has always been Prendergast. In 1892 he went to Paris for his first serious study of art, and worked in the Julian school on the Rue Dragon. . . . Here, for some two years, he spent each morning drawing and painting. . . . This familiar art mill. Essential, but, like a course of allopathic treatment, leaving a good deal to get out of the system.

The afternoons Prendergast spent with notebook in the cafés and the gardens, on the river, in the Bois, constantly sketching. Cabs, nursemaids, *sergents de ville*, boats— everything passes through his grist. Drawing moving life. Developing keen observation and memory of form and movement. He has found it of great value. It is, in fact, one of the bases of his art. . . . He lived this life until 1896, when he came back to Boston and made some illustrations, and much more to his taste, and with greater success, he painted on the beaches near the city [including Nantasket] and brought out the water-colors which first drew the attention of artists and picture-lovers to him. . . .

In 1898 he went to Venice. . . . Then to Padua with its Giottos. . . . At Sienna two months, then to Orvietto and to Rome. Here the fever attacked him. The fever for work. . . .

After a short rest in Naples and Capri, he returned for the summer and fall to Venice. The result of this Italian work was an exhibition at Macbeth's, in New York, and was the means of his being known to the men with whom he is now so strongly allied: Glackens, Henri, Sloan, Luks, Shinn, Davies, Lawson. The "Eight." Men who, like himself, believe a man should paint in his own way. . . .

Prendergast. What does that name bring to the mind? Pictures gay, joyous. Trees and silver skies. Deep blue sea and orange rocks. People in movement, holiday folk in their saffron, violet, white, pearl, tan. Quaint design. Color powerful, but not crude. Canvasses built up with overpainting—color dragged on color. A paint quality as delicious as an old tapestry. This is the art of Prendergast. . . . Trays of jewels. Rich brocades from eastern looms. And with all this beauty, and quality and joy, variety and downright individuality.

This short, white-haired, slight man, shut into his own world in a measure by his deafness, wiry, enthusiastic, strong in his likes and dislikes, indefatigable worker, has produced in his Boston studio on Mt. Vernon Street, an art gay, rich, personal, unique.

Charles Hovey Pepper, "Is Drawing to Disappear in Artistic Individuality?" *The World To-day* 19, no. 1 (July 1910): 717, 719

––––––––

The significant part of this story of his beginnings as an artist is that he never regarded all the careful and fastidious drawing of his school days, as anything but training for his mind, his eye, and his hand. He knew that this training would enable him to do as he pleased later on and that doing as he pleased would be in the style of his vacation sketches with their hasty notations in oil and water color of scenes that made him gay with their zest and animation. To suggest this movement of figures in park-like places checkered with sunlight and colored shadows, he needed to make his pigments vibrant and vivacious with a vitality of their own. He seems, even at the outset of his career, to have been already intent upon the lines which make motion and the contours which make form, and to have discovered for himself that by laying on small spots of color one over another, allowing the under colors to show through, he could make his tones flicker, his sunlight shift and sparkle and dance, his whole effect vivid and exultant with the actual sensations of his joy in living. Having demonstrated all this to his own satisfaction, he went back to Boston and painted scenes on the Common and on the sea beaches of his native land. . . .

. . . To convey a sense of the joy he felt in the presence of nature as he watched young people and animals of many shapes and colors, playing and idling under the trees in the silvery springtime, with a laughing breeze rippling the surface of a little bay, and a ship or two spreading white sails, and a white house or two on a neighboring shore—after all, what more in the way of a subject did he need, this poet? The inexhaustible variations in the

Prendergast repetitions of approximately the same theme, beach parties or picnics in the park, were the variations in the man's moods as he concentrated his dream upon this cross section of life, which he had chosen to make his own province, the realm of his own fancy. Just as Claude Monet delighted in painting over and over his hay ricks, poplars, and cathedrals . . . so Prendergast repeated his favorite fantasy, his midsummer daydreams, so delightfully inconsequential, with their strange air of being true to fact, true to real domesticated places and people, and yet very like fairy-tale towns, as if mortals had come down for a single happy holiday. . . . He lavished upon such themes his genius for infinitely various schemes of color—each concord of color-notes producing a tonality as subtle and as sumptuous as orchestral weaving of rare elfin sounds.

Duncan Phillips, "Maurice Prendergast," *The Arts* 5, no. 3 (March 1924): 125–26, 127–128

Provenance
The artist, Boston and New York, ca. 1900–1924

Descended in family to his brother and sister-in-law, Charles Prendergast (1863–1948) and Eugénie Van Kemmel Prendergast (married 1925), New York and Westport, Conn., 1924–1968

[Hirschl & Adler Galleries, New York, 1968]

John D. Rockefeller 3rd and Blanchette Hooker Rockefeller, New York, 1968–1979

FAMSF, 1979.7.83

Exhibition History
New York, Hirschl & Adler Galleries, *The American Impressionists*, 1968, exh. no. 67

Selected Reference
Carol Clark, Nancy Mowll Mathews, and Gwendolyn Owens, *Maurice Brazil Prendergast/Charles Prendergast: A Catalogue Raisonné* (Munich: Prestel-Verlag, 1990), cat. no. 839

Related Work
On the Pier, Nantasket, ca. 1900–1905
Watercolor and pencil on paper, 12⅛ x 18⅞ in.
Addison Gallery of American Art, Phillips Academy, Andover, Mass.

Oil on canvas, 14 x 14 in.
Signed lower left: *HARRY-ROSELAND.*

HARRY ROSELAND

b. Brooklyn, N.Y. 1868
d. Brooklyn, N.Y. 1950

Mr. Roseland, in his artistic performances, is essentially a story-teller. Fortunately for himself and for his work he is not in the least ashamed of this, which is as it should be. . . . He takes his stories, like a wise man, from the material just about him, and therefore the beauties of his paintings are appreciated by those among whom he lives and the little story that each tells is eloquent of meaning, even to the dull imagination of the average person. . . .

Mr. Roseland is a native of Brooklyn, and was educated there, where he still lives, and where, though he is just thirty, he has achieved great popularity. In the exhibitions in his own town his pictures have been conspicuous for ten years past; in New York there is rarely a show at either the Academy or the Society at which he is not represented. . . . Many of his paintings have been published, after being etched or engraved, and these have always met with a ready sale.

Jno. Gilmer Speed, "Story-Telling as a Motive in Painting," *Monthly Illustrator* 3, no. 10 (February 1895):241, 242

Mr. Roseland's talent has been recognized and rewarded not only by an extensive and lucrative sale of his pictures to private collectors, but also by honors awarded by the National Academy of Design, the Brooklyn Art Club and other organizations. All his sketches have been made direct from life, and they are admired for the masterly skill with which they are put on the canvas. Mr. Roseland believes an artist can do his best work by painting what he sees about him in his own times and he is continually searching for new subjects. . . .

He is especially effective in negro life, and these studies have been successful both from financial and artistic points of view. His types are portrayed with remarkable fidelity, and show a humorous spirit, originality and distinctive motives. . . .

Mr. Roseland is thoroughly American in his work and methods, for he has never crossed the ocean or come under the immediate influence of any of the fashionable painters at home or abroad.

"Studies from Life by Artist Harry Roseland Attracting Much Attention at Exhibition in National Academy," *(Brooklyn) World*, 5 January 1902

Provenance
[Carlen Galleries, Philadelphia, by 1968]

John D. Rockefeller 3rd and Blanchette Hooker Rockefeller, New York, 1968–1979

FAMSF, 1979.7.87

Related Work
Paying the Rent, 1901
Oil on canvas, 14⅛ x 20⅛ in.
Auction sale, Christie's, New York, 23 March 1984, lot no. 203

---

123 THE ICE FLOE, 1902

Oil on canvas, 25⅜ x 31⅞ in.
Signed bottom center: *Robert Henri*

ROBERT HENRI
b. Cincinnati, Ohio 1865
d. New York, N.Y. 1929

Robert Henri, although he always held that art knows no nationality and claimed for the artist world-citizenship, was born in the United States, and his work and, of course, his outlook on life were marked by characteristics unquestionably the product of the American environment. Marked qualities of all his canvases are preoccupation with life about him, scenes and people presented with what might be called studied nervous energy, and direct means of expression. . . .

Robert Henri gave as much of his life to helping others to free self-expression as he gave to his own work. His thirty years of teaching were devoted to the emancipation of the art spirit in the United States. His work and his inspiration as a teacher were factors in preparing for the earnest and growing interest in art which is so clearly in evidence in this young country today.

John Sloan, "Robert Henri," in *Catalogue of a Memorial Exhibition of the Work of Robert Henri*, exh. cat. (New York: The Metropolitan Museum of Art, 1931), pp. xi–xii

---

"The Ice Floe," a Winter scene in the East River, is the most satisfactory of the paintings [in the Macbeth Galleries exhibition]. There is such movement in the tugs; such expression in the smoke—for even smoke has its moods, governed by the condition of the atmosphere— and the ice floe gives to the tide. It is in such a picture that you learn what animation a free hand, not afraid of its own boldness, can give to whatever its owner has seen when he paints it as he feels it.

The Gilder [Stevenson], "Palette and Brush," *Town Topics*, 3 April 1902, Robert Henri Papers, AAA, roll 887, frame 99

Essentially a modern painter and imbued with the spirit of the times, Mr. Henri paints so as to recall vividly the sensations induced in his nature by things worth the seeing. . . . In "The Ice Floe" the chief theme is the luminous, brilliant, forceful sense of healthy, invigorating cold.

"Three Characteristic Canvasses," *Philadelphia North American*, 16 November 1902

Look again at the "Cumulus Clouds—East River," and note the poetic appreciation of the scene's real beauty of color and arrangement; the sky here is simply flooded with warm sunlight, and every shadow is transparent. Note the opposite effect in "Ice Floes," with its sense of all-embracing cold, its disquieting line of jagged ice cake and its steam from a tug, evaporating into a sky that holds no promise of light or heat.

Samuel Swift, "Robert Henri as a Painter of Emotion in Landscape," *(New York) Mail and Express*, 8 April 1902

Landscape is a medium for ideas. We want men's thoughts. It's the same in other things. It is said that [H. G.] Wells had the right idea about writing history when he wrote *The Outline [of History*, 1920], for his object was not so much to give us the dates of the various occurrences, as to tell us of the conditions of humanity. And so the various details in a landscape painting mean nothing to us if they do not express some mood of nature as felt by the artist. It isn't sufficient that the spacing and arrangement of the composition be correct in formula. The true artist, in viewing the landscape, renders it upon his canvas as a living thing.

Robert Henri, *The Art Spirit* (1923; Philadelphia and New York: J. B. Lippincott Company, 1951), p. 87

Provenance
The artist, 1902–1903
A. J. Crawford, New York and London, from 1903
Mr. and Mrs. Francis Sullivan, Washington, D.C., by 1962
[Kennedy Galleries, New York, by 1967–1968]
John D. Rockefeller 3rd and Blanchette Hooker Rockefeller, New York, 1968–1993
FAMSF, 1993.35.13

Exhibition History
New York, Macbeth Galleries, *Exhibition of Pictures by Robert Henri*, 1902, exh. no. 5
Philadelphia, Pennsylvania Academy of the Fine Arts, *Exhibition of Paintings by Robert Henri*, 1902, exh. no. 15 (as *The Ice Flow*)
Brooklyn, Pratt Institute, Art Gallery, *Exhibition of Landscapes and Portraits by Robert Henri*, 1902, exh. no. 15
Washington, D.C., The Corcoran Gallery of Art, *Picture of the Month*, 1962 (as *East River*), no publ.

Selected References
Robert Henri, diary, entries for 9 February 1901; 3 February 1902 (includes pencil sketch of painting and identifies it as *Ice Flow—East River*, "started about a year ago");
1 April 1902; 12 April 1902; 14 April 1902; 26 October 1902; 18 December 1902; 7 January 1903. Robert Henri Papers, AAA, roll 885

Related Work
Harbor Scene, ca. 1900
Lithographic crayon on paper, 6¼ x 7⅜ in.
Hirschl & Adler Galleries, New York, as of 1979

---

124 WOMAN WITH UMBRELLA, CA. 1904

Graphite on wove paper, 9¾ x 5¾ in.
Signed lower right: *EH*

EDWARD HOPPER
b. Nyack, N.Y. 1882
d. New York, N.Y. 1967

In 1899, after graduating from high school in Nyack, Hopper traveled daily to New York City to study illustration at the Correspondence School of Illustrating on West Thirty-fourth Street. His parents did not object to his becoming an artist, but they persuaded him to study commercial illustration, which offered a more secure income than did painting. The next year he enrolled at the New York School of Art on West Fifty-seventh Street. He remained there until 1906, studying with William Merritt Chase, Kenneth Hayes Miller, and Robert Henri. . . .

. . . At the New York School of Art, his talent was rewarded with prizes and scholarships. . . . In 1904, Hopper's sketch of a female model posing with an umbrella [closely related to the FAMSF work; Levin illustrates the FAMSF drawing to accompany this text] was among the student works reproduced in a magazine article about the School. Two of Hopper's classmates, Rockwell Kent and Guy Pène du Bois, recalled his precocious talent in their memoirs. But even a modest degree of success would be a long time in coming.

Gail Levin, *Edward Hopper* (New York: Crown Publishers, 1984), pp. 10, 13

No single figure in recent American art has been so instrumental in setting free the hidden forces that can make of the art of this country a living expression of its character and its people. . . .

Of Henri's renown as a teacher everyone knows; of his enthusiasm and his power to energize his students I had first-hand knowledge. Few teachers of art have gotten as much out of their pupils, or given them so great an initial impetus as Henri.

Edward Hopper, "John Sloan and the Philadelphians," *The Arts* 11, no. 4 (April 1927): 175, 176

Gifted with an instinctive sense of solidity and weight, he builds forms that are massive and monolithic. There are no unnecessary details; everything is severely simplified. With all his adherence to fact, his pictures are carefully designed. Nothing is accidental; every object is there because of its plastic relation to others and to the whole. The main constructive lines are never concealed. . . . His compositions are monumental rather than dynamic. Always they give a sense of the orderly balance of forces and the total harmony that are fundamental to all enduring art.

Lloyd Goodrich, *Edward Hopper*, exh. cat. (New York: Whitney Museum of American Art, 1950), p. 13

Hopper's viewpoint is essentially classic; he presents his subjects without sentiment, or propaganda, or theatrics. He is the pure painter, interested in his material for its own sake, and in the exploitation of his idea of form, color, and space division. In spite of his restraint, however, he achieves such a complete verity that you can read into his interpretations of houses and conceptions of New York life any human implications you wish; and in his landscapes there is an old primeval Earth feeling that bespeaks a strong emotion felt, even if held in abeyance. . . . It is this unbiased and dispassionate outlook, with its complete freedom from sentimental interest or contemporary foible, that will give his work the chance of being remembered beyond our time.

Charles Burchfield, "Edward Hopper—Classicist," in *Edward Hopper Retrospective Exhibition*. exh. cat. (New York: The Museum of Modern Art, 1933), p. 16

Provenance
[Kennedy Galleries, New York, by 1972]
John D. Rockefeller 3rd and Blanchette Hooker Rockefeller, New York, 1972–1979
FAMSF, 1979.7.57

Related Works
Woman with Soap, 1901
Pencil on paper, 10¼ x 8⅜ in.
Hirschl & Adler Galleries, New York, as of 1987

Woman Opening an Umbrella, 1904
Drawing reproduced in *The Sketch Book* (April 1904): 223

Transparent and opaque watercolor over charcoal on wove paper, mounted on paperboard, 20 x 28⅞ in.
Signed lower left: *A. B. Frost*

ARTHUR BURDETT FROST

b. Philadelphia, Pa. 1851
d. Pasadena, Calif. 1928

In 1890 A. B. Frost, his wife, and two young sons moved into the old mansion he aptly named "Moneysunk" on Treadwell Avenue in Convent Station, New Jersey. During the next sixteen years the artist reached the very zenith of his career as his illustrations appeared in nearly every edition of *Harper's* and *Scribner's* magazines, as well as in the volumes of many of the most prominent authors of his time. . . . In his career, which exceeded a half century, Frost's illustrations appeared in more than 110 published volumes plus numerous magazine short stories.

Henry M. Reed, *The World of A. B. Frost: His Family and Their Circle*, exh. cat. (Montclair, N.J.: Montclair Art Museum, 1983), p. 5

To Frost came not one but two or even three of the greatest immortalities to which an illustrator can aspire. His pencil gave the visual form to characters imagined by other men yet destined probably to live as long as America itself. Frost illustrated the works of Mark Twain and of Joel Chandler Harris. He created the physical semblance of Tom Sawyer, Huck Finn and Uncle Remus. He made them and all their friends as they appear today before our mind's eye. Without Frost we could not put these beloved friends into theatricals, we could not know them if we met them on the street. . . .

. . . Other artists have had similar bits of brilliant fortune. But A. B. Frost, the dean of our illustrators, had even greater luck. Down through the ages, when he and we are dead and gone, his genius will twinkle on in Huck and Tom and Ole Br'er Rabbit. What price monuments of stone?

New York Evening Post, 26 June 1928, quoted in Henry M. Reed, *The World of A. B. Frost: His Family and Their Circle*, exh. cat. (Montclair, N.J.: Montclair Art Museum, 1983), p. 11

His specialty was outdoor, sporting scenes that relate to the paintings of [Arthur Fitzwilliam] Tait and [Thomas] Eakins and were aimed at a broad, popular audience. Another tremendously prolific draftsman (in one year doing over two hundred drawings for publication), he was apparently the first American to draw "comic serials": here he showed both the quick graphic touch and the lively sense of humor that typify his work, and that appear in more finished form in the best of his illustrated books.

Theodore E. Stebbins, Jr., *American Master Drawings and Watercolors* (New York: Harper & Row, Publishers, in association with The Drawing Society, 1976), pp. 261–262

Provenance
Hirschl & Adler Galleries, New York, 1977–1978

John D. Rockefeller 3rd and Blanchette Hooker Rockefeller, New York, 1978–1979
FAMSF, 1979.7.43

Exhibition History
FAMSF, *As the Days Grow Shorter: A Winter Celebration*, 1981, no publ.

Related Work
After *Cutting Ice*
Color lithograph
Collier's 36, no. 24 (10 March 1906): 14–15

---

126 INDIAN BRAVE ON THE LOOKOUT, 1907

Opaque watercolor and glaze on wove paper, mounted on paperboard, 8¾ x 4¾ in.
Signed and dated lower right: *-FARNY-/◯/-1907-*

HENRY F. FARNY
b. Ribeauville, Alsace, France 1847
d. Cincinnati, Ohio 1916

The biography of Henry Farny fairly scintillates with action. To drag out from the high lights is like skimming through the pages of a favorite historical novel.

He was born in Alsace and when 4 years of age his parents decided the "new country" presented more opportunities for a growing family than their restricted French hills.

. . . After some months' moving about from place to place the Farny family finally located in the western part of Pennsylvania, where Farny, pere, found a sawmill to be a productive means of livelihood.

Still the West b[e]ckoned him on and, constructing a raft and loading his little family aboard, he set out for what was then the newer country.

In 1855 this crude means of transportation dug its prow into the sandbanks somewhere near this city [Cincinnati], and the members of the family decided that here could be found both fame and fortune. . . .

Buchanan Reid was one of the men to whose notice was brought the talent of the young man [Farny]. In the mid-sixties Reid received his appointment as Ambassador to Rome. He did not forget the energetic, struggling young art student in Cincinnati. Through his influence Farny received an appointment which took him to the Eternal City and gave him the realization of his cherished ambition—study under the masters in the galleries abroad.

Two years in Rome—in 1867 and 1868—were followed by further courses in Munich, Düsseldorf, and the art center of the world—Paris.

In 1873 he returned to Cincinnati, and there devoted several years to the production of water colors. In this line of painting Farny was a master. While many associate him with oils, and particularly Indian studies in oils, there are critics who say that his work . . . in water colors showed his true forte.

"Death Halts Brush of Henry F. Farny," *Cincinnati Commerical Tribune* (?), ca. 25 December 1916, Henry F. Farny Papers, AAA, roll 973, frame 263

When I was a small boy my father ran a sawmill in the backwoods of the Upper Allegheny River, and our lumbermen used to tell weird stories of the Indians around the fire at night in the logging camps, to which I listened open-mouthed and awe-stricken. . . .

You can imagine my horror, therefore, when I was chopping kindling in the woodshed one bitter cold day to hear a voice at my elbow . . . and on looking up I beheld an Indian who had come in noiselessly. . . . The Indian was Old Jacob, a famous Seneca hunter. . . .

. . . Of course, he and I became great chums. He would take me to his camp, show me how to make moccasins, and bows and arrows. . . .

The memories of those early days in the pine woods and laurel brakes of the Allegheny have always been my pleasantest ones, so that when I grew to be an artist it was but natural for me to find a more sympathetic subject for my work in the American Indian than in painting Arabs or Breton or Dutch peasants, as most American painters do.

Farny, quoted in "Artist Farny," *Cincinnati Enquirer*, 24 June 1900, transcription in Henry F. Farny Papers, AAA, roll 1233, frames 499–500

————

In 1878 he visited the West with George Smalley, the noted journalist of New York, and they took a canoe trip of 1,000 miles from the headwaters of the Missouri River to the Mississippi. In this trip Farny met many different tribes of Indians and added very much to his store of knowledge concerning their customs. Of course, he took notes and made many sketches for future use. . . .

While in the West he was adopted by one tribe of Indians, the Sioux, who, with much ceremony, made him a Chief and gave him the name of "Long Boots." They asked Farny, "How will we know your work?" and Farny replied, "By my sign in the corner."

Then the Chief said: "I will give you a sign that we will know." And so he gave Farny the sign with which we are all familiar—the circle with a dot in the center.

J. F. Earhart, "Henry Farny, the Artist and the Man," *(Cincinnati) Commercial Tribune*, 21 January 1917

———

Mr. Farny has painted the Indian and the land in which he lives just as he has seen them. . . . He has seen both with the eye of an artist, tempered by the mind of a poet, and verified by the fidelity of an illustrator. . . . Accuracy of conception, faithfulness of study and realism in depiction is a trinity thoroughly Farnyesque. . . .

The versatility with which the painter of these pictures works in varying and widely differing mediums is remarkable. The same equally agreeable effects are produced in [t]he various mediums of the palette, oil, watercolor, g[o]uache and pen-and-ink. He uses white paper, brown paper and blue paper with equal and unvarying skill. He paints over body color, he paints transparently, he uses washes, employs mediums and stipples with results that are always agreeable to the eye of the connois[s]eur and the transient optic of the casual admirer of art. Always and ever, however, he is Farnyesque in all that that coined descriptive implies. His water colors are exquisite in feeling, clear, brilliant and harmonious in tone. No harsh color-notes mar the harmony of his themes; there is lacking any indication of strained effort for purely color effects. The facility of the brush is subordinated to the effects sought by the realist. . . . Studied under a glass, Farny's pictures are full of admirably drawn and painted detail. The effect of the minuteness of detail is not, however, allowed to jar the harmony of the picture as a whole. Whether in oil or aquarelle, detail is painted with the fidelity to detail of a Meissonier and the broad sweep of a Gerome.

"The Paintings of H. F. Farny," *Cincinnati Commercial Gazette*, 14 March 1893

Provenance
Frank Bestow Wiborg (1855–1930), Cincinnati and Easthampton, N.Y., after 1907–1930

[Auction sale, Sotheby Parke-Bernet, New York, 12 December 1975, lot no. 45]

John D. Rockefeller 3rd and Blanchette Hooker Rockefeller, New York, 1975–1979

FAMSF, 1979.7.41

---

127 ROCKS AND LIGHTHOUSE, CA. 1908

Oil on canvas, 25 x 30 in.
Signed lower right: *W Glackens*

WILLIAM J. GLACKENS

b. Philadelphia, Pa. 1870
d. Westport, Conn. 1938

His subject matter, though I have called him the landscape painter type, is unlimited. From portraiture to still life it includes street, bathing and boating scenes, the entire gamut of things which contribute to the gaiety of the modern scene. He is undoubtedly a portrayer of life's most pleasant occupations, of the picnic spirit. Even his occasional unpeopled landscapes have a festive air, a feeling that nature is in celebration: little clouds race through amazingly blue skies, trees stand pert and independent against a ground itself gaily acclaiming the warmth and clarity and splendour of its friend and patron the sun. . . .

. . . His painting has had two definitely marked periods. These could bluntly be described as the dark and the light period. With the great variety of his interests, with his realization of the full glamour of outdoors he could not stay confined within the barriers of the dark period. . . . Renoir's palette, in any case, his enormous researches in the possibilities of color, his final realization of the qualities of light and form in one motive, may be said to have more greatly profited Glackens than the discoveries of any other artist.

Guy Pène du Bois, *William J. Glackens* (New York: Whitney Museum of American Art, 1931), pp. 13, 9

———

William J. Glackens is notable for his expressive drawing, his fine sense for the drama of everyday life, his extraordinary feeling for color, the ability to effect well-organized compositions and the command of his medium. In all of these he bears comparison with the great impressionists. . . . The resemblance to Renoir is due only in part to Renoir's direct influence; it springs perhaps chiefly from the psychological resemblance between the two men, the extraordinary feeling they have in common for color and its relations, for the picturesqueness that is all about us if we have eyes to see, and from their common spontaneity and ready expressiveness in the medium of paint.

  Albert C. Barnes, "The Art in Painting," in *William Glackens*, exh. cat. (New York: Kraushaar Galleries, 1949), n.p.

The grievance that gnawed at The Eight was the intolerance of their own profession. They looked beyond the outposts of society where people were real by default of riches. . . . Their predilection for such common subjects for their brush earned them the name of "The Ash Can School." The wind of enthusiasm was back of their canvas, and they voyaged out to find the things more vital to them than the gardenias and orchids wilting on the chests of those whose livers rivaled the emaculateness of their linen.

  Edward Shinn, "Recollections of The Eight," *The Eight*, exh. cat. (Brooklyn: The Brooklyn Museum, 1943), p. 13

Provenance
Descended in artist's family to his son, Ira Glackens (1907–1990), Conway, N.H., from ca. 1938–ca. 1962

[Kraushaar Galleries, New York, ca. 1962]

Daniel Fraad, Jr. (1912–1987), and Rita Fraad, New York, 1962–1966

[Hirschl & Adler Galleries, New York, 1966–1968]

John D. Rockefeller 3rd and Blanchette Hooker Rockefeller, New York, 1968–1979

FAMSF, 1979.7.45

Exhibition History
New York, the Glackens home, 10 West 9th Street, *Fourth Annual Memorial Exhibition of the Paintings of William Glackens*, 1942, exh. no. 7 (as *Rocks and a Light-house, Gloucester*, 1908, not for sale)

Manchester, Vt., Southern Vermont Art Center, *"The Eight": Fifty-five Years Later*, 1963, exh. no. 2

The Brooklyn Museum, *American Painting: Selections from the Collection of Daniel and Rita Fraad*, 1964, exh. no. 42

Washington, D.C., The White House, Rotating Exhibition Program, 1966, no publ.

New York, Hirschl & Adler Galleries, *American Paintings for Public and Private Collections*, 1967, exh. no. 93

Tokyo 1982, exh. no. 62

Selected Reference
The American Canvas, p. 245

---

128 THE SUMMER CAMP, BLUE MOUNTAIN, CA. 1909

Oil on canvas, 30 x 34 in.

MARSDEN HARTLEY
b. Lewiston, Maine, 1877
d. Ellsworth, Maine 1943

Amountain is not a space, it is a thing, it is a body surrounded by illimitable ethers, it lives its own life like the sea and the sky, and differs from them in that little or nothing can be done to it by the ravages of silent agencies. . . .

Mountains are things, entities of a grandiose character, and the one who understands them best is the one who can suffer them best, and respect their profound loneliness.

Marsden Hartley, "On the Subject of Mountains," quoted in *The Mountains of Marsden Hartley*, exh. cat. (Minneapolis: University Gallery, University of Minnesota, 1979), n.p.

For like every revolutionist, I've gone through my "periods,"—and have now come back I think to the original child within me namely the romanticist, albeit not perhaps a romancer of love as of madness for the mountain madness is on me and the bizarrerie of the hills gives me stranger thoughts than ever. . . .

But you'll be interested in my new pictures—my "Romances Sans Paroles" I call them—my "Autumn Impressionals" as I call them though I like Romances Sans Paroles better I think—I want to exhibit them in some unique place this winter in New-York for I consider that they represent me at my best in intention—though naturally not in achievement. They are the product of wild wander and madness for roaming—little visions of the great intangible—You'll like them—You couldn't help it with your sense of the strangely beautiful. At Mrs. Ole Bull's house last year I had a little exhibition and some said they saw in the pictures that light that "never was on sea or land."—What will they think now since I've got back to dreaming again. Some will look and say "he's gone mad—pitiable one"—and others will look and say ["]he's looked in at the lattices of Heaven and come back with the madness of splendour on him." And both will be right— . . . and you know I'm on my way (dreamway) to California & Alaska—lands of the majesty and splendour of dream— . . . O yes the Wander lust is on me now and I cannot choose but go for when the mountain spirit woos—him must follow follow follow always—Everywhere—"through silent valleys where pale stars shine" up and on, down and forward all ways that lure with mountain madness in them.

Hartley to Shaemas O'Sheel, North Lovell, Maine, 19 October 1908, Marsden Hartley Papers, The Beineke Rare Book and Manuscript Library, Yale University

---

At the beginning of May a small collection of paintings by Marsden Hartley of Maine found shelter at the hospitable Little Gallery of the Secessionists. They were examples of an extreme and up-to-date impressionism. They represented winter scenes agitated by snow and wind, "proud music of the storm"; wood interiors, strange entanglements of tree-trunks;

and mountain slopes covered with autumn woods with some island-dotted river winding along their base.

The depth and distance across the valley to the mountain, the plastic modeling and faithful detail, the hardiness and vigor of representation, showed knowledge of form and sincerity of sentiment. It was the color scheme, however, that startled the beholder. It produced a strictly physical sensation. It irritated the retina and exhausted it. After leaving the gallery Fifth Avenue looked more grey than usual. A melancholy vocation for such a robust phase of art!

Hartley's technique is interesting though not necessarily original. It is a version of the famous Segantini "stitch," of using colors pure and laying them side by side upon the canvas in long flecks that look like stitches of embroidery. . . . I for my part believe that he has invented his method for himself, up there in Maine amidst the scenery of his fancy, and that only gradually he has learnt to reproduce nature in her most intense and luminous coloring.

[Sadakichi Hartmann], "Unphotographic Paint: The Texture of Impressionism," *Camera Work*, no. 28 (October 1909), quoted in Jane Calhoun Weaver, ed., *Sadakichi Hartmann, Critical Modernist: Collected Art Writings* (Berkeley and Los Angeles: University of California Press, 1991), p. 189

————

There was much talk pro and con about my pictures in this little room [Stieglitz's Photo-Secession Gallery, 291 Fifth Avenue], mostly con, I seem to remember, with the dissensions coming largely from the Parisian element. I had no voice in the matter, for I was not a talking person. I only knew I had had some kind of definite experience with nature, the nature of my own native land. I could only tell at what I had been looking and from whom my release had come. Steichen's remark to Stieglitz then was, I don't see, Stieglitz, what you see in those pictures, why you bother about them or him, there is nothing there.

Stieglitz replied, I don't think so, though you may be right—I don't think so—something makes me think something is happening.

Marsden Hartley, "291—and the Brass Bowl," in *America and Alfred Stieglitz: A Collective Portrait* (New York: The Literary Guild, 1934), p. 240

Provenance
[Alfred Stieglitz, New York, 1909]
[Charles Daniel Gallery, New York]
[Bertha Schaefer Gallery, New York, 1952–ca. 1968]
[Hirschl & Adler Galleries, New York, by 1968]
John D. Rockefeller 3rd and Blanchette Hooker Rockefeller, New York, 1968–1979
FAMSF, 1979.7.47

Exhibition History
New York, Photo-Secession Galleries, *Exhibition of Paintings in*
Oil by Mr. Marsden Hartley of Maine, 1909, exh. no. 4 (as *The Summer Camp*)
New York, Bertha Schaefer Gallery, *Marsden Hartley—A.H. Maurer: Landscapes, 1907–1931*, 1954, no publ.
New York, Bertha Schaefer Gallery, *Marsden Hartley—A.H. Maurer: American Pioneers, 1868–1943*, 1956, exh. no. 10 (as *Blue Mountain*)
New York, Hirschl & Adler Galleries, *Twenty-five American Masterpieces*, 1968, exh. no. 24
San Francisco 1976, exh. no. 99
New York, Whitney Museum of American Art, *Marsden Hartley*, 1980, exh. no. 4 (shown only at University Art Museum, University of California, Berkeley)
Tokyo 1982, exh. no. 63
Washington, D.C., Smithsonian Institution Traveling Exhibition Service, *New Horizons: Painting, 1840–1910*, 1987 (organized for travel to USSR), exh. no. 53

Selected Reference
The American Canvas, pp. 210–211, 245

Related Works
Carnival of Autumn, 1908
Oil on canvas, 30¼ x 30⅛ in.
Museum of Fine Arts, Boston

The Ice-Hole, Maine, 1908
Oil on canvas, 34 x 34 in.
New Orleans Museum of Art

Cosmos, 1908–1909
Oil on canvas, 30 x 30⅛ in.
Columbus Museum of Art, Columbus, Ohio

Landscape, ca. 1909
Oil on board, 9 x 12 in.
Auction sale, Sotheby Parke-Bernet, New York, 1 December 1988, lot no. 244

---

129 BRINGING IN THE FIREWOOD, 1912

Opaque watercolor on wove paper, mounted on paperboard, 6⅛ x 8½ in.
Signed and dated lower right: -FARNY-/⊙/-1912-

HENRY F. FARNY
b. Ribeauville, Alsace, France 1847
d. Cincinnati, Ohio 1916

The name of Farny is inseparably associated with Indians and portrayals of the disappearing race as they are. Farny paints not the idealized red man, but the Indian as he exists—as he is to be seen in the West today. The greatest proof of his success is the number of imitators that he has. He is a realist; his subjects are real and he paints them with a fidelity that is wonderful.

To paint Indian pictures one must be a singularly versatile artist: he must be a landscape painter, a painter of figures and an animal painter. His pictures have in them something dramatic that makes them of the deepest interest. The broadest sympathies, the keenest insight into human nature, and the most thorough appreciation of the emotions of the heart are put into Farny's pictures. . . . Farny is a master of the touch of nature that makes the whole world kin.

"In Farny's Studio," *(Cincinnati) Commercial Tribune*, 6 October 1895, transcription in Henry F. Farny Papers, AAA, roll 1233, frame 440

Provenance
[Hirschl & Adler Galleries, New York, 1971]

John D. Rockefeller 3rd and Blanchette Hooker Rockefeller, New York, 1971–1979

FAMSF, 1979.7.40

Related Work
Nomads, 1902
Oil on canvas, 22 x 40 in.
Museum of Western Art, Denver

130 SPRING FLOOD, 1931

Oil on canvas, 26 x 50 in.
Signed and dated lower left: *CEB/1931* (initials in monogram)

CHARLES E. BURCHFIELD

b. Ashtabula Harbor, Ohio 1893
d. West Seneca, N.Y. 1967

Raised in the small midwestern town of Salem, Ohio, Charles Burchfield early displayed a talent for drawing and a profound sensitivity to nature. A shy and often lonely child, he spent long hours wandering through the woods or reading the works of the naturalists Henry David Thoreau and John Burroughs. After high school he worked one year at a desk job in a factory before entering in 1912 the Cleveland School of Art, where he encountered the more exotic inspirations of costume designs, fanciful illustrations, and Oriental art. In the fall of 1916 Burchfield went to New York, thinking "it was the thing to do." He felt isolated as a student at the National Academy of Design, unable to find "an artist in the school to feel the beauty and poetry of nature as existing for its own sake." He stayed only two months before homesickness overcame him. Returning to Salem, he began to paint watercolors evoking the memories and feelings of his childhood. Inducted into the army in 1918, he served in South Carolina before his discharge in 1919, and then returned to his factory job and continued to paint. In fall 1921 Burchfield accepted a design position with a wallpaper company in Buffalo, New York; he later became head of the design department, but resigned in 1929 to devote himself full time to painting. In 1936 and 1937 he was commissioned by *Fortune* magazine to depict railroad yards in Pennsylvania and coal mines in West Virginia. He began to teach summer classes in 1949 and painted nearly until the time of his death at the age of seventy-three.

> Sally Mills, in *The American Canvas: Paintings from The Fine Arts Museums of San Francisco* (New York: Hudson Hills Press, in association with The Fine Arts Museums of San Francisco, 1989), 228

I'm going to turn out some good oils or die in the attempt.

> Burchfield to his dealer Frank K. M. Rehn, 13 October 1930

I am developing my handling of oil and am, I think, arriving at an individual treatment. . . . I intend to dedicate my larger themes to oil.

> Burchfield to his dealer Frank K. M. Rehn, 12 June 1932

It is the romantic side of the real world that I try to portray. My things are poems—(I hope).

> Burchfield to his dealer Frank K. M. Rehn, 2 October 1940; all the above quoted in John I. H. Baur, *The Inlander: Life and Work of Charles Burchfield, 1893–1967* (Newark: University of Delaware Press; New York and London: Cornwall Books, 1982), pp. 157, 157–158 (there misdated to 11 March 1932), 152

I thought, as I squatted on my heels and gazed into the warm amber-colored water with its teeming life, that if one could but read it aright this little watery world would hold the whole secret of the universe. At least I had the feeling I was gazing into infinity.

> Burchfield, quoted in *Charles Burchfield*, exh. cat. (New York: Whitney Museum of American Art, 1956), p. 11

[*Spring Flood* is] unique and interesting—has wonderful movement of a rushing flood. Burchfield was influenced by Chinese ptgs. at the Cleveland Museum. He was not an imitator but the influence opened up a new technique in painting. He rarely painted in oil. Subject is entirely unlike anything he has done—much like Homer. A powerful picture.

> E. P. Richardson to John D. Rockefeller 3rd, December 1976, FAMSF departmental files

Provenance
[Kennedy Galleries, New York, by 1977]

John D. Rockefeller 3rd and Blanchette Hooker Rockefeller, New York, 1977–1979
FAMSF, 1979.7.20

Exhibition History
Tokyo 1982, exh. no. 65

New York, The Metropolitan Museum of Art, *Charles Burchfield, 1893–1967*, 1984, no exh. no.

Selected Reference
The American Canvas, pp. 228–229, 247

131 RAILROAD IN SPRING, 1933

Transparent and opaque watercolor over graphite on wove paper, mounted on paperboard, 28 x 42 in.
Signed and dated lower right: *CEB./1933* (initials in monogram)

CHARLES E. BURCHFIELD
b. Ashtabula Harbor, Ohio 1893
d. West Seneca, N.Y. 1967

They were immensely set up at the Frank K. M. Rehn Galleries because of the selling to the Boston Museum of a water color by Charles Burchfield. . . .

. . . I don't see why they didn't buy the vastly more important "Railroad in Spring," which is also in Mr. Burchfield's vintage of this year. This picture has a good deal of the savagery of intention that I always say Mr. Burchfield has when at his best. . . .

But for that matter I practically like everything that Mr. Burchfield does. I like helpless honesty such as his. I like honesty of any sort. . . . So the absence of floss and delicate persiflage and double meanings doesn't worry me at all in the Burchfield oeuvre. I am more than content with his determined insistence upon the truth and nothing but the truth about Buffalo and places in that neighborhood.

H[enry] McB[ride], "Burchfield's Implacable Art," *(New York) Sun*, 10 February 1934

He interprets, often supremely, the drab, ramshackle ugliness of old sections in our urban communities. The abandoned farmhouse offers him congenial material. A viaduct underpass can yield surprising vistas, now somber, now drenched in sunlight. And he has made himself all but undisputed maestro of that redoubtable American institution, the freight car.

But Burchfield, however, is really an artist whose interest in subject goes far beneath the surface and does not traffic with superficial aspects of the picturesque. . . .

The surprise implicit in sharp contrast again and again charges the artist's work with significant, always legitimate, visual excitement. Tender Spring green lifts hopeful leaves toward the sun and is relentlessly offset by the smoke-blackened faces and roofs of frame dwellings huddled beside the tracks of the railroad. No matter how bedraggled and forlorn a scene may be, the visioning eye will perceive some vestige of choked or persisting loveliness.

Edward Alden Jewell, "Art of Burchfield Glorifies the Drab," *New York Times*, 8 February 1934

P.M. Walk north along R.R.—sunshine & loose clouds, growing colder—

How good the earth, revealed now after months of snow—how exciting bits of things in the dirt—cherry pits, walnut halves, broken glass etc.—

Walking by string of cars, the shaggy grassy hummocks on other side of me. The sight of the grassy turf, old golden-rod heads against the sky—a flash of sunlight over the ochre grass, a train whistle abruptly interjects itself—and suddenly the moment becomes too poignant to endure. Vague memories arise to saturate the mood, and pain & pleasure are mingled to an agonizing degree.

Burchfield, journal entry, Gardenville, N.Y., 2 March 1936, in J. Benjamin Townsend, ed., *Charles Burchfield's Journals: The Poetry of Place* (Albany: State University of New York Press, 1993), p. 326

A walk at 10 P.M. along the railroad. These powerful locomotives represent the spirit of the age—and I thought how strange it was that what an age is absorbed in should be this

particular thing; the world did without Industrialism once, so it is not a necessity; but it means that every age must be dominated by something, it matters little what, whether it is religion, art or commerce.

There is no thrill equal to that produced by one of these monsters rushing headlong down the steel road. So the prehistoric trees and plants were packed away in the earth thousands of years ago in order that now they might come forth in rolling clouds of smoke from these rushing locomotives, from great square chimneys and stacks, and to make red glares in furnaces on stormy nights.

Burchfield, journal entry, Salem, Ohio, 23 January 1921, in J. Benjamin Townsend, ed., *Charles Burchfield's Journals: The Poetry of Place* (Albany: State University of New York Press, 1993), p. 455

––––––––––

The work of Charles Burchfield is most decidedly founded, not on art, but on life, and the life that he knows and loves best. From what is to the mediocre artist and unseeing layman the boredom of everyday existence in a provincial community, he has extracted a quality that we may call poetic, romantic, lyric, or what you will. By sympathy with the particular he has made it epic and universal. No mood has been so mean as to seem unworthy of interpretation; the look of an asphalt road as it lies in the broiling sun at noon, cars and locomotives lying in God-forsaken railway yards, the steaming summer rain that can fill us with such hopeless boredom, the blank concrete walls and steel constructions of modern industry, midsummer streets with the acid green of close-cut lawns, the dusty Fords and gilded movies—all the sweltering, tawdry life of the American small town, and behind all, the sad desolation of our suburban landscape. He derives daily stimulus from these, that others flee from or pass with indifference.

Edward Hopper, "Charles Burchfield: American," *The Arts* 14, no. 1 (July 1928): 6–7

293

Provenance

[Frank K. M. Rehn Galleries, New York, 1934]

John L. Robertson

Lawrence A. Fleischman (b. 1925) and Barbara Greenberg Fleischman (b. 1924), Detroit, by 1960–1966

[Kennedy Galleries, New York, 1966]

John D. Rockefeller 3rd and Blanchette Hooker Rockefeller, New York, 1966–1979

FAMSF, 1979.7.21

Exhibition History

New York, Frank K. M. Rehn Galleries, *Paintings and Watercolors by Charles Burchfield*, 1934, no publ.

Milwaukee Art Center, *American Painting, 1760–1960: A Selection of 125 Paintings from the Collection of Mr. and Mrs. Lawrence A. Fleischman, Detroit*, 1960, no exh. no.

Tucson, The University of Arizona Art Gallery, *Charles Burchfield, His Golden Year: A Retrospective Exhibition of Watercolors, Oils, and Graphics* 1965, exh. no. 53

San Francisco 1976, exh. no. 95

New York, The Metropolitan Museum of Art, *Charles Burchfield, 1893–1967*, 1984, no exh. no.

FAMSF, *Viewpoints VII: Twentieth-Century American Landscape Drawings*, 1989, no publ.

Selected References

Joseph S. Trovato, *Charles Burchfield: Catalogue of Paintings in Public and Private Collections* (Utica, N.Y.: Museum of Art, Munson-Williams-Proctor Institute, 1970), cat. no. 814

John I. H. Baur, *The Inlander: Life and Work of Charles Burchfield, 1893–1967* (Newark: University of Delaware Press; New York and London: Cornwall Books, 1982), p. 153

132 DINNER FOR THRESHERS, 1934

Oil on hardboard, 20 x 80 in.
Signed and dated lower left: *GRANT WOOD/1934* ©

GRANT WOOD

b. near Anamosa, Iowa 1891
d. Iowa City, Iowa 1942

You may now uncross your fingers and take your tongue out of your cheek when you say the middle west is to become the art center of the country. New York has already accepted that prediction for the future as a reality of the present.

Easterners are actually as wistful over the middle west as Iowans were over New York ten years ago. They're not only wistful, they're envious—so envious and so fed up with the futility of their own stamping grounds as to be planning to follow Horace Greeley's advice to go west, young man, go west. The first hand information on the Iowan's rapidly quiet transition from "yokel" to artist returned with Grant Wood from New York last week. . . .

His most recent painting, "Dinner For Threshers," is making its formal debut to the public today in the Carnegie International show in Pittsburgh, and it is already sold. Mr. Clark, chairman of the purchasing committee of the Metropolitan Museum in New York, saw only the photograph of the canvas . . . and indicated his desire to purchase it; whether for himself or for the Metropolitan, the highest hall of fame in which paintings can be placed in America, has not yet been revealed.

The photograph also so impressed Miss Treacy, art editor of Fortune magazine and a guest at the reception honoring Mr. Wood, as to give her the idea that Mr. Wood's Iowa City mural painters might take each character out of the picture and paint them in other surroundings to illustrate a series of articles on the middle west in Fortune, to be climaxed with the composite painting.

Adeline Taylor, "Easterners Look Wistfully at Midwest as Nation's Art Crown Brought to It: Grant Wood Lionized on N.Y. Visit," *Cedar Rapids Gazette*, 21 October 1934

———

"Dinner for Threshers" is from my own life. It includes my family and our neighbors, our tablecloths, our chairs and our hens. It was painted with my paint and my brushes on my own time. It is of and by me and readers have no right to attempt to force upon me their families, their clothing, their hens or their screen doors.

Grant Wood, "How Threshers Eat," *Time*, 21 January 1935, p. 4

———

I lived in Paris a couple of years myself and grew a very spectacular beard that didn't match my face or my hair, and read Mencken and was convinced that the Middle West was inhibited and barren. But I came back because I learned that French painting is very fine

for the French people and not necessarily for us, and because I started out to analyze what it was that I really knew. I found out. It's Iowa.

> Wood, quoted in "Iowa Cows Give Grant Wood His Best Thoughts," *New York Herald Tribune*, 23 January 1936

———

But the very fact that the farmer is not himself vocal makes him the richest kind of material for the writer and the artist. He needs interpretation. Serious, sympathetic handling of farmer-material offers a great field for the careful worker. The life of the farmer, engaged in a constant conflict with natural forces, is essentially dramatic. . . .

Let me try to state the basic idea of the regional movement. Each section has a personality of its own, in physiography, industry, psychology. Thinking painters and writers who have passed their formative years in these regions, will, by care-taking analysis, work out and interpret in their productions these varying personalities. When the different regions develop characteristics of their own, they will come into competition with each other; and out of this competition a rich American culture will grow.

> Grant Wood, *Revolt against the City* (1935), quoted in James M. Dennis, *Grant Wood: A Study in American Art and Culture*, rev. ed. (Columbia: University of Missouri Press, 1986), pp. 233, 234

Provenance
[Ferargil Galleries, New York, 1934 (as agents for the artist), sold for $3500 from Carnegie International Exhibition]

Stephen C. Clark (1882–1960), New York, 1934–1935

[Maynard Walker Gallery, New York, 1935, reportedly sold for $5000]

Edwin Hewitt (b. 1909), New York, 1935

[Maynard Walker Gallery, New York, probably before 1939]

George M. Moffett (1883–1951) and Helen Wilmot Moffett (d. 1956), Queenstown, Md., and New York, probably before 1939–ca. 1956

Descended in family to their son, James A. Moffett II (1907–1988), Glen Head, N.Y., ca. 1956–1970

[Wildenstein, New York, 1970]

John D. Rockefeller 3rd and Blanchette Hooker Rockefeller, New York, 1970–1979

FAMSF, 1979.7.105

Exhibition History
Possibly Des Moines, Iowa State Fair, 1934

Pittsburgh, Carnegie Institute, *The 1934 International Exhibition*, 1934, exh. no. 5

Chicago, The Lakeside Press Galleries, *Loan Exhibition of Drawings and Paintings by Grant Wood*, 1935, exh. no. 63

New York, Ferargil Galleries, *Grant Wood*, 1935, exh. no. 34

New York, Maynard Walker Gallery, *Paintings by Six Americans*, 1935, exh. no. 12

The Art Institute of Chicago, *The Fifty-third Annual Exhibition of American Paintings and Sculpture*, 1942, exh. no. 10

San Francisco 1976, exh. no. 103

Tokyo 1982, exh. no. 67

The Minneapolis Institute of Arts, *Grant Wood: The Regionalist Vision*, 1983, exh. no. 43

Selected References
Thomas Craven, "Grant Wood," *Scribner's Magazine* 101, no. 6 (June 1937): 21–22

Darrell Garwood, *Artist in Iowa: A Life of Grant Wood* (New York: W. W. Norton & Company, 1944), pp. 18, 161–162, 166–172, 176, 192–193

James M. Dennis, *Grant Wood: A Study in American Art and Culture*, rev. ed. (Columbia: University of Missouri Press, 1986), pp. 134–136, 159, 208, 218–219, 241

The American Canvas, pp. 13, 224–226, 246–247

Related Works
Dinner for Threshers (2 sections, left and right ends of composition), 1933
Pencil and gouache on paper, each 17¾ x 26¾ in.
Whitney Museum of American Art, New York

Dinner for Threshers, 1934
Pencil and chalk on paper, 18 x 72 in.
Private collection, Conn., as of 1984

Black and white crayon, graphite, black ink, and white opaque watercolor on brown wove paper, 25⅝ x 20 in.
Signed and dated lower right: © *GRANT/WOOD 36*

GRANT WOOD

b. near Anamosa, Iowa 1891
d. Iowa City, Iowa 1942

Prof. Grant Wood, who looks at American life with both aesthetics and humor, has done it again. This time it is a set of nine illustrations for a special edition of Sinclair Lewis' "Main Street." . . .

. . . Local persons posed for the illustration[s], but Professor Wood has explained, "I didn't try to make likenesses, but adapted them to my material." . . .

The drawings, which Professor Wood completed in January, were done in black and white pencils on brown wrapping paper. In "The Perfectionist," we see [the fictional character] Carol Kennicott, sitting in a window, looking out with somewhat precious disdain on Gopher Prairie. It is significant that she is shut away from the sordidness of the town by the lace curtains.

Audrey Hamilton, "Wood Draws for *Main Street*," *Daily Iowan*, 22 May 1937

———

"Is that the real tragedy, that I never shall know tragedy, never find anything but blustery complications that turn out to be a farce?

"No one big enough or pitiful enough to sacrifice for. Tragedy in neat blouses; the eternal flame all nice and safe in a kerosene stove. Neither heroic faith nor heroic guilt. Peeping at love from behind lace curtains—on Main Street!"

Carol Kennicott, in Sinclair Lewis, *Main Street* (1920; New York: The Library of America, 1992), p. 403

———

Not since Copley has America seen his equal in the delineation of people, and in subtle analysis of character and inventive design, he surpasses the Colonial master. By dealing unreservedly with local psychologies, he has created characters which, though rooted in the Iowa soil, belong in the gallery of American types—men and women as native and as faithfully studied as those of Sinclair Lewis, and much more affectionately fashioned.

Thomas Craven, "Grant Wood," *Scribner's Magazine* 101, no. 6 (June 1937): 21

———

I leaned strongly to the decorative, and also I endeavored to paint types, not individuals. The lovely apparel and accessories of the Gothic period appealed to me so vitally that I longed to see pictorial and decorative possibilities in our contemporary clothes and art articles. Gradually as I searched, I began to realize that there was real decoration in the rickrack braid on the aprons of the farmers' wives, in calico patterns and in lace curtains. At present my most useful reference book and one that is authentic is a Sears, Roebuck catalog. And so, to my great joy, I discovered that in the very commonplace, in my native surroundings, were decorative adventures and that my only difficulty had been in taking them too much for granted.

Wood, 1932, quoted in *This Is Grant Wood Country*, exh. cat. (Davenport, Iowa: Davenport Municipal Art Gallery, 1977), p. 27

———

Contrary to many a layman critic Grant's painting is not realism, nor is it realistic. He formalized and characterized his subjects. That was his special talent, his unique ability. He could make one face in a picture represent and interpret the lives and souls of a whole group of people.

John Steuart Curry, *Demcourier*, May 1942, quoted in *This Is Grant Wood Country*, exh. cat. (Davenport, Iowa: Davenport Municipal Art Gallery, 1977), p. 35

Provenance
Commissioned by Limited Editions Club, New York, for special edition of Sinclair Lewis, Main Street, 1935

[Maynard Walker Gallery, New York, 1937]

[Hirschl & Adler Galleries, New York, by 1960]

Lawrence A. Fleischman (b. 1925) and Barbara Greenberg Fleischman (b. 1924), Detroit, by 1962–1966

[Kennedy Galleries, New York, 1966]

John D. Rockefeller 3rd and Blanchette Hooker Rockefeller, New York, 1966–1979

FAMSF, 1979.7.106

Exhibition History
Iowa City, Iowa Union, State University of Iowa, 1937

The Art Institute of Chicago, *International Water Color Exhibition*, 1937, exh. no. 511

The Detroit Institute of Arts, *American Paintings and Drawings from Michigan Collections*, 1962, exh. no. 143

Tucson, University of Arizona Art Gallery, *American Paintings, 1765–1963: Selections from the Lawrence A. and Barbara Fleischman Collection of American Art*, 1964, exh. no. 104

Philadelphia, Pennsylvania Academy of the Fine Arts, *Small Pictures of Large Import from the*

Collection of Lawrence A. and Barbara Fleischman of Detroit, Michigan, 1964, exh. no. 50

San Francisco 1976, exh. no. 104

The Minneapolis Institute of Arts, *Grant Wood: The Regionalist Vision*, 1983, exh. no. 56

Selected References
"A Midwest Artist Views *Main Street*," *Saint Louis Post-Dispatch*, 23 May 1937

Darrell Garwood, *Artist in Iowa: A Life of Grant Wood* (New York: W. W. Norton & Company, 1944), pp. 202–204

James M. Dennis, *Grant Wood: A Study in American Art and Culture* (Columbia: University of Missouri Press, 1986), pp. 121–129

Related Works

Booster, 1936–1937
Charcoal, pencil, and chalk on paper, 20½ x 16 in.
Private collection, as of 1983

General Practitioner, 1936–1937
Charcoal, pencil, and chalk on paper, 20½ x 16 in.
Location unknown

The Good Influence, 1936–1937
Pencil, gouache, and ink on paper, 20½ x 16 in.
Pennsylvania Academy of the Fine Arts, Philadelphia

Main Street Mansion, 1936–1937
Charcoal, pencil, and chalk on paper, 20½ x 16 in.
James Maroney and Hirschl & Adler Galleries, New York, as of 1983

Practical Idealist, 1936–1937
Charcoal, pencil, and chalk on paper, 20½ x 16 in.
James Maroney, New York, as of 1983

The Radical, 1936–1937
Charcoal, pencil, and chalk on paper, 20½ x 16 in.
Private collection, as of 1983

Sentimental Yearner, 1936–1937
Crayon, gouache, and pencil on paper, 20½ x 16 in.
The Minneapolis Institute of Arts

Village Slums, 1936–1937
Charcoal, pencil, and chalk on paper, 20½ x 16 in.
Private collection, as of 1983

---

134 KITCHEN, WILLIAMSBURG, 1937

Oil on hardboard, 10 x 14 in.
Signed and dated lower right: *Sheeler–1937*

CHARLES SHEELER
b. Philadelphia, Pa., 1883
d. Dobbs Ferry, N.Y. 1965

Two years ago Mr. Sheeler was commissioned by Mrs. John D. Rockefeller Jr. [Abby Aldrich Rockefeller, John D. Rockefeller 3rd's mother] to paint portraits of two Williamsburg buildings—the Governor's Palace and Bassett Hall. While he was at Williamsburg, he made notes of the kitchen in the Governor's Palace. This painting, from The Downtown Gallery in New York, is the result. One generally associates "notes" with a casual sketch or mere indications, but this little oil shows the height of care and precision. The painstaking method Mr. Sheeler has devised for qualifying machine-age subjects has been applied here, and yet he differentiates between the machine-made and hand-made surface, indicating feelingly the wear and age of all these utensils and furnishings.

"Kitchen, Williamsburg: A Painting on Gesso by Charles Sheeler," *Christian Science Monitor*, 8 December 1937

For Charles Sheeler . . . life in America is just one museum piece after another.

He lives in Ridgefield, Conn., surrounded by fine old Shaker furniture. To a large extent his art reflects the tidy perfection of his domestic arrangements.

When he lifts the latch and steps into the outer world he carries with him the same unbroken preoccupation. He interprets a vast industrial complex like the Ford plant as a study in pure pattern. Its "clean lines" appeal to him, as do the simple contours and plain surfaces in the historic early American kitchen at Williamsburg, Va., which he has also painted.

Sheeler's art is thus a study in isolates. He has created an American scene undisturbed by the swarm of mortals. It is an esthetic order of breathless serenity.

Jerome Klein, "Modern Museum Shows Sheeler's Pure Americana," *New York Post*, 7 October 1939

Any picture worth hanging, is of this world—under our noses often—which amazes us. . . .

Charles Sheeler gives us such a world, of elements we can believe in, things for our associations long familiar or which we have always thought familiar. . . .

Sheeler had especially not to be afraid to use the photographic camera in making up a picture. It could perform a function unduplicatable by other means. Sheeler took it that by

its powers his subject should be intensified, carved out, illuminated—for anyone (I don't know that he said this to himself) whose eyes might be blurred by the general fog that he might, if he cared to, see again.

William Carlos Williams, introduction to *Charles Sheeler: Paintings, Drawings, Photographs*, exh. cat. (New York: The Museum of Modern Art, 1939), pp. 7, 9

––––––––

My theories about the technique of painting have changed in direct relation to my changed concept of the structure of a picture. In the days of the art school the degree of success in the employment of the slashing brushstroke was thought to be evidence of the success of the picture. Today it seems to me desirable to remove the method of painting as far as possible from being an obstacle in the way of consideration of the content of the picture. . . .

My interest in photography, paralleling that in painting, has been based on admiration for its possibility of accounting for the visual world with an exactitude not equaled by any other medium. The difference in the manner of arrival at their destination—the painting being the result of a composite image and the photograph being the result of a single image— prevents these media from being competitive.

Charles Sheeler, "A Brief Note on the Exhibition," in *Charles Sheeler: Paintings, Drawings, Photographs*, exh. cat. (New York: The Museum of Modern Art, 1939), pp. 10, 11

Provenance

[The Downtown Gallery, New York, 1937, sold for $750 to Mrs. John D. Rockefeller 3rd]

John D. Rockefeller 3rd and Blanchette Hooker Rockefeller, New York, 1937–1993

FAMSF, 1993.35.24

Exhibition History

New York, The Downtown Gallery, *Fall Exhibition*, 1937, exh. no. 2

New York, The Museum of Modern Art, *Charles Sheeler: Paintings, Drawings, Photographs*, 1939, exh. no. 39

Boston, Institute of Modern Art, *Ten Americans*, 1943, exh. no. 23

Andover, Mass., Addison Gallery, Phillips Academy, *Charles Sheeler: A Survey Exhibition*, 1946, no exh. no.

Minneapolis, Walker Art Center, *Charles Sheeler*, 1952, no publ.

Los Angeles, Art Galleries, University of California at Los Angeles, *Charles Sheeler: A Retrospective Exhibition*, 1954, exh. no. 19

New York, Brearley School, no exhibition title, 1958, no publ.

New York, M. Knoedler & Co., *A Family Exhibit*, 1959, exh. no. 38

Iowa City, University of Iowa, *The Quest of Charles Sheeler: Eighty-three Works Honoring His Eightieth Year*, 1963, exh. no. 44

Washington, D.C., National Collection of Fine Arts, *Charles Sheeler*, 1968, exh. no. 83

Selected References

Constance Rourke, *Charles Sheeler: Artist in the American Tradition* (New York: Harcourt Brace, 1938), pp. 173–174

"Sheeler Finds Beauty in the Commonplace," *Life*, 8 August 1938, p. 42

Frederick S. Wight, "Charles Sheeler," *Art in America* 42, no. 3 (October 1954): 205

Martin Friedman, *Charles Sheeler* (New York: Watson-Guptill, 1975), p. 95

Susan Fillen-Yeh, *Charles Sheeler: American Interiors*, exh. cat. (New Haven: Yale University Art Gallery, 1987), pp. 19, 67

Related Works

Williamsburg Kitchen, 1935–1936
Gelatin-silver print
The Lane Collection, as of 1987

Kitchen, Williamsburg, 1936
Conté crayon, 7½ x 9½ in.
Private collection, as of 1987 (ex-coll. Edith Gregor Halpert)

Kitchen, Williamsburg (Aunt Mary), ca. 1936
Gelatin-silver print
Private collection, as of 1987 (ex-coll. William Carlos Williams)

---

135 THE TRIAL OF JOHN BROWN, 1942

Oil on canvas, 16½ x 20⅛ in.
Signed and dated lower right: *H. PiPPiN. 1942*

HORACE PIPPIN

b. West Chester, Pa. 1888
d. West Chester, Pa. 1946

If art were to be studied by the case history method, Horace Pippin could be taken as an example of the "self-taught" artist who has succeeded in breaking through the barriers of lack of formal training and of physical disability to make his own direct and evocative statement. It happens that he makes use of subject matter of American, including Negro, history—episodes from the lives of Lincoln and of John Brown—as well as his experience of daily life today. However, if there were no topical or subject interest in his work, it would still be significant for contemporary American, including Negro, culture. For Pippin's is a true cry from the soul, a voice not to be denied, the inevitable compulsion of the artist to speak, in his own terms, of what he knows best and most deeply. . . .

. . . A wild poetry sings in his work. Lincoln at midnight in a tent on the battlefield, Lincoln the boy reading his first book in the dark attic, Lincoln the Good Samaritan; or John Brown reading his Bible, standing trial, and going to be hanged—these are the intense symbols of a profound knowledge Pippin has of life. This is not knowledge on the historical level, perhaps, or the political. It is, rather, a kind of intuitive knowledge which transmutes the great popular movements of history into symbols of the new horizon to come.

Elizabeth McCausland, "American Negro Art in Two Exhibitions," *Springfield (Mass.) Sunday Union and Republican*, 20 February 1944

The colors are very simple such as brown, amber, yellow, black, white and green. The pictures which I have already painted come to me in my mind, and if to me it is a worth while picture, I paint it. I go over that picture in my mind several times and when I am ready to paint it I have all the details that I need. I take my time and examine every coat of paint carefully and to be sure that the exact color which I have in my mind is satisfactory to me. Then I work my foreground from the background. That throws the background away from the foreground. In other words bringing out my work. The time it takes to make a picture depends on the nature of the picture. . . . My opinion of art is that a man should have love for it, because my idea is that he paints from his heart and mind. To me it seems impossible for another to teach one of Art.

Horace Pippin, "How I Paint," in Holger Cahill et al., *Masters of Popular Painting: Modern Primitives of Europe and America*, exh. cat. (New York: The Museum of Modern Art, 1938), pp. 125–126

———

All of the children [Pippin and his four sisters] would listen not only to Christine's [their mother] patient Bible readings, but to the tales she would tell of the past, and most especially to the one tale handed down to her from her mother, the tale of John Brown.

Brown, a fanatical white abolitionist, had staged his armed attack on the arsenal at Harpers Ferry, Virginia, on October 16, 1859, and Christine Pippin's mother had watched his hanging at nearby Charlestown December 2 of that fateful year.

Years later Horace would paint three of his best pictures about this legendary hero of his childhood. . . .

The second picture depicts the trial. The bearded Brown, still suffering from the wounds he received at Harpers Ferry, did indeed lie on a stretcher at the foot of his twelve bearded jurymen (Brown's Southern counsel-for-the-defense did not challenge any one of them). And Brown did indeed carry his documents—his maps, his Constitution, his "Vindication of the Invasion," and his letters from Frederick Douglass and other Northern Abolitionists—in a flowered carpetbag. (There is one such still lying in the basement of the Chester County

Historical Society's Museum, which Horace haunted at the time he was painting these pictures, and which he no doubt copied.)

Selden Rodman and Carole Cleaver, *Horace Pippin: The Artist as a Black American* (Garden City, N.Y.: Doubleday & Co., 1972), pp. 28, 29

———————

On October 16, 1859, Brown, along with twenty-one armed followers, seized the federal arsenal at Harpers Ferry, in hopes of inciting a rebellion among the blacks in the region. After relocating to an adjacent fire-engine house and a day and a half of hostage-taking, sniping, and arson, Brown and his six remaining marauders were eventually subdued by the U. S. Cavalry and Marines.

Captured, jailed, and then placed on trial that same month, John Brown instantly became a national figure, and consequently, the Harpers Ferry assault became an incident of nationwide concern. A wounded John Brown, as Pippin depicted him in *The Trial of John Brown*, lies on a cot before a Virginia jury of twelve men and a prosecuting attorney in shirtsleeves.

Richard J. Powell, "Re-Creating American History," in Judith E. Stein, *I Tell My Heart: The Art of Horace Pippin*, exh. cat. (Philadelphia: Pennsylvania Academy of the Fine Arts, 1993), pp. 74–75

———————

Virginians, I did not ask for any quarter at the time I was taken. I did not ask to have my life spared. The Governor of the State of Virginia tendered me his assurance that I should have a fair trial: but, under no circumstances whatever will I be able to have a fair trial. If you seek my blood, you can have it at any moment, without this mockery of a trial. I have had no counsel: I have not been able to advise with any one. I know nothing about the feelings of my fellow prisoners, and am utterly unable to attend in any way to my own defense. My memory don't serve me: my health is insufficient, although improving. There are mitigating circumstances that I would urge in our favor, if a fair trial is to be allowed us: but if we are to be forced with a mere form—a trial for execution—you might spare yourselves that trouble. . . . I have now little further to ask, other than that I may not be foolishly insulted only as cowardly barbarians insult those who fall into their power.

John Brown to grand jury, Circuit Court of Virginia, Jefferson County, 25 October 1859, quoted in Thomas J. Fleming, "Verdicts of History, III: The Trial of John Brown," *American Heritage* 18, no. 5 (August 1967): 29, 32

———————

We defy an instance to be shown in a civilized community where a prisoner has been forced to trial for his life, when so disabled by sickness or ghastly wounds as to be unable even to sit up during the proceedings, and compelled to be carried to the judgment hall upon a litter.

Lawrence (Kans.) Republican, October 1859, quoted in Thomas J. Fleming, "Verdicts of History, III: The Trial of John Brown," *American Heritage* 18, no. 5 (August 1967): 92

Provenance
[The Downtown Gallery, New York, 1942–1944, sold for $350]

Arnaud d'Usseau, New York and Hollywood, Calif., 1944–after 1960

Dr. and Mrs. Marvin Radoff, New York, after 1960–1977

[Terry Dintenfass Gallery, New York, 1977]

John D. Rockefeller 3rd and Blanchette Hooker Rockefeller, New York, 1977–1979

FAMSF, 1979.7.82

Exhibition History
New York, The Downtown Gallery, *H. Pippin: Exhibition of Paintings*, 1944, exh. no. 12

New York, Whitney Museum of American Art, *1943–44 Annual Exhibition of Contemporary American Art*, 1943, exh. no. 75

New York, M. Knoedler & Co., *Memorial Exhibition: Horace Pippin, 1888–1946*, 1947, exh. no. 15

Washington, D.C., The Phillips Collection, *Horace Pippin*, 1977, exh. no. 28

FAMSF, *American Folk Art: A Sampling from Northern California Collections*, 1986, no exh. no.

Philadelphia, Pennsylvania Academy of the Fine Arts, *I Tell My Heart: The Art of Horace Pippin*, 1994, no exh. no.

Selected References
Selden Rodman, *Horace Pippin: A Negro Painter in America* (New York: The Quadrangle Press, 1947), pp. 17–18, 48, 84

Oliver W. Larkin, *Art and Life in America*, rev. ed. (New York:

Holt, Rinehart and Winston, 1960), pp. 428–429

The American Canvas, pp. 216–217, 246

Related Works
John Brown Reading His Bible, 1942
Oil on canvas board, 16 x 20 in.
The Crispo Collection, Charleston, S.C., as of 1994

John Brown Going to His Hanging, 1942
Oil on canvas, 24 x 30 in.
Pennsylvania Academy of the Fine Arts, Philadelphia

Watercolor over graphite on wove paper, 22 x 30 in.
Signed lower right: *Andrew Wyeth*

ANDREW WYETH
b. Chadds Ford, Pa. 1917

Since the beginning of his career, Wyeth has preferred to paint the people and places that are familiar to him in the vicinity of his two homes in Pennsylvania and Maine. Near his Chadds Ford farm, in the Brandywine Valley of Pennsylvania, there stands a small, octagonal, stone schoolhouse built by the Quakers in the 19th century. In the 1930s and early 40s, the building was used as a church by local blacks and was known as Mother Archie's Church, after the congregation's leader.

Wyeth painted the building's interior on several occasions, almost always including the elaborate chandelier. . . . Wyeth must have had a particular fondness for this building as Arnold Newman took his photograph there in 1949, under the chandelier at an angle reminiscent of the McDonough [the FAMSF] watercolor.

E. John Bullard, *A Panorama of American Painting: The John J. McDonough Collection*, exh. cat. (New Orleans: New Orleans Museum of Art, 1975), p. 55

———

Scattered through the countryside around Chadds Ford are a number of small octagonal stone schoolhouses. Built in that form, it is said, so that the sun would light the interior at all times of day. They had now been for the most part abandoned or turned to other uses. One on the dirt road from Wyeth's home over the hill to Koerner's farm had been taken over by a preacher called Mother Archie. In 1945 it was already abandoned and it is now gone. One day in very early spring Wyeth went into the empty building. A storm had just passed over. The sun gleamed on the brilliant green of the winter wheat outside. Inside there was no sound but the cooing of pigeons. The walls seemed filled by the half darkness of the storm.

That is the moment in the life of the building he painted in the Andover picture [*Mother Archie's Church*, 1945]. Yours is different. Wyeth told me that he had tried to buy the building. Some negroes he had known were buried around it. The dark heads in your watercolor are, I suppose, that memory.

E. P. Richardson to John D. Rockefeller 3rd, 28 March 1978, FAMSF departmental files

His growth toward an art of air and light was an instinctive development. . . . [H]e turned from pen-and-ink to the use of pencil and colored washes, then to watercolor drawings in which the Negro citizens of Chadds Ford made their first appearance. When he saw Winslow Homer's watercolors, at about age sixteen, they helped him to move in a direction he had already discovered, toward a bold, rapid impression of light and tone.

E. P. Richardson, "The Artist: His Life and Work," in *Andrew Wyeth*, exh. cat. (Philadelphia: Pennsylvania Academy of the Fine Arts, 1966), p. 11

These paintings suggest one of the most disconcerting vantage points used to "float" the spectator in the 1930's: that of looking down upon or up at a scene, the so-called bird's- or worm's-eye view. Such views were extraordinarily popular and inspired a wide range of pictorial and psychological effects. Charles Sheeler created startlingly inventive abstractions by looking up at skyscrapers or down into rooms of early American furnishings. Grant Wood used such views panoramically to create storybook vistas of small Midwestern towns. . . . N. C. Wyeth, Andrew's father, looked down from a great height to survey the details and gloom of people gathering to attend a funeral on a small island in Maine.

Andrew Wyeth similarly likes to take us with him as he suddenly shoots up from below . . . or . . . as he looks down from some point above to contemplate his universe. . . . Such views in Wyeth's hands continually displace and disorient the spectator, never giving him a firm horizon or ground line and often leaving unresolved ambiguities. . . . This . . . is part of the elusiveness of Wyeth's art; we feel suspended and detached, not quite present in any physical sense.

Wanda M. Corn, "The Art of Andrew Wyeth," in *The Art of Andrew Wyeth*, exh. cat. (Boston: New York Graphic Society, for The Fine Arts Museums of San Francisco, 1973), pp. 108, 109

Provenance
Mrs. Josiah Marvel, Greenville, Del., to 1959

[M. Knoedler & Co., New York, 1959]

The W. B. Connor Foundation, Danbury, Conn., from 1959

The City College Fund, New York, by 1972

[Auction sale, Sotheby Parke-Bernet, New York, 24 May 1972, lot no. 204 (as *Schoolhouse*)]

Dr. John J. McDonough, Youngstown, Ohio, 1972–1978

[Auction sale, Sotheby Parke-Bernet, New York, 22 March 1978, lot no. 59]

John D. Rockefeller 3rd and Blanchette Hooker Rockefeller, New York, 1978–1979

FAMSF, 1979.7.108

Exhibition History
New Orleans Museum of Art, *A Panorama of American Painting: The John J. McDonough Collection*, 1975, exh. no. 60

Related Works
Mother Archie's Church, 1945
Tempera on hardboard, 25 x 48 in.

Addison Gallery of American Art, Phillips Academy, Andover, Mass.

Memorial Day, 1946
Watercolor on paper, 14 x 20 in.
Museum of Fine Arts, Boston

The Corner, 1953
Watercolor and dry brush on paper, 13½ x 21½ in.
Wilmington Society of the Fine Arts, Wilmington, Del.

Watercolor over graphite on wove paper, mounted on paperboard, 21¾ x 48 in.
Signed and dated lower left: *CEB/1949–56* (initials in monogram); inscribed on old backing paper on reverse:
IN SEPTEMBER, BRILLIANT SUNLIGHT SEEMS/ALWAYS TO HOVER JUST BEYOND/BLUE HILLS TO THE SOUTH

CHARLES E. BURCHFIELD
b. Ashtabula Harbor, Ohio 1893
d. West Seneca, N.Y. 1967

I feel happier than I have felt for years. . . . I'm going to give you more sounds and dreams, and—yes, I'm going to make people smell what I want them to, and with visual means.

> Burchfield to his dealer Frank K. M. Rehn, 21 September 1944, quoted in John I. H. Baur, *The Inlander: Life and Work of Charles Burchfield, 1893–1967* (Newark: University of Delaware Press; New York and London: Cornwall Books, 1982), p. 197

The full glory of September—warm and gentle S.W. wind.

Asters and goldenrod in such great profusion—I cannot get my fill of looking at them.

Hill road to Springville & then to E. Otto via the Cannoirturally [*sic*] Rd.—South of E. Otto

Near the crossroad, wild hedge along the road—Nondescript bushes overgrown with virginia creeper (now blood-red) and Virgin's bower (in fluffy seed)—Great clumps of goldenrod & asters—I thought of the Biblical "Purple, Scarlet & Golden"—

> Burchfield, journal entry, Gardenville, N.Y., 26 September 1953, in J. Benjamin Townsend, ed., *Charles Burchfield's Journals: The Poetry of Place* (Albany: State University of New York Press, 1993), p. 532

All afternoon on a Study of clouds, with the sun beating thru. I aim at an absolute conventionalized [*i.e.*, conventionalization], far removed from superficial realism. It was difficult to keep up the tempo, so that when it came to the foreground, I had to fight against realism.

> Burchfield, journal entry, Gardenville, N.Y., 22 August 1946, in J. Benjamin Townsend, ed., *Charles Burchfield's Journals: The Poetry of Place* (Albany: State University of New York Press, 1993), p. 509

To Zimmerman Rd painting—

A glorious day packed full of delightful impressions from beginning to end.

Parked at the open fields to the north of the main woods. The moment I landed, I felt at once that it was a special day—brilliant sun, hot dry wind from the southwest blowing of [*i.e.*, off] the meadows of bleached grass, asters and golden-rod.

I decided to do a painting featuring the asters and dry grass—almost from the first, the picture took the lead and I had to follow as best I could—and it was difficult to invent rapidly enough the semi-abstract conventionalizations that the power and beauty of the wind, sunlight and sky demanded [*Wind-blown Asters*, 1951; Burchfield Art Center, Buffalo].

> Burchfield, journal entry, Gardenville, N.Y., 21 September 1951, in J. Benjamin Townsend, ed., *Charles Burchfield's Journals: The Poetry of Place* (Albany: State University of New York Press, 1993), p. 525

What a pleasure it is working on this large scale. . . . I feel free and unhampered; it is as if I could better let the forces of nature control my brush.

> Burchfield, journal entry, 25 April 1955, quoted in John I. H. Baur, *The Inlander: Life and Work of Charles Burchfield, 1893–1967* (Newark: University of Delaware Press; New York and London: Cornwall Books, 1982), p. 197

Provenance

[Frank K. M. Rehn Galleries, New York]

Frederick Tomkins (1894–1977), Orange, N.J., by 1962

[Kennedy Galleries, New York]

[Auction sale, Sotheby Parke-Bernet, New York, 21 April 1978, lot no. 164]

John D. Rockefeller 3rd and Blanchette Hooker Rockefeller, New York, 1978–1993

FAMSF, 1993.35.2

Exhibition History

Williamstown, Mass., Williams College Museum of Art, *An Exhibition of Works of Art Lent by the Alumni of Williams College*, 1962, exh. no. 13 (as *Summer Landscape: New York State*)

Middlebury, Vt., The Christian A. Johnson Memorial Gallery, Middlebury College, *Spirit and Nature: Visions of Interdependence*, 1990, exh. no. 3

138 GANDHI, 1964

Black ink on wove paper, mounted on paperboard, 36¼ x 25⅝ in.
Signed lower right: *Ben Shahn*

BEN SHAHN

b. Kovno, Lithuania 1898
d. New York, N.Y. 1969

Shahn's evolution as a painter is the story of the artist as an American. . . . As a young artist seeking to emulate the "pure" painting of the modern French masters, Shahn was thoroughly unhappy and maladjusted. . . . He didn't "find himself" until the age of thirty-four when he turned to the theme of the social martyrdom of Sacco and Vanzetti. He became our outstanding mural painter when he associated himself wholeheartedly with the "useful" reforms of the New Deal. And by the time he had "arrived" at the age of forty-nine with a one-man retrospective exhibition at the Museum of Modern Art, he was already locked in a struggle with himself to prevent his work from becoming sterile in celebration of the social creeds he had become more and more involved with as a political being.

Son of a carpenter who came of a family of woodcarvers, and apprenticed in childhood to a lithographer, Shahn once told Lionel Trilling that he'd rather be a commercial artist working regularly at his craft than teach painting and "create" for three months in the summer. At the very time that big corporations were seeking him out and were making him one of the most highly paid "commercial" artists in the country, he was donating his time to the CIO and to Henry Wallace's lost cause, and writing an indignant letter to the Chrysler Corporation to refuse a commission because the choice of subject had not been left entirely to him.

Selden Rodman, *Portrait of the Artist as an American: Ben Shahn* (New York: Harper & Brothers Publishers, 1951), p. 6

Not known particularly as a portrait artist, Shahn was able to combine the physiological characteristics with the particular personality and intellectual attributes in a way which not only identified the subject but gave insight into his personality as well. Seldom flattering, his portraits carry the unmistakable reliance on line, which is so characteristic of Shahn's mature work. . . . The serigraph *Gandhi*, 1965, is derived from an almost identical brush and ink drawing, commissioned by *Look* magazine in 1964 to accompany a feature on the Indian leader. In *Gandhi*, Shahn has caught the essence of the character of this slight and venerable man, whose moral strength made him a leader of monumental stature.

> Kenneth W. Prescott, *Ben Shahn: A Retrospective, 1898–1969*, exh. cat. (New York: The Jewish Museum, 1976), pp. 25–26

Shahn recognized greatness in men who served humanity above themselves. His portraits, whether in painting, drawings or prints could never be confused with a photographic likeness; yet, each contained the essence of the man, focusing sharply on the distinctive features in a manner that created a sense of the monumental about the portraits. They seem larger than life in spite of the scale, and this, of course, is the role Shahn stated that they played in life.

> Kenneth W. Prescott, "Ben Shahn: His Life and Arts," in *Ben Shahn*, exh. cat. (Tokyo: The National Museum of Modern Art, 1970), p. 7

When Shahn has an idea for a picture he develops as many drawings for it as his imagination allows. . . . These drawings may be used immediately, or at some later date, and may develop into paintings, gouaches, finished drawings, prints, book illustrations, posters, stained-glass windows, or even tapestry. There is nothing sacred about their purpose, and the artist feels that he may use them as freely as he wishes, repeating them in various media; because the image is more important than the medium.

> Kneeland McNulty, "Ben Shahn as a Printmaker," in *The Collected Prints of Ben Shahn*, exh. cat. (Philadelphia: Philadelphia Museum of Art, 1967), p. 7

He was born Mohandas Karamchand Gandhi, in 1869, and was married off by his parents at 13. Excruciatingly shy, intensely sensuous, he studied law in London, then went to South Africa as a barrister. He suffered insults and humiliations because he was "colored," and urged his despised, disenfranchised compatriots to unite for peaceful disobedience, which he had learned from reading Thoreau. He told them to end the ancient rancors that split Hindu from Moslem, Parsee from pariah; to be clean of body, no less than spirit; to set a moral example to their overlords by absolute truthfulness. ("Not even for the freedom of India would I resort to an untruth.") He led 2,000 Indians from Natal across the Transvaal border, defying the law that forbade Asians to immigrate; returned by force to the coal mines, they refused to work. Beaten, starved, they held fast. Fifty thousand joined the *Satyagraha*, until the hamstrung government passed the Indian Relief Bill.

Gandhi set up an *ashram* (retreat) of ascetics devoted to prayer and meditation, in a search for godliness. Later, he left his lucrative law practice, returned to India and established a Tolstoyan retreat to which he admitted untouchables—horrifying even his Hindu wife, who warned that a place so defiled would fail. When funds finally ran out, Gandhi said, "We shall go to live in the untouchable quarter." He was often stoned, vilified, almost lynched. . . .

With Jinnah, the Moslem leader, and Lord Mountbatten, he framed India's independence in 1947, desperately opposing partition into Hindu and Moslem (Pakistan) states. When hideous fighting broke out, he toured the Bengal villages, pleading for an end to bloodshed. At a great prayer meeting in New Delhi, he was assassinated—by a Hindu fanatic who blamed him for India's partition. The irony was as supreme as the injustice. His ashes were strewn into the sacred river Ganges at Allahabad, and his great disciple Nehru said, "The light has gone out of our lives, and there is darkness everywhere."

[The article was illustrated with a photo-reproduction of the FAMSF drawing, on p. 60, with the caption:] "This remarkable brush-and-ink portrait was drawn especially for LOOK by the distinguished American artist, BEN SHAHN."

Leo Rosten, "They Made Our World . . . Gandhi," *Look*, 25 August 1964, p. 61

Provenance
[Kennedy Galleries, New York, by 1968]

John D. Rockefeller 3rd and Blanchette Hooker Rockefeller, New York, 1968–1979

FAMSF, 1979.7.91

Exhibition History
San Francisco 1976, exh. no. 102

Selected Reference
Kenneth W. Prescott, *The Complete Graphic Works of Ben Shahn* (New York: Quadrangle/The New York Times Book Company, 1973), p. 59

Related Works
Broadside: Gandhi and "The Mysterious Stranger," 1965
Collotype reproduction of ink drawing, 31½ x 21 in.
Edition of 200
Printed by Meriden Gravure Company, Meriden, Conn.

Broadside: Gandhi and "The Mysterious Stranger," 1965
Photo-offset reproduction of ink drawing, 17 x 11 in.
Printed by Meriden Gravure Company, Meriden, Conn.

Gandhi, 1965
Serigraph, 40 x 26 in.

Face of Gandhi, ca. 1965
Ink brush on paper, 7½ x 8¾ in.
Kennedy Galleries, New York, as of 1969

Gandhi, ca. 1965
Crayon on paper, 11 x 10¼ in.
Kennedy Galleries, New York, as of 1969

Transparent and opaque watercolor and ink over graphite on wove paper, 19⅞ x 28 in.
Signed lower right: *Andrew Wyeth*

ANDREW WYETH
b. Chadds Ford, Pa. 1917

For me, the paintings have that eerie feeling of goblins and witches out riding on broomsticks—damp rotting leaves and moisture—smell of make-up—as a child, the smell inside of a pumpkin when a candle is lit—the feel of your face under a mask walking down a road in the moonlight. I love all that, because then *I* don't exist anymore. To me it's almost like getting inside of my hound, Rattler, and walking around the country looking at it through his eyes.

What I'm trying to say is that I start every painting with an emotion—something I've just got to get out. These immaculately painted things—you'd think I was a very calm mathematician. Truth is, I use tempera partly because it's such a dull medium—those minute strokes put a brake on my real nature—messiness. My wild side that's really me comes out in my watercolors—especially of snow, which is absolutely intoxicating to me. I'm electrified by it—the hush—unbelievable. A white mussel shell on a gravel bank in Maine is thrilling to me because it's all the sea—the gull that brought it there, the rain, the sun that bleached it there by a stand of spruce woods. Most artists just look at an object and there it sits. . . .

I think in my life the real turning point—when the emotion thing really became the most important—was the death of my father, in 1945. . . . We had a wonderful friendship. Of course, he'd been my only teacher, and he was a wonderful, remarkable person. When he died, I was just a clever watercolorist—lots of swish and swash. When he died—well—now I was really on the spot and had this terrific urge to prove that what he had started in me was not in vain—to really do something serious and not play around with it, doing caricatures of nature. I had a vast gloomy feeling. Fortunately, I had always had this great emotion toward the landscape and so, with his death, I seemed to—well—the landscape took on a meaning—the quality of him. . . .

. . . I prefer winter and fall, when you feel the bone structure in the landscape—the loneliness of it—the dead feeling of winter. Something waits beneath it—the whole story doesn't show. I think anything like that—which is contemplative, silent, shows a person alone—people always feel is sad. Is it because we've lost the art of being alone? . . .

I've spent most of my life up to now pretty much alone. And I like it. I was the youngest of five kids and wasn't very well—sinus trouble. They went to school; I was just left alone. As often happens with the youngest, I grew up on the outskirts of the family, unconsciously without too much scrutinizing. . . . [A] lot of the time [I] just wandered over these hills, in this little territory right here, looking at things, not particularly thinking about art—hell no, just being perfectly to myself, but being very much alone. An ideal life for an artist. So, whenever I paint an open field or the inside of a house with loneliness implied, it's not a concocted dramatic thing—it's natural for me.

Wyeth, in Richard Meryman, "Andrew Wyeth: An Interview," *Life*, 14 May 1965, reprinted in Wanda M. Corn, *The Art of Andrew Wyeth*, exh. cat. (Boston: New York Graphic Society, for The Fine Arts Museums of San Francisco, 1973), pp. 55, 58, 60, 66

———

I work in drybrush when my emotion gets deep enough into a subject. So I paint with a smaller brush, dip it into color, splay out the brush and bristles, squeeze out a good deal of the moisture and color with my fingers so that there is only a very small amount of paint left. Then when I stroke the paper with the dried brush, it will make various distinct strokes at once, and I start to develop the forms of whatever object it is until they start to have real body. But, if you want to have it come to life underneath, you must have an exciting undertone of wash. Otherwise, if you just work drybrush over a white surface, it will look too much

like drybrush. A good drybrush to me is done over a very wet technique of washes. . . .
Drybrush is layer upon layer. It is what I would call a definite weaving process. You weave
the layers of drybrush over and within the broad washes of watercolor.

> Wyeth, quoted in Thomas Hoving, *Two Worlds of Andrew Wyeth: Kuerners and Olsons*, exh. cat.
> (New York: The Metropolitan Museum of Art, 1976), p. 33

Provenance
[M. Knoedler & Co., New York,
1967–1968]

John D. Rockefeller 3rd and
Blanchette Hooker Rockefeller,
New York, 1968–1993

FAMSF, 1993.35.27

Exhibition History
Boston, Museum of Fine Arts,
Andrew Wyeth, 1970, exh. no. 79

San Francisco 1976, exh. no. 106

Princeton, N.J., The Art Mu-
seum, Princeton University,
*Princeton Alumni Collections:
Works on Paper*, no exh. no.

Tokyo 1982, exh. no. 69

Related Work
Nick and Jamie, 1963–1964
Drybrush watercolor on paper,
14½ x 19⅜ in.
Virginia Museum of Fine Arts,
Richmond

Transparent and opaque watercolor over charcoal on illustration board, 20 x 30 in.
Signed lower left: *Philip Jamison*

PHILIP JAMISON
b. Philadelphia, Pa. 1925

The things I paint are close to me: the hills that surround my home, the houses among the hills, the flowers that grow nearby, my children. In all these I see a beauty that I attempt to capture for myself and others. In many instances this may be the less obvious appeal of a neighbor's mailbox or of a snow-trodden clump of weeds. My subjects are all derived from nature. It does not matter whether they have existed for hours, days or centuries, or whether only I can see their beauty. . . .

Since I often try to express the patina of time, an effect which cannot be achieved with a few bold strokes, my paintings tend to be subtle in color and handling. I also tend to use neutral colors because for me they are less tiring than bright ones. They reflect a personal sensitivity, an introversion perhaps, that enables me to say with pictures what I cannot express articulately in conversation. During the past two years my watercolors have also become increasingly darker in key. I disagree with those who read depression in such colors. A painting can have color without being colorful. If a man wears a dark suit, for example, it does not necessarily follow that he is an unhappy fellow. More likely he simply prefers dark suits.

For some years I did all my watercolors outdoors. Recently, however, I find myself working more and more in the studio. I am, of course, constantly in the field studying nature for inspiration. During the actual painting, however, the scene tends to be a deterrent to my creativeness. I don't wish to be bound by factual observation, for I paint by feeling and emotion rather than from the subject. Consequently, although I have a so-called "realistic approach," my finished paintings often bear little resemblance to the sources of inspiration. I try, in short, to transfer to paper or canvas the way I feel about the subject rather than how it actually looks.

Jamison, "Philip Jamison Discusses His Motivations for Painting Watercolors," in *Watercolors, Oils, Drawings by Philip Jamison*, exh. cat. (Durham, N.C.: Duke University Art Museum, 1969), n.p.

In 1936, while in grade school, he [Jamison] met William Palmer Lear who was to be one of the people most influential in his life. Lear was his art teacher in junior and senior high school, his scoutmaster and, in fact, a "second" father to him. Though he did not encourage his young protégé to become an artist or to pursue a career related to art, he was a source of wisdom and provided a strength on which Philip Jamison could rely. . . .

While a student [at the Philadelphia Museum School of Art], Philip Jamison met the second artist who was also to be a major influence in his career: his watercolor instructor in 1949 and 1950, W. Emerton Heitland. . . . Until his death in 1969, Heitland remained Philip's close friend. . . .

. . . In the 50s the Jamisons began to visit Vinalhaven, Maine, in the summer and gradually these visits increased in length so that now they spend each summer there. The landscape and architecture of Maine were added to his subject matter studies.

Bruce St. John, introduction to *Philip Jamison: Recent Watercolors*, exh. cat. (New York: Hirschl & Adler Galleries, 1971), n.p.

Provenance
[Hirschl & Adler Galleries, New York, 1971]

John D. Rockefeller 3rd and Blanchette Hooker Rockefeller New York, 1971–1979

FAMSF, 1979.7.61

Exhibition History
New York, Hirschl & Adler Galleries, *Philip Jamison: Recent Watercolors*, 1971, exh. no. 6

THE ROCKEFELLER COLLECTION OF AMERICAN ART
at The Fine Arts Museums of San Francisco

is produced by the Publications Department of the Museums.
Ann Heath Karlstrom, Director of Publications,
and Karen Kevorkian, Editor.

The book is designed by Robin Weiss Graphic Design, San Francisco.
The display type is Copperplate Gothic, and the text type is New Caledonia.
Photocomposition is by Mackenzie-Harris Corporation, San Francisco.
The book is printed on 135 gsm matte art paper by La Cromolito, Milan,
through Overseas Printing Corporation, San Francisco.